Manager of Giants

Manager of Giants

*The Tactics, Temper
and True Record of John McGraw*

LOU HERNÁNDEZ

McFarland & Company, Inc., Publishers
Jefferson, North Carolina

Library of Congress Cataloguing-in-Publication Data

Names: Hernández, Lou, 1958– author.
Title: Manager of Giants : the tactics, temper and true
record of John McGraw / Lou Hernández.
Description: Jefferson, North Carolina : McFarland & Company, Inc., 2018 |
Includes bibliographical references and index.
Identifiers: LCCN 2018039552 | ISBN 9781476670706 (softcover : acid free paper) ∞
Subjects: LCSH: McGraw, John Joseph, 1873–1934. | Baseball managers—United
States—Biography. | New York Giants (Baseball team)—History.
Classification: LCC GV865.M3 H47 2018 | DDC 796.357092 [B] —dc23
LC record available at https://lccn.loc.gov/2018039552

British Library cataloguing data are available

ISBN (print) 978-1-4766-7070-6
ISBN (ebook) 978-1-4766-2988-9

Front cover image: John McGraw wearing his "good luck" black broadcloth
uniform at the 1911 World Series. In 1905, McGraw had commissioned
identical uniforms for the World Series and won. He was not as successful
with the tailoring change this second time around (author's collection).

Printed in the United States of America

*McFarland & Company, Inc., Publishers
Box 611, Jefferson, North Carolina 28640
www.mcfarlandpub.com*

For my siblings,
Liz and George

Acknowledgments

The slew of old newspapers available online helped this project come alive. For that I have newspapers.com most to thank. No matter how often one delves into these digital time machines there is always something wondrously fresh and energizing about reading and seeing (through photos) the way we were.

The Society of American Baseball Research's Biography Project provided great background on many of the supporting players within this work. My thanks to those bioproject authors.

The McGraw family tree was obtained from ancestry.com.

This is my sixth book with my publisher McFarland & Company. Therefore, an overdue mention with gratitude is due the crack staff there who make me look as good as possible.

Table of Contents

Preface

Rarely has a manager identified so closely, so synonymously, with his team. The Giants were McGraw and McGraw was the Giants. In the newspapers, it was just as often *McGraw's clan, McGraw's forces, McGraw's outfit, the McGraw nine, McGraw's machine, McGrawmen*, as it was *the Giants*. By extension, it was on to *McGrawville* for a visiting team, or back in a *McGraw uniform* for a convalesced player.

McGraw's fame came from the winning brand of baseball his clubs consistently exhibited. It is often repeated that a manager is given too much credit for a team's success and too much blame for its lack of it. With the backing of the extensive New York press, McGraw benefited greatly from the first half of that credo. His name developed a prestige among his peers, and he came to be universally regarded as the sport's greatest manager.

McGraw's stature and reputation as a winning manager insulated him from a litany of vocational improprieties. Though Teflon had not been invented in McGraw's time, the Giants leader, in retrospect, could easily be described as having a Teflon-coated career—because nothing bad ever stuck to his persona. He racked up suspension after suspension after suspension for his raucous conduct on the field. Even in baseball's Rodney Dangerfield–era of umpires getting no respect, McGraw's personal aversion for the field judges—his chief agitators—often manifested in personally contemptible actions. For the longest time, McGraw held the dubious record for most ejections as a player and manager, until he was surpassed by Atlanta Braves Hall of Fame skipper Bobby Cox in 2007. Neither Cox nor any other manager amassed as many suspensions as McGraw did. All but 14 of McGraw's 137 (by my count) early showers came as a field general.

The whims of fortune seemed to be on his side as well. In 1927, McGraw avoided a substantial lawsuit over one of his failed land speculations in Western Florida when the plaintiff died before the trial began. While he could not avoid punishment for his blatant on-the-field infractions, away from the diamond McGraw repeatedly evaded gambling scandals and a public drinking scandal—avoiding prosecution from the latter during the nascent years of Prohibition. As a public figure, he was sued many times. Through it all, he came out none the worse for wear. Most anyone else would not have been as resilient—or fortunate.

He was called, among other things in the press, the "live wire of baseball" and the "little god of the Polo Grounds" and McGraw was unquestionably both. On and off the field, he had more fights than Ty Cobb, Leo Durocher, Billy Martin and anyone else you can think of—combined. His record in his many pugilistic encounters, it must be said, was nowhere near as good as his managerial one. McGraw physically fought with everyone (with the exception of the opposite sex). He had fights with: teammates, underlings, opposing players, other managers, umpires (of course), fans (including a 13-year-old boy), policemen, and generally people from all walks of life. And he often verbally clashed with his authoritative elders, as it were. He caustically tongue-lashed league presidents and owners alike.

The "little god" was not as omnipotent at the Polo Grounds, or other parks, as his career record indicates, however. Simply put, John McGraw has been given credit for managing, and winning, many more games than he actually did—at least 571 games (3¾ seasons worth) in which he was not on the bench and nearly 300 victories that he did not direct.

Using Charles C. Alexander's acclaimed *John McGraw* biography as a blueprint, along with the newspapers of the day, I have been able to trace to a much more accurate degree the number of games McGraw managed, which differs from the accepted record, found in most online and print sources. Managers' records do not appear to receive the same rigorous degree of scrutiny as other more glamorous players' categories in our statistically disposed game. The pious Branch Rickey, for instance, never managed on Sunday, yet his dugout ledger has not been amended to account for all the games he missed in a ten-season career. As recently as 2011, Tony LaRussa—the manager with the second-most wins in history—missed several games due to shingles, but no one has taken an interest in debiting those contests from his lifetime won-lost mark.

McGraw's greatness as a field manager might seem to be diminished as a result of his new standing among all-time winningest pilots. It is not. In fact, he won a greater *percentage* of games than previously believed. Most of his absences were due to illness, which eventually forced his retirement. Only Joe McCarthy had a better winning percentage among managers with over 2,000 career wins. To this day, as both a player and manager, McGraw has had few, if any, equals in the game.

In his *Evaluating Baseball's Managers,* author Chris Jaffe reminds all of McGraw's heady achievements and skill set in getting the most from his players:

> McGraw won ten pennants in 30 years based on his ability to work with players like Fred Merkle and Fred Snodgrass. McGraw coaxed four consecutive pennants out of teams led by Ross Youngs, George Kelly, Dave Bancroft and a foundling Frankie Frisch from 1921 to 1924. In comparison, Connie Mack had Lefty Grove, Jimmie Foxx, Mickey Cochrane and Al Simmons in their primes at the same time—yet that squad won only three pennants."[1]

McGraw lost six World Series, however, and he had no one to blame but himself for three, possibly four, of the defeats. (McGraw won the third-most World Series games, but lost the most of any manager; his record was 26–28, with two ties.) The Giants manager preferred to open the 1912 World Series with a rookie pitcher when he had Rube Marquard, who despite slumping down the stretch had won 19 games in a row during the season, available. McGraw also had Christy Mathewson waiting in the proverbial wings. The decision cost him dearly in the eight-game setback. In back-to-back World Series losses in 1923 and 1924, "the little round man," as McGraw was often called by his players, stayed too long with his starting pitchers in elimination games. In both instances, the Giants held late-inning leads. Making matters worse in those cases, McGraw stubbornly refused to learn from past mistakes. He had made an inexplicably poor decision in the 1917 World Series, when he permitted a no-longer-effective Slim Sallee to cough up a seventh-inning lead in the pivotal Game Five—and then let the pitcher come out for the eighth frame to disastrous results.

McGraw's greatest flaw, therefore, was managing World Series games in a way different from regular season contests. As a manager at the fore of fledgling bullpen use, this reflects perhaps more disappointingly on him. McGraw's heart, which was a big one, got the best of him at the worst possible times, to the ever-lasting detriment of his club and fans.

Al Bridwell, Giants shortstop from 1908 to 1911, provided what was in my view one of the most telling McGraw quotes, originally offered to Lawrence Ritter in *The Glory of Their Times*. As someone who has drawn close to McGraw through an examination of his life and career, I have been most (tickishly) struck by Bridwell's straightforward characterization of his former boss. In closing with Bridwell's words, I can no better prepare the reader with a sense of my subject's personality and personality traits.

> *[McGraw] was a wonderful man.... I got along with him fine. He only suspended me once, for two weeks. It was on account of I socked him.*[2]

Introduction

John McGraw sits fourth on the list of all-time-winningest managers—not second, as has long been catalogued. As often happens in the course of researching a topic, unanticipated discoveries are unearthed. In writing the *1933 New York Giants,* published in 2016, I discovered errors in the managerial record for the man who was perhaps baseball's most famous manager. McGraw established his reputation starting as a standout player in the 1890s with the Baltimore Orioles, and then as the long-enduring and successful manager for the New York Giants, then the flagship franchise of the National League. As a player, McGraw finished with the third-highest on-base percentage ever recorded. His .466 mark stands behind only legends Ruth (.474) and Ted Williams (.482). (It should be noted that from 1891 to 1900, McGraw benefited from a rule that did not count non-bunt fouls as strikes.)

John McGraw emerged from the 1890s "rowdy ball era" of professional baseball, when players routinely insulted (and sometimes assaulted) one another and engaged on-field shenanigans intended to give their teams an edge. Though he had a small build, McGraw not only survived but thrived in this rough-and-tumble atmosphere. As a gentler, more sportsman-like approach to playing the game was adopted by early 1900s league executives, McGraw was loath to turn over a new leaf.

As a manager, McGraw began to differentiate himself as soon as he arrived in New York to take command of the Giants in 1902. Baseball, at the turn of the 20th century, was a game in which pitchers completed a vast majority of the games they started. Though he was blessed early on with pitching linchpins like Christy Mathewson and Joe McGinnity, McGraw was not averse to using other pitchers to finish games and gain what decades later were called "saves." From 1903 to 1909, a Giants pitcher headed the league in games finished four times. If saves had been an official stat during that seven-season span, the Giants would have accounted for nearly one-third of the total recorded in the National League. Hardballtimes.com writer Shane Tourtellotte wrote that McGraw's use of secondary pitchers may have been influenced by Baltimore Orioles manager Ned Hanlon, whose 1894 team posted the highest retroactive save total of the 19th century with 11, although from 1895 through 1899, the Orioles cumulatively would have secured only ten saves, including two campaigns with none.

McGraw also pioneered the ready use of mid-game substitutions, including pinch-runners. "From 1903—McGraw's first full season managing the Giants—the number of position-player substitutions in the major leagues began to increase every year," wrote Bryan Soderholm-Difatte in the Fall 2016 SABR *Baseball Research Journal.* "Every year from 1908 to 1912, McGraw's position-player substitutions were more than double the major league average. By 1912, the number of in-game position-player substitutions over the course of a major league season tripled from an average of 23 per team in 1903 to 69 per team." Eventually, McGraw became sold on the concept of platooning, after Boston Braves manager George Stallings utilized the technique to achieve miraculous success with the 1914 Boston Braves.

Contrary to other managers, McGraw reassessed the long-held view on bunting.

According to *The Bill James Guide to Baseball Managers,* this occurred about a decade into his role as dugout strategist. "From 1909 on the Giants bunted less often than any other National League team," wrote James. "The Giants were last in the league in sacrifice hits in 1909, 1912, 1913, 1915, 1920, 1925, 1926, 1931 and 1932. In almost all the other years, they were near the bottom of the league."[1] The following item from a 1917 issue of *Sporting Life* reinforces the overview and touches on the alternative strategy McGraw preferred to employ: "John McGraw still clings to the idea that the sacrifice hit doesn't obtain the desired results. In this belief the leader of the Giants stands practically unsupported by the major league field marshals, yet he points to the fact that his teams in former championship years came out on top by adopting the hit-and-run style of attack."[2]

Managers of McGraw's era were responsible for all personnel. McGraw utilized a network of friends and former players, and later scouts, to help enrich his teams. He was best at recognizing pitching talent and especially keen at turning previously mediocre pitchers into winners, after acquiring the hurlers in trades or other transactions. McGraw's focus on winning—before he was slowed by illness—was second to none.

Uniquely, this concentrated desire made him a forward-thinking man during a time when mainstream baseball had no interest in looking outside of its comfortably segregated box. During spring training in Hot Springs, Arkansas, in 1901, an enterprising McGraw tried to recruit a light-skinned black player named Charlie Grant and pass him off as a Native American, as a way of conforming to the "gentlemen's agreement" existing throughout organized baseball. Working as a bellhop at the Eastman Hotel in Hot Springs, Grant had been employed by the Chicago-based Columbia Giants the previous summer. His association with the all-black team led to his being exposed, as publicity from McGraw's intentions began to circulate throughout the country. Under rigid pressure from Ban Johnson and Charles Comiskey, McGraw was forced to scuttle the deceptive but, in many ways, admirable attempt.

McGraw is most often compared to contemporary Connie Mack, who, because of ironclad job security (and good health) was able to manage for more than 50 years. "Although Mack and McGraw were products of essentially the same cultural background," assessed James in his guide, "McGraw would eagerly have signed black players, had he been able to. Mack might not have."[3] It is reasonable to believe that had he not been so thoroughly countermanded by league bigwigs in 1901 with Grant, because of his connections with Cuban baseball, McGraw would have attempted to bring José Méndez to the Giants a decade later. Edward Mackall, a black trainer, was an integral part of the conditioning of McGraw's teams from his Baltimore days until Mackall's death in 1922. In 1923, McGraw replaced him with two other African Americans, Waller Irvin and Emmett Parker. Later, Johnny Jamieson, another black and decorated soldier in the First World War, also served as trainer of the Giants under McGraw.

The first player to steal second, third and home in the same inning (July 4, 1899), John McGraw was elected to the National Baseball Hall of Fame in 1937, part of the institution's second class of electees. McGraw's second wife, Blanche, outlived him by 28 years, passing away in 1962 at the age of 81. Through her nearly three decades of widowhood, she remained close to the New York Giants franchise, often throwing out first pitches at games. Blanche appeared with Claire Ruth and Eleanor Gehrig at the New York Yankees' 1961 home inaugural, kicking off what was to be a historic, home run-filled championship season, the type of which her late husband may not have been too fond.

ONE

John Joseph Gets His Start

"When I first broke in there were leather-neck, tobacco-chewing characters in the game whose mannerisms were objectionable."—John McGraw

Delivered by a veteran Civil War surgeon, John Joseph McGraw was born in Truxton, New York, on April 7, 1873. The Village of Truxton lies 27 miles south of Syracuse and 68 miles west of Cooperstown.

McGraw's Irish immigrant father, John William McGraw, came to the United States in the mid–19th century. During the Civil War, he enlisted, or was drafted, into the Union Army. Following the end of the conflict, McGraw settled in upstate New York. Within a few years, now a maintenance worker for a railroad company, McGraw married Ellen Comerfort, a young lass from neighboring Onondaga County. In 1871, when she was 18, the ingénue Ellen gave birth to the first of their eight children. Two years later, John Jr., joined his sister Mary, the family's first male child. The Truxton couple had six more offspring over the next ten years.

When John, Jr., was ten years old, tragedy struck his family in a recurrent and crushing manner. An outbreak of diphtheria ravaged the general area of Truxton and especially so the McGraw clan. The infectious disease took the life of not only 30-year-old Ellen but three of her children. Ellen died on August 29, 1883, not long after giving birth to her fifth daughter, named Helen. Within a month of his wife's death, John McGraw Sr., would also have to bury seven-year-old Catherine McGraw, as well as first-born Mary and five-year-old Patrick Edmund. Mary and Patrick sadly perished on the same day, September 12.

After the hellish summer had passed and the calamity with it, the 39-year-old McGraw was left as sole provider for five children, ranging in age from a few months to ten years.

Following the tragic developments, John Jr.'s childhood continued to be cruelly stamped. John Sr. struggled with alcoholism and often physically abused his eldest son. One particularly severe beating caused McGraw to take up permanent residence at a neighbor's rooming house. Baseball was sometimes the accelerant source of the older McGraw's fury. John Jr. had taken to playing the game on the streets and had a penchant for hitting the ball through neighborhood windows. The affronted neighbor would invariably pound on McGraw's door, seeking several coins to cover the cost of the window pane repair. John's father could not grasp the appeal of baseball, could not fathom his son's preoccupation with the game, and could not imagine it as a potential full-time occupation.

Despite his father's objections, in his mid-teens, John McGraw, Jr. committed himself to playing baseball for a living. As a 16-year-old, the inspired athlete latched on with the local Truxton Grays team. "I had been quite a pitcher in Truxton and got as much as $5 a game to go to Homer and pitch for that club,"[1] McGraw later reminisced.

The following season, through his association with Truxton's manager, McGraw wedged his way into a roster spot with the Olean club of the New York–Pennsylvania League. After a poor start, he was removed from the starting lineup and later released. "I'll never forget the day I was told to sit on the bench and let someone else try the job," McGraw said of the occurrence. "I was a pretty cocky kid, and getting benched was a splendid thing for me. It had a great effect on the rest of my career. I never forgot it in handling young men later."[2] Undaunted, the young player found work in the Western New York League.

The undeniably talented teen reached baseball's highest level a year later, in 1891. In August, he left the Cedar Rapids Canaries of the Illinois-Iowa League to sign with the Baltimore Orioles of the American Association. At a time when the pitcher stood 50 feet from the batter and five balls were required for a walk, McGraw played 33 games for the Orioles at shortstop and hit .270. His major league debut came as a second baseman on August 26, against the Columbus Solons at Union Park. He was credited with one hit in four at-bats. It came against Solons' left-hander Phil Knell. McGraw scored one of his team's runs in its 6–5 victory.

In the field, he registered two putouts and three assists and was charged with an error. Future longtime friend and associate Wilbert Robinson was behind the plate for the victorious Orioles, who finished in the first division with a record of 71–64.

The same year he became a professional ballplayer, John McGraw made his first international foray. McGraw was only 17 years old when he first visited Havana, Cuba, in January 1891. McGraw was recruited for the journey by fellow minor league player Alfred Lawson. The British-born Lawson himself had reached baseball's top organized level in 1890, with brief stints as a pitcher with the Beaneaters of Boston and the Alleghenys of Pittsburgh. A budding promoter at all of 22 years of age, Lawson convinced a squad of mostly big-league players to make the foreign trip.

"From the time he first sailed through the narrow entrance to beautiful Havana harbor," disclosed Blanche McGraw in her 1953 biography of her late husband, "John was always fascinated by Cuba."[3] Cubans were the first foreign people the young McGraw had ever seen, Mrs. McGraw added, and he was very taken with their developed zeal for baseball.

Lawson outfitted his team in bright yellow uniforms. During the five-game competition (all won by the North Americans), McGraw's spunky play at shortstop earned him the nickname of *"El Mono Amarillo"*—The Yellow Monkey. It was a nickname that was fondly used by the Cuban press in years to come, in trumpeting the established McGraw's arrival or pending arrival in the city.

In 1892, the Orioles joined 11 other clubs in an expanded National League. As a 19-year-old, McGraw participated in 79 contests and hit .269 for his last-place club. McGraw batted from the left side of the plate and threw right-handed. He was short in stature, though not for the era—5'7"—and weighed a wispy 125 pounds. He was described by sports reporter Jack Veiock as a man with a square jaw and steel blue eyes.[4] McGraw had a high-bridged nose and thin, bow lips. He parted his dark hair down the middle, as was the typical male grooming of the time. Toward the end of his playing days, he would add another 30 pounds, and subsequently be was unable to prevent a ballooning weight in middle age.

The infielder cranked his first major league home run on October 1, against Brooklyn Bridegrooms pitcher George Haddock, with two men on base. The Bridegrooms topped the Orioles, 10–9, at Eastern Park. The high-scoring, Saturday afternoon affair, stopped after seven innings due to darkness, was attended by 1,976 fans. The three-run four-bagger was one of 13 (four of the inside-the-park variety) that McGraw hit in his 17-year career as an active player.

McGraw became a full-time starter in 1893—the year the pitcher's mound was moved back to 60 feet, six inches from home plate and the ball's deliverer was required to maintain foot contact with the rubber slab until he released the pitch. The new pitcher positioning resulted in a hitting bonanza for major league hitters. McGraw, as did many, benefited from the rule change—though everyone now was swinging with a conventional round bat, as opposed to previously allowed flat-sided ones. Playing shortstop, he hit a career-best five home runs in 127 games and hit over .300 (.321) for the first of ten seasons. McGraw not only stood out with his play on the diamond, but also with his conduct. "That spring, for the first time," biographer Charles C. Alexander pointed out, "McGraw began to display the belligerent, quarrelsome, unprincipled on-field personality that would become basic to his reputation as a player and manager—and the McGraw legend."[5]

In a prime example of his boundary-crossing behavior, the third-year player suffered his first expulsion from a game on the July 5. Playing at Exposition Park in Pittsburgh, McGraw was run from his defensive infield position for arguing balls and strikes on the opposing hitter. The *Pittsburgh Daily Post* provided an early account of the on-field temperament for which McGraw would become known throughout his baseball life.

> McGraw took exception to some of [umpire] McLaughlin's decision on balls and strikes while [Frank] Killen was at bat. He was warned and then sent to the bench. While leaving the diamond he took the trouble to go out of his way to say mean and nasty things to the umpire. He was fined $25, and as he still continued his vile language McLaughlin called for a policeman to take the blackguard out of the park. McGraw hurried to the bench, hastily put on his jacket and was at the exit when the big policeman hove in sight.[6]

Pitcher Killen shut out the Orioles, on five hits, 2–0.

Against the New York Giants on July 26, the disputatious McGraw earned the first extended write-up from the newspaper that would long and closely chronicle his career. "McGraw, the Baltimore shortstop, distinguished himself by having a couple of tilts with umpire [Pop] Snyder," outlined the *New York Times.* "On one occasion he was fined $5, and roundly abused the official who immediately added $25 to the fine already imposed, and ordered the player out of the game, [Hughie] Jennings taking his place."[7] The Orioles were trailing, 4–2, at the time of McGraw's fifth-inning dismissal, and lost by a final score of 5–4.

McGraw had no more serious run-ins with the field arbiters over the rest of the season. He played in all but three of the Orioles' 130-game campaign. On August 16, Orioles hurler Bill Hawke became the first pitcher to toss a no-hitter under the present-day mound distance. Hawke defeated the Washington Nationals at Boundary Field, 5–0. He struck out six and walked two. McGraw recorded four putouts and two assists in the historic encounter.

The Orioles produced an overall 60–70 mark. Although an improvement from the terrible 46–101 record of 1892, the team was excluded from the first division spoils. The eighth-place club finished 26½ games in back of the league-topping Boston Beaneaters.

The following year, the Orioles became champions of the circuit, claiming the first of three consecutive league titles. Ned Hanlon, in his second full season as Orioles manager, oversaw the dramatic improvement. The Maryland club soared to the top of the league with an 89–39 record. Left fielder Joe Kelley enjoyed a breakout season, leading all teammates with a .393 average and a slugging percentage .602. Pitcher Sadie McMahon solidified his station as the team's ace with a 25-win campaign. Baltimore was aided immensely by a trade that delivered veteran first baseman Dan Brouthers and young outfielder Willie Keeler in the off-season from Brooklyn. Brouthers, in his last starring season, hit .347 and led the club in home runs with nine and RBI with 128. Keeler was a small, 22-year-old outfielder, measuring 5' 4½". More colloquially known as "Wee Willie," the lightweight flychaser smacked the ball at a .371 clip, collecting over 200 hits for the first of eight consecutive seasons.

McGraw was the starting third baseman (displaced at shortstop by Hughie Jennings); he hit .340 and scored 156 runs in 124 games, in the runs-prevalent environment. He was not tagged with any ejections for the year, although he was fortunate to be spared one on May 15. Per SABR Games Project writer Terry Gottschall, McGraw was involved in some otherwise game-banishing conduct at Boston's South End Grounds. "Unexpected fireworks broke out on the field," wrote Gottschall. "As the Beaneaters' Tommy 'Foghorn' Tucker slid into third base, the Orioles' John McGraw kicked him in the face.... The umpire broke up the ensuing brawl."[8] In the very next inning, fire swept through the park's wooden grandstand, halting the incomplete game in the third inning.

Every member of the starting lineup hit over .300, and six of them scored at least 134 runs (in a 130-game schedule!), as the 1894 Orioles outlasted the second-place New York Giants by three games to grab the National League's coveted stanchion. The champs clinched the flag on their final road trip of the season and received a hero's welcome upon their return home.

> When the team's train reached Baltimore, it was met at the depot by one of the largest throngs that has turned out in a long time, and the players were driven to the best hotel in the city. The night after the return of the team to Baltimore one of the most magnificent banquets was given the players. At the banquet was the mayor of the city, judges of the court and state officials.[9]

The 1894 season begat a tradition in which the top two teams played each other for what was known as the Temple Cup, a sporting trophy donated by the president of the Pittsburgh Pirates, William C. Temple. The best-of-seven-game engagement was intended to leave no doubt as to who was the league's top team. The Temple Cup competition lasted for four seasons.

The inaugural square-off, which began a few days after the Orioles' triumphant return to Baltimore, did not come off without a hitch. As late as a few hours before the start of the first game, on October 4, there was doubt that the event would proceed. The issue had to do with players' compensation. Some Orioles had balked at the proposed winners' and losers' disparate gate split, preferring an even division of the receipts regardless of the series' outcome. They based their position on already being crowned league champions. But the incentive-driven division of proceeds won out. "The agreement to play the series of games under the condition that the winner take 65 percent of the receipts was made only a few minutes before the game was called," divulged one newsprint report.[10]

An Eastern newspaper revealed that McGraw had been among the leading dissenters. "It was not until play was about to be called that Jennings, McGraw, Gleason, Kelley and Keeler came to terms," said the *Brooklyn Daily Eagle*. "However ungracefully the Baltimore players may have acceded to the ultimatum of the Temple Cup trustees, the victory gained by Messrs. Byrne and Young and in general the league will tend to create added confidence among baseball enthusiasts."[11]

Not enthused were those hometown supporters in Game One, as the Giants' Amos Rusie suppressed the league champions, 4–1, on seven hits. McGraw collected two of the safeties and scored the only Orioles run. Another New York daily interestingly described the Orioles' attire for the game as "uniforms of solid black, with 'Baltimore' inscribed in orange letters across the breast, an orange colored belt and two orange colored stripes around the calf of the stockings. The cap is an Eaton one, with an oriole's wing embroidered on the front."[12]

The following day, with 11,000 fans on hand at Union Park (roughly 1,000 fewer than the previous day), Giants pitcher and 33-game winner Jouett Meekin outlasted Orioles hurler Kid Gleason, 9–6. Meekin was reached for seven hits and three earned runs. McGraw went hitless. The series moved to New York on October 6. Rusie, a 36-game winner for the Giants on the season, repeated his Game One effort (on one day's rest) and downed Baltimore, 4–1. An estimated 20,000 fans watched his seven-hitter at the Polo Grounds.

After a Sunday off-day, on Monday October 8, Meekin cruised to his second win, 16–3. Half the number of spectators were in attendance as the previous game, due to threatening weather. Gleason suffered his second loss. The blowout was called after eight innings due to darkness. McGraw singled and stole a base. (A speedy runner, McGraw stole 78 bases during the season, second-best in the league to Billy Hamilton's 100.) Spearheading the 88-win Giants to the series' victory were two pitchers who had earned an incredible 78 percent of the team's regular season wins. Two umpires, Tim Hurst and Bob Emslie, officiated the four games.

In 1895, Hanlon's Orioles repeated their showing as the National League's best team. The club's 87–43 record bested the second-place Cleveland Spiders by three games. But the Cy Young–led Spiders outshone the league champions, four games to one, to win the Temple Cup.

Slowed that year by what was diagnosed as a strain of malaria, McGraw missed 36 of his club's 132 games, yet swiped 61 bases. He hit an impressive .369 in 388 at-bats, seemingly unaffected by the new rule that allowed the catcher and first baseman to use gloves or mitts of "any size, shape or weight."[13] All other fielders had to manage with regulation ten-ounce gloves with a maximum circumference around the palm of 14 inches.

Although two umpires were used in the Temple Cup series, with few exceptions, one was the norm per game in the league. McGraw's developed defiance toward those holding field authority has probably been given too much credit for helping steer baseball at this time toward the two-umpire system. On defense, as a third baseman, McGraw was said to use underhanded means to try and prevent runs from scoring. In an attempt to delay an advance home on a potential sacrifice fly, McGraw would routinely hook his fingers into a tagged-up runner's belt. He would pull his fingers out the moment the sole umpire, watching the flight of the ball, spun around to check that the runner had not left the base prior to the catch. The unprincipled tactic was said to have saved his pitchers numerous runs, with many of the initially impeded runners being thrown out at the plate. Protests by the other teams were rarely upheld as the umpire was not able to catch McGraw in the act. Some rival players began unbuckling their belts in anticipation of McGraw's unprincipled move, leaving history with perhaps exaggerated stories of McGraw standing at third base with an opposing player's belt in his hand.

Future teammate Mike Donlin supported the basis that the additional field umpire was inspired by McGraw, but offered a varying reason. "In those days he never touched a base if he could help it," stated Donlin, a fascinating figure who became a stage and silent screen actor *during* and after his baseball career. "With McGraw on second, when I batted behind him, I knew we were sure of a run if I could force the third baseman to handle the ball. The umpire looking at the play at first could not watch third, too, and he never would see Mac until he came sliding into the plate. So they put another umpire on him to see that he touched all the bases."[14]

The Temple Cup opened in Cleveland on Wednesday, October 2. The Spiders scored twice in the bottom of the ninth inning to make Cy Young a winner, 5–4. McGraw had three hits and scored twice, with one caught stealing. The following side note to the game indicated that the disorderly climate surrounding the sport was not limited solely to players: "An opposing fielder was interfered with by a crank. In the eighth inning Zimmer sent a long fly to Kelley, and as he was about to catch it, a wild-eyed fan ran up to him and knocked the ball out of his hand. Zimmer took second base but after a lengthy wrangle he was called out."[15]

One thousand more "cranks"—a 19th century term for "fans"—than the 7,000 for the first game, turned out the next day at League Park. Cleveland scored three times in the first inning against the Orioles' top pitcher, Bill Hoffer, and won, 7–2. Hoffer, 31–6 on the season, permitted but three earned runs. McGraw took the collar in four trips.

Following a day off, the third game was also played in Ohio. Cy Young was in better form than three days earlier, downing the visitors, 7–1. McGraw, the leadoff hitter, opened the game with a bunt single but was erased trying to steal. Young was touched for six more hits the rest of the way. Orioles pitcher Sadie McMahon lost his second game of the series. As big a crowd as the game before came out, with twice as many patrons willing but unable to gain access to the ball park grounds.

The series shifted venues and resumed on Monday, October 7, after the mandatory Sabbath observation. At Union Park, the Orioles' number three man in the rotation, Duke Esper, shut out the Spiders, 5–0. The five-hitter by Esper was not the only indignity the Cleveland team was made to suffer. "Paper balls, peanuts, one or two eggs and finally a rock were thrown at Spiders players," it was reported, "as they left their hotel for the grounds, and after reaching there they were hissed by a small part of the crowd, but this was frowned upon by the majority, and there were no further attempts at insult during the game."[16]

The Spiders wrapped up the series the next day, with Young (35–10 during the campaign), winning his third game in seven days. A blustery day kept the crowd to an estimated 4,100, less than half of yesterday's Union Park total. Young allowed eight hits and two runs; the final was 5–2. McGraw registered two of the hits and scored one run. Hoffer was the loser.

Once again, Hanlon's pennant-winners had dropped the Cup Series to the runner-up club.

In 1896, for the second year in a row, McGraw contracted a potentially fatal disease.

Dressed in the high-end men's fashion of the era, clockwise from top left, Willie Keeler, McGraw, Hughie Jennings and Joe Kelley. Representing the pre–20th century Baltimore Orioles' best position players, the quartet was referred to as the "Big Four."

Prior to his 23rd birthday, McGraw was stricken with the new ailment. "The champion Baltimores are compelled to begin [the season] without their great third baseman John McGraw," explained a spring training report. "Typhoid fever is a great weakener and recovery is discouragingly slow."[17]

McGraw was admitted to St. Joseph's Infirmary in Atlanta. On the verge of being released, he suffered a relapse during the second week of May. It took nearly a month for him to recover sufficiently to leave the hospital's care. He rejoined his club in July but played sparingly. The severe affliction limited McGraw to only 26 games. Jim Donnelly took over the third base bag during McGraw's lengthy incapacitation.

The Orioles were the class of the league without McGraw, winning a stupendous 90 of 132 contests. Hanlon's club outdistanced the second-place Cleveland Spiders again, this time by 9½ games. Hughie Jennings, who had become the Orioles' star shortstop, hit .401. He was also struck by pitched balls *51* times—a record that has endured through the game's different and evolving "eras," through today. Though he accepted only 19 walks in nearly 600 plate appearances, Jennings accumulated a great on-base percentage of .472.

Left fielder Joe Kelley topped the circuit in stolen bases with 87 and knocked in 100 runs, second to team leader Jennings' 121. He also hit .364. On the strength of 210 hits (one more than Jennings), Wee Willie Keeler improved his batting average to .386 from last year's .377.

In their second Temple Cup meeting with Cleveland, the Orioles this time reaffirmed the dominance they had shown throughout the season. A freight train wreck on the Baltimore and Ohio Railroad delayed the Cleveland team from reaching Baltimore in time for the first scheduled game on October 1. The third Cup Series opened the following day, Friday. Despite favorable weather, only 4,000 fans came out to see the match—a 7–1 victory for the home team. Orioles ace Bill Hoffer displayed fine form in subduing the invading hitters to the tune of only five hits allowed. Last year's Orioles' mound nemesis, Cy Young, was roughed up for 13 hits. McGraw recorded a hit and a run scored. Perhaps still not physically up for the challenge, he was replaced by Joe Quinn after two at-bats.

McGraw played the entirety of game two behind winning pitcher Joe Corbett, who tamed the opposition, 7–2, surrendering seven hits and one earned run. The game was called after eight innings on account of darkness. McGraw duplicated his offensive efforts from the first game, adding two stolen bases. A second disappointing crowd of 3,100 was on hand.

Hoffer, a 25-game winner, returned to the mound for the third engagement, also in Baltimore, on October 5. He was slightly less effective than in his Game One start but, nevertheless, pitched his team to victory, 6–2. He allowed ten hits, but only one over the last four innings. McGraw was the offensive catalyst for the winners. He hit safely twice, scored a pair of runs and stole two bases.

Poor weather postponed the scheduled fourth game in Cleveland until October 8. Hanlon called on Corbett again, and the late-season acquisition did not disappoint. The right-hander, who was the younger brother of heavyweight prize fighter "Gentleman Jim" Corbett, cinched the Cup for the Orioles with a 5–2 triumph. He and Keeler were the hitting stars with three hits apiece. The attendance of only 1,500 implied that Cleveland rooters held out little comeback hope for their team. Spiders first baseman and captain Patsy Tebeau sprained his back in the first game and did not see action for the rest of the series. Young also did not pitch again in the series following his first game start, presumably due to a physical ailment.

The extra spending money from the series expectedly came in handy for McGraw, who married four months later. On February 3, 1897, he took as his bride a young Baltimore native named Minnie Doyle, the 20-year-old daughter of a civil servant named Michael Doyle. McGraw, though still shy of his 24th birthday, had made enough of a name for himself at this time for the nuptials to be recorded in a broad range of East Coast newspapers.

One such daily inscribed the happy occasion in this manner:

St. Vincent's Church was packed to the doors this evening with baseball "fans" and rooters to see the marriage of popular third baseman John McGraw. Hughie Jennings, as best man, looked as happy as the groom himself as he walked up the aisle with Miss Margaret Tighe on his arm and his face as full of blushes as it is when girls applaud him for a grand-stand play. The other bridesmaids were Miss Ella Doyle, sister of the bride and Miss Catherine Sweeney. The ushers were Joseph J. Kelley and Willie Keeler, the other members of Baltimore's "big four." Seven Catholic priests, friends of the popular ball player, were in the sanctuary. After the ceremony there was a reception at the home of the bride's parents.[18]

Two and a half months hence, McGraw's already seventh big league season began with a bit of a setback. Incurring an injury, possibly on Opening Day, the infielder missed nearly two full weeks before he made another appearance, pinch-hitting on May 5 at Eastern Park in Brooklyn.

On May 20, he had been back in the lineup on a regular basis when unsportsmanlike conduct on his part resulted in a banishment from a game against the Cincinnati Reds at League Park. McGraw was thrown out at home plate and became enraged at the call by umpire Jack Sheridan. "He will not be whiter when he is in his coffin than he was when he charged Sheridan," reported the *Cincinnati Enquirer*.[19] Venomously denouncing the call, with clenched fists, McGraw was directed off the field and fined $25. The incident occurred in the eighth inning, the same frame Cincinnati rallied for six runs to take an 11–9 lead. The final was 11–10.

The next day against the same team, McGraw was also given the heave-ho by Sheridan. The poor sportsman deliberately spiked the heel of first baseman Farmer Vaughn on a routine play at the bag. Vaughn threw the ball at McGraw's head but missed. Umpire Sheridan, and others, intervened to prevent a fight between the two players. "Every time McGraw came down to first he tried to cut me down," Vaughn said after the game. "In the eighth, the play was close and I did not get my foot off the bag before he could catch me. He caught me in the heel with his plates and cut the shoe in three places. There ought to be some way of protecting players from spikers and leg breakers."[20] Satisfyingly for Farmer and his teammates, the Reds won, 6–5.

At season's end, Hanlon's Orioles (90–40) slipped to second place, two games behind the pennant-grabbing Boston Beaneaters. Keeler led the league with a .424 batting mark, amassing 239 hits in 129 games. McGraw, appearing in 106 games, topped the circuit in on-base percentage, .471. Pitcher Joe Corbett, one of last year's Temple Cup standouts, won 24 games. He was one of three 20-game winners on the Orioles' staff.

The last of the Temple Cup series opened at South End Grounds in Boston, October 4. On a pleasant fall afternoon, in front of a large crowd of 10,000, manager Frank Selee's Beaneaters scored two runs in the bottom of the eighth inning to pull out a come-from-behind, 13–12 victory. Only four of Boston's runs were earned. The Orioles made four errors, including one each by McGraw and Hughie Jennings. McGraw registered three hits and the same number of runs scored. Jennings recorded five hits and two runs in the losing cause. Ted Lewis, in relief of Kid Nichols, was the winning pitcher. Jerry Nops (20–6) was the starter and loser for Baltimore.

Behind Joe Corbett, the Orioles evened the series the next day, winning 13–11. Five of the winning team's runs—like four charged to the record of Corbett—were unearned. The Orioles hit three home runs, including one by victorious hurler Corbett, who had three other hits. Among the 17 safeties batted out by the Orioles, McGraw recorded a triple. The Orioles defeated Fred Klobedanz, a 26-game winner and Boston's number two pitcher behind Nichols. Orioles center fielder Jake Stenzel recorded nine putouts.

The final game in Boston was played on October 6. The sloppy play of the past two days carried over into a rain-shortened contest won by Baltimore, 8–3. Ted Lewis (21–12) opened for the home club. Early wildness forced his removal in the second inning, when the Orioles scored four runs. Klobedanz, yesterday's starter, relieved. He permitted four more runs to the visitors in the third and four more in the eighth. A heavy rain shower forced postponement of the game in the same uncompleted inning. The score reverted to the seventh inning, ending at a final of 8–3. Only two of the Orioles' runs were legitimately made. McGraw went 1-for-4 with two runs. Twenty-two-game-winner Bill Hoffer was the victor.

The first three games drew approximately 21,000 spectators. When the series moved to Baltimore, the local enthusiasm displayed a direct contrast. Only 2,600 fans showed up for the Saturday, October 9 match-up. It seemed that the hearts of Boston's players were not into the endeavor either, as the Orioles scored 11 runs in the first two innings. Jack Stivetts, the Beaneaters' number four starter, was knocked out early and supplanted by Ted Lewis.

Boston staged a comeback in later innings when Baltimore starter Nops apparently tired and had to be rescued by Corbett. The final was 12–11. Nine of the Orioles' runs were unearned. McGraw notched a hit in his only official at-bat. The Beaneaters outhit their counterparts, 16–14. Center fielder Stenzel led the Orioles' attack with four hits.

By the time of the next game, Monday, October 11, it seemed that interest from all involved parties had been lost. "A crowd so small that management refused to give the exact number," conveyed one account of the apathy surrounding the game, "and so utterly devoid of enthusiasm that scarcely a ripple of applause occurred, saw one of the shortest games on record."[21]

Regulars Joe Kelley (LF) and Jack Doyle (1B) sat out the contest for the Orioles. For Boston, pitcher Jack Stivetts (0-for-5) played center field in place of speedster Billy Hamilton, the league leader in runs scored. Stivetts committed one of three Boston errors. Baltimore won handily, 9–3, two-thirds of their runs unearned. Scattering 15 hits, Bill Hoffer won for the second time. McGraw went hitless in five chances. The game was played in one hour and 20 minutes. It was officiated by Tim Hurst and Bob Emslie, completing their second Temple Cup partnering and third each, individually.

The lack of fan support toward the end and the players' noticeable devaluation of the competition led to the discontinuance of the series. At the owners' meeting in Philadelphia the following month, it was unanimously agreed to abandon the Temple Cup series. (The *Pittsburgh Post* circulated that New York Giants owner Andrew Freedman was originally the sole dissenting vote, feeling that his club was ready to make a move to the top of the league. Freedman, it was later explained, changed his position in order to make the vote unanimous.)

Shortly after the mid–November decision, W. C. Temple requested from Baltimore owner Harry von der Horst that his loving cup be shipped to him "express collect" in Pittsburgh.

The 12-team National League lengthened their schedule to 154 games in 1898 and assigned two umpires per game on a more recurring basis. The 102-win Beaneaters repeated as champions. McGraw led the league in runs (143) and bases on balls (112). He hit .342 in 515 at-bats, with 176 hits (career high), in his best offensive season since 1894.

During this period, McGraw and teammate Keeler began devising measures to upset their opponent's defensive schemes. (Keeler won his second straight batting title, hitting .385 in 1898.)

The pair have often been credited with developing what became known as the hit and run play and the "Baltimore chop"—purposely swinging down on the ball to cause a high enough bounce on the infield to enable the hitter to beat the fielder's throw to first. A different McGraw teammate, however, went on record early in the 20th century as being co-responsible for coming up with the interconnected strategy. "None of us had ever heard of a hit and run…. It came up accidentally the first game of the 1894 season," attested Joe Kelley. "We were playing New York. McGraw got on first base and started to steal. I saw him going, and when the ball came over the plate I swung for it. Johnny Ward had left his position to cover second base to get the throw, and I hit it through his position. The play struck us as being a corker. The next day we were all at the park early and we practiced that play."[22]

McGraw's fateful run-ins with the umpires increased this season. He was ejected four times due to discordant behavior. Three 20-game winners and a 16-game victor helped the Orioles to a 96-win season, their best under Hanlon. But the manager's squad finished in second place, six games off the pace. Despite winning 96 games in 1898, the Orioles drew poorly. The club had the tenth-worst attendance in the league (123,416). After seven years at the helm, manager Ned Hanlon sought to make a change. Whether he had soured on his team or city's lack of support, or was struck with a rush of ambition—or was simply influenced by his boss—Hanlon and Harry von der Horst initiated a large-scale transaction prior to the 1899 season that would place Hanlon at the head of another team and hasten the end of major league baseball in Baltimore for more than half a century. At a time when owners wielded supreme power, especially the wealthier ones, von der Horst, along with Hanlon, purchased interest in another ball club while maintaining ownership of the Orioles. By exchanging controlling shares of half of one team for half of the other, the Baltimore and Brooklyn ownership groups became equal partners in both teams.

This naturally bred a favoritism that was inclined to benefit one team. In this case, Baltimore ended up as the poor stepchild in ownership's eyes. Hanlon brought the majority of his star players with him to Brooklyn, including Kelley, Keeler, Jennings and 23-game-winner Jay Hughes. Eight former Orioles players were "assigned" to the newly renamed "Superbas" of Brooklyn. Hughes led the league with 28 wins, and the 101-win Superbas won the pennant by eight games.

The same off-season, a similar situation came to pass between the magnates of franchises in St. Louis and Cleveland. Frank and Stanley Robison, Cleveland owners, capitalized on the bankrupt state of the St. Louis Browns franchise and in the bargain indifferently left the Spiders destitute. The brothers' purchase of the Midwest franchise exposed a stark conflict of interest, after Spiders manager Patsy Tabeau gutted his former team to bring playing with him to St. Louis, under his newly appointed managerial tutelage. While there had been 19 previous instances of owners with stakes in more than one club, this new, broader extension into what historically became known as "syndicate baseball" proved detrimental to the game. The 1899 Cleveland Spiders, having lost 17 players to St. Louis, would finish the season with 20 wins and 134 losses, the worst record and winning percentage (.130) in baseball history.

Meanwhile, John McGraw, who had established business interests in Baltimore, along with Wilbert Robinson, could not be lured east by Hanlon. Robinson also stayed in Baltimore. Either one of the pair seemed the logical choice as the next Orioles manager. The 34-year-old Robinson was the longest-tenured Oriole, having first joined the club in 1890. Based on experience, he seemed to be the front-runner. But von der Horst and Hanlon decided on greater youth. McGraw's appointment as Orioles manager was confirmed during a meeting between executives of both teams in Baltimore on March 10.

McGraw's first game as player-manager came on April 15 and ended on a winning note. In front of a Union Park Opening Day crowd of 4,000, the Orioles outplayed the visiting New York Giants, 5–3. Frank Kitson, a second-year player, picked up the win. In the third game of the series, April 18, Joe McGinnity made his professional debut. McGinnity, a 28-year-old right-hander who pitched in the Western Association the prior year, topped the Giants, 8–4, benefiting from eight runs scored by the home team in the eighth inning. The hurler, who would be nicknamed "Iron Man"—derived from an off-season metal casting job—went the distance, allowing eight hits and two earned runs.

Two days later, the Orioles visited New York, where "six thousand persons, the smallest Opening Day crowd on record at the Polo Grounds, saw the New Yorks win a drawn-out but exciting game."[23] The Giants won, 5–4, scoring the deciding run in the bottom of the eighth inning, following an obstruction call on McGraw. The Orioles' third baseman grabbed Giants runner George Davis by the arm to prevent him from trying to score following a base hit.

Umpire Ed Andrews ("assistant" to John Gaffney, behind the plate) flagged McGraw and allowed Davis to score. McGraw was fined $5 for objecting too intensely to the decision. Robinson joined McGraw in protest but went too far and was booted from the game—the first ejection of his 14-year-career. The sprightly McGraw registered two hits, stole two bases and scored three-fourths of his team's runs.

The Orioles, under McGraw, were 23–18, 7½ games behind Brooklyn on June 5, the day the player-manager sustained the first of his five expulsions for the campaign. Ed Swartwood, a third-year umpire, tossed McGraw for squawking too strenuously on a strike called against him in the eighth inning of a 9–3 game, in favor of the visiting Chicago Orphans. The final was 9–4. Swartwood also ejected Chicago pitcher Clark Griffith for his objections to the strike zone in the third inning. "Swartwood gave an exhibition of bad umpiring and cowardice," wrote a non-impartial staff correspondent of the *Chicago Tribune*, "He permitted McGraw to do as he pleased. Once, after he put McGraw out of the game, he ordered the belligerent midget off the field, whereupon McGraw sat on the grass near the plate and heaped abuse on the umpire to the end, defying him to carry out his order."[24] Bill Phyle picked up the win in relief of Griffith, and McGinnity took the loss for the Orioles.

On June 18, McGraw made his first player deal as a manager that did not involve Brooklyn and, therefore, one that could be considered as his first as head of the ball club. He sold backup second baseman John O'Brien to the Pittsburgh Pirates. O'Brien, a weak hitter, concluded his six-year big league career with Pittsburgh in 1899. No matter how minimal a cash exchange was involved, McGraw came out ahead.

A month later, McGraw was again up to his dirty tricks, defending his position, and it cost him. "Cincinnati won today … the game being hotly contested and winding up in a fight between McGraw and [Tommy] Cochran," augmented one wire report. "The scrappy third baseman attempted to block Cochran, while running to third and a war of words followed. Cochran did not take kindly to an epithet applied by McGraw and struck him squarely in the face. [Umpire Tom] Lynch put both players out of the game."[25] Spurred by the ninth-inning incident, overheated Orioles fans spilled out onto the field in defense of McGraw. A swarm of police were required to restore order. The Reds won, 7–5.

Nine days afterward, on July 27, the Orioles played the worst team in the league and swept a pair of games. McGraw was ejected from the second game "for kicking at one of Snyder's decisions."[26] The Cleveland Spiders, forced to play the majority of their games on the road because they could not draw at home, fell to the Orioles at Union Park, 8–5 and 9–4.

"Kicking" was a term used to describe excessive or repeated complaints by a ballplayer directed at an umpire. "Kicking on the decisions of one of the umpires"[27] was also the cause of McGraw's next ejection on August 26. It came in Louisville. The Colonels scored three runs in the eighth, the inning of McGraw's dismissal, and won, 5–1.

The next day, the Orioles attempted to play two games in Louisville's Eclipse Park. The Orioles won the first game, 7–3; the second game was called a 4–4 tie due to darkness.

McGraw was not around for the nightcap. Before the finish of game one, he had been called away from the dugout by a telegram informing him that his wife was seriously ill. McGraw left the team immediately and headed home. The Orioles were playing at a better than .600 winning clip (.607). The team was in fourth place, 7 ½ games behind the potent Superbas. The team captain as well as manager, McGraw was having a fine season at the plate, especially when it came to getting on base. He had been the first player in the league to score 100 runs. But everything took a back seat to the news in the telegram.

Tragically, Minnie McGraw died after five days at Maryland General Hospital and four days after her ballplaying husband had been summoned to Baltimore via telegram.

The rookie manager was apart from his team for a two-week interval following the death of his wife, who passed away from complications of a ruptured appendix. Hughie Jennings, who had been best man at their nuptial ceremony, served as one of the pallbearers on Minnie's burial day. "The funeral took plae 31 months to the day of the wedding," announced a special wire report from Baltimore, "and the wedding gown served for the funeral shroud."[28] Other pallbearers were Joe Kelley and Wee Willie Keeler.

Wilbert Robinson took over managing the Orioles in McGraw's absence, and then he too took a brief leave to attend Minnie McGraw's funeral. After missing 15 games, including one tie, McGraw returned to the team on September 11 in Baltimore. It must have been extremely difficult for McGraw to suddenly become a widower. One can hope he used the game as a bracing tonic, in some way, to cope with the heartbreaking loss of his young wife, only 22 years old. McGraw did not put himself back into the lineup until September 21, almost three weeks since his Minnie's death.

McGraw's ninth big league campaign ended with the final games on the schedule, October 14. He did not play in most of the October games after being hit by a pitched ball on October 3. He hit a career-high .391, leading the league in both runs scored (140) and walks (124) for the second consecutive season. Playing in a reduced 117 games, he also topped the circuit in on-base percentage (for a second time) with a staggering .547 mark—an all-time high for pre-modern era baseball.

Before the 1899 campaign was completed, John T. Brush, owner of the Cincinnati Reds, made an overture to McGraw for him to come to Cincinnati as manager of the

Reds for the 1900 season. McGraw resisted. A few months later, the Baltimore franchise disbanded, a victim of contraction in the 12-team league that also claimed three other clubs. Tied through common ownership to Brooklyn, McGraw was assigned to the Superbas on March 9, 1900, and then was sold by that club to the St. Louis Cardinals (the franchise owned by the Robison brothers) the following day.

Brooklyn received $19,000 from the Cardinals in exchange for McGraw, fellow Baltimore infielder Bill Keister and catcher Wilbert Robinson. McGraw and Robinson, because of their long-standing business and personal ties, did not want to uproot themselves to the western degree of the Mound City. "I wish you would say for me that we are not going to play in St. Louis," McGraw said, speaking for Robinson as well. "We will play in New York or Philadelphia, if the league will make arrangements to that effect, but we will positively not go to St. Louis."[29] To back their position, McGraw and Robinson did not join their new club and threatened to retire.

St. Louis ownership convinced the players otherwise, using the usual persuasive inducement. McGraw was offered a salary of $6,000 and Robinson $4,500, with the players also dividing half of their sale price. It was too lucrative a deal to pass up. After missing 16 games of the Cardinals' schedule, the hold-out players arrived in St. Louis and played their first game on May 12. "McGraw made his debut in a St. Louis uniform, and despite the street car strike 7,300 rooters turned out to welcome him," chronicled one report. "McGraw got a great reception, as did Robinson, both receiving numerous floral gifts."[30] The veteran third baseman made a throwing error, contributing to three ninth-innings runs the visiting Brooklyn Superbas scored to extricate a 5–4 victory. The 35-year-old Robinson started behind the plate. He stroked three hits and scored a run, along with McGraw.

Three weeks later, on June 2, McGraw drew his and his new team's first ejection of the season. In a game replete with runs, hits and errors, the Cardinals defeated the Boston Beaneaters, 17–16, in ten innings. At South End Grounds, Boston lashed out 23 hits off three St. Louis pitchers, and committed eight errors—three more than the visiting team. St. Louis cranked out 14 hits in helping forge their runs. The game lasted 3 hours and 32 minutes. McGraw missed most of it, having been run in the third inning by the game's sole umpire, Bob Emslie, for indelicately disputing an out call at first base on teammate Jesse Burkett. (The shrunken league, undoubtedly with costs in mind, returned—with few exceptions—to the one-umpiring system in 1900.)

One week afterward, McGraw was spiked on the ankle by former teammate Jack Doyle on a hard slide into third base. McGraw was removed from the contest and did not return to the lineup until June 25. Completely healed, the testy player experienced his second early dismissal from a game the following month. At the Polo Grounds on July 19, McGraw objected to a second-inning safe call at first base on Giants pitcher Win Mercer by Adonis Terry. McGraw trudged over from third base to the pitcher's mound, where he railed at the nearby Terry, a retired pitcher trying his hand at umpiring. McGraw slandered Terry's decision more than the umpire could stand and swiftly lost his playing privileges. Mercer and the Giants were victorious, 8–3, pleasing the majority of 2,000 folks present.

In August, McGraw contracted a case of the boils, causing him to miss more action while he healed from the skin inflammation.

That same month, another example of the exceedingly roughhouse style of play that McGraw adhered to surfaced in a newspaper column. "In the eighth round," wrote famed baseball writer Charles Dryden, with a scrutinizing poke at the player's current princely salary,

> McGraw saw himself caught at third and shot both fists into the bagman's eye, knocking [Harry] Wolverton flat on his back and creating a mouse-colored lump under Wolverton's left eye. In the old days, at a meager pittance of $4,500 per, "Mugsy" would have been content to use one fist. But now with the $9,500 salary of a U.S. Senator, he must slam both hooks into the visage of an inoffensive player.[31]

The occurrence came during a Cardinals 10–3 win over the Philadelphia Phillies on August 13. A tiny home crowd of 700 applauded McGraw's unprincipled tactics.

Also during the same dog days of August, a news item surfaced from Cincinnati that team owner John T. Brush had again put out his prior, gainful $10,000 offer to McGraw to come to the Reds and manage in 1901. It was speculated that Brush would offer a top pitcher and cash to the Cardinals (who were still referred to by their 1899 founding nickname of "Perfectos" in most newsprint outlets). It was widely known on the underachieving Cardinals—several games under .500 and out of pennant contention—that McGraw and manager Patsy Tebeau did not get along. On August 19, the 35-year-old Tebeau abruptly quit. McGraw, wanting to avoid what he deemed as an unappealing situation with the second division team, refused the offered role as replacement chief. Club secretary Louie Heilbroner took over for the last 50 games of the season, with McGraw, some complained, rendering only half-hearted assistance.

On September 8, at the Polo Grounds, McGraw was thrown out at the plate on a close play in the first inning and unleashed his well-known ire on umpire John Gaffney. The arbiter would not stand for all McGraw had to say and put the incendiary character out of the game. In the third frame, left fielder Jesse Burkett joined his banished teammate when he was "not particular in his remarks" after Gaffney called Wilbert Robinson out at third base. "McGraw and Burkett planted themselves in right field in the last inning and burned newspapers over their head,"[32] noted one broadsheet. The cause behind the petulant gesture by the men, aimed at none other than umpire Gaffney, was that of calling attention to descending darkness over the park. The game, in fact, was called in the eighth inning with the Cardinals batting (and having scored two runs). Reverting back to the last completed inning, the visitors won, 6–5.

Eleven days later, Gaffney was behind the plate in a different New York borough when another altercation involving McGraw and Robinson brought a discreditable ending to a game at Washington Park. A third-inning close call at the plate instigated a forfeit in favor of the Brooklyn Superbas. Catcher Robinson was so incensed at a safe signal by Gaffney on runner Duke Farrell that he threw the ball hard at the arbiter's feet, and he leveraged his corpulent body to push Gaffney forcibly. Staggered, Gaffney swung his mask at Robinson in self-defense, barely missing his face. Expectedly, Robinson, and then McGraw, who jumped into it, were both tossed from the fray. The St. Louis squad, indisputably influenced by McGraw, refused to put a substitute catcher on the field. After delaying too long in providing another catcher for the game to continue, Gaffney awarded the game to Brooklyn by the 9–0 forfeit score.

With the loss, the sixth-place Cardinals fell 19 games behind Brooklyn, the same position and number of games they would trail the pennant-winners by when the season ended in four weeks.

TWO

Birth of a Baseball Legend

"He used to tell me there were things he would not stand in a ballplayer, and those were crookedness, dumbness and disobedience."—Blanche McGraw

For the game of baseball, the off-season of 1900–1901 was historic. A minor league executive named Byron Bancroft Johnson organized a new major circuit, which he would call the American League. Along with Charles Comiskey and the financial resources of coal magnate Charles Somers, Ban Johnson established a new eight-team loop that debuted, with great success, in 1901. Johnson, the league's first president, was intent on re-establishing the Baltimore franchise that had dissolved the prior year. Johnson was also intent on branding a new type of baseball that stressed integrity, fair play and sportsmanship as its common characteristics. These aspired-to "wholesome" values were in direct contrast with the National League's sometimes unscrupulous and commonly gritty, hard-nosed type of play.

Johnson reached out to the 28-year-old John McGraw to come back to his familiar port city for the inaugural year of his new circuit as player-manager. McGraw gladly returned in the offered capacity and led (on paper but not as everyday manager) the 68–65 Orioles to a fifth-place finish, while playing fewer than half of the team's games as its third baseman.

Johnson's choice of McGraw—the antithesis of his desired new make-over for the game—has been understandably questioned. The league's head grossly misjudged McGraw's ability to toe the new comportment line. Johnson's overall marketing sense, however, was much better in the area of fan comfort for the Charm City. He gave his blessing to the construction of a new playing venue for the inaugural season of the American League team, carrying with it the name of Oriole Park.

Perhaps some reasoning for Johnson appointing McGraw can be extracted from the following November report out of Washington, where a meeting of AL bigwigs took place: "John McGraw, the kingpin of the present baseball situation in the East, spent the best part of today in conference with Messrs. Johnson, Somers, Comiskey and [Connie] Mack, of the American League."[1] It seemed clear that Johnson knew that he not only had a big drawing card, at hand, in McGraw, but also a legitimizing figure for his ambitious new venture.

"I came over here to learn what Mr. Johnson had to offer me as far as a strong circuit," said the coy McGraw after the initial meeting.

I am waiting for the best offer for Baltimore. We have given Baltimore good ball in the past, and I am looking for the league that will come nearest equaling it next year. It is not a question of salary. Whatever I am doing is thoroughly proper. My contract with the National League has expired, and at any rate, the fact of the St. Louis club owing me money, according to National League law, would nullify my contract.[2]

The posturing by McGraw was brief in duration. He and Wilbert Robinson became part of a local ownership group of the reborn Orioles. The American League matched the National not only in teams but in length of schedule, opting for the reduced 140 games the older circuit had endorsed in 1900. National League teams were required to cut their rosters to 16 by May 15.

The new rival league opened the season with a roster of 15 players per team and decided to match their older counterpart in settling—for the most part—on one umpire per game.

Once he became manager, McGraw began the work of hiring his employees. Besides Robinson, he brought with him from St. Louis shortstop Bill Keister. Cardinals outfielder Mike Donlin also reunited with his former captain, after a fallout with team owner Frank Robison. In mid–March, in an early show of spotting promising talent, McGraw signed untested Roger Bresnahan. A 20-year-old who had debuted in the major leagues as a pitcher, Bresnahan would become the innovator of protective catching equipment and a valuably versatile player for McGraw in Baltimore and then New York. The young player had been released by the Chicago Orphans in September. Later in the month, McGraw inked Jimmy Williams, who skipped out on Pittsburgh to become the Orioles' starting second baseman. Primarily a New York Giants pitcher for the past five years, Cy Seymour was signed by McGraw a few days prior to the season. Cursed by wildness, Seymour was transitioned into a full-time outfielder by his new manager in 1901 and in 134 games would hit .303 (coincidentally his lifetime batting average).

McGraw's biggest signing coup was that of Joe McGinnity, snatching him away from Ned Hanlon and the Superbas. "Turning down an offer of almost twice as much to return to Brooklyn," wrote SABR biographer Michael Wells, "McGinnity signed for $2,800 with the Baltimore franchise in the new American League."[3] If true, this was quite a testament to McGraw (or a disdain for Hanlon and the Superbas) on McGinnity's part. Brooklyn also lost another pitcher, Harry Howell, to the Orioles in the same unrestricted manner.

During the McGinnity contract deliberations, Hanlon had stated that he was not worried about being able to sign the star pitcher or any of his players for the upcoming campaign. "Instead of the usual contacts, which attempt to reserve a player forever and therefore of doubtful validity," he said, "the Brooklyn contracts contain a special clause which give the club a special option on the players' services for one, two, or three years. Before the team disbanded, I notified all players that the option was exercised and their contract renewed for another year."[4]

Clearly, Brooklyn's contract option clauses, as well as the "reserve clause" throughout the National League, did not stand up or were not legally enforced by owners. "By the time the American League was ready to start its first season as a major league," wrote Charles Alexander, "111 of the 185 players under contract to its eight clubs had experience in the National League."[5]

The Orioles opened the season April 26 at Oriole Park. Ban Johnson threw out the ceremonial first pitch, and an overflow crowd happily watched a 10–6 Orioles win over the Boston Americans. McGinnity notched the first of his 26 wins and 39 complete games on the year. McGraw, batting in his customary leadoff spot, recorded a double and scored one of the Orioles' runs.

McGinnity's former Brooklyn moundmate, Harry Howell, won the next day, 12–6, prior to the Orioles commencing an eight-game road trip. In Philadelphia on May 7, in the last game of a so-far 3–4 road journey, McGraw and another player lost their cool with rookie umpire John Haskell, and both paid with an ouster from the competition. "Today's game was characterized by heavy hitting and continued objections to umpire Haskell's decisions," apprised one newspaper account. "On several occasions the Baltimore players surrounded the umpire, who in the sixth inning ordered McGraw and ["Crazy"] Schmit out of the game."[6] The Orioles outlasted the Athletics, 14–10, at Columbia Park. Haskell forwarded a report to Ban Johnson, delineating the worst of McGraw's behavior toward him, which included umpire baiting and rampant, abusive language for an hour's duration. (This would be Haskell's only year umpiring. He would be punched and physically assaulted by players—one an Oriole—in games later in the season.)

Also against Philadelphia, on May 15, McGraw, who had been called the "former snapping turtle of the National League"[7] in one castigating exposé, showed that he would rather act contemptibly toward the field authority than bathe in the limelight of a personally heroic deed. McGraw delivered a key, late-inning base hit to lift the Orioles over the Athletics, 8–5, at Oriole Park, but preferred not to defuse his ire with the accomplishment.

> With the scored tied and two out in the eighth inning McGraw came to bat and quarreled fiercely with [Joe] Cantillon's judgment of strikes. In the midst of it pitcher [Wiley] Piatt put a straight one over, and McGraw banged it against the fence for three bases. Without waiting to catch his breath on the third base bag, McGraw continued to give the umpire back talk and was ordered to the bench, which he took, but cordially invited the umpire to come to the clubhouse, promising him a bath in the vat there.[8]

Two days later, Ban Johnson made an early stand; he suspended McGraw for five days, stemming from his conduct with Cantillon. The suspension proved a minor slap on the wrist. The Orioles played but once, due to rain and off-days. But the stern notice made clear the honeymoon period between the league's chieftain and chief agitator was over.

It did not take long for the firebrand player-manager to run afoul, once more, of the upholders of the law on the diamond following the resumption of the Orioles' schedule on May 25. Three games hence, during the club's first trip to Chicago, McGraw was given the boot two innings into the proceedings at South Side Park. From third base, McGraw's calumnious speech toward umpire Al Mannassau was responsible. The White Sox scored five of their ten runs in the first two frames, on the way to the 10–3 victory.

On the last day of May, a heated wrangle with the umpire resulted in a forfeit by McGraw's crew, in the third set of a four-game series in Detroit. The Baltimore battery of Harry Howell and Wilbert Robinson were ejected for arguing a safe call at the plate by umpire Jack Sheridan. When a semblance of order was restored, the ejected men's teammates refused to continue the game. Though McGraw was not the instigator of the trouble, he did not exercise his authority to order his men back on the field.

Baltimore finished May and the first six weeks of the season with a 13–12 record, seven games off the front-running pace of the Chicago White Sox. The Orioles improved to 27–20 by the end of June, aided by their longest winning streak of the season (11 games).

Wearing the collared uniform of the day, McGraw is at the ready during pre-game practice drills.

With his club 5½ games out of contention on July 12, McGraw dislocated his right kneecap following an infield collision with Washington Senators outfielder Irv Waldron. The feisty field marshal did not return to the Orioles' bench until July 24 in Cleveland, missing nine games. The club went 5–4 under interim skipper Robinson.

No sooner had McGraw taken back command of his team when a story surfaced that raised tensions yet again between him and Ban Johnson. Through a third party, McGraw, Johnson alleged, had approached two AL teams to move, with the Orioles, to the National League, in 1902. Those teams' representatives blew the whistle on McGraw. Johnson decried McGraw as an ignominious traitor in the press.

"So the 'Julius Caesar' of the league calls me a 'Benedict Arnold' does he?" responded McGraw. "I should like to know upon what evidence he bases that assertion. I have my good money invested to a pretty considerable extent and I am anxious that the league should meet with success."[9]

Because of his injury, McGraw did not return to third base on a regular basis until August 9. The Orioles split a pair of games in Boston that day and trimmed half a game off a 7½-game deficit to the White Sox. On August 15, McGraw was removed from a contest in Baltimore for making derogatory comments about a strike called on him by Tommy Connolly, insisting the pitch was wide of the plate. "McGraw injected some of his famous remarks of the aqua fortis brand and took his customary walk to the dressing room,"[10] one learned sportswriter said. The Orioles were batting in the bottom of the ninth inning, trailing 9–5. Bill Karns finished McGraw's at-bat. No hometown rally materialized thereafter.

Four days later, the same umpire in the same place threw out two other Orioles, Joe McGinnity and Roger Bresnahan. The demonstrations that followed so incited the crowd of just under 2,000 that Connolly required police protection after the game. The Orioles won, 4–3, over the Detroit Tigers. The following day, August 20, with his team in third place and four games behind league-leading Chicago, McGraw tore cartilage in the same rehabilitated knee. He was lost to the Orioles as a player for the remainder of the campaign.

A 5–2 loss to the Tigers did little to placate any of the Oriole Park crowd's lingering animosity toward Connolly—again umpiring by himself. After the final out, a police presence had to guarantee Connolly's safety for the second day in a row.

The distasteful happenings in Baltimore did not escape the league's hierarchy. "President Ban Johnson yesterday sent a caustic letter to manager 'Mugsy' McGraw of the Baltimore club concerning the treatment of umpires in that city," it was widely published, "and incidentally imposed a few small fines for offenses of that kind. Pitcher McGinnity was barred from the coaching lines for a period of ten days. Fines were assessed as follows: McGraw, $5; McGinnity, $10; Keister, $5; Bresnahan, $5. This action of Johnson will widen the breach between the scrappy Baltimore manager and himself."[11]

The final game of the Detroit series, on August 21, was the worst of the lot, though McGraw was not present because of his injury. A fourth-inning out call at first base, on McGraw's replacement Jack Dunn, brought the entire Baltimore team out on the field in protest. In the ensuing rumpus, McGinnity lost control and spit tobacco juice in the umpire's face, the Tigers' Kid Elberfeld and the Orioles' Mike Donlin engaged in fisticuffs, and police and spectators rushed the field. Connolly again was escorted away from the angered gathering of 1,500 patrons, after the harassed official ejected McGinnity and forfeited the game to Detroit.

McGraw did not manage for an initial recovery period from August 21 to September 16, a span of 27 games. He returned to the bench for the Orioles' final homestand, beginning September 18, per Alexander. Curiously, the Baltimore Sun makes no mention of McGraw's return to playing or managing during the 11-game stand. McGraw took advantage of his disabled time to travel to New York, where the teams from St. Louis and Chicago were visiting. The recruitment jaunt launched a future trend of similar travel tours McGraw would make during the baseball season.

Shelved by his injuries, McGraw's season was curtailed as a player. He participated in slightly more than half (73 games) of the Orioles' schedule. But he hit .349 in 232 at-bats and posted a monstrous .508 OBP. A marked man around the league by pitchers, or just a plate-crowder, he led the league in being hit with pitched balls with 14. The Orioles faded over the second half and slipped into the second division, saddled with a final 13½-game shortcoming to the American League's first champions—the Chicago White Sox.

The time away from the bench may have helped temper the running feud McGraw had developed with Ban Johnson and had continued with his sworn adversaries in blue. One suspects he would have accrued more than his four ejections had he been around more or been more mobile in the latter half of the season. Recalling here the evocative quote about McGraw's temperament by former National League opponent and later Giants coach Arlie Latham, it might be easier to grasp why McGraw was routinely at odds with a varied segment of the populace and, in particular, authority figures: *McGraw eats gunpowder every morning for breakfast and washes it down with warm blood.*

Evidently, McGraw was not the same fire and brimstone spewer when it came to matters of the heart. He announced his engagement on October 24, 1901, to Miss Mary Blanche Sindall, a well-known Baltimore belle, and married her the following January 8. The ceremony took place at 6:00 p.m. at St. Ann's Roman Catholic Church, three miles north of where today's Camden Yards ballpark is located. Willie Keeler, Wilbert Robinson, Joe Kelley and Hughie Jennings were all in attendance.

The presiding pastor and evident baseball fan, Father Cornelius Thomas, sent the just married couple from the altar with this benediction: "Let selfishness be no barrier to your happiness, but understand that each must often give up much, renounce himself, that both may enjoy delightful fruit. For you know that it is the sacrifice hits that adds to the number of runs and wins the game."[12]

The bride and groom spent the first 24 hours of married life at the upscale Raleigh Hotel in Washington, D.C. They traveled to Savannah, Georgia, where McGraw informed his bride, "You know we're coming back here to train in about six weeks."[13] The newlywed couple continued from there to Florida. They returned to Baltimore, before departing once again for spring training in Savannah.

With players plainly unimpeded from jumping teams, McGraw ably retooled his starting eight in 1902. Only second baseman Jimmy Williams and right fielder Cy Seymour retained their positions. Bresnahan was shifted to third base. Assuming the bulk of the catching duties was 37-year-old Wilbert Robinson. Dan McGann, who had deserted the St. Louis club last September, was signed to fill the void left at first base by Jimmy Hart. An Orioles rookie, Hart was the player who punched umpire Haskell. Suspended and fined $25, Hart quit the Orioles late in the summer when the team refused to pay his fine. Billy Gilbert stepped in at shortstop for Bill Keister, who signed with the Washington Senators over the winter. Gilbert was a second-year "free agent" acquisition from the Milwaukee Brewers. Kip Selbach and Joe Kelley were courted away from the New York Giants and Brooklyn Superbas, respectively, to play the outfield.

The Orioles manager played sparingly in 1902, apparently not fully recovered from his leg injuries from 1901. One game McGraw sat out was the first of the season, April 19. He was far from idle, however, receiving the first and only Opening Day ejection of his career. At Huntington Avenue Grounds in Boston, McGraw picked one too many bones with Tommy Connolly, the official at the center of last summer's deplorable string of games versus the Detroit Tigers. He was commanded off the field of play by Connolly, to the rabid pleasure of a large crowd of more than 14,000. The Orioles lost, 7–6.

The Oriole Park opener came four days later. Joe McGinnity was defeated by Connie Mack's Philadelphia Athletics, 8–1. The game carried two historic notations. It was the last game played by hitting star Napoleon Lajoie for the Athletics. Lajoie had made a cross-town jump from the National League Phillies to the Athletics in 1901. The move by Lajoie elicited a legal challenge from the Phillies. After a year, the Pennsylvania Supreme Court ruled in favor of the player's former employer. The decision prohibiting Lajoie from playing with the Athletics was handed down during the game and wired to manager Mack in the dugout. Mack was forced to remove the elite player for the final inning. He inserted Colombian-born Luis Castro to take Lajoie's place. With his appearance, Castro became the first Hispanic major league player of the 20th century. (All ended well for Lajoie, who sat out a month before he signed with another American League team, the Cleveland Blues, for the hefty sum of $7,000.)

The season was not yet two weeks old when McGraw again trampled over the boundaries of sporting etiquette. On May 1, Jack Sheridan ruled that McGraw intentionally let himself be hit by a pitched ball—more than once. Each time, Sheridan refused to allow McGraw to take his base. "On the last denial, in the ninth inning, McGraw simply sat down in the batter's box and refused to move until Sheridan ordered him off the field."[14] Ahead at the time, Boston won, 6–4. Riled-up Orioles fans targeted Sheridan afterwards and a Baltimore policeman suffered a facial laceration while attempting to protect Sheridan.

Ban Johnson reacted. He slapped the chief instigator of the skirmish with a five-day suspension on Sunday, May 4. The disciplinary action encompassed four games on the schedule. The Orioles lost all of them. Their leader returned on May 9 in Philadelphia. Seemingly inspired, the team responded with a 13–6 win over the Athletics.

McGraw endured a rough two days, May 23 and 24, at Oriole Park, as he tried to motivate an 11–13 Orioles squad. He protested an interference call by umpire Silk O'Laughlin on Joe Kelley and was sent to the dressing room. Bresnahan, who was behind the plate, moved to third base as McGraw's fill-in, and Wilbert Robinson entered the game in Bresnahan's place. The Orioles and Joe McGinnity lost, 3–2, to the visiting Detroit Tigers. There were no reports of overt unruliness from the congregation of 3,100.

The next day, McGraw and Tigers outfielder Dick Harley were involved in a fight in the first inning. On a double steal attempt, Harley slid hard into the Orioles' third baseman, spiking him severely in the calf. Harley was called out; McGraw tossed the ball to pitcher Tom Hughes and then went after Harley. The aggrieved hometown player had to be pulled off the 5'10½" Harley. When he was finally subdued by teammates, it was noticed that the orange and black stocking of McGraw's leg was soaked in blood from the spiking.

McGraw was sidelined for a month, an infection to the wound initially hampering his recovery. Prior to his return to the club, McGraw traveled to Philadelphia with team owner Harry Goldman and his attorney, to press the issue of outfielder Jimmy Sheckard jumping the Orioles to sign with Brooklyn. They hoped to be heard by the same sympathetic court which had handed down the Lajoie verdict. Brooklyn manager Ned Hanlon showed up and resolved the issue by forking over nearly all of the $1,000 Sheckard had received from Baltimore as an advance salary before quitting the team.

Satisfactorily recuperated, McGraw came back to the team on June 24 in Baltimore. He made an appearance as a pinch-hitter—without success—the next day. Equally unsuccessful were the sixth-place Orioles, who were beaten by the Athletics, 8–6, to drop their record to 25–29. McGraw was separated from the team for 26 games. The Orioles won 12 as Robinson again filled in for his friend and teammate on the bench.

Just four days later, for a home game against the Boston Americans, McGraw made out the lineup card for the last time as a Baltimore Oriole. The truculent skipper became embroiled in a contentious argument with home plate umpire Tommy Connolly. It stemmed from an alleged missed tag of a base by Baltimore baserunner Cy Seymour. When ordered off the field by the arbiter, McGraw refused to go. Connolly forfeited the game to Boston. The contest was in the eighth inning with Boston ahead, 9–4. On June 30, McGraw was suspended indefinitely by Johnson for his obstinate actions. (Joe Kelley, though not ejected by Connolly, was also suspended indefinitely by Johnson for abusive language. The outfielder returned to the Orioles' lineup on July 4.)

As early as July 3, the *Brooklyn Daily Eagle* leaked that John McGraw had been in negotiations with New York Giants owner Andrew Freedman to manage his National League club. Freedman was quarrelsome and arrogant, antagonized and alienated ballplayers, managers, umpires, owners and sportswriters alike—and seemed to like doing so. It had been Ban Johnson's logical intent to place an AL franchise in the nation's largest city. But he had been stymied by Freedman and his political connections.

Those connections had now waned, and it was an open secret that Johnson was planning on moving the Baltimore franchise to New York in 1903—with supposedly the native New Yorker remaining as manager. But as the season progressed, a continued affiliation between Johnson and McGraw became less and less tenable.

Luckily for McGraw, during the turmoil with Johnson, he found a kindred recalcitrant in Freedman, who admired McGraw's combative fire and had a similar dislike for Ban Johnson's "toned down" game. Surely, in part, to spite Johnson for intending to infringe upon his territorial rights, Freedman offered McGraw the mid-season managerial reins of the last-place New York Giants. The Freedman-McGraw association would be a relatively brief one, as the Giants owner agreed to sell his club before the end of the season. But the short-term alliance helped elevate the New York City National League baseball landscape for the next three decades.

On July 8, the directors of the Baltimore Baseball Club granted their highest-profile employee his release. Principal owner John J. Mahon (and father-in-law of Joe Kelley), purchased McGraw's stake in the club, amounting to $6,500. "I appreciate the kindliness which has prompted the Baltimore club to give me the release I ask," McGraw said, "and I wish to assure them publicly that in consideration of this kindness I shall not tamper with any Baltimore players."[15]

In its afternoon edition the same day, the *Brooklyn Daily Eagle* was one of the first New York papers to announce McGraw's coming to Gotham. The paper indicated that McGraw had been given a two-year, $20,000 deal by Freedman. The now ex–American Leaguer took some parting shots at the infant circuit, saying the league was in debt and financially unsound and that its president acted with the greater interest of only the teams in Philadelphia, Chicago and Boston. Johnson and Philadelphia A's owner Connie Mack sternly refuted the allegations. Mack went so far as to publicly wager $1,000 with McGraw to prove to all that the A's were not losing money.

Freedman eventually sold out to Cincinnati's John T. Brush, who was involved in back-door dealings with Baltimore officials before McGraw's release. With the convenient assent of the Orioles' trustees, Brush purchased controlling interests in the Maryland team. The result was that several of the Orioles' top players, including Dan McGann, Roger Bresnahan and hurler Jack Cronin, gained their easy release and followed McGraw to New York, while Joe Kelley and right fielder Cy Seymour became Cincinnati Reds (Kelley as player-manager).

Ban Johnson survived the obvious treachery by replenishing the Baltimore club with new players from the minors and from other AL clubs, in order to keep the franchise afloat.

In light of Brush's involvement, it appears clear that McGraw knew all along that he would be obtaining a fresh injection of players from Baltimore in his new job and that his statement on July 8 was part of a treacherously hatched scheme against Johnson.

The beginning of a whole new life and career, and the birth of a baseball legend, began on Saturday, July 19, 1902, for John J. McGraw. Playing shortstop and hitting second in the order, McGraw managed his first game for the New York Giants. At the Polo Grounds, scoring four runs in the third inning, the Philadelphia Phillies defeated the Giants, 4–3. McGraw collected one of the home team's six hits and scored one of the runs. Joe McGinnity—another of the Baltimore players who followed McGraw from the Orioles to the Giants—was the starter and loser.

The first transaction by McGraw in his new post came on July 21. He purchased out-fielder George Browne from the Philadelphia Phillies. Browne would become the Giants right fielder for the next five and a half years, and he led the league in runs scored (99) in 1904.

The first victory for McGraw as New York Giants manager came in the team's next game, on July 23. At Brooklyn, behind pitcher Luther "Dummy" Taylor, the road squad defeated the Superbas, 4–1. McGraw was hitless but recorded eight assists at shortstop. No less than 12 former Orioles players played for the two clubs.

Over the remainder of the summer and early fall, the Giants continued the losing ways to which the team and its fan base had grown accustomed under the two previous managers that season. Of the 63 games remaining when McGraw took over, the Giants would win only 25. As McGraw became acclimated with his new National League club, he maintained designs for remaking it under its own innate identity. "I may make a few changes in the team before the season is over," he announced. "This is not going to be a Baltimore team, but a New York team—a team that will stand a good chance of walloping anything in the league."[16]

Pursuing those changes, the new manager spent more than two dozen games away from his club, visiting other cities, trying to sign up players in anticipation of the 1903 campaign. One striking acquisition was Chicago White Sox outfielder Sam Mertes, who agreed to play for McGraw while still catching flies for the Chicago team. Slightly under six feet tall and 190 pounds, Mertes was a barrel-chested figure whose speed and agility in the outfield belied his physique. He was nicknamed "Sandow," after a turn-of-the-20th-century, Prussian strongman named Eugen Sandow.

In games managed by McGraw, the Giants were 15–20. The team finished dead last, with an overall 48–88 record, a cavernous 53½ games below the pennant-winning Pittsburgh Pirates.

In McGraw's first full season at the helm of new owner John T. Brush's refitted New York Giants, he directed a sharp turn-around. The team won 84 games and lost 55 in 1903, one of only two National League clubs to win at least 60 percent of their games.

As a department store magnate based in Indiana, Brush not only held title as principle owner of the Cincinnati Reds but was a minority stockholder of the New York Giants as well. A New York state native, Brush sold his majority interest in the Reds to a local alliance of businessmen that included August "Garry" Herrmann, and then took control of the New York Giants by paying Andrew Freedman $200,000, some of it borrowed from other National League owners. Brush, like Freedman, vehemently opposed the placement of an American League franchise in New York. A decade earlier, the retail mogul had been criticized in the press by Ban Johnson, then a sportswriter, for improper roster manipulations involving the Reds and the minor league Indianapolis Hoosiers, which Brush also owned. Under pressure from the scrutiny, the Midwest businessman sold his minor league club. When Ban Johnson pushed through the relocation of the Baltimore Orioles to Manhattan as the New York Highlanders, Brush joined forces with McGraw with renewed animus toward the American League president.

Six weeks prior to the 1903 season, an interesting impasse occurred that reflected the player autonomy that existed for those strong-willed enough to pursue it. McGraw thanked infielder Heinie Smith, who led the league in games played and putouts at second base, and managed the team during McGraw's player recruitment jaunts during the second half of the season, by trading him to the Detroit Tigers for Kid Gleason. But the former Philadelphia Phillies and Orioles pitcher-turned-second baseman did not want to play in New York. With a home in suburban Philadelphia, Gleason had his heart set on returning to the Phillies. McGraw used former Orioles infielder Billy Gilbert to take over Smith's spot at second base, while he hoped things would sort out.

John McGraw's first Opening Day as manager of the New York Giants dawned on April 17, 1903, at the Polo Grounds, versus the Brooklyn Superbas (delayed a day by rain). The Giants' home field, which accommodated twice the crowd of McGraw's former 9,000-seat park in Baltimore, was the last of four stadium precursors to the yet-to-be-glorified, steel and concrete Polo Grounds of later baseball lore. It was a sun-splashed spring day, and a capacity crowd was in attendance. Giants and Superbas players marched shoulder to shoulder in a tight line from the outfield to the tune of a ragtime band. Both teams sported the collared uniform of the period. The Giants wore dark caps and leggings with the simple lettering NEW YORK across their chests. Photographers took careful aim at Mrs. John T. Brush tossing out the ceremonial first ball. Christy Mathewson started and lost, 9–7. The 22-year-old pitcher had won 20 games for the Giants as a rookie in 1901, but slipped to 14–17 in 1902. Mathewson, though, led the league in shutouts with eight and posted a 2.12 ERA with his under–.500 record.

Joe McGinnity, who, combined with Mathewson, would start 90 of the Giants' 142 games, took the mound the next day and evened his team's record with a 6–1 win. A 20-game winner since his rookie year in 1899, McGinnity permitted one hit, and the run was unearned. In 1903, McGinnity would establish career highs in starts (48), complete games (44) and innings (434), in a mind-boggling pitching campaign in which he was both a 30-game winner and 20-game loser (31–20). The right-hander from northern Illinois also saved two games and finished four others in relief. His ERA was 2.43.

Nine years Mathewson's senior, Joseph Jerome McGinnity mastered pitching from different arm angles that did not tax his arm—the key to the amazing volume of work he was able to deliver. McGraw compared his two aces shortly into their New York careers. "The style of the two men is essentially different," he said. "Mathewson is a pitcher of great speed, and his arm is subjected to a severe strain whenever he goes through a game.

McGinnity with his varying style, really saves himself by alternating first with one kind of pitching and then another."[17]

The Giants' offense was led by Sam Mertes, the outfielder McGraw had brazenly pulled away from Charlie Comiskey during the New York manager's first few weeks on the job last summer. A deceptively speedy outfielder, Mertes led the league in doubles with 32 and RBI with 104. He also scored 100 runs while hitting .280. Roger Bresnahan was asked to play the majority of his games in the outfield; he hit .350. Right fielder George Browne, playing the most games in the league (141), scored 105 runs and registered a .313 batting mark.

Though only 30, McGraw had relegated himself to a bench player at this stage of his career. The leg injuries of the past seasons had unquestionably taken their toll. He appeared in the Giants' third game, substituting for left fielder Roger Bresnahan following that player's eighth-inning ejection by umpire Augie Moran. The Giants and Brooklyn played 11 innings, to a 5–5 tie, called because of darkness.

A week later, a freak—and painful—accident caused the Giants manager to miss four early season sessions. Working out in the infield during a morning practice prior to the April 27 game versus the Boston Braves, he was caught unaware by a throw from the outfield that struck him in the face. The ball broke McGraw's nose and prohibited his participation later in the game in any way—though he did return briefly to the Polo Grounds after being treated at J. Hood Wright Hospital. (The ball was thrown by Dummy Taylor, the hearing- and speech-impaired pitcher who had given McGraw his first win as Giants manager.) No doubt in extreme discomfort, the tough pilot sat out the next two home games and then accompanied his team to Philadelphia. After apparently gritting through the game on April 30, McGraw began experiencing severe nose bleeds and was confined to his Philadelphia hotel room by a physician's order, while his team moved on to Boston. He returned to the dugout on May 6, as New York's own *Evening World* described him, "looking seven ways at once out of his blackened eyes"[18] at a 20–2 Giants romp at Washington Park. Weather issues and a Sunday off-day in Boston limited McGraw to only four games lost.

In the interim, the Smith-for-Gleason exchange became entangled in the front offices of the major circuits, whose heads were jointly trying to prevent the unchecked inter-league player movement of the past two seasons—with the ultimate goal of having both leagues independently grow and flourish. Gleason took his objections to court, expectedly in Philadelphia. Biding his time until a ruling came down, Gleason played minor league ball in Wilmington for $100 a week, a massive amount for a minor league player. Not willing to expend the effort, or perhaps scared away by Gleason's set going rate, the Giants pulled back on their rightful claim to the ballplayer. Gleason was free to play where he wished, and did so for the first time on May 16, joining the team of his preference in the City of Brotherly Love.

That same day, against Pennsylvania's other Senior Circuit team, the Giants recorded their biggest Polo Grounds crowd, "the official count being 31,500"—the largest in the city's history. The *Pittsburgh Daily Post* recorded that it was "the largest crowd that ever attended a baseball game in this country." Mathewson pitched his club to a 7–3 win over the Pittsburgh Pirates. Three days later, Mathewson gained a two-inning relief win, when the Giants pushed across a run in the eighth inning to edge the visiting Pirates, 4–3. In the same frame, McGraw was bestowed his first National League ejection. Umpire Bob Emslie ruled a pitched ball had not struck Giants third baseman Billy Laudner in the hand, and he would not allow the player the free base. McGraw raucously expressed his disagreement with the call and was run.

Watching the proceedings from John T. Brush's field box was the National League's president, Harry Pulliam. A former Pittsburgh Pirates executive, Pulliam, only 33, had been elected to office six months earlier. He also held, in joint capacity, the league's secretary and treasury posts. The next day, May 20, Mathewson pitched a 2–0 shutout over the Pirates, giving the series nod to the Giants, three games to one.

Umpire Emslie was also responsible for McGraw's next premature exit. On June 6 at West End Grounds, McGraw backed first sacker Dan McGann's complaints on balls and strikes and was expelled—along with McGann—in the third inning. Disappointing a large Saturday afternoon crowd of 15,000, the Giants won the contest, 7–4, over the Chicago Cubs. Dummy Taylor was the victor. The game was part of a four-game sweep of the Cubs by the Giants (McGinnity won twice, Mathewson once), as McGraw's team climbed into a first-place tie with Chicago with a 29–13 record.

A month later, Fred Clarke's Pittsburgh Pirates had ensconced themselves in first place, comfortably ahead of both the Cubs and Giants by the close of July.

On August 1, McGinnity started and completed both ends of a doubleheader at Boston's South End Grounds. McGraw made a rare start, at third base, in the opener. McGinnity won the two games, 4–1 and 5–2. According to news clippings, the Giants hurler insisted on pitching the nightcap. He gave up six hits in each game. A week later, the 32-year old moundsman duplicated the "iron man" feat, in front of a packed house at the Polo Grounds. Winning the first game, 6–1, against the Brooklyn Superbas, McGinnity was made a 4–3 victor in the afterpiece, following a two-run Giants rally in the bottom of the ninth inning. Pinch-hitter George Van Haltren, batting for McGinnity, singled in the winning run.

Though the workhorses McGinnity and Mathewson kept winning consistently, the Giants lost traction in the standings as the season progressed. On August 26, Augie Moran pinned McGraw with his third ejection notice for disagreeing beyond the norm to his out call at home plate on runner Roger Bresnahan. The Giants second baseman was also tossed for his protestations. Playing the Boston Beaneaters in the first game of a road doubleheader, the Giants fell, 6–5. A 3–2, nightcap victory by Jack Cronin, the Giants' fourth starter, kept the team 20 games over .500, at 65–45, and 7½ games off the pace of the league leaders.

Pittsburgh cruised to the pennant in September. The much-improved Giants, 84–55, placed second, 6½ games behind the first National League World Series representative. The Bucs were defeated by the AL champion Boston Americans, five games to three, in the inaugural Fall Classic.

McGraw's first season in New York was, by even the most critical of that city's standards, a success. The perennial last-place Giants had soared high into the first division.

McGraw's own comportment with the officiating could be viewed as temperate. He had received a fourth and final ejection in late September for directing abusive language at Hank O'Day, but there had been not one incident of the ugly, crowd-provoking histrionics that his clashes with umpires had previously wrought. Could it be that the turning 31-year-old McGraw was showing signs of not only maturing, but of dialing his abrasive temperament down a few notches? He had endured extreme personal tragedy during his young life, more than enough to send one less driven or with less resolve than he into psychological despair. Yet he had persevered to become one of the most widely known professional athletes in the country and now the leader of the most prominent baseball club in the nation's burgeoning metropolis.

Any conception of McGraw turning a softer personality page would be resoundingly put to rest in 1904 and for the next quarter-century. It simply would have been too much in contrast to the inherently defiant being he incarnated on the baseball field.

> In playing or managing, the game of ball is only fun for me when I'm out in front and winning. I don't give a hill of beans for the rest of the game. The man who loses gracefully loses easily. Sportsmanship is all right, but … once a team of mine is on the diamond, I want it to fight. Namby-pamby methods don't get much results.[19]

McGinnity and Mathewson were more than spectacular again in 1904. In the previous season, they had won 61 games between them. "Any time that either Matty or McGinnity walked out to the box there was a feeling of security on the bench,"[20] their manager recollected after the pitchers' retirement. It was easy to see why. The powerhouse pair were both 30-game victors once more, with McGinnity raking in a career-high 35 wins and the 24-year-old Mathewson nabbing 33 triumphs. Dummy Taylor posted a 21–15 record, and rookie fourth starter George "Hooks" Wiltse added a fine 13–3 mark. A high-quality purchase, on McGraw's part, from the New York State League in January of that year, Wiltse won his first 12 decisions (a rookie record he co-holds with Butch Metzger). The quartet of hurlers were too overwhelming a mound force for any team in the National League to overcome.

Christy Mathewson was the Opening Day starter on April 14. The Giants squared off against Brooklyn's Trolley-Dodgers, as the *Evening World* often referred to Ned Hanlon's team. An early morning dusting of snow did not discourage the planned pomp surrounding the opening. As part of the initial game's ceremonies, Hanlon's club crossed over to lower Manhattan to meet the Giants and escort them over the Brooklyn Bridge to Washington Park. Near the bridge's Brooklyn tower, a big wagon drawn by four horses that carried a brass band collided with one of the automobiles transporting McGraw's players. Some team members were dumped onto the roadway. But no one was injured in the mishap. After reaching the ballpark, the same band played the *Star Spangled Banner* as Brooklyn team president Charles Ebbets pulled a rope to unveil the flag atop the grandstand. Harry Pulliam threw out the ceremonial first ball, to the cheers of over 17,000 fans. There was not much cheering for the home team during the game that followed, as Mathewson tossed a three-hitter, defeating Brooklyn, 7–1. The Giants stole three bases, including one by Mathewson.

McGraw made base running an important facet of the Giants' offensive game. In the off-season, the keen strategist had traded his rookie shortstop, Charlie Babb, and pitcher Jack Cronin to Brooklyn for veteran shortstop Bill Dahlen. The Giants added $6,000 to sweeten the deal. The 34-year-old Dahlen led the league in RBI with 80 during the 1904 campaign. Tying Sam Mertes for the team high, Dahlen also stole 47 bases, as McGraw's lads led all of baseball in swiped bags with 283. The Chicago Cubs were a distant second with 227.

Three games into the season, tragedy struck the Giants' family. Second baseman Billy Gilbert's wife died. Gilbert missed only four games of the schedule, returning to the Giants on April 23. McGraw filled in twice during his absence.

On April 18 at the Baker Bowl, McGraw exchanged some unkind words with Phillies catcher Red Dooin around the second base bag. After the game, in which the Giants scored twice in the ninth to turn starter Christy Mathewson into a winner, 7–6, McGraw "hurled a vile epithet"[21] at Dooin. The offended player grabbed a bat and went after McGraw, who was protected by a policeman. Outside, incited fans threw stones and dirt at the carriage in which McGraw left the ballyard. Passenger Joe McGinnity was hit in the face by a thrown object but did not sustain a lasting injury. Sparked by seven wins from Mathewson and McGinnity, New York closed April with a 9–2 mark.

The Giants pushed the base-running limits even when they were not attempting straight steals. On May 12 at the Palace of the Fans in Cincinnati, George Browne was thrown out at third base, trying to go from first to third on a sacrifice bunt down the third base line. The over-aggressiveness resulted in a double play. The play indicates that Browne may have been off with the pitch or the third baseman was lax in returning to the bag. In any event, the play must have been close because McGraw, on the third base coaching lines, catapulted into battle against Bob Emslie, who made the demonstrative ruling. The manager was officially shown the gate for latching onto the arbiter's arm during his dissent.

While leaving through the players' exit under the grandstand, McGraw encountered a splinter group of heckling Reds fans and threatened to fight each and every one of them, except for one person who was, by 1904 standards, indelicately termed a cripple. McGraw was heard to tell the disabled person that the only thing that saved him from a thrashing was that he was not a whole man. A policeman eventually broke things up. On May 15, the *Pittsburgh Press* ran with the exaggerated story that McGraw had "threatened to fight a cripple." In the contest, tossing one of his 33 complete games, Christy Mathewson absorbed one of his 12 losses on the season, 13–7.

In the same series, three days hence, McGraw collected the final hit of his playing career—number 1,309 lifetime. It was a meaningless single in Cincinnati's lopsided 13–2 victory. McGraw was forced into the action when Sam Mertes was ejected for arguing a strike call by Bob Emslie. McGraw moved Roger Bresnahan, playing shortstop, into Mertes' left field slot and took the shortstop position. McGraw recorded a pair of assists and putouts but short-armed a throw to first which allowed two runs to score. A portion of the near-record crowd of over 21,000 stood five-deep behind ropes in the outfield.

Singularly exemplifying the Giants speedy style of play was Dan McGann on May 27. The first baseman stole five bases at the Polo Grounds. Establishing a modern National League record that would stand for more than nine decades, McGann stroked two hits and a scored a run in a 3–1 Giants win hurled by Mathewson over Brooklyn. "He can carry those 'old pounds' as rapidly as any six-footer in the history of the national game," said one news account of the 33-year-old, 190-pounder. "He is quick to start and gets such a lead when slipping away from the bag that he is a rod or so ahead of the pitcher when the latter delivers the ball."[22]

Two days later at Washington Park, New York City's first National League Sunday game of the century was played in Brooklyn. More than 20,000 patrons, many hailing from surrounding Long Island and New Jersey, overflowed the Park Slope grounds. Hooks Wiltse pitched the Giants to a 7–3 win. Having no problem working on the Sabbath, Messrs. Jim Johnstone and Hank O'Day were the umpires assigned to the game. Outside of the more Puritan-based legislature of the Eastern cities of Boston, New York, Philadelphia and Pittsburgh, baseball had been played on Sundays in St. Louis, Chicago and Cincinnati for years.[23]

Continuing to win over a legion of lifelong fans, Christy Mathewson twirled a one-hit shutout over the Chicago Cubs at the Polo Grounds on June 10. Cubs catcher Johnny Kling spoiled the no-hit aspirations of the Giants' exceptional pitcher. First-year umpire Charles "Chief" Zimmer ejected three home team players, in the third, fifth and sixth innings. The first to go was McGraw, from the third base coaching box, for obnoxiously objecting to Zimmer's overall management of the game behind the plate. Sam Mertes was next, while at the plate, over a strike call. And the speech- and hearing-impaired Dummy Taylor was thrown out for making shrill, shrieking sounds from the coaching lines. It was not clear whether Taylor had taken over for the banished McGraw or was stationed all along at the other coaching box. The final was 5–0. A Saturday crowd of 5,000 were treated to the pleasing exhibition.

Six days later, the Giants embarked on an 18-game winning streak that raised the team's half-game lead in the standings to a fat, 10½-game cushion. The scalding club's record zoomed to 48–16 on the Fourth of July.

In August, the manager set a personal high of four ejections in one month, all coming within a two-and-a-half-week period. The second came on August 19, as the 72–29 Giants faced the Pittsburgh Pirates at the Polo Grounds. In the sixth inning, Art Devlin was called out on a steal attempt of second base. McGraw and Frank Bowerman raged over the call. Both were ejected. The Giants were defeated, 3–2. Four days later, the manager was notified that he had received an indefinite suspension from National League President Harry Pulliam for "the part he took in the scenes of disorder during the last game with Pittsburgh in New York—the day he went into the tool box and refused to come out when ordered by umpire Johnstone to leave the field."[24]

The suspension was lifted after only two days. A Pittsburgh newspaper accused Pulliam of bowing to pressure from John T. Brush. One year on the job, Pulliam, it was conjectured, was counting on the influential Brush to support his re-election at the next annual league owners' meeting.

On September 5, the New Yorkers swept a doubleheader from the Boston Beaneaters. The second game of the Labor Day twin-bill was won on a Sam Mertes single in the bottom of the ninth inning. The thrilling climax to the successful day inspired a group of zealous fans to carry McGraw off the field on their shoulders. The unrestrained lot, however, accidentally dropped McGraw and he was nearly trampled by the surrounding swarm that was part of the doubleheader's huge attendance. McGraw suffered a sprained ankle in the celebration gone awry. The injured manager was placed on crutches and kept away from his club for a healing period of ten days.

The Giants continued their winning ways and easily won their first pennant under McGraw. The major leagues had expanded from a 140-game season to 154 for the first time, and the Giants smoked the competition winning a remarkable 106 contests (losing 47). The team clinched the pennant on September 22. Five days afterward, the juggernaut club won its 104th game, besting the Pirates' record set in 1901, albeit in a longer schedule. The Cubs, with 93 victories, finished well back in second, 13 games in arrears.

No World Series was played because of McGraw's and Brush's shared personal enmity toward Ban Johnson. In his autobiography, released in the early 1920s when McGraw's word on baseball was considered gospel, McGraw sided on the matter with his owner, saying, "[Brush] did not see why we should jeopardize the fruits of our victory by recognizing and playing against the champions of an organization that had been formed to put us out of business."[25]

The opinion of Brush was not shared by the organization's main employees. The

Giants team held a meeting on September 19, after which it announced to the press that the players were intent on playing the American League's best representative in a post-season series. "Each of us can make a few thousand dollars, and we are not going to lose that amount merely because Brush and McGraw are hostile to Ban Johnson," read part of the bold players' statement. "Brush cannot prevent us from playing the after-season contests, as our contracts expire on October 17, and we are at liberty to do what we please after that date."[26]

Brush became angry, but put his feelings aside and summoned Mathewson, McGinnity and Taylor, the day after the players' meeting, to his office. He agreed to pay them $1,000 each to forget about the interleague playoff, and, presumably, a near-equal amount to each of their teammates. Brush also underwrote a theatre event, held at the New York Theatre on October 2, throwing much of the rich proceeds his players' way. "Every sporting man in town has applied for one or more tickets and has paid liberally for them," reported the *Evening World* a few days prior to the event. "During the evening, manager McGraw and his 18 Giants will be called to the stage in a body and presented with the pennant."[27] Andrew Freedman bought a pair of orchestra tickets for $500. Brush did not attend the event due to illness.

The players were appeased. But by the following fall, after a second consecutive pennant, both McGraw and Brush would be forced to shed their personal, if not petty, grievances against the American League under the weight of public demand and simple business acumen.

In spite of the team's success over the course of the 1904 season, McGraw surpassed all managers in baseball with eight ejections. In 1905, the high-strung skipper maintained the top wallet-draining position in the league, accumulating 11 early-shower invitations. McGraw showed soon off that he could not be content with being a "rocking chair" manager.

On a beautiful spring day, a reported 40,000 New Yorkers gathered for the new season's inaugural game on April 14. The throng was crammed in and around the Polo Grounds, for the number exceeded what the stadium could hold by almost double. Among the national notables in attendance were Adrian "Cap" Anson, baseball's champion segregationist, and undefeated prizefighter James J. Jeffries. Prior to New York Mayor George B. McClellan, Jr., throwing out the first pitch, McGraw and his team headed a parade of 15 flag-draped automobiles along Fifth Avenue. The caravan, which included the visiting Boston Beaneaters, took a roundabout trip down the main street to Washington Square in lower Manhattan before turning up along Broadway and then Eighth Avenue, all the way to the Polo Grounds, 150 blocks to the north. The extended trip passed through the heart of the former Longacre Square, renamed Times Square almost a year earlier by Mayor McClellan after the prestigious New York newspaper that had relocated its offices to the area. If the ride seemed long to the Beaneaters, Joe McGinnity made the afternoon even longer, pitching a three-hitter. The Giants scored ten runs and Boston one. The next day, Mathewson and Hooks Wiltse combined for a 15–0 shutout of the New Englanders.

On the momentum of the dominant, two-game sweep of Boston, the Giants captured seven of their first nine games. The seventh victory was hurled by Leon "Red" Ames on April 27 at Brooklyn. A 22-year-old right-hander, Ames was a New York State League purchase of McGraw in 1903. He had joined the club last season and this year beat out Wiltse as the fourth starter. He utilized a roundhouse curveball to a great degree of success, the pitch not yet commonly thrown in baseball for fear of the strain it placed on the arm and elbow. Ames had all of his pitches working, allowing six hits to the Superbas in a 4–0 whitewash of the home team.

In the eighth inning, Mike Donlin was caught napping off second base by alert Brooklyn catcher Bill Bergen. McGraw did not see eye to eye with the call made by Jim Johnstone. The manager made too much of an issue of it and was booted from the game.

Mike Donlin had been obtained by McGraw from the Cincinnati Reds in a three-way trade last August. A rare .300 lifetime hitter in the Deadball Era, Donlin was a known carouser who preferred having a good time to a good batting average. Somehow he managed to balance both pretty well. He had several run-ins with the law over the course of his career, though. A disorderly conduct arrest and brief jail time had turned him into Reds trade fodder. Donlin was a terrific pickup. A speedy flyhawk, he joined with Sam Mertes and George Browne in solidifying the Giants' outfield corps, permitting Roger Bresnahan to move behind the plate. The 27-year-old left-handed slasher scored the most runs in the league (124) and hit a preening .356 in 150 games. Donlin also accumulated a .908 OPS.

On May 15, during a shutout effort by McGinnity, McGraw got all in a huff over what he viewed as a balk that was not called on pitcher Mordecai "Three Finger" Brown of the Chicago Cubs. At the Polo Grounds, the bases were loaded at the time. Venting too vociferously from the coaching lines, McGraw's premature removal from the contest was dictated by first-year arbiter William Joseph Klem. The 31-year-old Klem was starting his second month as a big league umpire, on his way to a 37-year career calling balls and strikes. Establishing a no-nonsense persona from the get-go, Klem handed out a league-leading 26 ejection slips in his rookie season. Incidentally, the McGinnity shutout was the Giants' third in four games, with another to follow the next day.

During the same homestand, against the Pittsburgh Pirates on May 19, McGraw became too verbally abusive toward umpire Jim Johnstone and lost his managerial privileges as a consequence. That day, McGraw established that no member of the opposition was competitively off-limits to his maligning mode of engagement. Pirates owner Barney Dreyfuss was in attendance and also became the object of McGraw's scorn on this and the following day. On May 20, McGraw and Pirates manager Fred Clarke were thumbed out by Johnstone for hurling invectives at one another and inciting members of both clubs to rush onto the field. (Christy Mathewson, on the coaching lines, was later ejected by the same umpire for disputing a foul call on a ball hit down the line by the Giants' Bill Dahlen.) The Giants won both games, behind Dummy Taylor and McGinnity.

Picking on Dreyfuss was a mistake. The team president was outraged enough to submit a written complaint to league president Harry Pulliam. The *Pittsburgh Daily Post* published its contents:

I desire to and herewith make formal complaint against John McGraw, Manager of the New York baseball club, for his conduct at the Polo grounds, May 19 and 20. On Friday, May 19, I was sitting in a box and was annoyed by McGraw's frequent and sneering personal remarks to me. On Saturday, I was watching the game and talking quietly with a friend when McGraw, who had been put off the field for using bad language, appeared on the balcony of the New York clubhouse and shouted: "Hey, Barney." I did not answer that too familiar greeting nor did I respond to any of his several attempts to attract my attention. He then urged me to make a wager. With that he accused me of being crooked, of controlling the umpires, and made other false and malicious statements.

I beg that steps be made to protect visitors to the Polo grounds from the abuse of said John McGraw.[28]

Pulliam, a former Pirates executive, responded with a 15-day suspension for the bad boy of the league. The decree came down on May 27 and would expire on June 10, provided McGraw also paid a $150 fine. McGraw did not take the punishment from the National League president lying down. In a legal twist, he sued and won an injunction, in a Massachusetts court, which McGraw interpreted as allowing him to return to the field—which he did, three days early, on June 7. His team won eight out of ten games in his absence. Not inclined to challenge the court, Pulliam withdrew the fine because of the verdict, which did not resolve anything and was simply a legal writ delaying action until a further ruling could be made.

But a victory was claimed by the plaintiff, who was able to don his uniform a few days sooner than expected. McGraw rejoined a team that was running away from the league, having opened a nine-game lead after 45 games played.

Coinciding with the suspension, McGraw's received news that his 66-year-old father was gravely ill, suffering from an ear abscess. He used some of his forced vacation time to visit the sick man, who was residing with McGraw's sister, Margaret Bowker, in Fulton County, New York. McGraw Sr. recovered.

The following month, Christy Mathewson again reached the pinnacle of his craft. On June 13, the right-hander no-hit the Chicago Cubs at West Side Grounds. It was the second no-hitter of Mathewson's career and his first under McGraw. Two runners reached base on infield errors, and one of them made it to second on a steal. The other was erased after a fine running catch toward the infield by right fielder George Browne, who threw to first to double up the surprised runner. Mathewson faced only 28 men in the 1–0 decision over Three Finger Brown. Bill Dahlen's single knocked in Dan McGann with the only run in the final inning. The Giants lead was seven games at this point.

On the eve of the traditional July 4 "half-way point of the season," McGraw, shortstop Bill Dahlen and catcher Roger Bresnahan were all given the heave-ho in the same game. McGraw and his catcher were ejected for giving the business to umpire Bob Emslie from the Giants' bench, and Dahlen for disputing a call by the same umpire. The team was not slowed by the loss of the two players. The defending champions slammed the Philadelphia Phillies, 9–1, at the Baker Bowl. Taylor orchestrated the win from the mound. The Giants' record stood at 49–19, with a lead of eight games over Pittsburgh.

McGraw's unabating ire toward umpires was particularly on display later that summer. He was ejected three times in four games, August 21–24, and five times overall for confrontational incidents during a stretch of 11 games. Four of the expulsions were handed out by Jim Johnstone, the same umpire McGraw had been such a headache to back in May. The *Washington Post* reported that Johnstone was roughed up by "hoodlums" on his way to the Polo Grounds during this time. The paper implied that McGraw was behind it. A year earlier, a Cincinnati paper had accused McGraw and John T. Brush of hiring "Hessian loudmouths" to inflict chaos and disorder when their team played the Giants.

Over the final five weeks of the campaign, McGraw tempered his act with the men in blue and concentrated on managing his team to the pennant, incurring not a single disciplinary incident. Only a potent Pittsburgh Pirates club prevented the Giants from making a shambles of the league. Winning 105 games, the Giants easily became repeat NL champions—although the clinching of the flag did not come until October 1, with eight games remaining.

Sealing the deal at Cincinnati, the Giants defeated the Reds, 5–4, in the opener of a twin-bill. The game ended on a spectacular, one-handed catch by Sam Mertes in the tenth inning. A decade later, McGraw remembered the play with clarity: "It seemed certain that the ball would go over his head. By a sprint, though, Mertes got back and with a jump speared the ball with his bare hand, crashing into the fence as he fell. But he saved the game and won the pennant."[29] Adding to the degree of the play's difficulty was the existence of a treacherous "sun field" at the time. Mertes had hit an RBI triple in the top of the inning that Reds center fielder Harry Steinfeldt lost in the sun. Knowing his experience with the Polo Grounds' own "sun field" in left, McGraw cannily moved Mertes from left field to center in the bottom of the inning, after seeing center fielder Donlin struggling in the harsh glare. Following the marvelous play, Mertes brought the caught ball back to the dugout and casually let it fall to the ground. Per a Cincinnati writer's post-game notes, McGraw sent reserve infielder Boileryard Clarke to retrieve it. "That's the ball that won the championship," McGraw was quoted as saying as he dropped the pellet into his satchel to keep as a personal souvenir.

The never-challenged team once more led all of major league baseball in steals with 291. Third baseman Art Devlin was the league's stolen base king with 59. Devlin had been snagged out of the Eastern League by McGraw two years earlier. Dan McGann had another standout year at first base, missing a .300 batting average by a single point. Billy Gilbert and Bill Dahlen were effectively steady up the middle, although Gilbert missed a chunk of games due to a foot injury. Bresnahan received the majority of the playing time behind the plate and hit .302. The Giants scored more runs (780) than any club in either league.

The pitching was headed by Christy Mathewson, who had taken the mantle from McGinnity as the Giants' unquestionable ace. The tall, blonde-haired, blue-eyed matinee idol had posted his third straight 30-win campaign (31–9). He struck out more batters than any other pitcher for the third season in a row, 206, and his ERA was an unrivaled 1.28. McGinnity went 21–15, while Red Ames made a big splash with a 22–8 mark. Dummy Taylor won 16 games and Hooks Wiltse 15, as the Giants used only *six* pitchers all year. Claude Elliott, the only other member of the staff, was winless in ten appearances, but saved six games.

Trying to correct last year's misjudgments, it had been agreed several weeks before the end of the season that the Giants would battle for National League pride against the American League champions in the World Series. Those champions were the Philadelphia Athletics, managed by Connie Mack. In early October, the Athletics were in a tight pennant race. "It makes no difference who gets the American bunting, we will take them into camp," stated a confident McGraw, adding his preference of opponents. "I would rather it be Chicago, as I believe the series would not be so difficult with the White Sox as with the Athletics, but as I said, we will win no matter who opposes us."[30] Mack's squad nosed out the White Sox for the pennant by two games. (The 92–56 Athletics would have finished third in the National League.)

On October 2, Garry Herrmann, chairman of the National Commission,[31] announced from Cincinnati that the first game of the World Series would be hosted by Philadelphia (decided by a coin toss). Two umpires, one from each league, were chosen to judge the games. The *Washington Post* said that Harry Pulliam had selected Jim Johnstone, but McGraw's complaint(s) over the selection caused a change to Hank O'Day. McGraw also did not like Ban Johnson's choice of Jack Sheridan, but the American League president stuck to his guns.

The first game was held at Columbia Park on Monday, October 9. A paid crowd of 17,955, some roped off in the outfield, packed the cramped arena, with thousands more denied entry. The Giants arrived by rail in Philadelphia on game day at 10:00 a.m. Following a parade down Chestnut Street, led by the Catholic Protectory Band (brought from New York as escort), the players trotted onto the field at 2:15 for the anticipated 3:00 start. Prior to the game, at home plate, McGraw was presented with a small, hand-carved white elephant by the home club's captain, Lave Cross. The gag gift was accepted by McGraw with a slight blush and a doffing of his cap. In a parting shot against the Athletics in 1902, during the war of words against the startup American League, McGraw had referred to the Philadelphia team as a white elephant, predicting their short demise. (Connie Mack adopted the pachyderm representation as part of its team logo.)

Mack and McGraw managed from the dugout, with Mack in street clothes. Eddie Plank opened for the home team. The 24-game-winner was tagged for ten hits and three runs. It was more than enough support for Mathewson, who had completed 32 games on the year. He allowed four hits, walked none and choked off all Athletics scoring attempts. One batter reached third, and he was cut down trying to score by Mathewson himself.

At Columbia Park, prior to Game One of the 1905 World Series, an amused McGraw accepts a small, pedestaled model of a white elephant from Athletics captain Lave Cross. Home plate umpire Jack Sheridan seems focused on the lineup card in his hand (courtesy Boston Public Library).

The first New York World Series game was played on October 10, using a National League ball, as opposed to the standard American League balls utilized in Philadelphia. On the heels of the Game One victory, the novel excitement expected at the Polo Grounds was energized twofold. Nearly 25,000 were privy to the historic contest. The outfield was cordoned off for the overflow crowd. The contracted band played "He Climbed So High That He Reached the Sky" and "Give My Regards to Broadway" when the Giants appeared on the field, to loud applause. For effect, Christy Mathewson walked in from the club-house across the field to the Giants' bench by himself and received the loudest cheers.

Joe McGinnity, who had been upstaged by Mathewson on the season, took the hill for the Giants. Opposing him, Chief Bender was given the ball by Mack. Bender, a third-year right-hander, spoiled the intended New York celebration and defeated McGinnity, 3–0. An 18-game-winner, Bender was nearly as good as Matty the previous day, surrendering four hits, walking three and striking out nine. McGinnity's performance was just as luminous. He was reached for only five hits and no walks. Errors by McGann and Bresnahan resulted in all the Athletics' runs being unearned.

Following a rainout, Mathewson pitched the third game of the best-of-seven series, on October 12. Back at Columbia Park, the right-hander was towering again, scattering four singles in a 9–0 win. Dan McGann drove in four of the runs.

McGinnity then outdueled Plank on October 13, 1–0. The run off Plank was unearned. The game was played at the Polo Grounds. Fighting the sun, Sam Mertes pulled down the last out of the game, as he collided with the left field fence on a ball hit by Danny Murphy. The attendance at this game, like the second one held in Philadelphia, dropped off from the enthusiastically big openers greeting each home park.

Also in front of the New York fans, McGraw brought back Mathewson the following day, and the "golden boy" shined once more. He again was the last Giants player to come onto the field from the clubhouse and received a one-minute ovation from the capacity crowd. On one day's rest, Mathewson hurled his third whitewash, a five-hitter, and won, 2–0. Defeated was Chief Bender, the Game Two star. The Giants were the ultimate professional baseball champions for 1905. Mertes, who scored the only run in Game Four, and Mathewson, were the only Giants to cross the plate in the deciding contest.

Each Giant received roughly $1,100 as the winner's share of the interleague series. The losing Athletics were handed over close to $400 apiece. It was decided that royalties from only the first four games would be shared by the participants. Receipts from Games Five through Seven, if needed, were to be directed to the coffers of the club owners.

With Mathewson winning three games—all by shutout—in a span of six days, McGraw and the Giants won their first world championship trophy. McGraw used only three pitchers—Red Ames had relieved McGinnity for one inning in Game Two. In five games, the Athletics did not score an earned run. His incredible performance in the series provided Mathewson with the heroic achievement required to brand his All-American persona nationally. It was an image he calculatingly promoted, judged by his solo entrances into the Polo Grounds, but an image his very nature easily and authentically embraced. The clean-cut, former college man who spurned all types of vices (except gambling) became the representative ideal American sportsman and lasting idol to millions of people from all walks of life.

"Of all the World's Series that I have taken part," McGraw later reminisced, "I think the picture of that one stands out most vividly in my memory."[32]

The fond memories came from the easy time the Giants had of it and a change to their baseball attire. "I will never forget," said McGraw, "the impression created in Philadelphia and the thrill that I got personally when the Giants suddenly trotted out from their dugout clad in uniforms of black flannel, trimmed with white. The letters across the breasts were in white. The Athletics in their regular-season uniforms appeared dull alongside our champions."[33] McGraw had commissioned the new uniforms for the special occasion.

The victory in his first confrontation with the American League, combined with the impeccable performance of Christy Mathewson and fundamentally sound play from the remainder of his squad, generated a lifelong sentiment in McGraw that was perhaps steeped as much in euphoria as fact. "I regard the Giants of 1905 as the greatest ball club that I have managed,"[34] he would contend time and again.

THREE

"The Most Hated Man in Baseball"

"We all make mistakes. We are all fallible. I never held that up against Fred for a minute. I only felt sorry for him."—John McGraw

After two consecutive pennants, with a pitching staff anchored by Mathewson and McGinnity and complemented by stellar secondary components Ames, Taylor and Wiltse, a dynasty appeared to be looming for McGraw's Deadball Era Giants. However, a team from Chicago undercut whatever dynastic inclinations the New York manager may have nursed in 1906.

No one was going to challenge McGraw in the realm of salary, though. Shortly after winning it all, McGraw was rewarded with a new contract calling for $10,000 annually for three years. His compensation was thought to have surpassed the Pirates' Honus Wagner as the highest paid major leaguer.

It was not enough for McGraw that the Giants were undisputed champions. He had to find a way to remind everyone of the fact throughout the team's title defense. The manager chose to fiddle again with the Giants' uniforms, vaingloriously adopting flannels with "WORLD'S CHAMPIONS" printed across the chest. Apparel notwithstanding, the Giants, from the start, were struck with news that did not bode well for their cause. Fighting off a case of nasal diphtheria, Christy Mathewson would not be ready for Opening Day. He would not make his first start until May 5, more than three weeks into the season. The stacked Giants, however, did not miss him, compiling a 15–4 record to that date.

With the same starting eight from last season, the Giants downed the Philadelphia Phillies, 3–2, in the inaugural action of the campaign on April 12. Red Ames claimed the first victory in the four-hit, complete-game effort.

The Giants were 4–3 and ready to take off on a ten-game winning streak, when they displayed their new uniforms for the first time at home on April 20. Early-morning, gloomy skies cleared over New York into a sunny, springtime afternoon that was perfect for baseball. Prior to the game, the championship banner was stretched out flat in the outfield, awaiting the arrival of McGraw and company, whose rank and file included the visiting Brooklyn Superbas. A halyard was run through one end of the large blue pennant, and McGraw and his Giants had a hand at hoisting the first world championship banner over the Polo Grounds. Pyrotechnic bombs were launched from two cylinder casings bestride the pitcher's mound, and the "Star Spangled Banner" was played by the Catholic Protectory Band. The championship banner was blue with yellow lettering, reading: GIANTS, Champion Baseball Team of the National League, 1905. Substituting for Mayor McClellan, Ida Brooks Hunt, a stage actress, gently tossed out the first pitch to lone umpire Hank O'Day. After the Giants took a 6–0 lead after two innings, the game was never in doubt. Red Ames won his second game of the season, 8–2. Every Giants starter collected at least one hit, Ames included.

Four days prior to Mathewson's debut, McGraw had been tagged with the second of nine ejections he accumulated on the season. At Boston's South End Grounds, the irascible manager incessantly badgered umpires Bob Emslie and John Conway. The latter threw the loudmouth leader of the Giants out of the game in the eighth inning. For the remaining two frames of the contest (won by New York, 7–5), McGraw "then stood in the runway between the center and left wing on the stand and yelled at the umpire."[1] For disobeying the umpire's order to leave the grounds, McGraw was handed a three-day suspension by NL president Harry Pulliam. Also suspended for their conduct in the game were Roger Bresnahan and Dan McGann.

Despite the earlier experimentation in Brooklyn, Sunday baseball was still prohibited in New York City—but not in other parts of the state or vicinity. It was common for all three professional teams of the metropolis to schedule exhibition games with minor league and amateur clubs in the surrounding area on the Sabbath. Right after his suspension ended, McGraw, his wife, John T. Brush and Mrs. Christy Mathewson were involved in an automobile accident as they were coming back from a trip to Newburgh, New York. The Giants had played an exhibition game with the local team. The two women suffered bone fractures, while McGraw, Brush and his chauffeur were not injured seriously in the May 6 mishap, in which the vehicle hit a tree as it swerved to avoid another car.

McGraw was in another type of conveyance when fortune frowned on him again—but this time the fault was all his. In Pittsburgh, May 17, the Giants suffered their second shutout loss in a row to the Pirates. On his way out of Exposition Park, McGraw and his players received a razzing on the Sixth Street Bridge from a group of goading fans, who obviously knew the route of the players. Crossing the bridge in an open carriage, McGraw grabbed the horse whip from the driver and lashed out at a 13-year-old boy riding in an express wagon that had pulled alongside. The boy was felled to the ground by the lash. McGraw's carriage was able to escape an increasingly angered mob. That evening, McGraw was arrested on a charge of aggravated assault and battery. He posted a $500 bond and was freed.

> I didn't hurt that boy, although he did all in his power to maim me by throwing stones at me. He hit not only me but some of my players. I did only what every man should do—defend myself from attack, and will do it again, only the next time I will use the butt end of the whip instead of the lash. For years visiting players have been assaulted by these gangs of hoodlums, and my men have been frequently badly hurt.[2]

McGraw may have still had fresh in his mind an incident from last August 24 in the same locale. After a particularly disorderly game in which he was ejected by George Bausewine and threatened with a forfeit, McGraw and his players were pelted by stones by unruly citizens along the route leaving Exposition Park.

McGraw's court date was scheduled for the morning of May 19, the last day of the Giants' four-day stay in Pittsburgh. In alderman J.J. Kirby's chambers, McGraw, "accompanied by a coterie of friends,"[3] faced his plaintiff, Neal Brady, and his father Edward. Allegations that young Neal's eye had been damaged were disproved when his facial bandage was removed. The boy's face was cut by the cracker of the whip, however. McGraw agreed to pay the elder Brady an undisclosed sum, plus all medical bills and the $25 alderman fee, in exchange for dropping the charges. The proceedings concluded,

McGraw ducked out of the office through a back alley. He emerged out of a Penn Avenue saloon that was next to the alderman's office in time to see the boy being photographed by the press contingent waiting outside. McGraw scurried away in time just as he was spotted by the press corps.

It had not been a good three days for McGraw in the Steel City. The Giants had lost the third game of the series the previous day, 7–6. Bill Dahlen, representing the tying run on second base with two outs in the eighth inning, was caught off the bag by Honus Wagner using the hidden ball trick. Sammy Strang had been announced as a pinch-hitter for starter Christy Mathewson moments before the successful deception. But umpire Bob Emslie ordered Mathewson to pitch the bottom of the eighth, despite loud protests from the Pittsburgh side.

Dahlen felt so bad about being caught off the base that the *New York Times* reported that he wept after the game. McGraw fined him, nonetheless, for his lapse. Dummy Taylor salvaged the final game of the series in Pittsburgh with a 5–1 win.

The Giants then traveled to Chicago, where they took three out of four games from the Cubs. The victories came all in a row and counted as the longest losing streak of the year for Chicago. Quickly establishing themselves as clear challengers to McGraw's champions, manager Frank Chance's club morphed into one of baseball's teams for the ages. The Giants and the rest of the league would turn powerless against them. Leading both circuits in runs scored (704) and fewest runs allowed (381), the Cubs won an amazing 116 games—the most regular season wins by a club in the 20th century—for a .763 winning percentage, the best in baseball annals.

The Giants (and Pirates) were still in the pennant picture in mid–July when McGraw tried to strengthen a previously weakened spot. Back on May 15, Mike Donlin had fractured his ankle sliding into third base in Cincinnati. The star outfielder would be lost to the Giants for most of their remaining games. On July 12, McGraw purchased Cy Seymour from the Cincinnati Reds for $12,000. The former acquisition of McGraw as Baltimore manager in 1901, Seymour, a left-handed thrower and hitter, had begun his career with the 1896 New York Giants. Arguably the best offensive player in baseball in 1905, Seymour, 33, was leading the majors in slugging and OPS. But the outfielder and another former Baltimore manager, Ned Hanlon, who was now guiding the Reds, could not see eye to eye on most things and were constantly butting heads. The incompatibility led to the acquisition, a pricey but positive one for New York.

The next day, McGraw acquired another outfielder, Spike Shannon, from the St. Louis Cardinals for Sam Mertes and infielder Doc Marshall. There was many a Giants fan disappointed at losing old "Sandow," who was a few weeks away from his 34th birthday. Mertes himself was crestfallen over the news. The trade appeared to affect his desire and commitment to play baseball at its highest level. He played his last major league game that September.

It was against those indomitable Chicago Cubs, on August 7, that McGraw conceded a forfeit rather than allow umpire Jim Johnstone to enter the Polo Grounds to conduct the scheduled contest. Fellow arbiter Bob Emslie declared the forfeit (upheld by the league) when his colleague was barred from entering the stadium by security personnel. McGraw completely disregarded the interests of the hometown fans, and an estimated 10,000 patrons inside the stadium angrily called for refunds but were given rain checks instead.

The previous day, Johnstone had ejected McGraw (number eight on the season), after a close call at the plate went against the home team. The play occurred in the fifth inning with the Giants behind, 2–0. Almost the entire team, headed by McGraw, rushed out to surround Johnstone in protest. McGraw called Johnstone "a damn dirty c—k eating bastard, and a low-lived son of a bitch of a yellow cur hound."[4] Some of the irritated patrons threw bottles onto the field. The Giants went on to lose, 3–1. A municipal paper chastised not only the fans' poor behavior, but also McGraw, for his part in inciting the disorderly actions. "The conduct of the New York baseball crowd at the Polo Grounds yesterday was a disgrace," admonished the *Brooklyn Daily Eagle*. "In this case, McGraw appealed to the unruly spirit of the crowd by making a riot over one of the umpire's decisions. But a captain who foments disorder when he is being beaten is worse."[5] After the contest, Johnstone required a police escort to exit the grounds.

The free win of August 7 gave the Cubs their 70th victory in 100 games. The first-place club moved 6½ games ahead of the Giants.

Impervious to Emslie's ruling, McGraw actually tried to play the game using two of *his* players as umpires (and he and Brush dishonorably attempted to blame Johnstone's exclusion on New York City policemen assigned to the game). When Cubs manager Frank Chance steadfastly opposed the use of two of McGraw's players as arbiters, one of the selected pair tried to forfeit the game *in favor* of the Giants. "It was a disgraceful quit on the part of the Giants," Chance said afterward. "They were afraid to play. [McGraw] did not try to win today's game through fair means. The decision of [Giants player Sammy] Strang in declaring the contest forfeited to the Giants was absurd. He had no more right to take that stand than any spectator present."[6] Chance did not hold back on who he thought was to blame for the embarrassing fiasco. "McGraw is the cause of all the trouble," the playing manager pointedly added. "He is the most hated man in baseball. He has done more to injure the game than any other man at present engaged in it."[7]

League president Pulliam suspended the Giants manager for his actions resulting in the forfeiture and those related to his expulsion the previous day. In the game in which the manager was ejected, Pulliam concluded in a public declaration that "McGraw used the most villainous language one mortal could use on another to umpire Johnstone on a ball field."[8]

But further proof that the league's top man did not wield complete power can be deciphered in the same published statement by Pulliam, which lifted McGraw's ban, effective August 25. "The proper penalty in this case is not in my power to decree. Someday the institution itself, the game and the league will take precedent over all,"[9] he said. McGraw was barred for 16 games from August 8th through the 24th. By the time of McGraw's return, his team had slid 11½ lengths behind Chance's Cubs.

On September 4, with the defending champions falling farther back from contention, McGraw appeared to be finding new ways to be expunged from games. "McGraw has about run the gamut of umpire baiting," one newspaper concluded. "He was chased off the field by [umpire Bill] Carpenter for rowdy coaching."[10] McGraw was canned in the fourth inning, his ninth and final ejection for the year.

The 96–56 Giants finished 20 games behind Chicago. Mathewson recovered sufficiently to make 35 starts; he went 22–12. Winning 27 games, McGinnity recorded his last outstanding campaign. Wiltse won 16 out of 27 decisions, and the dependable Taylor won 17 and lost nine. Ames added 12 more to the win column. Forty games above .500, the Giants were good enough to win the pennant most years, but in 1906 a team destined to be wrapped in National League lore impeded anyone else's lofty intentions.

The novelty uniforms of 1906 were largely forgotten when the new season rolled around on April 11, 1907. The Giants went back to their 1905 models, with large NY letters split over each half of the chest, in both home white and road grey flannels. Opening Day at the Polo Grounds was a cold, clear day, with heaped remnants of a days-old snow-storm visible around the open areas of the playing field. The diamond was still wet from a heavy rainstorm the previous day. McGinnity started against the Philadelphia Phillies. Through eight innings, Phillies pitcher Frank Corridon held a 3–0 lead and the home team had just one hit. The bulk of the crowd, which fell several thousand shy of a sellout, lost interest at this point and sauntered, in droves, onto the field. The wayward multitude became unmanageable. The unusual sight of a snowball fight at a baseball game made it into various newspapers when a mischievous few lugged in the packed, powdery stuff from the rear of the grandstand and began slinging compressed snow chunks about. Without a significant security presence to restrain them, umpire Bill Klem was forced to forfeit the game to Philadelphia. New York's police commissioner had warned Giants ownership that members of his force had to be contracted for games and, if not, were under no obligation to enter the sporting facility short of emergency or threat to the populace at large. Finally, four policemen entered the park and marched up the center of the infield. Their presence somewhat restored order. Two people were arrested. At home nursing a bad case of the grippe, McGraw missed the embarrassing spectacle.

Also absent was Mike Donlin. The outfielder, who had appeared in only 37 games in 1906 due to injury, asked for the same salary he had commanded following his sterling 1905 campaign, plus a bonus for staying away from the bottle. The amounts, totaling over $4,000, priced Donlin outside of the payroll budget. The player would not compromise, and when the Giants also refused to budge, he decided to try his hand at acting—not a far-fetched fling because the previous April he had married Mabel Hite, a noted vaudeville and Broadway comedic actress. The loss of Donlin was made easier by the presence of Cy Seymour and Spike Shannon. The pair joined George Browne to form the Giants' regular outfield trio.

The only change on the infield was at second base. In January, the team sold Billy Gilbert to Newark of the Eastern League. Gilbert, 30, had been slowed by injuries the past two seasons. He had to clear waivers from every National League team, and did. McGraw put Tommy Corcoran in his place. A natural shortstop, Corcoran was 38 years old and a recognized excellent fielder at his position for many years. McGraw had purchased him from the Cincinnati Reds over the winter.

McGraw's troops stepped off to a sensational start, winning 24 out of their first 27 games, including a 17-game win streak. Remarkably, the Chicago Cubs began the campaign nearly as well, with a 23–4 record. During the streak, McGraw incurred one of his four ejections on the season—a tempered total considering the 19 early terminations he compiled over the past two campaigns. On May 11, McGraw, from the bench, rode Hank O'Day excessively—or incessantly—and was kicked out. The Giants won, 9–6, over the Pittsburgh Pirates at the Polo Grounds.

The following month, McGraw played in his last big league game. He had not recorded a hit since 1904 and had consigned himself to the managerial chair almost exclusively for the past three years, appearing in only 12 games in that span. On June 18 in Cincinnati, the 34-year-old McGraw inserted himself as pinch-runner for Roger Bresnahan, who had been severely beaned by Andy Coakley in the third inning. (Knocked unconscious by the pitched ball, the Giants catcher was revived in the clubhouse and taken to the hospital. So dire did the situation originally appear that a Catholic priest was summoned to administer the religion's last rites to Bresnahan. A hometown newspaper reported that Bresnahan was left with a lump on his head the size of a hen's egg.) McGraw reached second base and was left stranded. Hooks Wiltse defeated the Reds, 4–3. It was the Giants' 33rd victory in 49 decisions.

Earlier in the week in New York, an assemblyman's bill for allowing amateur baseball games to be conducted on Sunday within city limits was heard by Mayor George B. McClellan, Jr. The bill, if passed, would inevitably pave the way for professional baseball. The mayor, whose namesake father was the discredited commander of the main Union Army in the Civil War, was currently overseeing a public works boom that was laying the groundwork to propel New York into a progressively international and commercial hub.[11]

"It simply makes merchandise of the Lord's day," offered opponents of the measure, who were led by prominent clergy of the New York Conference of the Methodist Episcopalian League and officers of the Anti-Saloon League. "These people are putting the law of God aside. If you are a man of family you'd rather have your children in Bible school than at a baseball game on Sunday."[12]

"I will ask these gentlemen if there is a minister here who will preach the gospel on Sunday without his annual stipend," said one of the main proponents. "These ministers seem to be afraid that the youths of the country will forget who the Lord is and if asked might say McGraw or Mathewson. These gentlemen have nothing else to do but hunt up ways of taking the pleasure of the working classes away from them."[13]

The mayor reserved the right to make a decision at a later date. Like his procrastinating father, he never addressed the measure again.

Three quarters of the way through the month of July, McGraw bought infielder Larry Doyle from the Springfield Babes for $4,500. McGraw wasted no time in replacing Corcoran with the 20-year-old Central League player. "There are few defects in Doyle's style of play," McGraw said of the player whose demeanor would win over a great many fans. "Above all, he has a good head, a fine pair of hands, and is lucky. That is all a player needs."[14] McGraw outbid two American League clubs in an "auctioning off" of Doyle, put together by Springfield's owner, R.F. "Dick" Kinsella. Well-known from his involvement in local politics, Kinsella would later become one of McGraw's most important scouts, responsible for the discovery of several future stars.

On July 28, the Giants lost a doubleheader to the Cincinnati Reds in the Queen City. During the first game, backup Danny Shay became entangled in an argument with a fan. A park policeman joined the unpleasant discussion. McGraw leaped to the defense of his player. For his rebuttal, the officer threatened to put McGraw off the field. The Giants manager scoffed at any such intentions, making it clear that the policeman had no authority between the white lines. The cop irritably withdrew. After the second game ended, the same authority figure walked over to McGraw on the bench as he was preparing to leave. The officer slugged McGraw flush on the jaw. As he prepared a second punch, Joe McGinnity grabbed his arm and stopped him. The next day, the aggressor, John Kramer, was fired from his park detail by Reds president Garry Herrmann, who issued a zero tolerance decree for fans and players alike who used abusive language or employed inappropriate conduct at his ballpark. For his part, Kramer admitted he was wrong in hitting McGraw, but offered in his defense that he had been "grossly insulted" by the Giants commander.

Despite the great start, by the end of July the Giants—and the rest of the league—

had once again fallen victim to the high-flying Chicago Cubs, who had opened double-digit leads over the other first division clubs, including New York.

On August 5 in Chicago, McGraw engaged in a protracted beef with Bill Klem over what the manager thought was a blown call at the plate, allowing the Cubs to score in the first inning. McGraw kept up the criticism from the bench and was banished. The manager continued to give Klem a personal dressing down, forcing the umpire to pull his watch and threaten to forfeit the game to the home team if McGraw did not leave the field. McGraw left, but not before lying prone in the center field pasture of West Side Grounds. The contentious flap at the plate also led to the ejections of shortstop Bill Dahlen, utility man Danny Shay and star pitcher Christy Mathewson, the latter players not being in the game. In an unrelated incident, first baseman Dan McGann sprained an ankle in the next inning and limped off to the sidelines. The depleted Giants overcame three first inning runs by the Cubs and rallied to beat the first-place team, 5–4. Red Ames was the winner.

Two days later in Pittsburgh, as the Giants continued their road trip, McGraw received a telegram from league president Pulliam, informing him that he had been suspended for three days for his hostilities toward Klem. "It's too bad," said an unrepentant McGraw of the news. "I just had to tell Klem what I thought of him in Chicago for he was even worse than usual which is saying a lot. I have nothing to say about my suspension save that I am sorry that it came about at this time."[15] The Giants won two out of the three games from which McGraw was excommunicated.

In September, the Giants selected half a dozen players in the minor league draft. Among them were infielder Charles "Buck" Herzog and pitcher James "Doc" Crandall. Both would make the team next year. Later in the month, the big club purchased the contract of a Southern Michigan League player named Fred Merkle. The first baseman was called up and participated in 15 games. During this busy transactional period, a Midwestern newspaper took note of McGraw's pioneering strategy in a news "round-up" of National League teams: "Manager McGraw is this season making more substitutions at bat than any other major league manager."[16]

As the season wound down, McGraw and the third-year umpire Klem again clashed. The first altercation began prior to the opening game of a series in Pittsburgh, on September 23. The Giants, although 21 games over .500, had been eliminated from contention by the powerful Cubs. Klem initially showed great self-restraint with McGraw before running him from the contest and doggedly chasing him from the field. It began with Klem objecting to the presence of Roger Bresnahan in the Giants' starting lineup. The umpire was expecting the Giants player to be suspended for his actions the day before with Klem associate Bob Emslie. A thorough recount of the occurrences saturated evening and morning news sources. One such recount read:

> McGraw insisted that Bresnahan was not suspended until official notice was received.
> Klem went over to the New York players' bench to get the batting list. McGraw was drinking a cup of water. During the argument he threw water in the face of the umpire.
> Klem stood the dose like a stoic. Between the sixth and seventh innings [Ed] Abbaticchio drove a ball over third base. Klem called it fair. McGraw insisted that it was a foul ball. Klem ordered McGraw from the grounds. Instead of retiring, McGraw went to a small gate under the grandstand and coached the team. Klem went after him and drove him out of the grounds entirely."[17]

The game, a 2–1 Pirates victory, was delayed 12 minutes at the start, and Art Devlin was also ordered out of the contest by Klem when he stubbornly maintained an opinion similar to McGraw on the Bresnahan matter.

The following day, as Christy Mathewson threw his league-topping eighth shutout of the year, Klem banished four Giants. Included was Sammy Strang, for allowing his bat to move perilously past Klem's face on a swinging strike. McGraw escaped the wrathful Klem this day and somehow managed to avoid a suspension for his scornful intolerance of the previous day.

The Giants lost their last seven games of the season and finished in fourth place, 82–71, 25½ games behind the 107-win Chicago Cubs. The Cubs avenged their stunning 1906 World Series loss to the crosstown White Sox, defeating the Detroit Tigers in five games in the 1907 Fall Classic.

In the off-season, McGraw worked on retooling his regressing team. Two months after the World Series, he traded his first baseman, shortstop and left fielder to the Boston Doves for their first baseman Fred Tenney, shortstop Al Bridwell and backup catcher Tom Needham. McGraw also included *his* second-string catcher, Frank Bowerman, and bullpen pitcher Cecil Ferguson in the five-for-three deal.

A strong point of McGraw was recognizing the decline of position players and cutting future losses, as it were. Dan McGann, Bill Dahlen and George Browne had all reached the end of their careers as productive players. McGann had missed nearly half of the Giants' games due to a broken wrist suffered in spring camp. He managed to hit .298 in those appearances, but had put on weight and become lethargic around the bag and on the bases. His first campaign in Boston would be the final one of his 12-year big league career. Dahlen hit .207 in 1907, and his first year in Boston would be his last as a major league starter. But the 37-year-old had justified McGraw's faith in him since his pick-up from Brooklyn four years earlier. (In terms meaningful to readers today, we can say that Dahlen had seasons of 5.6, 5.5, and 3.2 WAR from 1904 to 1906.)

Browne, McGraw's first acquisition as new Giants manager in 1902, had been a steady, if unspectacular, player during his time in New York. He would hang on the big league scene for a few more years as a marginal and mostly part-time contributor. The aging Bowerman would continue as a backup receiver with Boston. He was probably most missed by Christy Mathewson. The 39-year-old Bowerman caught the most shutouts by the iconic hurler with 26, and his second no-hitter in 1905.

Before he executed the deal, which was consummated at the NL owners meeting on December 13, McGraw paid a visit to the home of Mike Donlin in Champaign, Illinois. McGraw acceded to the player's year-old contract demands and named him captain of the Giants (which provided the bonus Donlin had been seeking). The signing of Donlin, who had played semipro ball in the Chicago area over the summer—in between sporadic stage engagements—was greeted with enthusiasm in New York.

On Opening Day at the Polo Grounds, April 22, 1908, the inside of the stadium was steeped with fans like never before. Under sunny skies, an estimated 25,000 rooters crammed their way inside the upper Manhattan ballpark. A good many of them were given standing room privilege on the field, not only in a half-ring around the outfield but also behind the plate. Stretching out along the lower grandstand toward each corner base, rows of fans, a compact four and five deep, resembled the very horseshoe configuration of the stadium. In a scene difficult to fathom today, patrons sat on the grass in foul territory and stood on chairs dragged onto the field from the lower boxes to better, or more comfortably, see the action. The starters for the four o'clock contest—Mathewson for New York and Harry McIntire for the visiting Brooklyn Superbas—warmed up on the sidelines with lines of people on either side of them—in the grandstand and on the field. The inaugural home game began with the unprotected fans behind home plate closer to the catcher than was Mathewson. (The Giants became accustomed to playing in front of large Polo Grounds crowds this season, averaging a major league record 11,375 fans in 80 home games—a mark that held held up until the 1920 New York Yankees averaged 16,746.)

The game developed into a pitcher's duel until the bottom of the ninth inning. Behind 2–1, Mathewson, the scheduled leadoff batter, was called back in favor of rookie Fred Merkle. The pinch-hitter delivered a ground-rule double into the right field crowd encroaching the field. He was sacrificed to third by Spike Shannon, the first-place batter. But Fred Tenney grounded into a fielder's choice, with Merkle thrown out at the plate. The new Giants captain came up. Donlin looked at four consecutive pitches, a ball, strike, strike and ball. Each bellowed strike call dampened the raucous din of the frenzied crowd. Donlin leaned into McIntire's fifth offering and sent it sailing into the right field bleacher section for a game-winning home run. Donlin, whose nickname was "Turkey Mike" because his strut resembled the wattled bird, was engulfed by shouting fans and partially carried off the field. A more successful homecoming by an athlete has rarely been made.

After opening the season on the road, the thrilling victory was the sixth in seven games for the Giants. But the team could not build on the early success. It lost the next three games to Brooklyn before Mathewson stopped the slide with a shutout at Boston.

The series with the Doves resulted in some off-the-field fireworks for the Giants' impertinent dugout leader. The club made it two in a row over Boston with a 3–2 win on April 28. Pinch-hitting, the Doves' Dan McGann hit into a rally-killing double play in the ninth inning. After the game, McGraw criticized McGann's speed on the play, referring to his former player as an ice wagon. There was bad blood between McGraw and all the players he had traded in December.

> The trouble between McGraw and the men started last summer, when McGraw found that the players were not trying to win nor keeping themselves in proper condition to play fast ball. Frank Bowerman and Bill Dahlen have been denouncing McGraw since the season opened. Bowerman has not been on speaking terms with the Giants manager for several years…. The men who were sent to Boston were dissatisfied because of a cut in their salary, and made many a threat to quit the team.[18]

"Proper conditioning" was usually a reference to breaking team conduct rules (set by McGraw), including curfew violations.

McGann was irked sufficiently by McGraw's post-game comments, which went beyond just the comparison to the slow-moving vehicle, to confront his former boss. As it happened, the Giants and McGann were staying at the Copley Square Hotel. That evening, McGann went looking for McGraw and threw a punch at him in the hotel's pool room.

> Hats were knocked off and there was a clash, but no damage was done except to rile McGann's Kentucky blood. The scrap broke up the billiard game after the players separated the combatants. McGraw went upstairs and was soon followed by McGann, who made a vicious pass at the Giants manager. McGraw ducked in time to get a blow on his shoulder. He was up in a flash, and the pair clinched again, but some of the players interfered before any blood was spilled."[19]

McGann was put out of the hotel by its owners and did not play the following day.

The Giants' start to the 1908 season was as sputtering as the McGann-McGraw fight. Joe McGinnity missed the first month of the campaign, battling a viral infection with prolonged fever. The illness sapped him of much of his strength and durability; he was limited to 20 starts, although McGraw used him almost as many times in relief. Hooks Wiltse moved into the number two pitching slot, behind Mathewson, and delivered a 23-win season. Red Ames, Dummy Taylor and Doc Crandall, the minor league draftee, split the remainder of the Giants' starts on the season save one.

At the end of May, the top six teams in the NL were separated by six games. Having completed their first trip to the Western cities of the National League, McGraw predicted that the league-leading Chicago Cubs would tumble once they left home for the first time to face their Eastern counterparts.

The last stop for the Cubs on their first trip east was New York. McGraw missed one of the anticipated games versus the Cubs at the Polo Grounds, on June 18. He had been suspended a few days earlier by Harry Pulliam for calling umpire Jim Johnstone, as one daily delicately put it, "a piece of cheese." The verbal denigration occurred at the Polo Grounds on Saturday, June 13, versus the Cincinnati Reds. A strike three call on Spike Shannon set McGraw off. Although he had been presented with the suspension notice earlier in the day, McGraw showed up in uniform for the continuation of the series on Monday the 15th. He stayed out of view under the grandstand, until the game was called due to rain in the fourth inning. He then became involved in a fist fight with a Pinkerton security man—or two—as the crowd was dispersing. Unbothered by the falling raindrops, McGraw came to the defense of Joe McGinnity, who had started the scuffle with the private police guard now employed at the Polo Grounds. McGraw entered into the lively scrap until broken up by New York City bluecoats, called in from their station outside the park.

Cincinnati sportswriter Jack Ryder conjectured that McGraw's suspension would be extended for his undisciplined actions.

> McGraw used considerably strong language to umpire Johnstone from his cubby hole. "This cubbyhole is a unique feature of the Polo Grounds. Whenever manager McGraw is put off the field or suspended he retires to it and is out of sight, but far from out of mind. Through a small hole cut in the boards he can survey the field, to say nothing of attacking the umpire at critical times."[20]

(The "cubbyhole" reference is presumably the same as the "toolbox" from an earlier chapter.)

Pulliam did not extend the suspension. "I don't see my way out of it," said the obviously frustrated circuit president. "The umpire certainly cannot leave the game and go swooping around behind the players' bench to find out if McGraw is there. It is a bad condition and I don't know what can be done about it."[21]

The McGraw-less Giants swept a doubleheader from the Reds two days later, June 17. Then the Cubs beat the Giants, 7–5, in the opener of their series. But with McGraw back in the saddle the next day, the club won three straight from the front-runners. The McGrawites improved to 29–24, three-and-a-half games behind the Cubs' pace.

In July, McGraw applied himself to improving his team for the immediate future. He made two much-publicized purchases on July 1. He bought pitcher Richard "Rube" Marquard from the Indianapolis Indians for $11,000, a record for a single minor league player at the time. A prolific minor league hurler with nearly 700 innings pitched in a two-year span, Marquard joined the Giants late in the season and made one start. Also from the American Association, the Giants laid out $6,000 for catcher John "Chief" Meyers of the St. Paul Saints. Meyers was also a late "call up" but did not see any action. Giants secretary Fred Knowles later divulged the $1,500 acquisition of infielder Art Fletcher from the Texas League's Dallas Giants.

McGraw was not finished spending John T. Brush's money. Within ten days, he bought outfielder Harry "Moose" McCormick from the Philadelphia Phillies and obtained pitcher Jake Weimer and infielder Dave Brain from the Cincinnati Reds, in exchange for pitcher Bob Spade and $5,000. While the latter trade was a complete waste of funds, it could easily be excused by the extremely good expenditures that preceded it. The pickup of McCormick was in direct response to Spike Shannon's alarming drop-off. Shannon was placed on waivers and claimed before the end of the month, with McCormick taking his spot in the outfield.

Not one to be replaced any time soon was Christy Mathewson. The Giants and McGraw were blessed with Mathewson's most prolific season in 1908. The Bucknell University graduate led the league in every positive pitching category. He started 44 games, completed 34 and appeared 12 other times in relief. Winning 37 games, he tossed 390⅔ innings and a career-best 11 shutouts; he led the league in strikeouts with 259 and posted the lowest ERA at 1.43. Yet the pitcher deluxe lost the Giants' most important game of the year—a season-closing, pennant-deciding contest at the Polo Grounds on October 8.

The Giants took first place in September, entering the month in a tight, three-way battle for the lead with Chicago and the Pittsburgh Pirates. The Giants played 24 home games in September, a schedule happenstance. Winning 18 of the first 19 September games, the Giants made it clear that the pennant would have to be taken from them. McGraw's club had won nine in a row when the second-place Pirates arrived in New York. A large crowd, supposedly topping 30,000, were enticed to the Polo Grounds for the opening of the series, a doubleheader on Friday, September 18. Mathewson did not disappoint his followers. He spun his 11th whitewash, while holding the visitors to five hits in the opener. In the nightcap, Hooks Wiltse, with relief assistance from McGinnity, pulled in a 12–7 triumph. McGraw's team moved 4½ games ahead of Chicago and five over the Pirates with two-and-a-half weeks to go on the season.

With his men having won 11 in a row, McGraw allowed himself the type of sports boast that invariably comes back to haunt the boaster. "I am not claiming any championship until the pennant is clinched," he said following the doubleheader win. "I am of the opinion, however, that we will win and win, too, with comparative ease. Easier, in fact than the race now shows."[22]

But following the dual wins, the Giants lost four straight to their closest rivals. The Pirates bounced back to win, 6–2, on Saturday. With still no Sunday baseball permitted in New York, Mathewson lost a tough 2–1 decision to the Pirates' Vic Willis in the Monday afternoon affair. McGraw was asked to leave the premises by Hank O'Day for arguing a safe call at first base on a Pirates hitter in the third inning. The runner eventually scored to further send the ousted manager's blood into a boil.

After the new invading team—the Cubs—won a twin-bill the next day to pull virtually even with the Giants in first place, McGraw brought back Mathewson, on one day's rest, in the next game of the series on September 23. The game's ending made one player infamous for baseball eternity.

Mathewson dueled with Cubs starter Jack Pfiester to a 1–1 tie entering the bottom of the ninth. In their last at-bat, the Giants strung together three hits between two outs and seemingly won the game. The runner at third base, Moose McCormick, came home with the assumed winning run, following a clean hit to center field by shortstop Al Bridwell. At first base, Fred Merkle did not advance to second and touch the bag. The play has been written about countless times. Coaching at first base, Joe McGinnity intercepted the game ball on its way back from the outfield and then flung it into the stands. Merkle was also physically impeded by opposition players as he attempted to go back and touch second base, after being made aware of the Cubs' intentions. Somehow, through the chaos of the happy crowd overrunning the field, the Cubs' Johnny Evers retrieved a baseball, touched second base and petitioned the umpires for a phantom force-out call from umpire Hank O'Day. A substitute baseball was used by Cubs manager Frank Chance for the alleged force out call on Merkle. Both umpires, Bob Emslie and Hank O'Day, would admit that they did not follow the unconventional ending on the bases to completion. With no possible way to clear the field, "no contest" was finally declared as descending darkness introduced another unmitigated factor.

Two of the most prominent newspapers in the country, the *New York Times* and the *Chicago Daily Tribune*, assumed the mantle of Merkle bashers and laid the foundation for the rookie player's more than century-old, ill-gotten reputation. From the *New York Times'* September 24 sports pages:

> Censurable stupidity on the part of player Merkle in yesterday's game at the Polo Grounds between the Giants and Chicagos placed the New York team's chances of winning the pennant in jeopardy. His unusual conduct in the final inning of the great game perhaps deprived New York of a victory that they would have unquestionably had he not committed a breach in baseball play that resulted in umpire O'Day declaring the game a tie.[23]

The *Chicago Tribune* chimed: "Minor league brains lost the Giants today's game after they had clearly and fairly won it by a score of 2 to 1. In the ninth round, Merkle did a bone-head base-running stunt."[24]

Gaining back sole possession of first place, the Giants defeated the Cubs, 5–4, the next day, as everyone awaited a ruling from Harry Pulliam on the previous game's outcome. Mathewson, appearing in his fourth game in seven days, saved Wiltse's victory.

Then came the league president's edict, upholding O'Day's ruling and cementing Merkle's enduring blame. "Much as I deplore the unfortunate ending of a brilliantly played game as well as the subsequent controversy, I have no alternative than to be guided by the law," Pulliam said. "I believe in sportsmanship, but would it be good sportsmanship to repudiate my umpires simply to condone the undisputed blunder of a player?"[25]

The Giants went 10–5 in their remaining 15 games, but could not shake the formidable Cubs. McGraw's club, in fact, had to win their final three games of the season to tie Chicago with a 98–55 record. The teams finished in a dead heat, requiring a replay of the "Merkle boner" game.

On Thursday, October 8, a mass of humanity descended upon 8th Avenue and 155th Street in upper Manhattan. Thousands of people, an enormous number of interested spectators never seen before at a sporting event in New York—or anywhere in the country—congregated in and around the Giants' home park in anticipation of the three o'clock ball game on tap to decide the National League pennant.

The Polo Grounds' 20,000-plus seating capacity was obliterated by ticket-buying fans, standing-room patrons and gate-crashers alike. "The 15-foot fence behind the grandstand, topped with barbed wire," was reported "scaled by scores of men and boys."[26] Young adventurers latched onto the girders under the top of the grandstand, usurping space normally belonging to pigeons. The roof of the grandstand was covered with fans. Looming behind those al fresco denizens, people congregated all over Coogan's Bluff. The elevated train line stop adjacent to the ballpark that brought so many of the throng was replete with hardy souls willing to risk injury for a skewered peek at the big game. Two hundred yards away, they perched atop the platform's roof and signal posts, some as high as 100 feet above the ground. One man died from a fall from his precarious placement. The local authorities had their hands full, particularly once the venue had reached its interior limit. "The police were swept aside like corks before a torrent," described one regional account of the mad scene around the park, "and the horses of the mounted men were pushed and jammed against the high walls of the grounds."[27]

"For the first time, men and boys clung to the narrow tops of all the towering dry goods and wet goods sign boards which overlook the ball field,"[28] wrote another reporter. By most conservative estimates, 50–60,000 people were in and around the Polo Grounds and Manhattan Field to the south on a warm, sunshiny autumn afternoon. It was stipulated by home plate umpire Jim Johnstone that any ball hit into the roped-off outfield crowd would count as a two-base hit. Bill Klem, on the bases, would be most responsible for making such rulings.

Christy Mathewson had last pitched on October 3, five days earlier. He had been beaten by Phillies rookie Harry Coveleski, 3–2. Mathewson was relieved in the eighth inning, trailing by two runs. Over the last 37 days of the season, as both a starter and reliever, Mathewson threw 110⅓ innings—equivalent to pitching a complete game every three days for five weeks. The grueling workload appeared to catch up to him at the worst possible time. So much so that on the eve of the pennant-deciding game, McGraw remained non-committal about using his one-of-a-kind pitcher. "It's something of a guess," he said. "Mathewson has not done any pitching this week, and though somewhat fagged last week, from the amount of work he has done, the rest he has had since then may have put him on edge for tomorrow's struggle."[29] No matter what McGraw communicated, everyone knew that if Mathewson could stand, he would pitch the critical game.

Several minutes before the designated start time, a mighty roar was heard as Mathewson walked in from the outfield "accompanied by the proudest small boy in the world."[30] To paraphrase one onlooker, the biggest collective cheer ever to reverberate off the rocky cliffs overlooking John T. Brush's ballpark was heard when Mathewson removed his long sweater and began warming up.

As was the custom, the crowd rose in unison and then sat down, right before the first offering was delivered, a dual gesture of acknowledgment and support for their pitcher and one indicating a "settling in" to be entertained. Amid a relentless clamor of cowbells and horns, Mathewson threw the first pitch of the game to the Cubs' Jimmy Sheckard. It was a ball. But Matty came back and struck out Sheckard on three more pitches, including a swinging strike three on his famous "fade away" pitch. The next hitter, Johnny Evers, grounded out to second, and Frank Schulte also whiffed. A loud percussion of horns and cheering lauded Mathewson on his walk to the Giants' dugout.

Perhaps remembering too much the game Jack Pfiester hurled against Mathewson on September 23, which had brought both teams to this all-or-nothing point in the season, manager Chance named the left-hander—the fourth-best pitcher on his staff—to oppose Mathewson once more. Pfiester, though 12–10, had done a fine job in 29 starts, but his numbers were no match for topline starters Three Finger Brown and Ed Reulbach. Brown, 29–9, had last pitched on October 4, with the 24–7 Reulbach last toeing the rubber on October 3. Both were amply rested to make the start versus Mathewson.

Pfiester hit the first Giants batter, first baseman Fred Tenney, on the right arm and walked the number two hitter, Buck Herzog. But the southpaw fanned Roger Bresnahan, and Herzog was picked off first base by catcher Johnny Kling. Cleanup hitter Mike Donlin lined a ball into the multitude in the outfield and was awarded a double, scoring Tenney. When Pfiester walked the next batter, Cy Seymour, Chance made a crucial, game-altering call to the bullpen. The manager summoned Brown. Striking out Art Devlin, Brown left Donlin stranded at second.

Mathewson had one errant inning, and it cost the Giants dearly. In the top of the third frame, the Cubs bunched four extra-base hits, plus a bunt single and a walk, enabling four runs to score. A double by Chance knocked in two of the Chicago tallies. Brown held the Giants at bay throughout the rest of the game, limiting the home nine to only one more run.

Mathewson was pinch-hit for in the bottom of the seventh by Larry Doyle and relieved by Wiltse in the eighth—McGraw's only moves of the game. After wisely replacing Pfiester with Brown in the first stanza and taking the lead in the third, Chance stayed pat and made no other changes.

With the 4–2 victory, the 99–55 Cubs won the pennant by one game over the Giants (and Pittsburgh Pirates).

"I do not feel badly about the game," said an uncharacteristically dispassionate McGraw afterward. "We merely lost something we had won before."[31] A day later, sounding a bit more like himself, McGraw wired the following well-wishes to former Orioles teammate and good friend Hughie Jennings, the current manager of the repeat AL champion Detroit Tigers: "If justice had been done, you would have been playing off with the Giants now. My hearty congratulations."[32]

The Cubs made it three pennants in a row in 1908—but not without historic controversy. It took a herculean effort to dislodge the three-time National League pennant-winning Cubs from the top spot of the circuit in 1909. Back-to-back World Series champions in 1907 and 1908, the Cubs won 104 games in 1909. But the Honus Wagner-led Pittsburgh Pirates claimed 110 victories to garner the title. McGraw's Giants won over 90 games again (92–61), but were simply outclassed by the two dominant teams ahead of them.

In McGraw's first six full years at the helm, the Giants had won two pennants and their only World Series, had barely lost another flag, and had never failed to place in the first division. The Giants had irrefutably shed their turn-of-the-20th century doormat roles.

The success was reflected at the box office. In 1908, the club led all of baseball in attendance for the second year in a row, attracting over 900,000 fans. As baseball took undisputed hold as the national game, the New York Giants—with major drawing cards in superstar Christy Mathewson and in McGraw's polarizing personality—evolved into the sport's most publicized team. Building on that national identity was the wide newspaper network that the country's largest city would engender.

John McGraw missed his second Opening Day in three years, Thursday, April 15, 1909. This time it was due to an operation the previous day on an infected finger that had been split by a spring training line drive. Coach Arlie Latham, a National Leaguer dating back to the 1880s, was McGraw's surrogate for this and other games missed by the Giants skipper early in the season.

Veteran Fred Tenney, the new captain of the team, was also identified as pulling the players' strings from the bench on more than one occasion. Tenney, a slick fielder at first base, was the former playing manager of the Boston Doves. In spite of a pedestrian batting

McGraw's "aldermanic paunch," as one newspaper described the Giants manager's waistline, is more evident in this photo next to the Cubs' rail-thin Johnny Evers—who would later become a Giants coach. Evers was involved in the infamous (for Giants fans) September 23, 1908, tie-game at the Polo Grounds.

average of .256, Tenney had scored 108 runs in 1908 to pace the league. (Tenney played in every game for the Giants in 1908, except for the 1–1 tie game versus the Cubs on September 23. His replacement, due to a stiff back, was Fred Merkle.) Richard Croker, former Tammany Hall boss, threw out the ceremonial first pitch moments prior to the four o'clock start. The sun was shining brightly over what was sometimes informally referred to as Coogan's Hollow.

The Polo Grounds had been built up over the winter with bleachers added in center field and an overhang of box seats attached to the upper pavilion. All except some seats in the center field bleachers were filled for the initial game of the campaign (delayed a day by rain), which came against the Brooklyn Superbas. Red Ames and Brooklyn's Irvin "Kaiser" Wilhelm hooked up in a scoreless, extra-inning duel. Wilhelm defeated Ames, 3–0, in 13 innings. The story within the game was that Ames held the visitors hitless through the first nine stanzas. Three innings after Ames permitted his first safety, a succession of four hits, mixed with a walk, accounted for all the Brooklyn scoring.

Also experiencing its share of building up was the Giants' outfield. Mike Donlin landed a co-starring role with his actress wife in a successful traveling play and not too reluctantly gave up baseball for the near future. Red Murray, a gifted outfielder who was landed by McGraw in a trade with St. Louis, assumed Donlin's old spot. The 25-year-old Murray would make right field at the Polo Grounds his home for five fruitful years.

Another new ballhawk conscript was Bill O'Hara. The Toronto-born O'Hara became the first Canadian to play for McGraw's Giants. He received the majority of the playing time in center, over the aging Cy Seymour. Moose McCormick, in his first full season in New York, played left field. In the infield, Tenney, who was 37, was retained. Larry Doyle was again the regular second baseman, although he missed the opening games of the season due to a contract dispute. Steady Art Devlin began his sixth year at the hot corner, while Al Bridwell covered short once more.

McGraw returned for the Giants' third game on April 17 and witnessed Rube Marquard garnish his first major league win—4–1 over the Philadelphia Phillies. Marquard was the minor league darling who had won 51 games over the past two seasons. Early on referred to as the "$11,000 Beauty" from the unprecedented purchase price McGraw had laid out for him, the hard-throwing left-hander tossed a three-hitter in his second major league start.

During the first week of the season, the name of the man at the center of a bribery probe, involving the Giants, came to light. Bill Klem had made public that prior to the first pitch of the pennant-deciding contest at the Polo Grounds last October, he and his colleague were offered $2,500 to call the game with a favorable Giants outcome in mind by a representative of the New York club. That man was now identified as Giants team physician Joseph M. Creamer.

Klem immediately ordered Creamer, who was acting on behalf of three Giants, out of the clubhouse. Creamer emphatically denied the bribery charges. Baseball, lacking impartial investigative authority and apparently unwilling to seek it, eventually swept under the rug the potential scandal involving its foremost franchise. It did, however, order Creamer banned from all league parks.

After missing the Giants' fifth game at Brooklyn because of his injured digit, McGraw excused himself from the team's first road foray, an eight-game excursion to Philadelphia and Boston. For his finger's sake, McGraw was remanded to a sterile environment as much as possible and stayed at his home. During the series in Philadelphia, Christy Mathewson made his initial start of the campaign on May 4. One report mentioned that "Big Six" had hurt his rib cage, while another indicated that McGraw was "saving him," by sparing his throwing in the cool spring weather.

Whatever the reason, the pitcher was not sharp. Mathewson was roughed up for nine hits in six innings by the Phils. He walked four and struck out the same number in suffering a 5–2 setback.

McGraw was back in the swing of things when the Giants returned to Harlem on May 11, and Mathewson made five more starts in May, including on the last day of the month. In that outing—the second game of a doubleheader against the Phillies—he slugged his second fence-clearing home run, to go along with three previous inside-the-parkers and one "bounced" four-bagger. He clouted a pitch from Lew Moren into the left field bleachers with plenty of room to spare. The solo blast, in the bottom of the eighth inning, broke a 4–4 tie and provided the margin of victory. With a win in the earlier contest, the Giants' record stood at a mediocre 17–17.

New York turned over half of their frontline pitching staff in 1909. Prior to the season, McGraw released both Joe McGinnity and Dummy Taylor, both stalwarts who had served McGraw well—in particular, McGinnity. It could easily be argued that the "Iron

Man" deserved better. Thirty-eight years of age when Opening Day rolled around, the indefatigable right-hander had seemingly been slowed by his age. Though he had hurled over 3,400 innings in ten big league seasons, he would show that he still had a lot more left in the tank. McGinnity could have continued as an asset for McGraw if the manager had looked past the salary ($5,000) he commanded. After McGinnity failed to throw 300 innings for the first time in his career in 1908, McGraw made too hasty a disassociation. None of the other miserly magnates in the league were willing to take on the pitcher's known asking price either. Joe McGinnity, therefore, was unceremoniously drummed out of the major leagues. He went on to pitch in the minors well into his 50s. He became a five-time 20-game winner in the lower levels, and won 30 games in another season. While owner Brush has been implicated as the driving force behind the release, McGraw could have intervened and found a way to keep the future Hall of Fame pitcher, if he had so desired.

The 34-year-old Taylor was a different story. Coming off a 15-start, 8–5 season, his best pitching days were behind him, and no one could fault McGraw for making a cold but prudent business decision. After the pitcher had a swollen gland in his right shoulder lanced over the winter, the rudimentary procedure accelerated his exit from the big time. Replacing the veterans were Marquard and Arthur "Bugs" Raymond, whom McGraw had picked up, along with backstop George "Admiral" Schlei and Red Murray, in the off-season trade with the Cardinals. In exchange for the trio, the popular Roger Bresnahan had been shipped to St. Louis, where he became the playing manager. Raymond, a tragic figure with an alcohol abuse problem, would prove less of a help and more of a headache to McGraw.

McGraw traded Bresnahan, who caught 139 games in 1908, at the right time. The 29-year-old catcher's career arc began a downward trajectory in his first year in St. Louis and never recovered.

Hooks Wiltse, the five-year veteran, and Red Ames, the Opening Day pitcher, were the other starters, as McGraw made a concerted effort to lessen Mathewson's responsibilities and spread the pitching workload. Perhaps the fateful make-up game, when a fatigued Mathewson had disappointed so many, still weighed on the manager's mind.

Raymond produced an ineffective start on June 5 in St. Louis, the first time McGraw was drummed out of a 1909 game. McGraw became too peeved over an out call on a close play at first base by Harry Truby. The Giants, trailing at the time of their manager's third-inning ejection, rallied to win, 8–7.

On July 16, facing the Cincinnati Reds, Mathewson pitched one of his many extraordinary games that year. In the seventh inning, home plate umpire Jim Johnstone called a high chopper off the dish fair, resulting in a double play when Art Devlin, the runner at first, was forced at second and batter Al Bridwell failed to run, thinking the ball foul. Protesting the play beyond the acceptable norm, McGraw was asked to leave the Polo Grounds premises in no uncertain terms by Johnstone. Mathewson finished a six-hit, 2–1 victory, in 80 minutes. His team bettered its record to 45–28, but were losing ground in the standings to the first-place Pirates.

On August 2, all scheduled games in the major leagues were canceled due to the funeral of Harry Pulliam, who had committed suicide a few days earlier. Only 40 years old, Pulliam had suffered a nervous breakdown in the months prior to taking his own life. The stresses and strains associated with his job, along with verbal attacks he took too personally, led him down the road to oblivion. His verdict on the "Merkle game," and its hotly debated aftermath, were especially damaging to his fragile psyche.

By the time of McGraw's third and final 1909 ejection, September 3, the Giants were playing out the string, 15½ games behind the Pirates. McGraw was exiled in the first inning, after too vehemently insisting that Cardinals third baseman William Barbeau had missed a swipe tag on Cy Seymour. Barbeau threw to first to complete a double play. From behind the plate, the game's sole umpire, Bob Emslie, made the ruling. The Giants ended up winning the contest, 7–4, over the visiting Redbirds.

Later that fall, the Detroit Tigers lost their third straight World Series, dropping a seven-game clash with the National League champion Pirates.

The first season of the century's second decade for the New York Giants began in the spring in Marlin, Texas. The small, north-central town with a population of about 4,000 was chosen by McGraw as a training locale in 1908 and would remain the Giants' pre-season base through 1918. A natural, hot mineral water deposit, discovered in the 1890s and soon promoted as curing physical ailments, had put Marlin on the map as an early health resort destination. McGraw found the secluded "hot springs" town most suitable for the single-minded purpose of getting his players in top shape, and Marlin never failed to welcome with open arms the Giants during their 11-year association. McGraw instituted a daily regimen for his team of walking the two-mile distance from their hotel to the ballpark, which was maintained by the city's fathers especially for the Giants. For the two-a-day workouts, in the morning and afternoon, the manager and his players habitually marched along railroad tracks taking them to the park outside of town.

The Giants left their Texas training facility the first week of April and headed north, playing exhibitions along the way. On April 4, McGraw traded backup infielder Buck Herzog and outfielder Bill Collins to the Boston Doves for outfielder Beals Becker. In July of 1909, Herzog had deserted the team and returned to his Baltimore hometown after receiving a merciless tongue-lashing from McGraw. He later returned to the squad but received very little playing time. Collins would make his big league debut with Boston and play four seasons in the majors, only one as an everyday player. Becker, who had led the league in strikeouts in 1909 with 87, would churn out above-average seasons in 1910 and 1911 as a reserve outfielder and then as the Giants starting center fielder in 1912. Herzog was the steadier player over the next two seasons, and consequently, the trade was more of a winner for Boston than the Giants.

Both Herzog and Collins were in the starting lineup for the Doves as Boston hosted the Giants on April 14 to open the season. Mayor John F. Fitzgerald, the grandfather of the 35th President, John F. Kennedy, threw out the ceremonial first ball. New National League president Thomas J. Lynch attended his first Opening Day celebration. The home team tied the score in the ninth with a single run and won the game two innings later. An error by third baseman Art Devlin facilitated the 3–2 Boston victory. Red Ames, the Giants' starter, pitched the distance. In relief of Al Mattern, Doves pitcher Chick Evans chalked up his only career major league win.

Two days later, Christy Mathewson picked up the Giants' initial win, a 3–1 triumph. The ace allowed six hits and lashed out two long hits himself. He doubled and drove a pitch over the South End Grounds left field wall to account for the Giants' final run. The home run was the seventh and final circuit clout of Mathewson's career.

Backing Mathewson in the win was a Giants lineup that differed a bit from last year. Sophomore Chief Meyers split the first-string catching duties with Admiral Schlei. Age, coupled with foot ailments, caught up to Fred Tenney; he was not resigned. Fred Merkle took his place at first base. Cy Seymour was back in the outfield, following the release of

Bill O'Hara. Josh Devore had won the third spot in the pasture. As compact a player as you could find, at only 5'6" and 160 pounds, Devore had been signed out of the Cotton States League in 1907. He hit .304 in this, his first season as a regular player.

The followers of the legion of McGraw had to wait out two days of rain prior to their team's home opener on April 20. After 48 hours of wet weather, a sunny but nippy day reigned over New York City. A capacity crowd of 25,000 rallied in support of the home club. Among them was new Gotham mayor William J. Gaynor, who occupied an upper box and tossed (or dropped) the first pitch down to home plate umpire Cy Rigler. The *New York Times* reported that the mayor "stood up and stretched like the rest of the fans" in the seventh inning. U.S. President William Howard Taft had become the nation's first chief executive to toss out the first pitch six days earlier in Washington. Taft is sometimes given credit for starting the "seventh-inning stretch" later in the same game. The *Times'* Gaynor reference made no mention to that recent event. It rather indicates that the tradition may have already been in vogue. Either that, or President Taft's unintended action had spread popularly in a very short period of time in an age of no instantaneous or repeated media coverage. Hoping his performance would be repeated often during the season was Giants starter Hooks Wiltse, who twirled a 3–0, three-hit shutout that day. The left-hander knocked in two of the runs with a double. He struck out two and walked no one in the grand effort.

The Giants, as they were prone to do, jumped off to a fast start. On May 2, Mathewson hurled a shutout and nearly the third no-hit game of his career. At Washington Park, he was reached for an eighth-inning infield hit by Brooklyn's Pryor McElveen, the only safety of the contest for the Superbas. The Giants won their seventh game in a row and improved to 10–3 with the 6–0 win.

Two days later, in the same venue, McGraw was bounced from a game for the second time already in the young season. McGraw became furious when Brooklyn outfielder Zach Wheat was called safe at third base on a close play in the bottom of the ninth inning. The Giants were holding a 2–0 lead. What ensued was one of the pugnacious pilot's better "shows." He raced up to field umpire Bob Emslie, who had made the call. Emslie did not appreciate being read the riot act and tossed the Giants' steersman.

> McGraw evidently did not get any satisfaction, so he hustled up to Mr. Rigler and did some pleading. The chief umpire merely shook his head, whereupon the leader of the Giants went back to Emslie. There followed the funniest bit of pantomime seen out of the circus. First McGraw advanced and retreated, then Emslie did the same. Bob ordered the little manager to the clubhouse and Mac went—about three feet at a time only to return two. Finally, Rigler stalked majestically down, tugging suggestively at his watch. Thereupon, McGraw faded away and disappeared."[33]

Starting pitcher Red Ames weathered the Cubs' intended rally—and the delay from McGraw's antics—and closed out a 2–1 victory.

On June 9, the Giants scored five runs in the bottom of the ninth inning, with two outs, to defeat the St. Louis Cardinals, 5–4, and make John McGraw jump around as if he had been stung by a wasp, as the next day's *New York Times* put it. Down to their last out and a man on second, the Giants used a walk, an infield hit and a two-strike double by Fred Merkle to plate two runs, initiating the improbable comeback. Another hit scored the third tally, and a throwing error by shortstop Arnold Hauser allowed the winning runs. Reliever Doc Crandall received the unexpected win.

McGraw experienced a respite from his running battle with the umpires, a rare, nine-week, expulsion-free period. The tolerable behavior ended on July 17 in Cincinnati.

Bellowing rudely over the lack of strikes called by Jim Johnstone for Red Ames prompted the expulsion in the fifth inning at the Palace of the Fans. Ames seemed unbothered by the tight strike zone, flinging a five-hit, 5–0 shutout. The Chicago Cubs swept a double-header from Brooklyn the same day and pushed out their first-place lead to four games over 43–31 New York. A Cincinnati writer speculated that McGraw would draw a suspension for the name-calling he inflicted on Johnstone during his subsequent walk of shame from the field. But McGraw avoided any such sanction.

In mid–August, the Pittsburgh Pirates arrived in New York to close out a long Giants homestand. The Pennsylvania club had temporarily slipped passed the Giants into second place. Christy Mathewson was matched up with Lefty Leifield in the first game of a double-header on August 15, the opener of a four-game set. The pitchers were at the top of their game, both hurling shutout ball into extra innings. In the bottom of the seventh inning, Cy Rigler called a liner over third base by Fred Merkle foul. On the coaching lines, McGraw did not see it that way one bit. He kicked up a storm around Rigler, and when McGraw threw his hat to the ground in disgust, Rigler ejected him. Leifield out-pitched Mathewson, gaining a 2–1 win in 11 innings.

McGraw could not let the incident go, and he continued his harassment of Rigler and partner Bob Emslie over the next two games, when league president Thomas J. Lynch happened to be present. McGraw, who had earlier skirted a suspension, could not avoid it this time around. The day after the Pittsburgh series concluded, August 18, Lynch issued this summary judgment:

> I will tolerate no longer this umpire baiting and these tactics of putting the crowd on the umpire. I have suspended manager McGraw of the New York club indefinitely for his actions in Wednesday's game. I am sure the high class patronage we now enjoy does not approve of the methods to incite spectators, and which are directly responsible for the spectacles of calling in the police to protect the National League's representatives.[34]

McGraw served a six-game suspension, missing the team's first two stops of a western road trip in Cincinnati and St. Louis. During his inactive time, McGraw decreed that Cy Seymour was going to be given his release and that his outfield position would be permanently taken by rookie Fred Snodgrass.

Seymour, long a fan favorite in New York from his early pitching days, was nearing 38 years of age, and McGraw recognized his playing days were numbered. The 15-year veteran was sold to Baltimore, now a minor league franchise in the Eastern League. Snodgrass was a California collegiate who had attracted McGraw's attention in exhibition play during the Giants' spring training on the West Coast in 1907. McGraw signed Snodgrass the following year. Not whiling away his time, McGraw also bought pitcher Charles Tesreau from the Texas League. A tall, burly right-hander, the 22-year-old Tesreau would turn into a bargain purchase for his $3,000 acquisition price. Tesreau would be called "Jeff" by his Giants teammates, drawing from a good-natured comparison of the pitcher's big frame to prizefighter James Jeffries.

McGraw quietly rejoined his third-place team in Chicago on August 25 for the start of a four-game series with the first-place Cubs. The Giants had slid 11 games off the pace. The prior day, McGraw had all but discounted his own squad's, and the Pittsburgh Pirates', eight-and-a-half games back in second place, chances of challenging Chicago the rest of the way. The field boss was quoted as saying the Cubs would not only win the NL pennant but also the World Series over Connie Mack's Philadelphia Athletics, who currently held a double-digit lead in the American League.[35]

The August 25 game at West Side Grounds, which the Giants lost, 6–1, featured an officiating oddity in that a player from each team served as umpire. Cubs pitcher Orval Overall called the balls and strikes, and Wee Willie Keeler made the decisions on the base paths. Scheduled officials Bill Klem and Steve Kane confused their assignments and traveled to Pittsburgh. Each was fined $25 by the league president for their mix-up.

NL umpires Cy Rigler and Bob Emslie handled the chores the next day. In McGraw's first game back from suspension with standard umpires, he was ejected. In a strange play at third base, Art Devlin, after taking a relay throw and wheeling around, mistook Cubs regular Harry Steinfeldt, who was coaching at third base, for a baserunner and tagged him out, while the actual runner scored. McGraw complained that Steinfeldt had over-stepped his boundaries and had intentionally fooled Devlin. McGraw's vehement protests were rejected by Cy Rigler, who ordered the steaming manager off the field. Three innings later, Frank Schulte and Joe Tinker hit back-to-back home runs to lift the Cubs to a 3–1 victory, pitched by Three Finger Brown. The Giants won one game in four to slip farther out of contention.

McGraw earned three more ejections during the next three weeks, bringing his circuit-topping total to ten for the year. His most animated act of the three came on September 16 at the Polo Grounds. Umpire Hank O'Day called Larry Doyle out on strikes, to which Doyle objected. McGraw picked up the argument and, in the process, tossed his cap—and Doyle's—into the air. He threw a nearby bat upward and heaved toward the heavens catcher Chief Meyers' mitt and mask as well. Doyle was also run out of the game by O'Day. The Giants edged Pittsburgh, 2–1.

Clan McGraw wrestled away second place from the Pirates over the next weeks and closed out the season with a record of 91–63.

The 104-win Chicago Cubs made McGraw look bad with a World Series loss to the Philadelphia Athletics in five games.

FOUR

World Promoter of the Game

"We always called him Mr. McGraw. Never John or Mac. Always Mr. McGraw. And how he hated Mugsy! That was a sore spot for him. Sometimes we'd call him that behind his back, but if he ever heard you, he wasn't your friend anymore."—Chief Meyers

The second-place finish of the Giants in 1910 continued a long string of first-division finishes under McGraw. Only twice in 29 years, leading up to the 1932 season, did McGraw's hirelings finish lower than fourth place. In 1915, the team tumbled to the bottom of the circuit standings, and in 1926, the club came in fifth. In between, Giants followers could point with pride to 11 second-place finishes, four third-place, and two in fourth position, along with a bountiful ten pennants.

Three of those flags came in succession, from 1911 to 1913. But McGraw was defeated in the World Series each year.

McGraw's early successes as a manager, not to mention having a boss who liked him, delivered the baseball man's biggest payday yet. On November 16, 1910, the *New York Tribune* revealed that John T. Brush had signed the 37-year-old Giants manager to a five-year contract, at $18,000 per annum. By comparison, earlier in the month, Brush had inked pitching stud Christy Mathewson for the 1911 season for $15,000. Judged by results and performances during the upcoming season, Brush was not short-changed by either man.

The Giants' Opening Day lineup in 1911 was virtually the same as in 1910. The only exceptions were Fred Snodgrass in center field and Chief Meyers behind the plate. Meyers, the $6,500 summer purchase of McGraw from the St. Paul Saints in 1908, did not start the first game of the 1910 season but assumed the mantle of the Giants' regular catcher during the campaign.

Left fielder Josh Devore led off, and second baseman Larry Doyle hit second. Snodgrass was the third-place hitter. Right fielder Red Murray followed him, with first baseman Fred Merkle assigned to bat fifth. The left side of the infield, shortstop Al Bridwell and Art Devlin, hit sixth and seventh, respectively. Meyers took his hacks from the eighth slot. Red Ames started his fourth inaugural game in six years, including his second in a row, on April 12, against the Philadelphia Phillies. At the Polo Grounds, Ames had the misfortune of drawing Phillies starter Earl Moore, who permitted only two hits to the Giants in spinning a 2–0 whitewash. Moore spaced eight walks in the triumph, which soured the vast majority of the 30,000 fans who had waited all winter to see top-brand baseball again, including Mayor Gaynor, who made a poor opening toss to Jim Johnstone. Devore stole the first of his team-leading 61 bases on the season.

Mathewson took the Polo Grounds mound the next day and laid an egg. The classy pitcher was rocked for 14 hits and five earned runs as the Phillies won again, 6–1. McGraw did not use Mathewson again until almost two weeks later. On April 25, the star hurler defeated the Boston Rustlers, 3–1. The seven-hitter by Mathewson pushed the Giants' record over .500, to 5–4. From there, the team went a scorching 94–50 in its remaining games.

Mathewson's first victory of the season came at home—but not at the Polo Grounds. It was hurled at Hilltop Park, the home grounds of the New York Highlanders, Manhattan's other professional baseball club. It was the fifth game the Giants played at the Washington Heights ballpark since a fire swept through parts of the Polo Grounds and rendered the location unsuitable for baseball. Luckily, the fire began around midnight on April 14, and therefore there was no loss of life.

The extent of the blaze's damage, however, can be derived from one of the first wire reports to circulate the news: "The Polo Grounds, the New York Nationals' magnificent home at the foot of historic Coogan's bluff—the biggest baseball arena in the country— was swept by fire during the early morning hours and at sunup everything inside was a blackened ruin except the left field bleachers and the clubhouse."[1] Beyond right field, the players' clubhouse was saved only because it was separate from the ballpark.

McGraw and Wilbert Robinson, who had joined the Giants that season as a coach, arrived at the burning ballpark around 2:00 am. Another Giants player to show up at the scene was Bugs Raymond, who lived at a hotel nearby. "I believe I know how it started," offered Raymond. "I was under the grandstand this afternoon with Hartley, the catcher. We came across a pile of blazing peanut shells. I called groundskeeper Murphy and the fire was put out. It is my belief the fire was smoldering somewhere else in piles of peanut shells."[2]

McGraw concurred with his pitcher. "I believe Raymond is right," he said. "There were piles of peanut shells under the grandstand, and matches are often dropped there as are lighted cigars and cigarettes."[3]

The Giants forged ahead, evicted from their ballpark by unforeseen circumstance but with a pledge from their owner to rebuild, using modern applications of steel and concrete. All of the Giants' home games were transferred to Frank Farrell's ballpark. The Highlanders owner graciously accommodated the National League team that had steadfastly opposed their move into New York less than a decade earlier. (The Giants and Highlanders had played a "Gotham Series" after the 1910 regular season, indicating that some of the past resentment on the part of Giants management had waned. McGraw's unit won the engagement for city pride. Christy Mathewson garnered three wins and saved a fourth victory. The Highlanders won two games, and one contest ended in a tie.)

McGraw, for one, did not seem to be as considerate as his temporary host. The Giants manager complained about Hilltop Park's rock-hard playing surface and its small seating capacity (15,000). McGraw seemed particularly irritable during three games played at Hilltop on May 12, 15 and 16; he was ejected from all of them.

Meanwhile, John T. Brush stepped up magnificently and began to rebuild his charred ballpark, starting on May 10. Showing his baseball commitment, Brush signed a new 25-year lease with the estate of James J. Coogan for the continued use of the flattened roll of hilly terrain buttressing the Harlem River, beneath the familiar monolith that had come to be known as Coogan's Bluff. The lease was an extension to the nine years remaining on the team's current tenancy.

Also in May, Rube Marquard began to blossom. The so-called "$11,000 beauty" had been anything but, posting a 9–18 record since McGraw had purchased him three years earlier. On May 13 at Hilltop Park, the Giants batted around in the first inning without making an out, on their way to scoring 13 runs against three St. Louis Cardinals pitchers. Starter Mathewson singled, drove in a run and scored. He was removed from the game after the first frame, with the apparent knowledge that he would be awarded the victory (his fifth) if the Giants did not blow the lead. They did not, and he was. Marquard finished the contest, a 19–5 romp. The winning club filched six bases on the day, including a steal of home by Fred Merkle, who also contributed seven RBI. The 24-year-old Marquard struck out 14 batters in the long relief exercise. (In September, Marquard would whiff 14 hitters in a ten-inning loss to the Braves. No other National League pitcher struck out more than 12 batters in a game that year.) With a 3–0 mark at the end of May, Marquard took off from that modestly good point to finish with a 24–7 mark and nearly catch Mathewson (26–13) for most wins on the pitching staff.

A month later, Mathewson gained his 14th win, a 3–0 blanking of the Boston Rustlers on June 28. The nine-hitter took place at the Polo Grounds. Only a lower deck of seating was available for the incredibly quick re-opening. The lower deck was designed with tiers of seats that scaled higher and further back than the previous wooden configuration. The lower deck seated 16,000, with the spared outfield wooden bleachers holding another 10,000.

About 10,000 patrons attended the rededication game. One local newspaper commented that the new grandstand was so big that it made hundreds of people look like a few dozen. Another indicated that work on constructing the upper grandstand would proceed from 7 a.m. until 2 p.m. daily on the dates the Giants were scheduled to play at home. Brush watched the happy proceedings from his automobile, parked near the right field foul line. At this stage of his life, Brush was not an outwardly mobile person. He was impaired by a muscular disease of the central nervous system that required his walking with two canes, and he customarily viewed home games in this mode.

The game also marked the home return of Mike Donlin to the Giants. (Donlin had pinch-hit the previous day in Brooklyn.) The popular player-turned-actor had agreed on a return engagement with the Giants. He was bestowed with an elaborate array of floral displays prior to the first pitch, all carried in from center field. Some floral harps Donlin received were six feet high, made of roses, violets and orchids. One incorporated the shapes of a large baseball and bat. The good luck offerings came mostly from his theatre friends. Donlin did not appear in the game, and his return would be of short duration.

On July 13, the team with baseball's first steel and reinforced concrete ballpark, the Pittsburgh Pirates, was at the Polo Grounds, where construction continued throughout the summer. In the fifth inning, Fred Merkle and Al Bridwell tried a double steal. Merkle, the lead runner, was called out at third base. Coaching at third, McGraw fumed at the call by umpire Bill Finneran. He was put off the field for the fifth time on the season. Chief Meyers later hit an inside-the-park home run, and the Giants scored four runs in the inning. Winning 9–4, McGraw's squad moved into a first-place tie with the Philadelphia Phillies with identical 47–31 records. The first hit of the game was a ground-rule double by Fred Clarke. The Pirates' player-manager hit a ball inside of first base that rolled down and under John T. Brush's car, stationed along the right field foul line.

Later in the month, prior to leaving New York for a western road swing, McGraw pulled off a trade that reacquired third baseman Buck Herzog from Boston. The manager

POLO GROUNDS GREETS DONLIN 6/28/11

This is from SPECIAL SPORT SERVICE of BAIN NEWS SERVICE. $5 a week. TRY IT!!

Homecoming Day on June 28, 1911, for the Giants' brilliant but distracted outfielder, Mike Donlin. The day also marked the re-opening of the Polo Grounds less than three months after a fire consumed most of the wooden structure. Chief Meyers can be seen standing at far right, facing forward. A partially obscured Larry Doyle is standing to the left of Meyers. Some members of the visiting Boston Rustlers, in their dark road uniforms, are positioned at left.

shipped off little-used first baseman Hank Gowdy and shortstop Al Bridwell. The trade allowed Art Fletcher to take over at shortstop, a position he held for the next eight and a half seasons. Fletcher had been one of the productive 1908 signings that also landed Marquard and Meyers.

At the beginning of the four-city trip, on July 24, the Giants were battling for first place with the Phillies and Chicago Cubs. A day into the trip, McGraw placed himself in disfavor with one umpire and one chief executive. At the Palace of the Fans, Jim Johnstone called the Reds' Mike Mitchell safe at the plate on a close play on a sacrifice fly. Out huffed McGraw, who registered ferocious displeasure at the decision. Showing admirable restraint, Johnstone sent McGraw back to bench. But when McGraw would not let up, the arbiter kicked him out. McGraw left the field, grudgingly, but not before giving harsher lip service to Johnstone. "Shaking his finger under the umpire's nose," wrote a Cincinnati scribe, "McGraw said in a voice loud enough to be heard all over the stand, 'You're a drunkard, that's what you are. You've been drunk all season. Look at your red face. You're drunk all the time. You're a drunkard and you can't deny it.'"[4] The run by Mitchell was an important one for the home team, which edged New York, 3–2.

Two days later, McGraw received the ominous yellow envelope. He was on the field preparing for the fourth game of the series versus the Reds. The Western Union telegram from NL president Lynch informed him of a three-day suspension for his verbal attack on Johnstone.

On the final day of his ostracized period, July 29, McGraw watched from the grandstand in St. Louis as Rube Marquard tossed his first career shutout and won his 11th game, 8–0. The Giants stole *nine* bases in the game.

On August 1, a scheduled off-day, McGraw sold Mike Donlin to the Boston Rustlers. The former captain had been used mostly in pinch-hitting situations and had received only 12 at-bats. Donlin's comeback attempt, at age 33, had flopped. McGraw had also recently relieved himself of self-destructive pitcher Bugs Raymond. The right-hander simply could not abide by McGraw's anti-carousing rules.

During summer's hottest month, McGraw's band found themselves in the thick of a pennant race with the Cubs and another new contender, the Pirates. With Mathewson and Marquard leading the way, the Giants slowly emerged as the best club. On August 21, Marquard raised his record to 15–5 with a ten-inning, 3–2 triumph over the Cubs in New York.

By this stage of construction, the new Polo Grounds' upper deck was partially completed, and about 2,000 of the 18,000 paying fans sat in the unfinished area—something completely unimaginable in public recreation facilities today. The Giants did not swipe a bag in the game, a rarity for them, as the team set a major league record for most steals in a season with a whopping 347. The win put the 66–42 Giants in a three-way tie for first place. McGraw was ejected for disagreeing with Bill Klem's called third strike on Art Devlin with the bases loaded. Larry Doyle took over for McGraw on the coaching lines, continued the argument and was also run. Arlie Latham manned the third base coaching box through to completion. A week and two starts later, Marquard (17–5) one-hit the Cardinals, 2–0, at the Polo Grounds. Only a seventh-inning single by Rube Ellis slightly scuffed the gem.

The Giants used separate winning streaks of eight, nine and ten games over the remaining seven weeks of the season to capture the flag rather easily. In September, McGraw's roadrunners averaged slightly better than three steals a game. The second-place Cubs trailed the league champions by 7½ games when the season ended. In the American League, the 101-win Philadelphia Athletics (two more than the Giants) ran away with their circuit over the last six weeks of play.

The World Series haphazardly began in New York on Saturday, October 14. Eight days earlier, at a National Commission meeting, Garry Herrmann flipped a quarter and Athletics part-owner Ben Shibe incorrectly called "heads," ceding the opener to John T. Brush's ballpark. The Giants pulled out all-black uniforms with white trim as they had for their first Fall Classic appearance in 1905. Behind their ace pitcher and inside the finished Polo Grounds, McGraw's club edged the A's, 2–1. Viewed by more than 38,000 spectators, Mathewson won his fourth World Series game in as many starts and allowed his first Fall Classic run.

But the Giants lost the next three contests, two of which were Mathewson starts.

The teams did not play on Sunday. In consecutive games on October 16 and 17, Philadelphia third baseman Frank Baker smacked home runs off Marquard and Mathewson to key victories and earn himself an enduring nickname. Part of the Athletics' famed "$100,000 infield," Baker clubbed a two-run circuit smash off Marquard in Shibe

Park in Game Two. The two-run blast broke a 1–1, sixth-inning tie. Eddie Plank, the Athletics' starter, closed out the contest without any further Giants scoring.

In Game Three, back in New York, Athletics pitcher Jack Coombs outdueled Mathewson, 3–2, in 11 innings. Baker ruined Mathewson's shutout bid with a solo home run in the top of the ninth, precipitating the extra frames. Giants baserunners were thrown out four times trying to steal second base, including the final out of the game. The disappointed crowd topped 37,000.

Mathewson was hit freely in his second start at Shibe Park on October 24. (The Series was interrupted for a week by rain.) He surrendered ten hits and four earned runs in seven innings. Chief Bender avenged his Game One defeat, winning 4–2.

At the Polo Grounds the next day, the Giants staved off elimination with a 4–3, extra-inning win in the fifth game. A proactive McGraw replaced starter Marquard, who was trailing 3–0, after three innings. (The runs off the left-hander were unearned.) Red Ames and Doc Crandall provided seven innings of scoreless relief. With things looking bleak, the Giants rallied for two, two-out runs in the bottom of the ninth inning to tie the score. Crandall doubled in the second run and scored the tying one on a clutch single by Josh Devore. In the tenth, Larry Doyle scored the winning run on a Fred Merkle sacrifice fly. A less than capacity crowd of 33,228 were rewarded for holding out hope.

But at Shibe Park on October 26, the A's shook off the loss and resoundingly beat up on starter Red Ames and Hooks Wiltse to win 13–2, and capture the world title in six games. Having pitched four scoreless innings the previous day, Red Ames allowed five runs, two earned, in four innings. Reliever Wiltse was pummeled for the remaining eight scores. McGraw chose to pitch the curveballing Ames on back-to-back days, rather than Marquard, or use Mathewson on one day's rest.

McGraw could do nothing but accept that his team was vanquished by a better one. "Under the circumstances, the best team won," he said. "Connie Mack is to be congratulated for having gotten together the fine team of clean ballplayers that beat the Giants."[5] Incidentally, the quicksilver club stole only three bases in the six contests—with nine caught stealing.

The Giants leader tried to get over his 1911 World Series loss by taking his first barnstorming tour of Cuba, which proved financially rewarding. Each Giants player was guaranteed $500 plus expenses by Cuban promoters. The team trained for a week in Jacksonville, then played exhibition games in that city, Miami and Key West, before sailing from Key West to begin play in Havana on November 25. During the excursion, the National League champions, led by Mathewson's and Doc Crandall's three wins apiece, won nine of 12 contests played at Almendares Park. Five victories came against the Habana club and four, in six tries, were wrestled from Almendares. José Méndez, of the latter team, was beaten twice, once each by the Giants' leading pitchers. Upon his return to New York, McGraw had this to say about the local talent he encountered: "The Cubans are dull thinkers. Fast on the bases, wonderful throwers and fair batters, but know absolutely nothing about inside baseball. Mendez, the so-called 'Black Mathewson,' is the best pitcher they have and is really a first class boxman, a man who could get a job on any big league team were it not for his color."[6]

Racial issues were at the bottom of some unpleasantries for McGraw during his trip. There was an incident in a game involving Almendares catcher Gervasio "Strike" González, umpire Cy Rigler and McGraw. Rigler tossed González for using foul language (presumably in English). The game, with McGraw backing Rigler all the way, was delayed over an hour as Cuban officials argued to get González, a top player, back in the contest. McGraw and Rigler were accused of being verbally abusive to all involved. Soon after the incident with González, a black player, the *New York Tribune* published the following report, datelined December 4 from Havana:

> John J. McGraw and Rigler, an umpire, have been fined $20 each for making alleged derogatory remarks about Cubans. Last night, while having dinner in a café, they were accused of making a public declaration that all Cubans were merely negroes, whereupon a policeman was called and he attempted to arrest the baseball men. McGraw and Rigler stubbornly resisted on account the policeman was a negro. Two white policeman were called and the two men submitted to arrest. They appeared in court today, where the fines were imposed.[7]

The Giants' regulars who did not make the barnstorm trip were Merkle, Meyers, Murray and Snodgrass. All were in the 1912 Opening Day lineup for New York, however, as the club began a successful title defense on April 11. At Washington Park in Brooklyn, the Giants upended the Superbas, 18–3, in a game shortened by darkness to six innings and marked by an overflow and often uncontainable crowd on the field. The Giants lashed out 21 hits; Rube Marquard was the winning pitcher.

The previous day, 32-year-old Art Devlin was sold to the Boston Braves. From 1904 to 1910, the steady third baseman had averaged 146 games played for McGraw. He hit respectably while fielding in a manner that contained more than a touch of wizardry. Sports authorities Frank Graham and Grantland Rice rated Devlin above all other Giants they saw at his position. In 1911, his legs began betraying him, and his playing time was cut to under 100 games. After filling in during most of Devlin's down time, Buck Herzog succeeded him on a full-time basis. Devlin played two more seasons with the Braves, only one as a first-stringer.

The defending champs lost the next two games, with McGraw ejected from the final contest. A tight force play at third base, in which the Giants' Tillie Schafer was called out, set him off. He was ordered off the diamond by umpire Garnet Bush.

On April 19, the Giants played their first home game, after poor weather the prior day delayed their scheduled opening. A crowd of less than half of the 38,000 capacity ventured to see the game. Gloomy weather and the grim news of the *Titanic's* sinking were reasons for the reduced gathering. Christy Mathewson hurled his team to a 6–2 victory. The ace was presented with a shiny new Columbia Knight car prior to the first pitch, a gift from his many, many admirers. McGraw saw only half of Mathewson's effort. In the fifth inning, he ran across the infield to object to an out call on an attempted steal of second base by Red Murray. Bill Finneran, who had expelled McGraw twice last season, rang up the ejection slip again. Insubordinate behavior (he refused to give up the third base coaching box immediately after being tossed) netted McGraw another suspension. Five days was the duration, but he missed only two games due to an off-day and rain-outs.

Bigger crowds would soon populate the Polo Grounds, drawn there by a top-notch team and a grade A baseball arena. John T. Brush had raised from the ashes of wooden grandstands and bleachers a steel and reinforced concrete phoenix of nostalgic stadia lore. The new, double-decked Polo Grounds was not only bigger and better, but safer as well for the public. Retaining its horseshoe layout, the enlarged structure was also visually unique with the "façade of the upper deck faced with decorative frieze, while the façade of the roof was adorned with the insignia of all National League teams. The box seats were designed upon the lines of the royal boxes of the Colosseum in Rome, with pylons flanking the horse shoe shaped grandstand on both ends."[8] The upper deck grandstand accommodated 8,000 ticket buyers, while the lower bowl and bleachers had seating for 30,000 more.

The home opener was one of nine straight wins and 18 out of 19 decisons that the Giants reeled off in April and May, to give them an early leg up on the rest of the league. During the streak, McGraw was stung with another game dismissal. On May 3, Bill Klem expelled both Larry Doyle and McGraw for questioning his strike zone. It was the fifth time since 1910 that McGraw had been ejected for questioning a strike call on the same infielder. On three of the occasions, Doyle joined him. Parenthetically, at the end of the campaign, Doyle won the Chalmers Award—the equivalent of today's MVP—named by writers from eight newspapers. Batting .330, Doyle topped the club in hits (184) and RBI (91). Tris Speaker was voted the AL recipient. A Chalmers automobile was given to each selectee.

From May 20 to 30, the Giants compiled their second nine-game win-streak of the season. The team followed that up, three weeks later, with a string of 16 victories in a row to improve their record to 54–11 and markedly wreck the pennant chances of the entire league. Prior to losing a doubleheader to Brooklyn on July 4, to end the impressive streak, the Giants had pulled 16½ games out in front of their nearest competitor.

The formidable 1–2 punch of Mathewson and Marquard again led the way from the mound, with the portsider outshining the veteran star much of the time. Four days after dropping the twin-bill to the Superbas, Marquard suffered his first loss of the year—after winning *19* straight decisions since Opening Day. The still-standing single-season record was brought to an end by the Chicago Cubs at West Side Grounds, 7–2. Marquard was touched for six runs on eight hits. He walked three and wild pitched home a run.

"The Hon. Mugsy McGraw was greatly distressed over Rube's fall," relayed one Chicago writer, who was unable to resist a reference to McGraw's burgeoning waistline. "He stood at the third base coaching lines with his arms folded over his stomach as an indication of great mental torture."[9]

The nickname "Mugsy" was one McGraw disliked immensely. McGraw himself explained the origin and his objection to the tag. "Back in Baltimore in 1891," he told New York sportswriter Frank Graham,

> there was a roughneck ward politician named McGraw, who was called Mugsy. It was rumored that I was his son, and one of the newspapers called me Young Mugsy McGraw. Soon the name caught on, but the Young was dropped. I asked the newspapers not to call me that anymore. But some of the fans in the other towns who didn't like me had picked up the name and, knowing I didn't like it, took delight in yelling it at me every time I appeared on the field. Since then every ____ who doesn't like me has called me that.[10]

Graham, a *New York Sun* reporter, wrote that the nickname grew repulsive to McGraw and caused him to snarl and want to fight those who, even innocently, applied it to him. Although newspaper writers and editors never desisted from using the cognomen, as he aged and his stature within the game grew, few referred to him by this name—to his face.

Another of McGraw's well-known nicknames was "Little Napoleon." A reference to his autocratic temperament, it was one that the diminutive manager seemingly did not mind. Who first pinned it on McGraw seems to be unclear. The earliest application of the label the author came across was from a January 1911 interview with Tip Wright. The New York writer made it clear in the piece, in which he visited the Giants manager at the billiards palace owned by McGraw in Manhattan, that the nickname was already in use. He also speculated that McGraw was baseball's highest annual earner on the field. McGraw boasted to Wright about the Giants outdrawing every team on the road the previous year, and engaged in some practical preaching. "No man can play baseball and highballs," he said. "He's got to drop one or the other. I'm against drinking and cigarette smoking. Both are bound to ruin the best batting eye that ever looked for a seam on a ball."[11] A life-long non-smoker, McGraw carried through into his personal life 50 percent of these vice warnings. McGraw also thought playing golf was bad for a player's swing. (Blanche McGraw mentioned neither sobriquet in her husband's biography.)

A determined Cubs team actually whittled the Giants' lead down to 4½ games by the end of August. But New York held firm and, with a final record of 103–48, copped the flag by 10½ games over the Pittsburgh Pirates. The Cubs came in third, two games in back of the Bucs. Remarkably, McGraw picked no more fights with umpires the rest of the long season—or none raucous enough to warrant a dismissal—following his May 3 ejection.

The Giants' opponents in the World Series were the Boston Red Sox, whose 105 American League victories edged out the National League champions' total. The championship series opened Tuesday, October 8, at the Polo Grounds—three days after the season's conclusion. Excluding 4,000 box and reserved seats, and 4,000 upper deck seats that went on sale a day earlier, approximately 30,000 tickets became available for initial purchase on the morning of the game (limit two tickets per buyer). The perplexing marketing strategy may have had something to do with the final turnstile count falling a few thousand short of capacity.

More perplexing was McGraw's selection of a starting pitcher, Jeff Tesreau, over Mathewson and Marquard. The rookie Tesreau had produced a fine season, winning 17 games with a league-leading ERA under two. He had started the Giants' final game of the schedule, three days earlier, and pitched five shutout innings before being removed. Twenty-six-game winner Marquard had started on October 4, thrown five runless frames and was relieved by McGraw. Mathewson (23–12) did not receive a "tune-up" start prior to the Series; he had not pitched since September 26 and was well-rested. McGraw had sent the idle Mathewson, along with Marquard, to Philadelphia on October 3 to scout the Red Sox as they played the Athletics.

Red Sox player-manager Jake Stahl went with his best—Smokey Joe Wood. The Red Sox right-hander had posted his 34th victory of the season in the game attended by the two Giants pitchers, culminating his career year of 34–5. Wood topped Tesreau, 4–3, striking out the last two hitters with the winning run in scoring position. Despite the tough loss, McGraw stated that he was satisfied with his young starting pitcher's performance, and that the Red Sox were not as good as the Athletics of last season.

The next day, at a not yet six-month-old Fenway Park, Mathewson pitched for the first time in two weeks—unhappily behind a defense that performed as if *it* were rusty from inactivity. Three errors by shortstop Art Fletcher and one by substitute catcher Art Wilson allowed the Red Sox to score six unearned runs. Matty permitted no other scoring. The Giants plated six runs of their own against two Boston hurlers, but the knotted contest was halted because of darkness after 11 innings. The game was declared a tie.

Marquard, arguably the Giants' best pitcher, pitched the third game at Fenway Park and was excellent. The swift southpaw defeated the home team, 2–1, losing his shutout in the ninth. Marquard allowed seven hits and fanned six, a few presumably on the sharp

Before one of the games of the 1912 World Series, a rotund Wilbert Robinson, McGraw and a sweatered Christy Mathewson have their attention drawn elsewhere.

curveball he had perfected to complement his speed ball and raise his pitching to a higher level.

Having the option of veterans Red Ames (11–5) or Hooks Wiltse (9–6), McGraw chose Tesreau again—on two days' rest—in Game Four, October 11. Wood also came back on short rest for Boston. The largest crowd of the Series turned out at the Polo Grounds—36,502. Having given up four runs in seven innings in Game One, Tesreau allowed only two runs in the same number of stanzas. But Wood, who won 16 games in a row during the campaign, tying Walter Johnson's American League record set earlier that year, was better. He threw his second complete game, winning 3–1. The Giants outhit Boston, 9–8.

The Red Sox also claimed an upstart rookie pitcher that season in Hugh Bedient. The right-hander and 20-game winner hurled the most memorable game of his life in defeating Mathewson, 2–1, in Game Five. The Giants' run was unearned. Attendance at Fenway Park numbered 34,683.

Two days hence, Monday, October 14, down three games to one, McGraw turned to Marquard. The left-hander did not disappoint. He rode a five-run first inning to a 5–2 victory. The pitcher's own error in the second inning prevented a shutout. Polo Grounds loyalists totaled 30,622.

In Game Seven the next day in Boston, McGraw remained fixed—or fixated—on Tesreau. Stahl, hoping for the clincher, went with Wood. The Giants jumped on the Red Sox ace for six runs in the first inning, ending the 34-game winner's afternoon after recording only three outs. Tesreau was caught trying to steal second for the final out of the frame. Buoyed by the big, early lead, the rookie right-hander went the distance, notching his first World Series win, 11–4. The showdown game was then set for Fenway Park, with a three-day-rested Christy Mathewson ready to start.

John McGraw's players often became infamous for mental and physical errors which ultimately denied the Giants greater team glory. The Fred Merkle error of omission of 1908 McGraw viewed as an unfair ruling by his personal scourges—the umpires. In the 1912 Fred Snodgrass error of commission—in which his "muff" in the bottom of the tenth inning of the final game of the World Series allowed the Boston Red Sox to mount a Giants championship-denying rally—McGraw advocated the consistent view of all managers that physical misplays cannot be faulted.

"Well, the Red Sox won," McGraw flatly expressed after Boston's extra-inning, 3–2 win in the deciding game. "We are not handing out alibis. My men came from behind and we put up a fight but the Red Sox beat us and that is the final answer. I am not blaming anybody."[12]

The October 16, 1912, game interestingly resembled the final game of the 2001 World Series, where the Arizona Diamondbacks scored twice, in the bottom of the ninth inning, against a seemingly invincible pitcher (Mariano Rivera) to pull out an exhilarating, 3–2 championship win. Down 2–1 in their last at-bat in Game Eight, the Red Sox scored twice, the winning run coming on a sacrifice fly—after Snodgrass had dropped a routine fly ball hit by the first batter of the inning, Clyde Engle. The misplay opened the door for the two-run rally.

The frame's next hitter, Harry Hooper, flied out to Snodgrass, who made a difficult catch; Engle advanced to third base. Mathewson then walked Steve Yerkes, and Tris Speaker followed with a game-tying single, with Yerkes hustling to third and Speaker taking second on the throw home. One of a trio of radiant outfielders, including Duffy Lewis and Harry Hooper, known as the "Speed Boys," Speaker was given new life in his at-bat when his catchable foul pop dropped in foul territory between a converging Mathewson, Meyers and Merkle. This was just as critical a gaffe as the misplay by Snodgrass. After an intentional walk to load the bases, Red Sox third baseman Larry Gardner hit a sacrifice fly to Josh Devore in right field to bring a joyful Yerkes to the plate.

Wood pitched the final three innings to get his third win. Mathewson absorbed his second loss of the Series, throwing his third complete game. A game-time temperature hovering around 40 degrees and a controversy involving seating arrangements for a block of hardcore Red Sox fans in Game Eight held down attendance to 17,034.

Incidentally, the final half-inning provided baseball with its first "Golden Pitch," a rare happenstance wherein a World Series victory—for either club—hinges on a single pitch. Mathewson threw a combined seven Golden Pitches to Yerkes and Speaker, the results of which could have delivered a victory for either team.[13]

"Snodgrass! Snodgrass did not lose the game," McGraw emphatically stated in one form or another in the game's wake. "The game was lost when Speaker's foul wasn't caught. Snodgrass is the best outfielder I have and one of the best in baseball. I'm going to give him a better contract next year than he's ever had."[14]

It all may have been academic if Mr. McGraw had not outsmarted himself in his starting pitching selections. His preference of the rookie Tesreau over Marquard in the Series can be viewed as baffling. In his two starts, Marquard was 2–0 with an 0.50 ERA in 18 innings. The Red Sox's two best hitters, Larry Gardner (.315) and Tris Speaker (.383) were both left-handed swingers. From another persepective, Tesreau had been McGraw's best pitcher in September, winning six games. The right-hander, who relied on a spitball, hurled a no-hitter on September 6; he benefited from a controversial official scorer's change *after* the game, in which a hit was changed to an error. McGraw may have also been influenced by Marquard's 7–11 mark following his 19-game unbeaten streak.

Had McGraw opened the autumn classic with Marquard, as the pecking order suggested, the "Snodgrass muff" may not have become an indelible term in baseball's historic lexicon.

The Giants manager hit the road again in the off-season following his World Series defeat. But this time he did not leave the country. He accepted a lucrative offer to appear on the vaudeville circuit, along with a close baseball friend. "John McGraw and Hughie Jennings have finally answered the call to the stage," alerted one wire report a few days after the World Series. "McGraw will draw $1,500 a week for 15 weeks. He will do a monologue act. The little Napoleon will open in Providence and after days' work in that city will appear at Keith's Theatre in Boston."[15]

McGraw traveled the country, performing in major cities six days a week. McGraw's acting gig was interrupted in late November by the death of John Tomlinson Brush. The Giants owner died on a train en route to southern California for a medically prescribed rehabilitation stay. Over the summer, the 67-year-old Brush had broken his hip in an automobile accident. He was lionized by his fellow owners and his most renowned employee. "He was a citizen of sterling worth, of high moral standard and correct business principles, and his death is not only a loss to us but to the community at large,"[16] read part of a joint statement released by the magnates of the National League baseball clubs.

"No man ever knew a brainier or more wonderful man that John T. Brush in baseball," stated McGraw, while making mention of the locomotor ataxia that debilitated Brush through much of his later life. "He was … as resourceful as a man in the fullest of grand health. The lower portions of his limbs, as you and I know, suffered intensely. Yet that head of his never suffered. This is a great battle, this game of life. No man fought it more nobly than he…. A gamer, a better man never lived."[17] Most ballplayers and the general press did not share the same high regard for the departed.

The holdings of the National Exhibition Company, the corporate name of the New York Giants, passed to Brush's immediate family, his wife and two daughters. Brush's eldest daughter Eleanor (by a previous marriage) was married to Harry Hempstead, a Brush department store manager in Indianapolis and recently elected vice president of the NEC. Hempstead became the Giants president following Brush's death. Two months prior to the 1913 season, Hempstead showed he had as much, or more, appreciation for McGraw as his deceased father-in-law. He signed McGraw to a new contract, voiding the remaining years on his current lucrative agreement. The new deal called for another five years with an annual salary of $30,000.

On February 16, McGraw left New York for Marlin, Texas. Accompanying him was a small entourage, including Christy Mathewson and Dr. E. Biers, a dentist McGraw had hired to promote the general health of his players. Many other Giants players were expected to join the group along the rail stops.

At Harrisburg, PA, coach Wilbert Robinson came aboard, along with Carlisle Indian

School product Jim Thorpe. The legendary sports figure had been signed by McGraw a few weeks earlier to a highly unusual three-year deal. The contract paid Thorpe, who months earlier had been stripped of his Olympic medals for previously playing minor league ball, $6,000 annually. Robinson was assigned to mentor the "world's greatest athlete."

Thorpe was not in the Giants' Opening Day lineup (he played sparingly throughout the season) on April 10. On a cold day under Coogan's Bluff, McGraw was presented with a floral horseshoe of Killarney roses prior to the game. The cheery gift was placed unattended down the right field line and was stripped within minutes, left knocked over on the ground by opportunistic fans. A ragtime band tried to keep the blood of the 22,000 fans circulating to their syncopated beats. The Polo Grounds displayed a new scoreboard which, among other things, registered the novelty of balls and strikes. A section of the 25-cent bleacher seats in center field had been painted green to help the hitter's "batting eye." On the receiving end of the first toss from Mayor William J. Gaynor was Bill Klem. The applause for the throw paled to that heard when Christy Mathewson earlier appeared on the field. The fans cheered him for so long that he was forced to doff his cap in acknowledgment.

The Giants unveiled violet and white uniforms, a tribute to New York University's school colors. McGraw's men performed like shrinking violets, losing 8–0 to the Boston Braves. Purposely or not, McGraw placed two fateful components of last year's World Series front and center on the inaugural stage. Giving up half the runs, Jeff Tesreau was the starter and loser. Fred Snodgrass batted leadoff and went 0-for-4. His reception in his first trip to the plate was mixed, at best.

Bad weather postponed the Giants' next two games. On April 14, Tesreau coughed up a lead, giving up a two-run home run to Brooklyn's Red Smith with two outs and a man on base in the top of the ninth inning. McGraw had called upon the right-hander to pitch the final inning in relief of starter Red Ames. The Giants failed to score in their turn and lost, 3–2. Impressively, last season in 243 innings, Tesreau surrendered only two home runs. The four-bagger by Smith was already the second allowed by the 6'2" pitcher, including one on Opening Day.

The Giants' most reliable pitcher earned the team's first win of 1913, three days later in Boston, after inclement weather kept the team from suiting up until then. Christy Mathewson defeated the Braves, 3–2, in ten innings at South End Grounds. On April 29, the pre-eminent pitcher picked up his third win and the Giants' eighth. Mathewson tossed a 13-inning, 6–0 shutout against the Brooklyn Superbas. It was the fourth shutout in six games endured by the Brooklyn team at their new, weeks-old ballpark named after their principle owner, Charles Ebbets.

The following day, McGraw fancied his eyesight from the third base coach's box as better in determining balls and strikes than home plate umpire Cy Rigler, who branded McGraw with the first ejection recorded at Ebbets Field. Arguing a called strike three on Art Fletcher, after Fred Snodgrass had been called out on strikes, drew the banishment from Rigler. The Giants were down, 5–3, and batting in the top of the ninth; the team did not rally. McGraw was fined $50 for the extracurricular action.

After 23 games, the Giants were 12–11. In their 24th engagement, a sloppy, 14–11 win over the Chicago Cubs at the Polo Grounds, McGraw reacted indiscreetly to an out call by home plate umpire Bill Klem on Chief Meyers at third base. Loud enough for many of the fans to hear, McGraw called Klem, among other things, "catfish," an unkind but common correlation made by disdainful players between Klem's countenance and that of the typical bottom fish.

McGraw's name-calling was rebuked by the league with a three-day suspension, instituted May 15—the day after the altercation—which was the start of a four-game, home series against Pittsburgh. On May 16, after Mathewson defeated the Pirates, 7–4, the suspended McGraw met sportswriter Grantland Rice and amateur golfer Oswald Kirkby on the field. The gathering, attended by Mathewson and other players, was arranged to settle a gentlemanly disagreement. McGraw had contended that a golf ball could not be hit over the center field bleachers from home plate. Both Rice and Kirkby took four swings at teed-up balls at the dish. Rice drove one ball over the center field fence and Kirkby two. The winning drives were estimated at carrying about 200 yards each. The distance to the center field wall at the Polo Grounds was 495 feet, with a 50-foot-high rear wall. McGraw and Mathewson lost undisclosed wagers to the long drivers.

A week later, with none of his starters except Mathewson (5–1) showing better than mediocre form, McGraw initiated a poor trade. He acquired 29-year-old Art Fromme from the Cincinnati Reds. A right-hander, Fromme had only one winning season since breaking into the majors with the St. Louis Cardinals in 1906. What McGraw saw in Fromme is unclear. But it must have been something promising, for he gave up pitcher Red Ames, outfielder Josh Devore, infielder Heinie Groh *and* $20,000. Turning 31 in August, Ames had been a pitching mainstay since his breakout 20-game campaign in 1905 and a solid fourth starter for the Giants. Devore, a regular for the past three years, had become expendable with McGraw's decision to promote George Burns. A 23-year-old rookie, Burns had been purchased from the New York State League for $4,000 at the tail end of the 1911 campaign. Groh, also 23, had been purchased the same year by McGraw for $3,500. The infield prospect came from the Decatur Commodores on the recommendation of team owner Dick Kinsella.

At the Polo Grounds, the 1–4 Fromme received his first Giants start on May 30, in the first game of a doubleheader. He recorded the win, 8–6, saved by Rube Marquard. The Giants also won the second game, 5–1, against the Philadelphia Phillies. In control all the way, Tesreau evened his record at 6–6. With a win the following day, McGraw's legionnaires began June with a 20–16 mark. Over the next four months, the team replicated its successes of the past two seasons—led, not coincidentally, by its frontline pitching. The spitballer Tesreau went 16–7 the rest of the way, and Marquard, a lackluster 3–2 through May, won 20 and lost only eight over the rest of the schedule. The dependable Mathewson won his seventh game on May 31, with 18 more to be registered in the win column.

As the Giants began to play better in June, McGraw said he had seven men who would steal 40 bases. Catcher Chief Meyers was the only regular excluded from the list. Meyers, however, would be the only Giants starter to hit .300 (.312), doing so for the third year in a row. George Burns stole exactly 40 bases. Fred Merkle, Larry Doyle, Tillie Shafer, Art Fletcher and Red Murray all topped 30.

On June 30, the Giants visited Philadelphia to play the Phillies, who were one-half game ahead of New York in the standings. The Giants won, 11–10, in ten innings; 27 hits were made and ten errors, five by each squad. Buck Herzog drove in Snodgrass with the game-winning base hit in the top of the tenth. Mathewson gained a win with four innings of relief work. Grover Cleveland Alexander was the loser, also in relief. Walking toward the Baker Bowl center field clubhouse after the game, McGraw was felled by punches from Phillies pitcher Addison Brennan.

Some initial reports portrayed McGraw as the victim, being kicked along the side of his face, at least once, while he was down. McGraw was cut and sustained a noticeable facial bruise. But a further investigation by league president Thomas Lynch placed equal blame for the incident on McGraw. Two days afterward, both men were fined $100 and suspended for five days. Lynch's ruling read that "evidence showed conclusively that both players were in violations of the rules in that they indulged in personalities during the game and that the feeling aroused thereby was the direct cause of the happenings when the players were leaving the field."[18] McGraw brushed off the Brennan public skirmish. "It reminds me of the old times,"[19] he said.

The Giants had gotten hot prior to the McGraw-Brennan blowup and remained that way. From June 23 until July 31, the team did not lose two games in a row. During the stretch, they accumulated a 14-game winning streak. McGraw's charges pulled away from the Phillies and the rest of the league. By the time of their next visit to Philadelphia at the end of August, the Giants had opened up a 12-game advantage. But the second-place Phillies made a brave stand, sweeping three games from the league's elite club.

On August 30, the final contest of the series, a riotous incident occurred involving another Brennan—umpire Bill Brennan—that made the McGraw-Brennan I skirmish look like a tea party. An overflow crowd required that the seats in center field be opened up to the public. In the ninth inning, with the Giants trailing, 8–6, Moose McCormick pinch-hit. There was one out and no one on base. McCormick complained to home plate umpire Brennan that the white shirts in the center field bleachers were blinding him. Brennan actually walked out to the bleachers and asked the people to either move or put on jackets. It was a fruitless endeavor. He tried to enlist the help of a Baker Bowl policeman and Phillies manager Red Dooin, but received a similar amount of cooperation. Brennan and co-arbiter Mal Eason conferred with McGraw, after which Brennan decreed the game forfeited in the Giants' favor. "Bedlam cut loose at that instant," declared the next day's *Philadelphia Inquirer*. "Screaming in rage the bleacherites by the thousands poured over the low rail into the playing field. In the grandstand, men rose and hoarsely shouted, 'robber! thief!'"[20]

Brennan had to dodge seat cushions and pop bottles all the way to the clubhouse. Several minutes later, upon exiting the grounds along with much of the Giants team, Brennan found about 5,000 angry fans milling about outside the park. The umpire needed a police escort to the North Philadelphia Railroad Station, not far from the Baker Bowl. What ensued was depicted by the *Inquirer* as a madcap finish to an ugly scene:

> Brennan and his guard reached the entrance to the station just at the instant McGraw and his players came fleeing around the corner at Broad Street. The police fortook the umpire to try and head off the larger crowd behind the New Yorkers. With drawn guns, they held them at bay for a few minutes. When Brennan turned into the station he found his way blocked by several hundred rooters. They jumped upon him by the dozens. He was beaten to the ground, rose, was beaten down again, and finally rose again, breaking away and fleeing into the station. Screaming "Murder!" at the top of his lungs, Brennan fled through the station. McGraw was running by his side. Together they jumped aboard a waiting train. It was an extra fare train to Pittsburgh, but that made no difference to them. The vestibule doors closed and the train moved off as the disappointed thousand came plunging through the station windows, around corners and out doorways, until the platform was packed by the howling mob.[21]

A Philadelphia protest was upheld by the league, and the last two outs of the previously forfeited game were obtained by the Phillies, on October 2 in New York, prior to the regularly scheduled doubleheader between the Giants and Phils.

The 101–51 Giants sailed to the pennant uncontested, by a 12½-game margin. McGraw, however, was challenged by several players on his team who broke or were on the verge of breaking curfew. In Cincinnati, the first week of August, McGraw found five players together away from the team hotel. The players were not ready to call it a night and were in no mood for a scolding from their chief. A day or two earlier, McGraw had traded Doc Crandall to the St. Louis Cardinals for catcher Larry McLean. (Chief Meyers had recently suffered a hand injury and his status was uncertain.) Crandall was a popular player among his teammates, and the trade was not viewed kindly from within the Giants' clubhouse. Two of the five players were identified as Buck Herzog and Fred Merkle. Heated words were exchanged, and McGraw emerged with a bloody nose. Less than two weeks later, McGraw reacquired Crandall from St. Louis in a straight-up cash deal.

The 1913 World Series, opening on October 7, was a rematch of the 1911 engagement. Fans began camping outside of the Polo Grounds just after midnight to be ready to snap up the limited unreserved and bleacher seats available early the next morning. A cloudy day emerged on those fans and all others, totaling over 36,000 for the day's turnout. Spectators had to observe new rules imposed by the National Commission, prohibiting standing on chairs or in aisles.

A bit of cat-and-mouse strategy developed with both distinguished managers prior to the call of "Play Ball!" Connie Mack warmed up right-hander Chief Bender and lefty Eddie Plank. McGraw had Mathewson and Marquard getting ready to pitch. While Mack picked his number one hurler (Bender, 21–10), McGraw elected not to use his best pitcher (again) to start Game One of the World Series. Bypassing Mathewson, McGraw chose Marquard to face the the American League champions (who had four left-handed hitters in their lineup). The three-time 20-game winner was not up to the task. He was beaten by Chief Bender, 6–4. "Home Run" Baker did it again, connecting for a two-run circuit clout in the fifth inning. Baker drove in another run with a single. Doc Crandall gave up the final run in relief. Both teams collected 11 hits. Bender did not walk a batter.

Mathewson was at his best in Game Two, throwing his fourth Fall Classic shutout, this one in ten innings. He was involved in the decisive three-run tenth inning, contributing a single and scoring a run. Art Fletcher delivered a big two-run single. Mathewson surrendered eight hits, walked one and struck out five, giving the Shibe Park crowd of 20,563 very little to cheer.

McGraw was forced to do some personnel juggling in the game. Chief Meyers was knocked out of the Series with a split finger after just one game. The injury was sustained during practice prior to the second contest; the catching duties fell on Larry McLean and Art Wilson the rest of the way. After Fred Snodgrass pulled up lame running the bases, Hooks Wiltse came in to play first base. Snodgrass was substituting for Fred Merkle, who was nursing a sprained foot. (Merkle was able to start the remaining encounters.) Wiltse performed flawlessly at the initial bag, handling 16 chances, including three assists.

On October 9, Bullet Joe Bush defeated Jeff Tesreau, 8–2, in New York. Bush, a rookie and one of only three pitchers used by the A's manager in the Series, tossed a five-hitter. Tesreau was removed in the seventh, with seven runs—five earned—attached to his

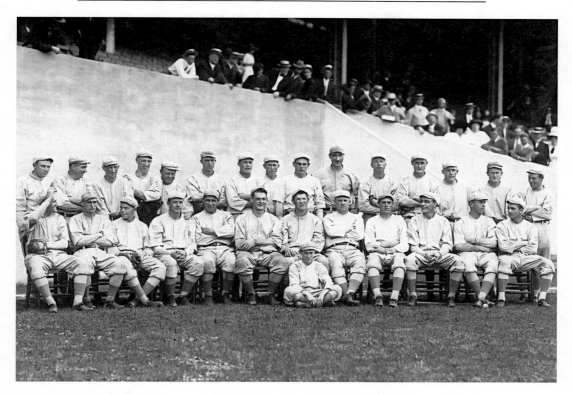

The 1913 New York Giants were defeated in the World Series for the second time in three years by Connie Mack's Philadelphia Athletics. Rookie Jim Thorpe is seated behind the bat boy. McGraw, arms folded, is seated to the right of the great athlete.

record. Nearly 37,000 Polo Grounds followers were let down hard for the second time in three days.

Integrating into the mound corps this season as the fourth starter was first-year hurler Al Demaree. The former Southern Association pitcher was purchased by McGraw in July of 1912 and put together a spiffy 13–4 record in just under 200 innings of labor. In Game Four at Shibe Park, the A's scored six unanswered runs in the first five innings—four off Demaree (two earned) and two off Marquard in relief. Chief Bender, on two days' rest, held on to win, 6–5. Merkle "bounced" a three-run home run into the left field bleachers to put the Giants on the board in the seventh inning.

On Saturday, October 11, another large, despondent crowd filed out of the Polo Grounds when the final out was logged. Eddie Plank, whom the Giants had beaten in Game Two and three other times in previous World Series appearances, stepped up, on short rest, in the clinching fifth contest. Tossing a shining two-hitter, "Gettysburg Eddie" beat Mathewson, 3–1.

"I felt confident last spring if Plank and Bender could pitch as they have done we would win both the American League pennant and world series," said Connie Mack afterward. "I wish to thank manager McGraw for his sportsmanlike behavior after today's game. He was the first man to reach me after the last play and his congratulations were deeply appreciated."[22] The 96-win Philadelphia Athletics once more outclassed McGraw's Giants, who lost all three home games.

McGraw outdid himself with off-season traveling during the winter of 1913–1914. He partnered with Garry Herrmann and Charles Comiskey to take a group of prominent players on tour around the world to promote the game that had made him famous. "Setting out from San Francisco [on the *Empress of Japan*], we sailed through fifty different bodies of water and railroaded through Japan, China, Australia, Egypt, Italy, France and England,"[23] McGraw recounted in his autobiography. McGraw invited Bill Klem and paid Klem from his part of the joint expenses. The other umpire, Jack Sheridan, was contracted by Comiskey.

The Americans played against native teams only in Japan and Australia. In London, the clubs were enthusiastically received by their "English cousins." McGraw was introduced to King George V of England, who was one of the 30,000 interested spectators on the day the touring teams played. Previously, during the Paris stopover, Damon Runyon had joined the traveling group in the City of Light. He wired back to his New York newspaper a story about accompanying McGraw on a visit to the Army Museum at *Les Invalides*. Standing in front of the tomb of Napoleon Bonaparte, Runyon (probably not truthfully) attributed McGraw as soulfully saying, "I too met the Duke of Wellington, only his name was Connie Mack instead of Arthur Wellesley."[24]

The first week of March, McGraw and company returned to New York from England on the *Lusitania*. The British passenger liner was destined to be sunk by a German submarine a little over a year later, in an eastward crossing of the Atlantic that cost more than 1,100 people their lives, including 128 Americans. Back home, the globe-trotting pilot was met with the news that a third major league had formed and his third baseman, Buck Herzog, had been traded, by Harry Hempstead, to the Cincinnati Reds. In the deal along with Herzog (who became player-manager of the Reds) was Giants reserve Grover Hartley. The Giants received outfielder Bob Bescher. It might be hard to say which upset McGraw more—losing Herzog, whose tenacious style of play he admired, or the breach of protocol on the part of Hempstead for not consulting his manager, who had full reign over player acquisitions under Brush.

McGraw plugged in 20-year-old rookie Milt Stock at third base, a player he obtained from the Boston Braves for a minor leaguer last September. Bescher became the starting center fielder. Otherwise, McGraw's group was the same that had won three pennants in a row, with one pitching exception. Doc Crandall, the Giants' excellent bullpen man and spot starter, had jumped to the new Federal League. Having led the league in games finished five years in a row, Crandall was the closest thing there was to a relief specialist for this era.

In the spring, the Giants played their usual lot of exhibition games before heading north. While in Houston on March 31, Houston Buffaloes manager Pat Newnam floored McGraw with a punch prior to the scheduled game. Art Fletcher intervened and knocked down Newnam before things could escalate. McGraw and Newnam had exchanged words during the previous day's battle. McGraw blamed his counterpart for starting the scuffle, saying Newnam had tried to antagonize one of his players, Fred Merkle. McGraw managed from the bench with a bandaged upper lip.

To begin the 1914 season, the Giants returned to Philadelphia, where they had lost the final game of the World Series six months earlier. Perhaps still haunted by the memory of Connie Mack's troops, New York dropped both games at the Baker Bowl to open the campaign. Rube Marquard and Jeff Tesreau were beaten.

Tesreau won the Polo Grounds home opener on April 23. It was a sunny and not unseasonable day, but only an estimated 20,000 decided to attend. As part of the pre-game frivolities, a large floral ball was wheeled out to the center of the diamond. Six-feet high and made up of white and red carnations, the baseball-designed arrangement was gifted by the Lambs—a professional theatre club in New York deriving its origin from the London-based association of the same name. In an individual ceremony, an encased gold bat and glass ball were presented to none other than Mike Donlin, once more wearing a Giants uniform. Like a bad penny that keeps turning up, Donlin had been signed again by McGraw, who had taken the irrepressible personality with him to Europe. Donlin served as McGraw's primary pinch-hitter on the year. He hit .161 in 1914 and finally called his career on the diamond to a close.

Recently elected Mayor James Purroy Mitchel gladly presided over the ceremonial first ball-tossing. From a lower box, the 34-year-old Mitchel flung a new baseball in the direction of Jeff Tesreau to signal the start of the home season. Tesreau had announced at the end of spring training that his goal was to take the title of best spitball hurler in the major leagues away from Chicago White Sox pitcher Ed Walsh. With Walsh nearing the end of his career, it was easy for Tesreau to reach his objective. Posting the first of his career-best 26 wins, the brawny moundsman defeated the Philadelphia Phillies, 12–4. Fred Merkle hit his second home run, with two men on base.

After stumbling to an 0–3 start and a 4–4 record in April, the Giants turned things around and steadily regained their brand of winning baseball. Tesreau evened his record at 2–2 with a shutout victory at Pittsburgh on May 16, which nearly produced his second career no-hitter. The Pirates' Joe Kelly lined a clean single to center with two outs in the bottom of the ninth inning. The disappointed pitcher retired the next batter to secure his 2–0 win.

Following a doubleheader sweep over the Brooklyn Suberbas on May 30, McGraw's minions edged into first place over the Pittsburgh Pirates and Cincinnati Reds. Four teams were bunched together further back. Trailing the entire NL circuit field, by 11 games, were the Boston Braves. Three weeks later, June 18, at the Polo Grounds, McGraw was run from a game for the first time on the season. Questioning an out call at third base on George Burns by Bob Emslie, McGraw declared that the decision was worthy of a Federal League umpire, and Emslie most took umbrage. The opponent Pirates won the game, 4–3.

On the last day of June, Tesreau (9–4) had his saliva ball working as he defeated Brooklyn, 3–1, at the Polo Grounds. After 60 games, the 37–23 Giants owned a five-game advantage over the second-place Chicago Cubs. The 26–35 Boston Braves maintained the lowest position in the league, 11½ lengths behind New York.

On July 17, one of baseball's all-time great pitching duels took place, and McGraw was one of the managers involved. The other was Pittsburgh skipper Fred Clarke (although Clarke was not around at the end, having been ejected). At Forbes Field, Rube Marquard defeated the Pirates' Babe Adams, 3–1, in *21* innings. Both pitchers hurled to the grueling finish. Larry Doyle hit a two-out, two-run, inside-the-park home run for the winning score. Marquard (8–8) allowed 15 hits, walked two and struck out an equal number. The pitcher recorded the last out of the contest on a comebacker. Adams surrendered a dozen safe hits and fanned six. He remarkably did not walk a batter. All the runs were earned.

On July 20, two days after receiving his third 1914 expulsion, an article McGraw wrote on the progression of the campaign, so far, appeared. Probably penned for the *New*

York Evening World—a paper which carried many of McGraw's musings (often ghost-written by Bozeman Bulger)—the article was circulated nationally.

> My big ambition in baseball is to win four straight pennants, and by copping this year I have a chance to make this record. I am afraid to ease up for a minute. I have too often seen other machines that looked as if they were on their way to a fourth pennant double up and blow, to be nosed out by some unexpected contender. The Cubs, Tigers and Athletics have all done this.[25]

McGraw—nor anyone in baseball—could have seen it coming, but the Boston Braves had already begun what would be an unbelievable rise from cellar dwellers to easy National League champions.

From July 27 through August 3, the Giants lost five out of seven games. McGraw was ejected four times. In the second clash of a Polo Grounds doubleheader on August 3, after the visiting Cincinnati Reds scored five runs in the top of the eighth inning to take a one-run lead, McGraw took out his displeasure on umpire William "Lord" Byron. Following the manager's dismissal, McGraw snatched Byron's watch, after the arbiter had pulled it out as a forfeiture warning for McGraw to leave the field. Swiftly, the league office responded. McGraw was suspended for five days. With Wilbert Robinson having left the Giants to become the pilot of Brooklyn, Larry Doyle became acting manager—as he had, and would, for all 12 games (a career-high) which McGraw was asked to leave early that year.

Upon McGraw's return on August 10, the Giants were still the team to beat, 5½ games in front of both the Chicago Cubs and St. Louis Cardinals. The Boston Braves were now one game behind the two second-place clubs. Within two weeks, the hot Braves caught up with the Giants, and jockeyed with McGraw's forces for first place into September. During the back and forth, McGraw released veteran pitcher Hooks Wiltse. The two-time 20-game winner was now strictly a back end of the bullpen man, being used in mop-up roles. The 35-year-old would sign with the Federal League in 1915 for one final big league go-around.

A morning-afternoon Labor Day doubleheader on September 7 brought out the biggest single-day Boston baseball crowd in history. Attending the early game, 35,000 fans gained entrance into Fenway Park. In the afternoon affair, another 40,000 were reportedly crammed into the three-year-old ballpark. Winning his 21st game (against eight losses), Jeff Tesreau salvaged a split for McGraw's aggregation in the nightcap, handily beating the home team, 10–1. In the opener, McGraw was ejected by Bob Emslie for arguing an out call on a Giants baserunner. "Naturally, McGraw was very angry at the start of the second game," addressed a news wire from Boston. "He declared that the morning penalty should not keep him idle during the afternoon; again the umpires disagreed with him. In walking from the field, McGraw gave free vent to his opinion of the arbiters. This got a rise out of the Braves [bench]."[26] The decision to ban McGraw from the premises for the second game, due to his conduct in the first, was probably an overreach of the umpires' authority. Three times during the season McGraw was excluded from participating in the second games of doubleheaders because he had been thrown out of the first. It is unclear whether this was a general practice for all managers or McGraw was singled out by the arbiters.

The Giants left Boston with a 68–54 record, a game behind the Braves. Incredibly, the next time the teams played, beginning on September 30, the Giants trailed George Stallings' New England team by nine games. The drastic turn of events affected McGraw.

In a glimpse at an unflattering, defeatist character trait that would come to light in future years, McGraw gave up his usual command spot on the field and hid in the dugout as his Giants squad unexpectedly fell by the wayside to the Braves. A write-up from the manager's penultimate expulsion of the season, on September 26, further explains:

> The game did accomplish one thing. It served to bring McGraw back to the diamond again. Ever since the period of the great depression began, the Little Napoleon has stuck to his base deep in the shelter of the players' bench. No matter how exciting the contest, he had refused to take his place on the coaching line. McGraw was impelled to show himself again because he felt he had a message. He delivered it to Cy Rigler, who received it close to his left ear, after deciding Mathewson's wild pitch was not a foul tip.[27]

The "Miracle Braves" won the pennant, the first team other than the Giants, Pirates, or Cubs to do so in the National League since 1900. The James Gaffney-owned team towered 10½ games over second-place New York and then swept the Philadelphia Athletics in the World Series.

A few days before the Fall Classic began, the Giants manager received a multi-year offer of $100,000 from Federal League owner Harry Sinclair to manage his Newark Peppers team, recently relocated from Indiana. McGraw never seriously considered it.

In January 1915, McGraw traveled to Cuba again. The trip commenced, with few exceptions until his death, what would become an annual winter pilgrimage for him and his wife to the island. Sailing with McGraw and Blanche were Christy Mathewson, Hans Lobert and their spouses. It was documented that McGraw spent time at the Havana race track—a side passion of his—and watched Cuban League games. He noted that Cubans had taken a big interest in the sport of boxing. McGraw also came back with a changed attitude on another sport. Probably prodded by Mathewson, McGraw played golf at the Havana Country Club, almost daily, during his month-long stay. McGraw eventually dropped his previous contention that the popular recreational game affected a player's swing and batting eye.

Prior to the 1915 season, as if to make a point to Harry Hempstead, McGraw traded Bob Bescher (along with some cash) to the St. Louis Cardinals for right-handed pitcher William "Pol" Perritt. The exchange reaped the biggest rewards for McGraw. Perritt proved a valuable addition to New York, while Bescher's skills began diminishing soon afterward. In January, six weeks before the Bescher trade, the Giants skipper made a deal that did not work out as well. He ill-advisedly moved the young Milt Stock, pitcher Al Demaree and backup catcher Bert Adams to the Philadelphia Phillies for third baseman and travel buddy Hans Lobert. The trade one-sidedly favored Philadelphia, as the 33-year-old Lobert contributed little to the Giants during the campaign, and even less afterward in his two remaining major league seasons. Demaree won 33 games for the Phillies over the next two seasons, and Stock matured into a top-end infielder for Philadelphia, and two other teams, in a 14-year major league career.

The Giants opened the season at home in fine fashion on April 14, drubbing Wilbert Robinson's Brooklyn club, 16–3. Jeff Tesreau was the complete game winner, and Hans Lobert collected three of the Giants' 18 hits and knocked in four runs. On a beautiful day, a regimental band entertained the early arrivals, and the players marched in unison across the field. New York City's "boy mayor," James Purroy Mitchel, got the real party started with his important duty of throwing out the first pitch. Heading her own important cause, Vira Boarman Whitehouse, a well-known suffragist, presented the Giants with an oversized bat festooned with satin ribbons. Neither the mayor nor Mrs. Whitehouse

was as photographed prior to the game as Christy Mathewson and Jim Thorpe, who garnered the most attention from the professional shutterbugs. Playing right field, Thorpe
contributed modestly with a hit and run scored.

The next day, Rube Marquard no-hit the Robins. Marquard, who lost 22 games last
season and was the athlete most speculated in the press as being on McGraw's chopping
block, faced only 30 batters in the 2–0 win. He walked two and struck out a pair. The
Giants then lost seven games in a row, slipping into last place.

Before the month's expiration, the Giants hosted the world champion Boston Braves.
The front page of the *Boston Daily Globe* of May 1 headlined events from the Battle of
Gallipoli, launched a few days earlier, as the great war in Europe—begun last summer—
raged forward. Much smaller page one news space was allocated to player Benny Kauff.
That story, continuing on the *Globe*'s sports pages, told readers how John McGraw tried
to insert Kauff into the lineup versus the Braves on April 29. Trouble was that Kauff was
a member of the Federal League's Brooklyn Tip Tops club.

> Considerable surprise was expressed by baseball fans today that McGraw was not disciplined for
> his remarkable actions on the field during the Kauff affair yesterday. Not only did the manager of
> the New York team try to force an ineligible player into the game but he grossly insulted the presi-
> dent of the Boston club while the latter sat in a box with his wife and daughter.[28]

Among the printable things McGraw called Boston team president James Gaffney
were "four-flusher" and "squealer," after Gaffney blew the whistle on McGraw's illegal
player to the umpires. Kauff could not have sufficiently helped the Giants, who lost, 13–8,
in a darkness-shortened, seven-inning engagement. The star player of the Federal League
in 1914, Kauff eventually reunited with Brooklyn and produced another near–MVP season.

May 18 was dubbed "Suffrage Day" at the Polo Grounds, with Vira Boarman Whitehouse and her constituents making a broader appearance—and appeal—than on Opening
Day. The suffragettes pre-sold 4,100 bleacher tickets, mostly to women. They handed out
small balloons and pamphlets, urging all registered voters to cast ballots in their favor
in the upcoming November elections. The local leader of the ladies' equality movement
did not forget the participants, offering $5 to every home and road player who scored a
run.

Sparing the ladies' operating fund a substantial loss was the pitching of Tesreau and
the Cubs' Bert Humphries. The Cubs pitcher outdueled his counterpart, 1–0. Frank
Schulte, who four years earlier had become the first 20th-century player to hit 20 home
runs in a season, scored the only run of the game. His wife, Mabel, was identified as collecting the prize afterward. Although the event may have provided some financial wind-
fall, the Giants' front office should be acknowledged for forward thinking and a good
brand of public relations in backing the worthwhile cause.

The Giants finished the month with a 14–19 record, and things did not improve.
Pitching, the club's mainstay for years, crumpled. The hurlers cumulatively finished seventh in ERA (3.11) in the circuit and allowed the most home runs (40). The team's legendary chucker had one victory to his credit on the first of June. On that day, Christy
Mathewson lost to Pat Ragan of the Boston Braves, 7–0, to drop his record to 1–4.
Although Mathewson had won 20 games in 1914 for the 13th time in his career, he had
also led the league in home runs and earned runs allowed. This season spelled the imminent end for one of baseball's iconic greats. Bothered presently by a bad *left* shoulder,

Mathewson's 1915 pitching ledger would read 8–14 in 24 starts, with an ERA of 3.58 (compared to the 2.75 league average).

With Mathewson not performing like his old self, the pitching load fell on Jeff Tesreau. The 27-year-old right-hander responded admirably, posting a 19–16 mark, with a 2.29 ERA, for what we now know to be a team-leading 5.7 Wins Above Replacement rating. But no other staff hurler came close to matching Tesreau. Trailing him were 12-game winners Pol Perritt and Pacific Coast League recruit Ralph "Sailor" Stroud. A right-hander, Stroud had come up with the Detroit Tigers in 1910. He had been selected from the San Francisco Missions by McGraw in the major league draft in September of last year. No other Giants pitcher reached the double-digit victory level.

In June, the Giants barely won more games than they lost (12–11). One of the losses was on June 23 to the Philadelphia Phillies. The score was 2–1, and it took 11 innings. The Giants used two pitchers and so did the winners. Keeping with pairs, only two balls were used in the game, according to the *New York Tribune*. The original ball lasted until the top of the 11th, when the Cubs' Gavvy Cravath lined a foul into the crowd down the right field line. A dozen balls were usually used per game at this period.

Earlier in the month, McGraw was involved in a highly publicized incident at a St. Louis hotel with third-string catcher Larry McLean. Disparaging words were spoken between McLean and Dick Kinsella, in the presence of McGraw and a handful of other players. McLean was upset at the new Giants scout for snitching on him to McGraw. A fight broke out, with McGraw in the mix, and at least one piece of hotel furniture was smashed. Afterward, McLean was suspended indefinitely by McGraw. The big, 35-year-old catcher left the squad immediately afterward and never played baseball at its highest level again.

The following month, the major league trial of Jim Thorpe all but concluded. Unable to earn any appreciable playing time the past two and a half seasons, Thorpe was sent to the International League. The transaction came on the heels of the release of Red Murray, a Giants starter in the outfield since 1909. McGraw had decided upon Dave Robertson for the near future. A left-handed-throwing flychaser, Robertson had been signed by McGraw on a recommendation from scout Mike Finn in 1912. Robertson, 22 at the time, was with a lower-level minor league team in the Virginia League. He spent 1913 with the Single-A Mobile Sea Gulls before joining the Giants in 1914. Toward the end of July, McGraw, always on the lookout for young blood, purchased 19-year-old George Kelly from the Northwestern League. From Northern California, Kelly was a first baseman with a prototype size for his position; he stood 6'4" and weighed 190 pounds.

With his team floundering in the second division, McGraw made more roster changes in August. He cut Fred Snodgrass on the 18th of the month. Having held a regular place in the pasture for five seasons, the outfielder had slumped badly and was hitting under .200 when he was released. He was shortly signed by the Boston Braves. The day after the Snodgrass decision, McGraw looked to strengthen his weak pitching. He bought underachieving, 25-year-old portsider John "Rube" Benton from the Cincinnati Reds, paying out the $3,000 waiver price to get him.

A few days earlier, McGraw had openly criticized his other pitching "Rube," something uncharacteristic of the Giants manager. (McGraw rarely called out a player on his team in public. Once the player left or was traded, it was a different story.) "Rube Marquard has been a big disappointment to me," McGraw flatly stated. "He looks to be in good shape, and he can show more stuff when he warms up than I ever saw on a left-hander, and I have seen a lot of them. But he can travel about five or six innings and then he blows [up]."[29]

On August 31, McGraw, Harry Hempstead, and team secretary John B. Foster were visited at the team offices in Manhattan by Wilbert Robinson. Also present was Marquard. The men agreed to terms for Marquard at the Class AA waiver price of $2,500. Robinson signed the pitcher for the remainder of 1915 and 1916. When he left the Giants, Marquard was 9–8 in 21 starts, including ten complete games. His ERA was an elevated 3.73. He pitched for ten more major league seasons, accumulating up and down won–lost records.

Looking toward the future, McGraw made more headlines when he signed high school pitcher Waite Hoyt. A product of Erasmus Hall High School in Brooklyn, Hoyt was only 15 and was proclaimed as the youngest person ever to sign a major league contract. His father, Arthur, was required to co-sign the contract.

As the team played out the string in September, the first Hispanic player in Giants franchise history debuted. The starting pitcher in the second game of a doubleheader at West Side Grounds on September 21, Emilio Palmero lasted but two-thirds of inning on the mound. Palmero was a 20-year-old left-hander signed by McGraw during his Cuban vacation. The pitcher allowed three runs to the Cubs, the result of two hits, three walks and a hit batsman. Losers in the first game to the Giants, 5–4, Chicago prevailed, 5–3, with Palmero absorbing the loss.

In his second start, on October 6, Palmero hurled the distance but came out on the losing end again, this time 1–0, to counterpart Tom Hughes of the Boston Braves. The foreign hurler would have another brief go of it with the Giants in 1916 and then would be gone from the major league scene for five years. In 1921, with the St. Louis Browns, Palmero would become the first left-handed Hispanic pitcher to win a major league game.

The day after Palmero's shutout loss, the Giants' season ended. The team's 69–83 record, although not terrible, placed them in last place. The club trailed the pennant-seizing Philadelphia Phillies by 21 games. The disappointing campaign can perhaps be best capsulized by the fact that John McGraw had more ejections (ten) than Christy Mathewson had wins.

The Federal League lasted two years, folding in December 1915 with the acceptance of a large remuneration package from organized baseball. The deal, contingent on the rival circuit dropping their filed lawsuit over OB's monopolistic player control, allowed two Federal League owners to gain control of major league clubs. The St. Louis Browns were purchased by Phil Ball, owner of the now-defunct St. Louis Terriers, forcing Browns manager Branch Rickey out. In the National League, the Chicago Cubs were bought by Chicago Whales owner Charles H. Weeghman and placed in the park he had built especially for the Whales. Weeghman later sold his interests in the team and the park to a chewing gum chieftain named William Wrigley. Only the Baltimore Terrapins refused to go along with the deal, preferring to continue the legal fight with the hope of reintegrating a new major league franchise into Baltimore.

As part of the monetary arrangement, every Federal League player under contract was put up for bid by his owner. McGraw zeroed in on Benny Kauff, this season's attempted roster ruse. Around Christmastime, McGraw paid Brooklyn Tip Tops financial backer Charles S. Ward $35,000 for the 26-year-old Kauff, who had led the Federal League in batting, on base percentage and slugging average (.342/.446/.509). McGraw signed Kauff to a two-year, $12,000 contract. Also plucked by the Giants from the short-lived league was outfielder Edd Roush, a former member of the Newark Peppers.

Kauff was the player McGraw coveted. Based on his fabulous two seasons in the rival loop, he had been dubbed the "Ty Cobb of the Federal League." Kauff was also gregarious and quotable; he was the type of flashy sensation that would come to be lustily craved by the New York media. He was another Mike Donlin, but with no distracting, second-career aspirations.

"I'm going to make the Giants live up to their contract with me," Kauff said shortly after his acquisition, referring to a $5,000 signing bonus he said he had been promised by Harry Hempstead but had not yet received. "Then I'm going to show those other birds in the National League how to play ball. Say, if Larry Doyle can hit around .330 in that league I'll hit .375. That right field stand at the Polo Grounds will be a cinch for me. And if I don't steal 40 bases they won't have to pay me."[30]

The mention of second baseman Doyle was to his league-leading .320 batting average in 1915. The former Chalmers Award winner had blossomed into a full-fledged star for McGraw. He also possessed an affable personality that ingrained itself with daily pleasure among the New York writers. "Laughing Larry," as he was dubbed by one of those scribes, was known for coining the glib phrase, "It's great to be young and a Giant." He paced the National League in hits for the second time in his career and was the Giants' best position player.

FIVE

The Irresponsible John McGraw

"You can ask anyone who knows me. They'll tell you that I am not a man to pick a fight. I haven't a quarrelsome disposition."—John McGraw

In the new year's first month, McGraw secured the services of another Newark Peppers player, Bill Rariden, considered the Federal League's best catcher. From the same talent stream, McGraw added pitcher Fred Anderson, a right-hander who had won 19 games for the dismantled circuit's Buffalo Blues. The reason for the Rariden acquisition became clear in mid–February when McGraw asked waivers on Chief Meyers. The catcher's production had slipped the last two seasons, most noticeably in 1915. McGraw was saved the Giants having to pay the last year of Meyers' three-year contract—about $6,500—when Wilbert Robinson claimed the 35-year-old backstop for his Brooklyn club. Meyers, by the way, caught more games of Christy Mathewson than any other catcher (186).

A few days before the 1916 season began, Hans Lobert fractured his leg in an exhibition game against the Yale collegiate baseball club. Lobert's first season had been curtailed to 106 games due to a knee injury. This new injury continued to compound McGraw with regret over the three-for-one trade that had brought Lobert to him in 1915. To replace Lobert, McGraw acquired Bill McKechnie—most recently the player-manager of the Newark Peppers—two days into the season. McKechnie had been in St. Louis with the American League Browns, where he had been "loaned" to the team by former Newark owner Harry Sinclair for the duration of spring training, in the hopes of obtaining a bid on him.

The Giants' 1916 season did not begin auspiciously. The team dropped two out of three in its opening three-game series in Philadelphia, then lost a single game to Brooklyn at Ebbets Field. The first home game of the season on April 20 did nothing to stem the losing trend. Mayor James Purroy Mitchel attended his third straight opener and, from a field box, tossed out the first ball. Unlike in past years, the ball was signed by McGraw, standing nearby, and returned to the chief executive (in compliance to a request). Presumably with other more pressing matters to attend, Mitchel left the contest with his souvenir in hand prior to the final outcome, one of the few in the crowd of 25,000 to do so. Against the visiting Philadelphia Phillies, McGraw's Federal League outfielders, Benny Kauff and Edd Roush, performed admirably, each collecting three hits, driving in two and scoring three runs between them. The game came down to a battle of relievers after both starters were pulled after five innings of work in a tie game. Emilio Palmero hurled six scoreless innings before he was touched for a run. The Phillies' Hugh McQuillan topped Palmero with seven runless frames and was the winning pitcher in the Phillies' 12-inning, 7–6 victory.

The Giants lost five more games in a row and 13 out of their first 15. Jeff Tesreau provided the only victories in the span.

In late April, during the string of setbacks, McGraw was thrown out of back-to-back games by Bill Klem at Braves Field. McGraw and Klem nearly engaged in a fist fight after the game on the second day, April 27. Klem associate Bob Emslie had to step between the two men to prevent them from coming to blows. The veteran umpire was in no mood to take any more guff. He had been serenaded by the Giants' bench with a chorus of "meows" after he called George Burns out at the plate in the fourth inning. The feline noise was a reference to his unflattering nickname. It got so bad that Klem prohibited all the visitors' substitutes from staying on the bench. McGraw himself was banished for not letting up on his protests over the Burns play that had gone against him.

On May 9, the 2–13 Giants opened an extended road trip with the Pittsburgh Pirates at Forbes Field. McGraw's tailenders pummeled the Pirates, 13–5. Tesreau pitched the first five innings, giving up all of the home team's runs. So desperate for victory was McGraw that he summoned Christy Mathewson to pitch the last 3⅔ innings. In an obvious psychological attempt to separate this year's club from last, McGraw had changed the design of the Giants' pinstripe uniforms and rounded crown cap design that the team had been wearing since 1911. "The Giants looked strange in their new traveling suits of putty hue and caps patterned after inverted soup tureens," critiqued one Pittsburgh sportswriter. "The togs are ornamented with prison stripes and the hosiery has a ring of red sandwiched between two bands of black."[1]

Nearly three weeks later, May 29, Mathewson hurled the 79th and final shutout of his magnificent career. At Braves Field, the box artist four-hit the Braves, 3–0, in a vintage one hour and 30 minutes. Mathewson's second win on the campaign was also the Giants *17th* victory in succession. The following day, Al Demaree, the pitcher McGraw had let go in the Lobert trade, halted the long winning streak. Demaree, hurling for the Phillies, puzzled the Giants, 5–1, in the first game of a doubleheader at the Baker Bowl.

On June 2, the Giants, 21–15 and in second place, returned to the Polo Grounds for the first time in nearly a month. In honor of their extremely successful road trip, each member of the team was presented with a silver loving cup. The gifts came from Eddie Leonard, a well-known vaudevillian of the day, who bestowed upon McGraw a cup that, according to the June 3 *New York Times*, "held several more quarts" than the ones received by the players. Perhaps not convinced yet by the Giants' turn-around, only 18,000 fans came out for the welcome home. The Giants proceeded to drop a 6–4, 13-inning contest to the Cincinnati Reds. Pol Perritt was the loser in relief of Mathewson, who had been taken out after just three innings. McGraw was ejected for the third time in 1916, verbally clashing with Mal Eason over his sixth-inning out call at first base on Fred Merkle.

On June 26, the roles of Perritt and Mathewson were reversed, and the outcome favored their squad. In the first game of a doubleheader at Ebbets Field, Perritt started and Mathewson finished, taking home a 13–8 triumph with 4⅓ innings of one-run relief. Benny Kauff was the hitting star with a double and two triples, one with the bases loaded in the seventh inning, deciding the contest. Rube Marquard earned Brooklyn, which was in first place, a split with a masterful 12-inning, 2–1 win in the nightcap. Mathewson's first-game victory was his 372nd lifetime and last as a New York Giant.

Mathewson made one more appearance in a Giants uniform; it came in the first game of a morning-afternoon July 4 doubleheader at the Polo Grounds. He was the second of four Giants pitchers McGraw used in a 7–6 loss to Brooklyn. The former brilliant hurler, six weeks away from his 36th birthday, was tagged with the defeat, allowing five runs, two earned, in 6⅔ innings. His record slipped to 3 and 4. Marquard pitched 8⅓ innings of one-run relief to secure the victory. Brooklyn captured the afternoon game, as well, 6–2, to move four games out in front of the pack. Close to 20,000 fans, more than double the morning game total, attended. The Giants, 30–33, slip into a tie for fifth place with the dual losses.

Later in the month, on the final day of a Giants' four-day stay in Cincinnati, McGraw was arrested by local police on a disorderly conduct charge brought by a local fan who accused McGraw of abusive language after the game, outside of the players' clubhouse. The fan, John T. Reed, was booked by police, under the same charge, when shortstop Art Fletcher, who was with McGraw, swore out the same complaint on Reed. McGraw posted a $100 bond and left with his team for Chicago, their next road stop. Six days afterward, July 20, McGraw was back in Cincinnati on strictly baseball business. He finalized a trade that for a few days had received speculative headlines in the press.

McGraw traded Christy Mathewson, Bill McKechnie and outfielder Edd Roush to the Cincinnati Reds, for Buck Herzog and utility player Wade "Red" Killefer. The deal was made with the understanding that the once-great Mathewson would take over Herzog's managerial duties with the Reds. Ironically, accompanying McGraw to the Queen City to meet with Garry Herrmann was Harry Hempstead, who had traded the plucky Herzog to the Reds a couple of years earlier without consulting with McGraw. By landing the 23-year-old Roush—a future Hall of Famer and a player Herrmann had been interested in signing since Roush's Class D days back in 1913—the trade turned into a coup for the Cincinnati owner. Mathewson immediately put Roush in center field. He won the first of his two battling titles for the Reds the following season.

Mathewson won one more game in his Cooperstown career before retiring after the season.

Further assessing the trade, in fairness to McGraw, Roush was the Giants' fourth outfielder. As McGraw planned, Kauff, George Burns and Dave Robertson, a heavy hitter McGraw had been grooming for several years, were the main outfielders. Moreover, McGraw was trying to promote Mathewson's advancement in the sport. And why not? Mathewson was the player most responsible for elevating McGraw's stature in the game as a manager. The two men had developed a deep friendship, if not bond, over the years. The pair, and their wives, frequently socialized and were often seen in public together. (During McGraw's first few years in New York, the McGraws and Mathewsons shared a two-family residence.)

But McGraw seemed to have as great a degree of interest in Herzog as he had altruism for Mathewson. "Charlie Herzog is the finest third baseman in the game," McGraw said less than a month after the trade was consummated. "He makes my club the best balanced in either league. His spirit and aggressiveness spur all the other players on to twice their earlier vim."[2] McGraw and Herzog, a versatile player who played every infield spot but first base, had clashed on numerous occasions as both subordinate and opponent. It would not be inaccurate to state that the pair developed a love-hate relationship, as the "pepper pot" infielder was a younger version of McGraw in his "take no prisoners attitude" against the opposition team. Indeed, the player's nickname of "Choke 'Em Charley" was derived from the personal credo he often passed along to writers: *When you get 'em down, choke 'em*. In his third go-around with the Giants, Herzog maintained his fiery but also headstrong temperament—attractive yet disruptive traits, in the eyes of McGraw.

As for the other "incidental" players in the big swap, Bill McKechnie was a few years away from evolving into a well-deserved Hall of Fame manager.

Red Killefer played two games for the Giants before being sold to the American Association, eventually becoming a player and manager in the Pacific Coast League.

Another player McGraw sold to the American Association was pitcher Rube Schauer. What can only be categorized as a "$10,000 bust" (Schauer's purchase price in 1913), the right-hander had managed a 3–13 record in trials with the team over the past few seasons. To compensate for the loss of Mathewson and Schauer, McGraw swung a cash deal to obtain hurler "Slim" Sallee from the St. Louis Cardinals. The Giants shelled out $10,000 to receive the experienced left-hander, christened Harry Franklin.

In mid–August, while the Giants were in Philadelphia, a minor league purchase was made that attracted little, if any attention, in New York. Ross Youngs, a 19-year-old outfielder hitting the cover off the ball in the Western Association with a batting average over .340, was signed. Two thousand dollars was the price for the 5'8", 160-pound Youngs. Scout Dick Kinsella was the man most responsible for bringing the youngster into the Giants' fold.

Just prior to the excellent acquisition, and with his team only a few games over .500, McGraw made a patently outlandish statement to the baseball community at large. "I not only have the greatest ball club in the world, but I also have the most valuable single player," he said. "My pennant winning teams of 1911, 1912 and 1913 do not compare with the present outfit. And I never had any one player that compared with Davy Robertson—that is, excepting the greatest pitcher of all time, Matty."[3] Robertson, McGraw's Virginia League purchase of 1912, was presently challenging for the league's batting and home run titles. At six feet tall and 190 pounds, Robertson was an early embodiment of the mid–20th century power hitter. He would top the circuit in home runs with 12 and hit .307. His 69 RBI finished a few behind Benny Kauff for the most on the team. On August 18 and 19, Robertson boosted over-the-wall home runs in back-to-back games at Weeghman Park, a feat not often seen during the present brand of baseball.

Weeghman Park's inhabitants, the Chicago Cubs, had a talented third baseman named Henry "Heinie" Zimmerman at this time. Zimmerman, a Triple Crown winner in 1912, outwardly, at least, had lost his focus—or as his manager Joe Tinker put it, "his interest in the game." Thus he became a dispensable commodity. Zimmerman was landed by McGraw on August 28 in a deal in which the Giants gave up three players, most significantly their captain, Larry Doyle. In doing so, New York beat out pennant aspirants Brooklyn, Boston and Philadelphia—all of whom had previously expressed a strong desire for Zimmerman. McGraw plainly had no qualms in parting with Doyle, his starting second baseman since 1908. The defending batting champion's average had slipped more than 50 points.

Proving further that managers and team executives had little patience when it applied to the perceived regression of a veteran player, Fred Merkle was exchanged for Brooklyn third-string catcher Lew McCarty on August 25. A regular for seven years, including the current campaign, Merkle's average had dipped from .299 in 1915 to .237.

The inexperienced Walter Holke was plugged in at Merkle's spot. A few days before August expired, the disorderly conduct case in Cincinnati against McGraw was dismissed. McGraw issued an apology to the aggrieved John T. Reed and paid all the court costs involved in order to bring the matter to an agreeable resolution.

Facing the second-place Boston Braves in a road doubleheader on September 2, McGraw was banished from the opener after a choleric dispute over a called strike three on Hans Lobert. The ejection was McGraw's sixth—his quota for the year. Pitching 5⅔ innings of one-hit relief, 31-year-old Slim Sallee gained his fifth win (against three losses) since joining the Giants. McGraw's team had to settle for the 4–1 win on the day, as the second contest ended in a ten-inning, 5–5 tie, called because of darkness. Pitcher Ferdie Schupp tossed four scoreless innings in relief.

The effort earned Schupp a start, five days later, against the Brooklyn Robins. At the Polo Grounds, the left-hander subdued the visiting squad, 4–1, on two hits. That win kicked off a historic winning streak for the Giants that did not end until the last day of the month. The Giants won a phenomenal *26* consecutive games, modestly interrupted by a tie game almost halfway through the span.

The record winning streak was stopped by an 8–3 loss to the Boston Braves in the back end of doubleheader on September 30. For the second time in as many home dates, a crowd exceeding 35,000 showed up to cheer on their invincibles in the split. Schupp won six games during the long, unblemished string. For the season, the 9–3 southpaw posted the lowest ERA by a starting pitcher of the 20th century—0.90, in 140⅓ innings.

In spite of the record run, the Giants managed only a fourth-place finish, while greatly improving last season's overall record to 86–66.

The season, which should have ended on a high note brought on by the victory parade, concluded with damaging controversy, however. The Giants' final four games were at Brooklyn. The borough team was in a fight with the Philadelphia Phillies for the National League pennant. After Brooklyn beat the Giants for the second day in a row, October 3, and the Phillies dropped a twin bill to Boston, Wilbert Robinson's club clinched the flag.

In the October 3 loss, in Brooklyn, McGraw grew peeved at what he discerned as indifferent play on the part of some of his players. Responding contrary to the responsibility of his position, McGraw left Ebbets Field in the fifth inning. "I simply would not stand for the kind of baseball my team was playing," he said afterward. "I do not believe that any of my players deliberately favored Brooklyn, but they simply refused to obey my orders and fooled around in a lifeless manner."[4] Evidently, the straw that broke the camel's back was Pol Perritt not pitching from the stretch with a man on first base, and the player then stealing second.

Because McGraw's statements could be taken to suggest that the Giants had purposely let Brooklyn win, there was an immediate backlash, especially due to the immediate pennant implications. "Personally," said AL president and old McGraw adversary Ban Johnson, "I think it was an outrage, and had it occurred in the American League there would be the devil to pay."[5]

McGraw, as he had shown over and over, feared repercussions from no one. He skipped the last two games of the schedule—simply did not show up for them. The day following his tendentious remarks, he appeared at the Polo Grounds, instead of Ebbets Field, and watched the tenant New York Yankees play a doubleheader with the Washington Senators. Buck Herzog piloted the Giants to a 1–1 record over the final two games.

The players, meanwhile, universally did not agree with their abandoned manager's opinion. "I can't honestly believe that Mac said the things which were printed," commented outfielder George Burns. "If he did it was unfair to our team. We did our best, fought hard, but couldn't win."[6]

"I don't know that McGraw said anything," said pitcher Fred Anderson. "But if he thinks the boys deserted him, he is mistaken."[7]

"The proposition that we quit is preposterous," added new team member Lew McCarty. "The Giants did their best and couldn't win. I heard the talk on the bench, and I know that they were in to win."[8]

Harry Hempstead and club secretary John Foster did their best to diffuse the situation with statements that supported the players' perspective. Hempstead downplayed things by saying the "wild Irish in McGraw rose to the top" when he thought his players were purposely not performing to professional expectations.

National League President John Tener declined to reprimand McGraw. "This is not a case for league consideration," he maintained. "It concerns the New York club. If there is to be any disciplining it must come from Mr. Hempstead or Mr. McGraw."[9]

The Giants' front office quickly made clear that neither McGraw nor any players would be fined or suspended, and then hoped for everything to blow over as the media shifted its focus to the World Series between the Brooklyn Robins and Boston Red Sox.

The National League owners' meeting was held December 12, 1916, at the Waldorf-Astoria Hotel in New York. Although Giants executives did their best to quell the matter, the serious issue involving McGraw and alleged dereliction of duty on the part of his players would not go away. This was partly due to commentary by Ban Johnson and the Giants' Buck Herzog, speaking on behalf of some teammates, which kept the potential scandal alive. While both had their own degree of self-promotion and self-interest in mind, the underlying core of the game's integrity was placed at the forefront.

The eight owners re-elected John Tener to another one-year term as league president and voted the secretary and treasurer of the league, John A. Heydler, to a four-year tenure in that same capacity. The magnates voted down, 6–2, a joint proposal brought forth by the Giants and Chicago Cubs to increase the major league rosters to 25 players. A compromise was reached, bumping by one the number of players carried per team from 21 to 22. The league also pledged its support for Clark Griffith's Bat and Ball Fund and was brought up to snuff on the pending lawsuit by the former Baltimore Federal League owners. The McGraw incident was not brought up and therefore, died.

Something that could not be ignored that off-season was a threatened strike by the "Players' Fraternity," a loose attempt at unionism, founded by former player Dave Fultz. Ban Johnson vowed that his American League would only engage its players individually and never as a representative body. McGraw took a more dismissive attitude than Johnson's hard-line approach.

> The only real harm that has arisen from the [proposed] ball players' strike is that I stayed in town to look after the details of our club and it has delayed my trip to Cuba. It looks as if it would be impossible for me to get in my month of golf now and I may not go at all. The players, you know, don't like for their teammates even to know the amount of their salaries. They won't pay much attention to the union business.[10]

By mid–February the weak unionism threat passed, with Fultz withdrawing strike threats on the condition that there would be no reprisals against the players by major league ownership. On February 23, McGraw left New York, by rail, for Marlin, Texas. A month later, from San Antonio, Harry Hempstead put aside any and all doubt on where he stood on the future of his team's controversial field commander. Hempstead confirmed a new five-year deal for McGraw, at an annual salary of $40,000. Effective this season, the contract replaced the last remaining year of McGraw's existing agreement.

Following the great September put together by the Giants, as the 1917 season rolled around, McGraw's months-old statement about having "the greatest ball club in the world" no longer sounded so outlandish. The substantial amount of money the team had spent on Federal League players replenished key roster positions, with Bill Rariden at catcher and Benny Kauff in center field. Though he was no Ty Cobb, of course, Kauff provided Giants fans with fielding and base stealing thrills. He fell well short of his indirect boast of winning the batting title, but in 1917 he raised his batting average over 40 points to .308.

The in-season trades of 1916 made by baseball's highest-paid manager indisputably upgraded the quality of the club for 1917. McGraw appeared to have succeeded in turning Heinie Zimmerman around. The third baseman hit .297 in 1917 and led the league in RBI with 100. He accumulated the third-best wins above replacement level on the squad at 5.3. The team's top player, analytically speaking, was shortstop Art Fletcher—for the second year in a row. A defensive specialist, Fletcher's 7.4 WAR topped his league-leading (among position players) 6.3 metric from 1916. As for the rest of the infield, Walter Holke and Buck Herzog adequately manned first and second base, respectively.

Teaming again with Kauff and George Burns in the outfield, McGraw's highest-praised player, Dave Roberston, led the league in home runs with 12 for the second year in a row. McGraw's high praise, in Robertson's case, implied no disdain for the long ball, but rather assessed it as a potentially powerful weapon. In left field, Burns paced the circuit in runs scored for the second consecutive campaign. Burns, Kauff and Robertson comprised the best outfield in the National League.

In the pitching department, McGraw was relying again on Jeff Tesreau and Pol Perritt. Both were coming off 18-win seasons. Rube Benton, the pitcher McGraw had purchased from the Cincinnati Reds in 1915 as a reclamation project, had enhanced his record from 9–18 to 16–8 the next year. In 1917, Benton would pull in 15 victories. Ferdie Schupp, who was brilliant in a limited role in 1916, carried over the dazzling mound work for an entire season and produced a 21–7 career year. With the emergence of Schupp and holdover Slim Sallee, McGraw utilized five starters throughout most of the season.

Sallee was the only regular starter over 30 years of age. He earned the Giants' first win on April 12, in the season opener (delayed a day by rain). On a bone-chilling day at Braves Field, Sallee pitched six innings in relief of starter Fred Anderson, allowing two unearned runs. The Giants used a six-run fourth inning to come out on top, 6–4. Six thousand of the Braves' faithful showed not only loyalty but spunk in being undeterred by the less than ideal conditions.

Eight days hence, with little weather improvement on the East Coast, the Braves were hosted by the Giants in their home inaugural. More colorful and patriotic imagery than usual was integrated into the Opening Day pomp, as the United States had officially entered World War I earlier in the month. Allied flags of Great Britain, France, Russia, Belgium, Italy and Japan flew from the Polo Grounds grandstand roof, interspaced between numerous banners of the *Stars and Stripes*. A few minutes prior to the game, the left field exit doors of the Polo Grounds swung open. A representation of the fife and drum corps marched out to the heart-fluttering strains of "Yankee Doodle" played by the regimental band behind them. Players from both squads lined up along the fouls lines holding American flags, while the "Star Spangled Banner" played. Pending the arrival of Mayor Mitchel, the game was delayed for several minutes. Finally, Giants treasurer John Whalen pinch-threw the opening toss. George Stallings' team then evened the inaugural

One of McGraw's many show business friends, vaudevillian actor Harry Fox, points something out to the Giants skipper. The pair are standing in front of one of the "Roman Colosseum–like royal boxes" that rimmed the field level seating at the Polo Grounds. The VIPs in the box seem intrigued by Fox's discovery as well.

day score, downing the Giants, 4–2, in 14 innings. Little-used bullpen man George Smith was tagged with the loss, after spelling starter Jeff Tesreau in the ninth inning. An estimated 18,000 fans watched the festivities.

A few days later, the Giants' roster was reduced by one when outfielder Jim Thorpe—whom the Giants did not seem to know how to use—was claimed by the Cincinnati Reds for the waiver price of $2,500.

The Giants played all home games in May and won 12 of 19 decisions. The flourishing Schupp won four times, including three victories over the occidental clubs. At 20–11, the McGraw ensemble held a precarious foothold on first place over the Cubs and Phillies, as the team began its initial western road journey on June 1. The second stop, in Cincinnati, coincided with "Registration Day." The June 5 date that President Woodrow Wilson had marked as the conscription obligation date for all able-bodied men between the ages of 21 and 31 drew nearly 10,000,000 men across the country. Among those eligible Giants were standouts: George Burns, Dave Robertson, Benny Kauff, Jeff Tesreau and Ferdie Schupp. Led by Schupp, who won his first eight decisions, the Giants emerged as firm early-season contenders. On June 9, Schupp improved to 7–0, shutting out the Chicago Cubs on three hits at Weeghman Park. McGraw was not on hand in his usual capacity to appreciate the effort. The manger had been suspended indefinitely by National League secretary John Heydler, acting on direct orders from president Tener, who was in Philadelphia answering the lawsuit brought against organized baseball by the stockholders of the former Federal League club from Baltimore.

The previous day, McGraw had been expelled from his game in Cincinnati by Lord Byron. McGraw scathingly contended that the Reds' Heinie Groh had left third base too soon on a sixth-inning sacrifice fly. Three innings later, Art Fletcher was tossed for arguing that baserunner Hal Chase deliberately hit his arm on a throw to first base, part of an attempted double play, which allowed Ivey Wingo to reach second. The Reds catcher promptly scored on a single by Jim Thorpe, and the Reds won, 2–1. After the final out, McGraw confronted the umpires as they headed toward their dressing area along the third base side of Redland Field. McGraw challenged Quigley associate Lord Byron to a fight. Byron had ejected McGraw earlier in the series and had pulled the forfeit-threatening stopwatch on McGraw earlier in the game when he had delayed vacating the field. The men ended up exchanging insults, and McGraw slugged the arbiter.

After the fight was broken up by the players and people around them, McGraw rushed to a Cincinnati notary. He did not deny striking Byron, but swore that he was not the aggressor (though he was) and that it was the first time in 27 years that he had ever laid hands on an umpire (though it was not). He said that he was provoked into throwing a punch by Byron's shouted accusation that he had been run out of Baltimore years back. Catchers Bill Rariden and George Gibson and first baseman Walter Holke were witnesses who also signed the affidavit. McGraw received no sympathy from Tener, however, as evidenced by his suspension.

On June 13, in Pittsburgh, McGraw received a telegram from Tener advising him that the duration of the suspension would be 16 days. He was also fined $500. The castigated skipper returned to the bench on June 25. During his inactive period, McGraw irritated some New York writers by denying that he had called Tener incompetent and accused him of misusing his power, in an interview he gave Sid Mercer of the *New York Evening Globe.*

The *Sun*'s Frank Graham printed a similar story with the same corroboration from McGraw. When the investigating Tener and board of directors (consisting of the club owners) of the National League accepted McGraw's quick denial, the case was conveniently closed. Claiming that their journalistic integrity was at stake, the New York Chapter of the Baseball Writers' Association of America petitioned Tener and the board to reopen the investigation.

McGraw's second day back featured a doubleheader between the Giants and the

McGraw, in the Giants' 1916 "prison-striped" uniforms, poses with Philadelphia Phillies manager Pat Moran. As manager of the Cincinnati Reds, Moran passed away prior to the 1924 season from Bright's Disease.

first-place Philadelphia Phillies at the Baker Bowl. Trailing the Phillies by one-half game, the Giants won the lidlifter, 4–3, plating all unearned runs. Jeff Tesreau (7–1) was the victor, aided by Slim Sallee's four-inning relief. Pete Alexander was the undeserving loser. The Giants lost the nightcap, 6–5, in 11 innings. The next day, the Giants completed the five-game set with a 4–2 triumph. The 35–21 New Yorkers moved back into the first place and never relinquished the position again.

Over the rest of the summer, the Giants began separating themselves from the rest of the league. In mid–August, a write-up in the *Pittsburgh Press* alluded to McGraw's purported influence in the league when it came to trades. The paper indicated that the Pirates, after returning prospect George Kelly to the Giants a day earlier, were the only

National League team without a former Giant on its roster. It also leveled a common and legitimate gripe frequently heard for decades to come concerning certain affluent New York ball clubs: "Many a manager develops a team with one or two weak spots, but he is not able to secure the one or two men needed to give him a winner, because he has not the open pocketbook at his disposal which McGraw has behind him."[11]

The last-place Pirates had no one but themselves to blame for giving up Kelly, who would emerge as a star for the Giants in the next few years. Pittsburgh had claimed the young first baseman on waivers from the Giants only three weeks earlier, further proving the difficulty of judging young talent.

Another player returned to the Giants the same way as Kelly was Jim Thorpe. The Giants were forced to accept Thorpe from the unsatisfied Reds on August 23. Also in August, apparently not completely content with his own pitching, McGraw recouped one of the former players he had spread throughout the league. He traded infielder Pete Kilduff to the Chicago Cubs for pitcher Al Demaree.

The Giants entered September with a nine-game advantage over second-place Philadelphia. Barring a collapse, McGraw's sixth flag was all but assured. Before reaping his pennant laurels, McGraw was slapped with an additional $1,000 fine for maligning John Tener in the aftermath of the earlier suspension. The punitive sum was in response to the New York BBWAA's petition filing in June. The somewhat contradictory league edict absolved the writers of not reporting the truth, but declared it was not proven that McGraw used the specifically quoted words to attack Tener. McGraw was blamed for allowing the writers to publish the offensive report when he had the power from the beginning to suppress it.

As expected, the team clinched the pennant the third week of September. The Phillies, who used only *seven* pitchers all season long, came in second for the second year in a row, ten games behind the Giants. Scoring the most runs in the league (635), and backed by the second-best team batting average (.261), the Giants completed a quick reversal of fortune from last to first in two seasons.

The World Series opened on Saturday, October 6, three days after the Giants concluded a 98–56 campaign. Only five Giants remained from the team's last World Series roster in 1913—Buck Herzog, Art Fletcher, George Burns, Jeff Tesreau and Al Demaree.

The American League representative was the Chicago White Sox, winners of an even 100 games. Comiskey Park hosted the first two games. The White Sox displayed patriotic conviction by donning red, white and blue-striped sanitary socks, eschewing the white stockings that were part of their uniform all season. The team also dotted the large "S" on the left side of their jerseys with white stars and imprinted undulating American flags on each sleeve. Also reflective of broadening nationalistic sentiments, in between innings, collections were conducted for the Bat and Ball Fund for soldiers in France.

In another stark contrast to today's coddling of pitchers, McGraw had Tesreau and Rube Benton throw batting practice prior to Game One, and warmed up both Slim Sallee and Ferdie Schupp before deciding on Sallee (18–7) as the starter. The 32-year-old Sallee was the more experienced southpaw. The White Sox's lineup had two left-handed batters and two switch-hitters, including starting pitcher Eddie Cicotte.

On about as fine a fall day as one can expect during the first week of October in Chicago, Cicotte hurled the first pitch of the game (a called strike) to leadoff hitter George Burns. Both Cicotte and Sallee worked in front of a capacity-filled stadium.

The guest list of big names, among the throng of 32,000 spectators, contained four state supreme court justices, numerous high-ranking community and regional politicians, and recognizable baseball figures from around the country, as well as Judge Kenesaw Mountain Landis, who had (inattentively) presided over the Federal League's lawsuit against organized baseball in 1915.[12]

With his wife Rose and an infant in her lap watching, Cicotte and his so-called "shine ball" bested Sallee and the Giants, 2–1. Each pitcher permitted seven hits. The game-deciding blow was struck in the fourth inning by Oscar "Happy" Felsch. The White Sox center fielder blasted a Sallee offering over the left-center field wall, a 400 foot wallop scarcely seen at Comiskey Park or anywhere. The long hit doubled the home team's early lead. (The Chicago South Side park and Braves Field had the biggest outfields in baseball.)

The World Series had been played on a Sunday only three times, and each time in the autumn showcases held in Chicago (1906, 1908, 1910). In Game Two on October 7 at Comiskey Park, Schupp opposed another White Sox spitballer, Urban "Red" Faber. The White Sox made it three Sabbath Fall Classic victories, in four tries by an Illinois team, when Faber twirled the White Sox to a 7–2 victory. Eddie Collins, Joe Jackson and Buck Weaver, all held hitless the previous day, slashed eight hits and drove in four runs collectively. Schupp started for the Giants and was replaced in the second inning by Fred Anderson, the Giants' top bullpen man, who had led the league in ERA with a 1.44 mark. Anderson was roughed up for four runs on five hits in just two innings of work. Pol Perritt allowed the final Chicago run. A crowd similar to yesterday's was overwhelmingly satisfied with the results.

"I have no excuses to offer," stated NL president John Tener. "New York was outlucked in the first game and beaten fairly [today]. I think Schupp will have his revenge in New York."[13] McGraw tried to remain upbeat. "We had bad breaks in both the games played in Chicago," he said, before making the trip back to New York. "The series is not ended yet. The advantage will be with the Giants in the coming games."[14]

Meanwhile, White Sox manager Clarence Rowland, flush with two victories on his home turf, seemed overly assured about where the Series winners' share would wind up. "My boys were confident from the start," he stated. "With such an advantage as they now possess the big profits are as good as split among them."[15]

McGraw turned to his fourth-winningest pitcher, Rube Benton, to salvage the team's World Series hopes. After an off-day and a rainout on Tuesday, some speculated that the Giants manager would come back with Sallee or Schupp. But McGraw stuck with his previously announced starter for Game Three. All Giants followers were glad McGraw remained true to his original conviction. Benton allowed only seven balls out of the infield, five of which were base hits, in hurling the first World Series shutout by a Giants pitcher not named Mathewson or McGinnity. Benton's 2–0 gem was untarnished by three Giants errors. Right fielder Dave Robertson tallied three hits and scored a run. A non-capacity crowd of 33,616 was present. With the unexpected extra off-day, Rowland elected to start Cicotte. The right-hander pitched well but was outclassed by Benton.

Before retailer Abe Stark placed his celebrated HIT SIGN WIN SUIT promotion at Ebbets Field, tobacco manufacturer Bull Durham sponsored wall advertisements at major and minor league ballparks throughout the country. The placards promised $50 to any player who hit the outfield sign with a batted ball. Prior to Game Four on October 11, Christy Mathewson returned to the field at the Polo Grounds to ceremoniously hand

Benny Kauff a $50 check for hitting the BULL DURHAM sign with a drive earlier in the season at, coincidentally enough, Ebbets Field.

Kauff shortly outdid his precise hitting in the Brooklyn ballpark that day with a two-homer game on the big stage against the White Sox. Backing Ferdie Schupp's 5–0 win, Kauff drove in three runs, becoming the third player in World Series history to clock two four-baggers in one Fall Classic game. (The others were Pat Dougherty, 1903, and Harry Hooper, 1915.) One of Kauff's home runs was an inside-the-parker. Surprisingly, fewer than 28,000 fans showed up on a clear and not unseasonably cool day. The diehards were treated to the first-rate exhibitions of pitching and hitting by Schupp and Kauff. Schupp allowed seven hits and whiffed a like amount. Red Faber took the loss for Chicago.

Beating in back-to-back encounters the two pitchers who had put them in a 2–0 hole, the Giants had completely shifted the momentum of the Series in their favor, even as they were scheduled to return to Chicago for the fifth game. McGraw had ditched his "prison striped" uniforms with "inverted soup tureen caps" for more traditional garb to start the season. The Giants went back to the narrow pinstripes for both home and away attire. Their road uniforms were battleship gray with an arched NEW YORK lettering across the front. The uniform color matched the team's somber mood after the pivotal game.

On the off-day before the Series resumed on October 13, a cold front passed through Chicago, bringing snow flurries to the city. Although a sunny day, the fifth game was played in frigid conditions. The inhospitable weather knocked attendance down by about 5,000 from the two previous Windy City meetings. A well-rested Slim Sallee started for the Giants and was rather effective for six innings, allowing two runs. The Giants jumped on Chicago's starter, Ewell "Reb" Russell, for two quick runs in the first. George Burns led off with a walk, Buck Herzog singled, and Benny Kauff doubled Burns home. Sox manager Rowland pulled Russell, fourth on the White Sox's pitching depth chart, and brought in Eddie Cicotte. The AL ERA champ (1.53) permitted another run to score (charged to Russell) before getting out of the inning. Pitching in his third game in eight days, Cicotte yielded two more runs (one earned) in six innings and then gave way to Claude "Lefty" Williams. The Giants scratched across a run against Williams (17–8) in the top of the seventh frame to increase their lead to 5–2. But in the bottom half of the inning, Chicago tied the score on three hits and an error by Herzog. The second baseman muffed a relay throw when Ray Schalk tried to steal second with a man on third base. Schalk was awarded a stolen base, with Arnold "Chick" Gandil scoring on the play.

Prior to the game, besides Sallee, McGraw warmed up Rube Benton, Pol Perritt, Jeff Tesreau, Fred Anderson and Al Demaree. With all these pitchers available, and although Sallee had surrendered a three-run lead in the previous inning and had allowed five runs, ten hits and four walks.... McGraw allowed Sallee to come out for the eighth. A leadoff hit, sac bunt, two more singles and a throwing error by Heinie Zimmerman plated two go-ahead runs. As if he had been frozen by the weather conditions, only then did McGraw overcome his outward immobility and turn to his bullpen to relieve his battered starter. Perritt permitted an inherited runner to score. Red Faber, who had replaced Williams to start the top half of the eighth, retired the six Giants he faced, and the White Sox won, 8–5.

Behind closed doors, Charles Comiskey had lost the coin flip to decide where the seventh game, if needed, was to be played. Comiskey called "heads," but the half-dollar came up "tails." After Game Six, the coin flip became a moot point.

Nevertheless, the best day of the 1917 World Series, weather-wise, greeted the players and fans of both teams at the Polo Grounds on Monday, October 15. The warm and sunny day helped generate the Series' largest attendance, 33,969. Rube Benton was called on once more by McGraw to rescue the Giants. Clarence Rowland, who used all four of his starters in Game Five, picked Red Faber to try and clinch it.

The game was decided in the fourth inning. The Giants made two errors and botched a rundown play that allowed a run to cross the plate. Zimmerman, who hit .120 in the six games (3-for-25), committed one of the two miscues and was chiefly involved in the badly executed rundown. (The Giants third baseman endured, on both sides of the ball, one of the worst World Series played by a single player in history.) The White Sox scored three runs, all unearned, before the Giants could record three outs. It was all the runs Faber would need. The Pale Hose pitcher completed a 4–2 victory, his third win of the Series (one in relief). He stumbled only in the fifth, when he was reached for a two-run triple by Buck Herzog. In relief of Benton, Pol Perritt hurled the last four innings and gave up the final Chicago run.

"I knew Faber could do it," proclaimed winning manager Rowland, while revealing designs for the unnecessary seventh game. "I wanted the sixth game badly, but even if we lost I am sure we could have won with Cicotte working in the seventh [game]."[16] Counting his World Series victory in Game One, the 33-year-old Cicotte won 29 games for Chicago in 1917 and pitched over 400 innings, if spring training is included.

More than a decade since his last Fall Classic victory, Charles Comiskey conveyed satisfaction in his post-celebratory comments. "I feel well rewarded for my 11 years of patiently waiting for a world series," he said, "and no praise can be too much for my team."[17]

After the final out, McGraw could be seen graciously shaking hands with White Sox players on the field, including his counterpart. The first person he sought out was Eddie Collins, who had earned McGraw's

McGraw and three-time World Series foe Eddie Collins (1911, 1913, 1917). As evidenced by his gesture, McGraw respected Collins and called him the game's best player on more than one occasion.

respect with his play in two prior World Series with Philadelphia. "I'm glad to congratulate the White Sox," McGraw said afterward. "Chicago has a well-balanced ball club, owned by a man who is a credit to the national game. I don't think my boys played quite the ball of which they are capable. But this is not the time to mention that. I hope we may meet again."[18]

The winning league's president now had four consecutive World Series triumphs over his former unrelenting antagonist. Privately, that must have provided him with a sense of nose-tweaking pride. Publicly, he stayed true to the high road his position demanded. "We are naturally elated over the victory for the American League," Ban Johnson said. "I think congratulations are due both teams."[19]

Three months before the 1918 season began, McGraw made his first trade of the winter. He parted ways with the man who, a year and a half earlier, he had called "the finest third baseman in the game"—Buck Herzog. For the third time in his career, Herzog, who had been named captain by McGraw, was shipped away from New York. The 32-year-old infielder was bothered by a bad back the past season, limiting him to 113 games. He hit only .235. But he continued to back down to no one, including the stern Giants manager. Herzog even stood toe to toe with Ty Cobb in a fight the two walking matchsticks had the previous spring. "I hate his guts," McGraw had said about Herzog, "but I want him on my club."[20]

But not when you are not hitting, apparently. And not when you publicly challenge your boss more than once. In 1916, Herzog had strongly disagreed with McGraw's contention that some of the players were not giving 100 percent in the final series versus Brooklyn. After the Giants had all but sewed up the 1917 pennant, Herzog had requested time away from the team, to rest his back for the World Series. McGraw refused, and Herzog deserted the team (for the second time in his career, doing so previously in 1909). McGraw suspended him. Herzog also questioned, in the press, McGraw's handling of Slim Sallee in the fifth contest of the World Series, saying he had lobbied McGraw, during the game, to remove the ineffective pitcher.

Herzog, therefore, had to go. He was sent packing to the Boston Braves for Larry Doyle and pitcher Jesse Barnes on January 8. Doyle had been part of the Braves organization for only a few days. On January 4, he had been included in a multi-player exchange with the Chicago Cubs.

Doyle was acquired to take the place of the military-enlisted Rabbit Maranville. McGraw had originally proposed pitcher Dick Rudolph and Doyle for Herzog. But George Stallings refused to part with Rudolph. As the record will prove, McGraw and the Giants would be filled with eternal gratitude that Stallings did not kill the deal as a result. Instead, Stallings offered 25-year-old pitcher Jesse Barnes, a 21-game loser but with an ERA well under three. The compromise speaks to Herzog's stature in the league. Stallings did not have to make the deal. He could have stood pat with the well-proven Doyle and kept Barnes, who appeared in 50 games, 33 as a starter.

Three months later, though, the accepted trade remained in the balance. Known as a tough negotiator when it came to salary, Herzog delayed in signing with the Braves. Despite spending all of spring camp with the Giants, Doyle and Barnes would have to be returned if the Braves and Herzog could not come to terms. The former player-manager inked a contract with Boston only hours before Opening Day.

"I am very glad to have Larry Doyle back with our team," said McGraw about the transaction. "He still can play good ball, and I would not have let him go in 1916 if I could have obtained Zimmerman in some other way."[21] It could be supposed that Doyle, though perhaps no longer youthfully impassioned at 31 years of age, still felt "great" about being a Giant once again. Less than two weeks later, McGraw left for Cuba. "The players are all satisfied," he stated prior to leaving, "and there will be no holdouts. With Doyle back and Barnes added to the staff, the New York club will be in the race from the start."[22]

McGraw plainly did not check with all of his players. It was reported in the *Pittsburgh Press* on February 24, and in other papers the next day, that he had to cut short his vacation in Havana to address the holdout problem of his team. Top players such as George Burns, Art Fletcher, Dave Robertson, Ferdie Schupp, Slim Sallee and Pol Perritt were all seeking better salaries than first offered.

Harry Hempstead personally invited New York native Burns to the Giants' Fifth Avenue offices to hammer out a deal, while McGraw took to the road to meet with the other unhappy athletes. McGraw traveled to the home states of Fletcher (Illinois), Schupp (Kentucky), and Sallee (Ohio), to convince the players to resign with the team. From Shreveport, Louisiana, a disillusioned Pol Perritt stated that he was preparing to take a job selling automobiles rather than play for the Giants' initial salary offer and that McGraw would be wasting his time coming to see him unless he wanted to buy a car. Long before players had agents working on their behalf, posturings in the press, such as Perritt's, were the standard negotiation tools used. Perritt subsequently put off his sales job, signed with New York, and became the club's top winner (18–13) of 1918.

One trip that was not fruitful for the trekking manager was to Norfolk, Virginia. McGraw and outfielder Dave Robertson could not come to terms. Following the impasse, the two-time home run champion and the Giants' leading hitter in the recently concluded World Series announced that he was pursuing a career as an agent in the Justice Department. Before the NL champions broke training camp, McGraw placed the man he had called "the most valuable single player" in the league less than two years earlier on the voluntarily retired list.

As luck would have it for Robertson, a shining new outfield prodigy emerged that spring in camp. The player's name was Ross Youngs, and he made Giants fans quickly forget about Robertson. Youngs, the under-the-radar Western Association purchase of 1916, had played in seven big league games in 1917. He had led the International League in hitting and stolen bases prior to being called up in September. A left-handed batter, Youngs turned 21 six days before the Giants' season began on April 16.

In their first season opener at home since 1915, the Giants defeated the Brooklyn Robins, 6–4. Batting leadoff, the speedy Youngs collected two hits and scored the Giants' first run in the first inning. Fred Anderson picked up the win, spelling Jeff Tesreau. The drum corps of the Pelham Bay Naval Reserves and a brass band from neighboring Fort Slocum provided the pre-game pomp, on a temperate spring day for nearly 30,000 attendees. Larry Doyle received the biggest cheers prior to the engagement. The first pitch was delivered by General William A. Mann, who had delivered the U.S. 42nd Division to France last winter. The 42nd, also known as the Rainbow Division, would be a heavily engaged and impactful fighting force on battle fields of western Europe in the upcoming months.

The Giants won their next eight games, lost to Brooklyn, and then reeled off nine more wins in a row. The 18–1 commencement to the season was the best by a McGraw-led Giants team. The unsustainable start tapered off, and the Giants finished May with a 25–11 mark, good enough for first place but only a game and a half ahead of the Chicago

Cubs. Newcomers Youngs and Barnes had as much to do with the Giants' fine early show-
ing as anyone. Youngs was hitting .329 with a .381 OBP, having started every one of the
Giants' 36 games. The right-handed Barnes was 6–1, with two shutouts and an ERA under
two. It was also Barnes' final ledger on the campaign, as he was inducted into the U.S.
Army before the end of the month. Earlier in May, Rube Benton had been called into
Uncle Sam's league.

The Giants were also dealt a blow with the loss of Doyle the first week of May. The
second baseman was tearing up the circuit with a .426 average and slugging over .700
when he was stricken by an illness. Originally thought to be a severe strain of the flu,
intestinal abscesses were eventually diagnosed. The colon disorder prevented his return
until July. The injury gave a second Havana signee of McGraw, José Rodríguez, a chance
to show his stuff at the big league level. But the Cuban (the franchise's first Hispanic
position player in 1916) could not hit a lick. The Giants claimed Bert Niehoff from the
waiver wire to add infield depth, but the former St. Louis Cardinals infielder was severely
injured after only seven games. The injury, sustained in a collision with Ross Youngs and
resulting in a fractured tibia, ended the 34-year-old Niehoff's major league career.

The Great War in Europe had not affected the National Pastime until this year.
Major league rosters had been depleted by more than 60 player enlistments—with more
to come. On May 27, the U.S. Federal Government announced intentions to increase
immediately passenger taxes on train fares. It was a blow to the traveling expenses of the
baseball owners, who had been jarred a week earlier with the War Department's "Work
or Fight Order." The national decree, effective July 1, mandated all males eligible for the
draft must be employed in war-related industry or face being drafted.

Pol Perritt, the would-be car salesman, took up the pitching mantle from the
departed Barnes. In front of 25,000 strong, the biggest crowd since Opening Day, the
right-hander won his sixth game in the first game of a Polo Grounds doubleheader on
Saturday, June 8. Defeating the St. Louis Cardinals, Perritt scattered seven hits and walked
one. In the afterpiece, Slim Sallee lost an 11-inning, 4–2 decision. Ross Youngs dropped
a fly ball in right field with two men on base to allow the deciding runs to score. Youngs
fell down on the play, and McGraw presented an unwelcome case to Lord Byron that
Youngs had held the ball long enough for a legal catch. The arbiter was not willing to
hear all of McGraw's overwrought arguments and excused him from the rest of the game.
An empty bottle, heaved from the second deck, landed near Byron in the aftermath.
(McGraw protested the game but it was later turned down by league head Tener.)

With the Giants still reluctant, or unable, to entertain Sunday baseball, the next
game in the series was scheduled for Monday, June 10. The contest was postponed because
of a threat of rain. The *Evening World* ran a headline on June 11 that read: M'GRAW HAD
HOT RACE TIP, SO THE GAME WAS CALLED OFF. "There may have been other reasons
for the Giant management deciding not to play the final game of the St. Louis series yesterday," Hugh S. Fullerton wrote, "but the fact that the limousine was waiting and that
McGraw raced for it with a hot tip on Superhuman and Wise Joan may indicate that
there are things more important than baseball."[23] Fullerton advised that no sufficient
amount of rain fell on the Polo Grounds to have stopped play, if it had begun, and that
Wise Joan was a winner.

Less than two weeks later, Benny Kauff answered the call to the colors. He played
his thought-to-be last game at Ebbets Field on June 22. Prior to the contest, the quotable
player was presented with a gold wrist watch by John McGraw. Eleanor Brush Hempstead

also gave Kauff a watch. "If I lose one arm over there, I'll still be able to tell time,"[24] morbidly commented Kauff.

Jim Thorpe filled in the majority of the time in Kauff's absence.

Through the unusual upheaval of players, McGraw kept an eye on the future. On the recommendation of old St. Louis teammate Jesse Burkett, McGraw signed Holy Cross pitcher Wilfred "Rosy" Ryan. Burkett was currently the baseball coach at the Worchester, Massachusetts, college, which happened to be located in Ryan's hometown.

As the "Work or Fight Order" neared, the Giants closed June with a 41–20 record. Eleven game-winner Pol Perritt (against only two losses) carried the team from the mound. Youngs continued to distinguish himself, along with outfield cohort George Burns. Only the Chicago Cubs, holding a 42–18 mark, bettered McGraw's bunch in the National League.

In the middle of July, the Giants lost one of their stalwart pitchers. Jeff Tesreau abruptly left the club. He had not pitched in more than five weeks and indicated he had expected McGraw to ask waivers on him. The strapping right-hander went to work for Bethlehem Steel and pitched in the industrial giant's internal baseball league. Tesreau, 30, was in "Class 4" of the Army draft, signifying a low chance at selection into service. His record was 5–4 at the time, and he may have thought his best days were behind him or had other personal justifications. The two-time 20-game winner never pitched in the major leagues again, eventually establishing himself as a long-tenured Ivy League baseball coach.

A few days after Tesreau's desertion, McGraw purchased pitcher Fred Toney from the Cincinnati Reds for an undisclosed amount of cash. A few days after that, the Giants absorbed their final Selective Service loss. On July 25, first baseman Walter Holke was called up by his St. Louis draft board. He followed Tesreau to Bethlehem Steel instead.

For the entire month, the Giants could manage no better than a .500 brand of baseball in 32 games, but stayed in pennant contention. The National League became a two-team race between McGraw's squad and the first-place Cubs, holding a 3½-game advantage on July 31. All other teams faced double-digit deficits.

Facing the national edict that would deplete their rosters and thereby decimate their product, major league baseball owners appealed to the Judge Advocate General of the United States Army, Enoch Crowder, to consider their sport's special mainstream place in America. The JAG officer was the administrative head of the U.S. Selective Service Act of 1917. With petitions pointing out that "baseball is the national game" and "it furnishes amusement and healthy recreation to a large portion of the war worried people,"[25] the sport succeeded in belaying Crowder's order and extending their operations.

The baseball magnates had proposed three solutions: simply ending the season on September 1; closing down on September 2 (Labor Day) and then playing the World Series; or release their eligible players on September 1, recruit younger players to complete the season, and proceed with the scheduled World Series in October. (Many of the prospects could be had from lower-level minor leagues, many of which had ceased or would be ceasing operations.) Receiving the blessing of U.S. Secretary of War Newton Baker, a compromise to the "Crowder order" was reached—the baseball season would be cut short by more than a month and the earliest World Series in history would follow.

That World Series did not involve the Giants, as a 14–17 finish to the abridged campaign left the New Yorkers with record of 71–53, a distant 10½ games behind the Cubs.

As a final footnote to the season, Benny Kauff received a 15-day furlough from the service in mid–August and spent the free time playing for the Giants. He played in 13 games, with his average dipping from .324 to .315. Kauff's curtailed number of at-bats excluded him from consideration in the batting championship.

The merciful end of World War I in November 1918 assured the continuance of baseball on its traditional level for 1919. Owners, to save money and try to recoup losses from last season, shorted the schedule to 140 games. Thinking of their own wallets and underestimating the public, the magnates were anticipating not being able to draw as many fans as a residue of the war's effect. They were badly—and gladly—mistaken. Even taking into account that most teams played fewer than 130 games in 1918, attendance in 1919 soared.

The Giants vastly increased their turnstile count by more than 450,000 from the prior season to 708,857—the franchise's best showing in ten years. Albeit hampered by only 54 home dates dates in 1918, Ebbets Field more than quadrupled its patronage to 360,721. The Giants, with the size advantage of the Polo Grounds, and the Chicago Cubs, with their large population base, usually ran 1–2 in the National League attendance charts. In 1919, the Cincinnati Reds, pulling in more than three times their total from a year ago, with a figure of 532,501, placed ahead of the Cubs but behind the Giants. The Ohio fan enthusiasm was in direct correlation to the team's grand performance on the field. The Reds captured the pennant with relative ease, posting a stupendous 96–44 record and .686 winning percentage. The Giants, no slouches themselves, accruing a .621 winning clip with an 87–53 mark, ended up nine games back, nevertheless. No other NL club finished within 21 games of first place.

McGraw began the new year with a trade that he hoped would solidify his catching position in the years to come. Two days into January, he struck a deal with minor league Rochester for Earl Smith. The 22-year-old backstop had been a sensation in the past International League season. McGraw gave up four players, plus cash, to acquire Smith. One of the trading chips was pitcher Waite Hoyt. The former teenage signee had debuted in July 1918 for New York; he pitched one inning, faced three batters and struck out two of them. McGraw sent him down to Newark for more seasoning. Hoyt did not take kindly to the demotion. During the past few seasons, he had been shipped to Hartford, Memphis, Montreal, and Nashville. Still only 19, the headstrong youngster had apparently had his fill of the minor leagues. Probably swayed as well by the looming national conscription order, Hoyt left the professional ranks and became a member of the Baltimore Dry Docks, a baseball shipyard team. Still claiming ownership of the young pitcher, the Giants included Hoyt in the package for Smith. But Hoyt refused the minor league assignment to Rochester and another to New Orleans, and went back to Baltimore. While pitching for the Dry Docks later in 1919, Hoyt happened to shut out the Cincinnati Reds in an exhibition game. The Boston Red Sox became aware of him and bought his rights from the Giants.

Hoyt was practically forgotten, two weeks after the trade to Rochester, when McGraw elevated his place within the New York Giants organization by purchasing, along with two others, a controlling interest in the team. The sale of the National Exhibition Company was agreed to by Harry Hempstead, who released the following statement on January 13:

> This day I have in conjunction with N.A. Lloyd, co-executor and trustee of the estate of John T. Brush, passed the stock to Charles A. Stoneham, Francis X. McQuade and John J. McGraw.... I have many regrets indeed, but I feel it was for the better interests of the estate and those

dependent upon it to accept the offer of Mr. Stoneham and his associates. It is fitting to say that in releasing the club that it continues in the hands of Mr. McGraw, who will be advanced to part ownership in the organization.[26]

As the principal buyers, McGraw was given the vice-presidency of the team and McQuade, who was a New York lower court judge, the treasurer's post. Stoneham, a Wall Street stockbroker and the biggest shareholder, assumed the presidency. The sale price was announced at $1,000,000—by far the largest sum paid for any sports team. For McGraw, it was a defining career moment combined with an ultimate personal achievement. "It has long been the ambition of the Little Napoleon to take a hand in the business end of baseball and there was no happier a man in the vicinity of Peacock Alley last night than John Joseph, who has finally seen his dream come true,"[27] analyzed one New York writer. The final transaction saw the appointment of a seven-man Board of Directors. Apart from the three main men, who all knew each other, the others were: Ross F. Peterson, John Whalen, Leo Bundy and Horace C. Stoneham, son of the principal buyer.

Many newspapers anticipated that there could be a new Giants manager, with McGraw leaving the field to assume his new executive position. Pat Moran, fired by the Phillies and recently hired by McGraw as a coach, was the name most bandied about. Another was Christy Mathewson, who was awaiting his imminent discharge from the chemical warfare service of the army. Mathewson had resigned from the Reds toward the end of 1918 to serve his country and was not expected to return to Cincinnati. But McGraw, soon enough, dispelled any notions that he would not be returning to the Giants' dugout. On January 31, he gave Pat Moran permission to negotiate with the Cincinnati Reds for their vacant managerial chair. On the surface, it seemed like a goodwill gesture on the part of McGraw, but he was seeking something in return.

On Valentine's Day, the Captain Edward L. Grant Memorial Association was formed in New York, for the purpose of erecting a "fitting memorial" to honor the fallen war hero. The former Giant, Grant was killed in battle on October 4, 1918, in the Argonne Forest in France. Spearheading the memorial drive, McGraw was aptly named president of the association. Other members included both major leagues' presidents, several members of the Giants' Board of Directors, New York Yankees co-owners Colonel Jacob Ruppert and Colonel T.L. Huston, and Clark Griffith, Grant's manager at Cincinnati. The Giants contributed $200, and an additional $300 was pledged from various baseball patrons on the day.

Five days afterward, McGraw traded veteran catcher Bill Rariden and first baseman Walter Holke to the Cincinnati Reds for checkered former star Hal Chase. Upon examination, it was one of McGraw's most head-scratching moves. Holke was in McGraw's doghouse for bolting from the team last summer to join the essential work force. Apart from that, first sacker Chase was currently a walking toxin to any big league ball club. A known collaborator with gamblers, Chase had strayed from the path that had led him to an elevated degree of stardom years earlier. He had been suspended by manager Mathewson the first week of August 1918 for "indifferent play" in a game in which evidence later pointed to his willingness to tank his own efforts to the detriment of his team.

Garry Herrmann backed Mathewson and accused Chase of "letting up" in several games. John Heydler, who became president of the National League in 1918, found no substantive proof to implicate Chase in the gambling conspiracy hearing that followed. (Mathewson was overseas and could not testify against Chase.) Heydler's ruling, a smack in the face of the National Commission chair, Herrmann, cleared the way for the trade.

A caveat from the Reds included that the Giants would have to come to some arrangement with Chase on his pending litigation with the Reds. The ballsy Chase, who had not played in a game since his suspension, had filed suit against the Cincinnati club for unpaid salary for the time he was suspended.

"Chase can't be half as hard to handle as Bugs Raymond," said a mitigating McGraw, who knew Chase personally for more than a decade.

> I once gave Raymond a brand new ball and sent him to the warming pit. Three innings later I called for him to come in. [Honus] Wagner met him with a three-bagger that tied the score. I found out too late that Raymond had run out of the Polo Grounds, sold the ball for half a dollar, bought as many drinks as he could, and came back to the game. There never was a troublemaker like him.[28]

By the end of the season, Chase made McGraw reconsider this last statement.

On March 7, the return of the Giants' first 20th-century icon was publicized. Christy Mathewson agreed to come back to the Giants in the coach's spot Pat Moran had left to take over managing duties with the Cincinnati Reds. "He merits in every particular the love and affection New York has ever been pleased to lavish upon him, even during the few seasons he was associated with a rival club," said a sincere McGraw. The Giants manager also made everyone privy to his intentions for the future, adding, "I cannot begin to tell you how much I have always appreciated Mathewson. To him I feel I can safely entrust the management of the club when I seek the repose of my physical craves."[29]

With the season fast approaching, McGraw's pitching was not altogether settled. Slim Sallee further muddied things when he threatened his retirement during contract negotiations. It was not as personal an indictment of McGraw and the Giants organization as one might think. McGraw placed Sallee, only 8–8 last season, on waivers. The Giants' most active off-season trading partner, the Cincinnati Reds, claimed the left-handed pitcher, providing a near-perfect fit for the Higginsport, Ohio native. Sallee, much to McGraw's chagrin, became a 20-game victor for a dominant Reds staff of six primary pitchers that also included a pair of 19-game winners.

From Shreveport, McGraw's top pitcher from last year, Pol Perritt, boasted to the press that he was making too much money in the "oil business" to consider inferior baseball wages. Perritt was placed on the holdout list. This left McGraw—surprisingly—with only one established hurler on his staff as the season neared its opening on April 23. And that pitcher, Rube Benton, was coming off a sparse pitching year (only two starts) due to military service.

Ferdie Schupp, who had injured his arm following the 1917 World Series and had not contributed to the Giants since, was still a question mark. McGraw was counting on Jesse Barnes, but Barnes possessed a losing record (28–37) after four big league campaigns entering the 1919 season. A day before Barnes threw the first pitch of Opening Day, McGraw purchased former Detroit Tigers right-hander Jean Dubuc from the Pacific Coast League. Dubuc, a Vermont native, was used primarily out of the bullpen. The Giants used 19 pitchers on the season, a number much more reflective of baseball in the 21st century than in 1919. Based on the Giants' outstanding record, McGraw should be recognized for possibly the most skillful generalship of his career. Barnes posted a career year at 25–9, Benton won 17 games, and Fred Toney, a pitcher McGraw re-signed in May, notched 13 victories. The other 32 team victories were divided among ten other hurlers.

The case of Toney was an atypical one, to say the least. Over the winter, he was given a four-month jail term at the Robertson County Detention Facility in Nashville, Tennessee, for violating the Mann Act. The pitcher had previously run afoul of the Selective Service office over alleged draft dodging. Toney had become a persona non grata in the Queen City, due to his immoral behavior (and 6–10 record), which preceded his purchase by McGraw the prior summer. Following his acquisition, the right-hander went 6–2 with a 1.69 ERA in nine August starts and two relief appearances, for the Giants. McGraw, understandably, wanted him back.

The Giants pilot sent scout and former American League player Herman "Germany" Schaefer to Tennessee in May to await Toney's prison release. Hired just this year by the Giants, Schaefer succeeded in inking Toney and was also instrumental in re-signing Pol Perritt the same month. Unlike Toney, Perritt was of no help to his team. Out of shape and badly ineffective, he quit the Giants in August, owning a 1–1 record and 7.11 ERA, in only 19 innings. Over the next two seasons, the disinterested Perritt put in similar cameo performances for the Giants and Detroit Tigers, before retiring. Parenthetically, Schaefer, who was on the Giants' coaching lines on Opening Day, died suddenly of a hemorrhage while on his way to upstate New York on May 16. He had received time off from the Giants and was traveling to Lake Saranac to rest and appease an existing tuberculosis condition. Some news outlets linked his death (erroneously) to influenza, which over a three-year span, 1918–1920, reached pandemic proportions and shudderingly killed approximately 650,000 Americans. It was a sad end for the 43-year-old Schaefer, who had been part of McGraw's around-the-world trip and had been known for his crowd-pleasing hijinks on the field.

A week before Opening Day, the major leagues were dealt a blow from the Baltimore Federal League lawsuit. The Supreme Court of the District of Columbia awarded $80,000 to the Terrapins' shareholders, increased to $240,000 by the presiding judge under the treble damages statute.

The Giants' inaugural home series of 1919 was a three-game set over the weekend of May 2–4. In the home opener, the president of New York's board of aldermen, Robert L. Moran, was privileged with throwing out the first ball. Giving up only two runs, Jesse Barnes coasted to his second win of the campaign. The Giants lashed out 16 hits and dented the plate 14 times—all against Philadelphia Phillies starter Milt "Mule" Watson, who pitched all eight innings. Benny Kauff cheerily returned to the Polo Grounds for the first time since his Army discharge. He doubled and drove in three runs. Hal Chase, in his first time donning the Giants home colors, managed a hit and scored two runs. Horace Stoneham contentedly presided over his first home inaugural victory, in the presence of 22,000 other fans.

After winning, 4–3, the following day, the Metropolis men came out for the sweep on May 4. Unlike years past, Sunday was no longer a statutory day of rest for players in the Empire State. New York fell in step with Illinois, Missouri and Ohio and legalized the playing of Sunday baseball throughout the state. The said-to-be largest non–World Series crowd in Polo Grounds history, approximately 35,000 people, came out to support the new measure resoundingly. A gorgeous spring day did not hurt the occasion. (Across the river in Brooklyn, Ebbets Field recorded its largest gathering—25,000—save for the 1916 Fall Classic.) The Phillies spoiled the day, winning their only game in the series, 4–3. For most of the contest, John McGraw coached at first base and Christy Mathewson manned the lines at third. But in the eighth inning, when the Giants loaded the bases with no one out, the men traded places. Failing at a chance for a big inning, the Giants scored only one run, on a bases-loaded walk. Rube Benton took the loss for the home team.

A few days later, McGraw sought to settle two open matters. With Rochester acquisition George Smith not ready to step in as a full-time catcher, the team architect attempted a trade that would upgrade the current deficiency and simultaneously close another unresolved situation. The dual issues were gnawing enough for McGraw to leave his team for a day, on May 8, and travel to Pittsburgh to meet up with Branch Rickey, who was in town with his St. Louis Cardinals.

McGraw proposed to the Cardinals manager a three-way deal in which the Giants would acquire catcher Mike González from Rickey's club, shortstop John "Doc" Lavan would be sent to the Cardinals from the Washington Senators, and the latter club would receive McGraw's former power-hitting, outfielder-turned-civil servant Dave Robertson. But four unnamed National League owners reportedly blocked the transaction on the grounds of not wanting to lose a player of Robertson's caliber to the American League. Ironically, Robertson, who had reluctantly come back to the Giants, made his only appearance of the season with the team (as a pinch-runner) in the game McGraw missed on May 8. A few days after Doc Lavan was sold to the Cardinals, Mike González conveniently cleared waivers and McGraw snatched him.

Blessed with the best outfield in the league again (Burns, Youngs and Kauff), Robertson was traded to the Chicago Cubs two and a half months later, after leaving the team. "I agreed to sign a contract with the Giants under the belief I was to be traded or sold to the Washington club," said Robertson after arriving at his home in Norfolk. "I had no intention of playing with the New York club then, and I have no intention now. So, I'm quitting. I shall never again play with the Giants."[30] Robertson agreed to play for the Chicago Cubs. In return, McGraw received a hard-throwing right-hander named Phil Douglas. The July 25 trade would reap greater rewards for McGraw than his trading partner.

McGraw's team moved into first place in May and held the position through the end of June. But the pitching-rich Reds passed them for good at the beginning of August. The Giants were in the process of being overtaken when McGraw again engaged in a player exchange. Ranking as one of the best deals he ever swung, McGraw acquired left-hander Art Nehf from the Boston Braves for four below-average players and $55,000. The deal for the five-year veteran was consummated on August 1, a day after Nehf's 27th birthday.

The runner-up finish to Cincinnati in 1919 was soured as the season was winding down. On September 15, with the Giants eight games behind the Reds, McGraw skipped out on the team in Cincinnati. It was originally reported that McGraw left the club in the hands of Christy Mathewson so that he could travel to Texas to make arrangements for next year's spring training. The truth would eventually come out after McGraw sped home to huddle with Charles Stoneham. McGraw was concerned with addressing revelations of "game-fixing" swirling around two of his players, Heinie Zimmerman and Hal Chase. In this, the year of the "Black Sox" World Series, the fact that McGraw thought it was more important to get ahead of this potentially dirty state of affairs than it was to stay with his team, demonstrated the susceptible state of the game to nefarious forces.

Zimmerman had been suspended indefinitely by McGraw on September 11, on the road trip's previous stop. The reason given was "curfew violation." But the sanctioned third baseman met with his bosses in New York, all but confessing his unscrupulous behavior and undeniably implicating Chase as well.

Chase had performed questionably during a key series with Cincinnati during the first week of August, and he and Zimmerman periodically attempted to bribe teammates thereafter, until word finally reached McGraw. Chase would not be disciplined within the organization and escaped public reprimand again. But both baseball cads never wore a major league uniform after this season. The dubiously nicknamed "Prince Hal" remained with the Giants after McGraw's departure, a situation acting manager Mathewson must have found extremely awkward, given his past history with the first baseman.

Chase, however, did not bother to show up for the final day of the campaign, September 28, at the Polo Grounds. He missed the fastest nine-inning game in major league history. In the first game of a doubleheader, Jesse Barnes grabbed his 25th victory, defeating the Philadelphia Phillies, 6–1, in an elapsed time of only 51 minutes. Belying the short duration were the number of runs scored and 18 total hits made, along with three walks issued. There were two double plays, both by the Phillies.

McGraw also was not present for the game. He never rejoined his club after leaving it in Cincinnati in mid–Steptember. As in 1916, when he turned his back on his men with a pair of games to play, his extended absence from the team this time around can only be described as inexcusable behavior for a man in his position. On the surface, his abandonment would suggest that he was trying to distance himself from potential scandal. There does not seem to be any other message that he could have been sending other than self-preservation. It was a weak performance—especially in his (non-) handling of Chase—from an otherwise tough man.

McGraw wrote a syndicated column from New York during the World Series and then left for Cuba with Charles Stoneham immediately afterward.

SIX

A Second Eluded Dynasty

"McGraw just sat sphinxlike on the New York bench with arms folded."—
Harold Burr, *Brooklyn Daily Eagle*

"They are going to have a tough time getting that boy out of there," said Johnny Evers. "I have seen many of them get their start the same way. Good ones like this lad seldom go back to the bench."[1] The celebrated former infielder was speaking about Frank Francis Frisch in August of 1919. On the recommendation of its college baseball coach and former Giants third baseman Art Devlin, Frisch had been signed off the Fordham University campus months earlier. He had gotten a chance to play due to a leg injury to Larry Doyle. Heinie Zimmerman's suspension opened the way for more playing time for the 20-year-old Bronx native toward the end of the season.

The veteran Giants infield of 1919 underwent a near-complete overhaul for 1920. Thirty-six-year-old Hal Chase and 32-year-old Heinie Zimmerman were gone for good. Art Fletcher, 35, was transitioned to back-up shortstop. The life-long Giant had been a rock-solid infield component of the club since becoming a first-stringer in 1911. The Giants' top player (according to 21st century analytics) of the most recent campaign (once again), Fletcher would be displaced following a trade in early June. In that eye-opening exchange with the Philadelphia Phillies, the Giants sent $100,000 to the Phillies for 29-year-old Dave Bancroft, a player to whom McGraw had taken a liking. Larry Doyle hung on to second base. (Fletcher and Doyle's value over the years to the Giants is reflective in their career WAR totals of 42. Only 13 players in franchise history, including San Francisco, have compiled higher ratings.)

The new corner infield men were the aforementioned Frisch, at third base, and George Kelly. The player McGraw lost and then recouped from Pittsburgh in 1917, Kelly played in every one of the Giants' 155 games and paced the circuit in RBI with 94 in his first season as a starter. After waiting in the wings behind Fred Merkle, Walter Holke and Hal Chase, the 24-year-old Kelly and Frisch, 22, simultaneously became starring infield anchors for McGraw over the next half-dozen seasons. The tall drink of water first-sacker was called "Long George" or "High Pockets" throughout his career by the New York press. McGraw finally obtained the steady presence at catcher he had sought. Dealing Ferdie Schupp, whose arm never came around fully, to the St. Louis Cardinals, he secured Frank Snyder. Kelly, Frisch and Snyder, a nine-year veteran, would all participate prominently in the Giants' run at championship glory over the next five years.

The flipping of new calendar pages not only ushered in the 20th century's third decade, but brought with it a rules reform on the diamond that changed the game of baseball for the better and increased its popularity exponentially. Tighter-wound baseballs with better quality yarn were manufactured, and these baseballs traveled farther when struck squarely. The spitball and any application of foreign substances to or defacement of the baseball were outlawed.

McGraw had called the spitter both "dirty and dangerous" back in 1918, when baseball began to contemplate its banning. "My position as regards the spitball is well known. I have always been opposed to it," he said. "It is disgusting, unscientific and dangerous. I was the last manager in the major leagues to sign a spitballer—Jeff Tesreau. Now, we have in addition [Fred] Anderson, but I am in favor of the abolition ... with a year's notice to the pitchers in the league."[2] The pitchers were not given a year's notice, but those known moist-finger men were exempted under a "grandfather clause" in the rule. Now, two years later, Tesreau and Anderson were no longer part of McGraw's pitching staff.

The major leagues also agreed to return to a 154-game schedule, and more new baseballs were introduced into games by umpires to enable them to enforce the "dry ball" and "non-scuffing" mandates. Thus, with the simultaneous emergence of a farther-traveling ball, the eventual extinction of the spitball, and an American League goliath named Babe Ruth, the pitching-dominant Deadball Era gave way to the runs-happy Liveball Era.

The dawn of the Liveball Era broke over New York on April 14, a chilly day at the Polo Grounds that drew 20,000 patrons. Among those in a group of military and civic officers marching on the field during pre-game ceremonies were General Douglas MacArthur and New York Mayor John F. Hylan—the man who signed into law Sunday baseball in New York City last year. In a separate contingent, New Jersey governor Edward Edwards, a staunch opponent of the 18th Amendment, paraded across the field and was met by what the *New York Times* described as a "decidedly anti-prohibitionist reception" by the fans. ("And Oh! Boy! Didn't the crowd enjoy the music," reported the next day's *Daily* News, "as the band played 'How Dry I Am' as Gov. Edward I. Edwards ... entered his box.) MacArthur, accompanied by club director John Whalen, took a seat in a flag-draped box. When the regimental band grew silent, McGraw received a floral horseshoe from silent screen child stars Katherine and Jane Lee. McGraw and Giants players posed for photographs with the Giants' mascot, a baby Texas wildcat named "Bill Pennant." The unusual sight of aeroplanes flying overhead captured much pre-game attention. From a similar box seat location as MacArthur and Whalen, Mayor Hylan threw out the first ball to home plate umpire Hank O'Day. Later in the game, the same umpire visited Braves pitcher Hugh McQuillan on the mound to rebuke him for suspected "doctoring" of the baseball.

With McGraw and Mathewson on the coaching lines, the visiting Boston Braves marred the day for the home folks, tripping up the Giants, 6–3. Done in by a five-run second inning, Jesse Barnes was the starter and loser for New York. Arnold "Jigger" Statz, a year removed from the Holy Cross college campus, drove in two of the Giants' runs. McGraw planned on platooning Statz in center field with Benny Kauff.

The Giants commenced the season with a slow start. They lost Frankie Frisch to appendicitis ten days into the campaign. He was out for nearly eight weeks. Prior to their initial western road junket, McGraw induced Johnny Evers to join the 6–11 club as a coach. Evers had just taken the baseball coaching job at Boston College, but was able to escape the commitment. It was on that first tour away from home that McGraw lapsed into the adverse trend he had developed with the Senior Circuit's top field administrators.

On May 18, McGraw was ejected at Cubs Park by Charlie Moran "for having too much to say, or saying it the wrong way,"[3] in the bottom of the tenth inning, after the Cubs had tied the score at four apiece. In taking out the home team's rally against the umpire, McGraw delayed the game with an extended reluctance to leave the field. The Giants won the extra-inning contest, scoring two runs in the top of the 12th frame, 8–6. Art Nehf was the relief winner.

Judged by the diminished number of ejections McGraw had received over the past three campaigns (four in three seasons), the militant manager had seemingly turned over a new leaf. The previous day, following a tough, extra-inning loss to the Pittsburgh Pirates, McGraw engaged in a diatribe against Bill Klem—after the game. The back-to-back incidents with the umpires brought McGraw his first suspension since 1917. The duration was five days. Evers was given primary control of the team in McGraw's absence.

At the end of May, with the Giants five games under .500, the good luck mascot "Bill Pennant" was released. McGraw gifted him to pitcher Fred Toney, who shipped him to his home in Nashville, Tennessee.

On May 31, a Decoration Day morning-afternoon doubleheader at the Polo Grounds attracted a single-game record crowd. In the first game, 11,500 early birds came out, while the afternoon affair jammed the most people into the Polo Grounds yet—38,688. McGraw and the Giants, meanwhile, were in Brooklyn, playing a twin-bill against the Robins. The tenant New York Yankees, engaging the Washington Senators, were Coogan's Bluff's big draw. Babe Ruth hit a home run in the nightcap against Walter Johnson. (The pinstriped lessees would go on to become the first big league club to attract over 1,000,000 fans in a single season.)

McGraw took ill and left the club for five days, including an off-day. Mathewson was put in charge. McGraw returned on June 6 and "was still a bit shaky and did not don his uniform."[4] McGraw was well enough to consent to the Art Fletcher trade on June 7. He said goodbye to his team captain to obtain Dave Bancroft. Larry Doyle was appointed captain. The same day, Jigger Statz was claimed off waivers by the Boston Red Sox.

Barely two months into the season, it was clear that the new restric-

Opening Day 1920 at the Polo Grounds: McGraw's hands are full with a loving cup and the Giants' baby cheetah mascot named "Bill Pennant." Though overrun with greying hair and baggy eyes, McGraw still manages to flash a boyish smile that hints at youthful times past. Some background players are more captivated by the unusual sight of planes flying overhead than the photographer's lens.

tions placed on pitchers were resulting in many more safe hits and runs since the 1890s. McGraw weighed in on the matter. "The new pitching rules are too drastic," he said. "In my opinion the rule which prevents a pitcher from using resin on their fingers to remove the gloss from the cover of the ball is largely responsible for the fact they are not getting enough stuff on it. So far this season there has been too much slugging—too many home runs. I think the rules should be amended immediately."[5]

On the last day of June, the Giants dropped a home doubleheader to Brooklyn, which curiously was being referred to as the "Dodgers" in most New York newspapers but the *Brooklyn Daily Eagle*. The borough paper uniformly maintained the "Robins" nickname. The Giants slipped to a 30–35 record and were denied any improvement on their seventh-place position in the standings.

Days later, news circulated that coach Christy Mathewson was stepping down permanently, due to bronchial trouble. He would retreat to the same Adirondacks town that Germany Schaefer had attempted to reach before his fatal hemorrhage. By month's end, the release of a shocking report that the famed pitcher had contracted tuberculosis shook baseball to its core. "Baseball has lost the greatest idol it has ever known," reflected one sports diarist over the news. "The big, quiet, slow spoken fellow whose baseball life has inspired tens of thousands of kids and who, by clean sportsmanship made himself the best beloved of players, has quietly left the New York Giants and is seriously ill at Lake Saranac."[6]

Somewhat lost in the initial Mathewson news was the trade of Benny Kauff to the Toronto Maple Leafs for Vern Spencer, a highly-touted center fielder who would flop with the Giants. The colorful Kauff had to clear waivers from every other NL team. Despite his .274 average, a legal cloud was hanging over Kauff from a shared stake in an auto repair business he had locally opened. Although later absolved of any wrongdoing in a court of law, Kauff was not permitted to return to the game by baseball's recently elected first commissioner, Kenesaw Mountain Landis, a decision seen by many as unjust. Intended by McGraw to accompany Kauff was Bill Hubbell. But the right-handed pitcher was claimed by Philadelphia, and the Kauff deal had to be sweetened with cash instead.

On July 16, two pitchers displayed an unwillingness to let go of the pitching-centric past. Rube Benton hurled 17 scoreless innings, finally defeating the Pittsburgh Pirates, 7–0, at Forbes Field. It was only his fourth win, against ten losses, as the left-handed pitcher was experiencing a tough follow-up to his most recent 17–11 campaign. Pirates hurler Earl Hamilton tossed 16 scoreless frames before blowing up in the top of the last stanza. "I feel quite sure that we are getting quite close to our real form," McGraw said prior to leaving Pittsburgh, "and will continue to win regularly."[7] His statement proved correct. The Giants climbed above the .500 mark as the month was expiring and, earning 20 wins in August, found themselves in a pennant race with two other clubs.

On Saturday, August 7, the Chicago Cubs set back the Giants, 6–2, at the Polo Grounds, snapping a six-game New York winning streak. Sometime afterward, McGraw ended up at the Lambs Club. The exclusive theatre club was now doubling as a posh Manhattan speakeasy, as Prohibition had constitutionally swept over the lexicon and law of the land. (The banning of alcoholic beverage sale, production and transport throughout the United States lawfully began in January 1920.) At the club, McGraw was involved in a late-night fight with another patron.

McGraw pulled an all-nighter that also left a second man, 50-year-old John C. Slavin, with life-threatening injuries, sustained in a mysterious manner. After sharing a cab ride with McGraw, Slavin was said to have fallen outside of McGraw's 109th Street apartment early the next morning. A musical comedy actor, Slavin was a friend of McGraw's and reasonably sure to have been in McGraw's company at the Lambs Club. He was taken to St. Luke's Hospital by the taxi driver who dropped McGraw off at his residence. Another individual, Winfield Liggett, also accompanied McGraw home in the cab and assisted in the transport of the unconscious Slavin to the hospital. Every major New York newspaper carried a page one report of the incident in its August 9 editions. Ensuing information leaked out that McGraw's membership at the midtown establishment had been temporarily revoked because of a previous fight with a member identified as Walter Knight. It was made known McGraw had been welcomed back recently, and that another actor, William H. Boyd, had come forward as the "other" man in the after-hours incident. Boyd attested that the fight, which left McGraw with a forehead welt, blackened eyes, and swollen nose and lips, was entirely provoked by the intoxicated Giants manager. There subsequently turned up seven other corroborating witnesses.

Police raided the Lambs Club and seized 15 cases of whiskey, champagne and sherry. In the near aftermath, one hometown paper went as far as to publish, perhaps a bit derisively, McGraw's more celebrated brawls, with the heading:

John McGraw's Record as Maiden Class Fighter[8]

Place	Opponent	Winner
Philadelphia	Addie Brennan	Brennan
Boston	Dan McGann	McGann
Cincinnati	Umpire W. Byron	Byron
Houston	"Pat" Newnam	Newnam
Havana	C.A. Stoneham	Stoneham
Lambs Club	W.H. Boyd	Boyd

McGraw dragged himself to the Polo Grounds on Sunday, August 8, but did not leave the clubhouse and almost surely did not stay for the game. Not returning to the ballpark again, he was out of commission for 12 days, recovering from his own facial and head wounds. With Johnny Evers suspended, Larry Doyle guided the Giants. Holed up in his apartment, behind the shielding orders of his physician, McGraw refused to comment to the press and delayed beyond a reasonable period in speaking to authorities about the sensational story.

When McGraw failed to answer a subpoena, New York District Attorney Edward Swann released this statement: "It is very apparent some unseen influence is at work to befuddle the authorities in their work in the investigation as to how Slavin received his injury. The truth will be obtained despite this and no influence can be exercised to prevent the guilty man from being punished if we can get the necessary proof."[9] The story told about Slavin by McGraw, Liggett and the taxi driver was that he must have received his head injury after tripping on the sidewalk in front of McGraw's apartment. None of the three said they saw the "accident" happen.

No longer able to avoid the wheels of justice, McGraw came forward and pleaded amnesia. "From the moment I was struck by Boyd until Monday morning my mind was a blank," he stated. "I have no idea how Mr. Slavin was hurt."[10] He alluded to being hit on the head by a water bottle at the Lambs Club, but also had to disclose that he had consumed four quarts of whiskey in order for his memory-loss stance to fly.

Shortly thereafter, McGraw was permitted to leave New York (no doubt glad of it) and rejoin his team in Chicago. The squad had won seven out of 11 games in his absence and climbed ten games over .500. On August 20, the same day McGraw re-established his field authority over his men, funeral services were held at St. John's Roman Catholic Cathedral in Cleveland for Ray Chapman. The Cleveland Indians player had been beaned four days earlier by New York Yankees pitcher Carl Mays, causing the only field fatality in major league baseball history.

Moundmates Rube Benton's and Art Nehf's infant daughters happened to be born on July 20, 1920. On August 27, Nehf established another bond, this one of the professional nature, with Benton. Nehf flung 17 innings against the Cincinnati Reds, equaling Benton's marathon performance five weeks earlier. Nehf's 6–4, road victory was not as virtuoso a performance as Benton's shutout masterpiece, but it gained the same results in the standings for the Giants. Nehf allowed 16 hits and did not strike out a batter; three of the runs were earned. Ray Fisher was the Reds' complete-game loser. The win brought the 65–53 Giants to within 3½ games of first-place Brooklyn. The Reds were 2½ games ahead of New York, in second place.

Incidentally, nine days earlier, both Benton and Nehf's daughters were assured the right to vote when they came of age with the announced ratification of the 19th Amendment.

McGraw signed Slim Sallee off the Reds' waiver wire on September 5 to bolster his pitching staff. Sallee responded with a 5–1 road triumph over the Boston Braves in his first start on September 8. Then at the Polo Grounds, Nehf pitched a one-hitter on September 16 for his 19th win. The score was 4–0, and the lone hit was an infield single by Pittsburgh Pirates outfielder Billy Southworth.

During the last week of September, McGraw was requested to appear before the Cook County grand jury in Chicago. The full-scale investigation into the fixing of the 1919 World Series by Chicago White Sox players, and gambling in baseball in general, was under way. McGraw was asked to testify about the Heinie Zimmerman suspension he had imposed and the reason behind the eventual release of Hal Chase. Rube Benton had previously been called and testified that Buck Herzog had tried to entice him with $800 to throw a game between Herzog's Cubs and the Giants in September of 1919. Sworn affidavits were secured from Christy Mathewson on the Hal Chase incidents and a similar one involving Lee Magee. Baseball and its fans were in for other shocking revelations soon to come.

McGraw returned to New York briefly. He was met with the news that John C. Slavin had been released from a nearly two-month-long hospital stay and that a Mr. Wilton Lackaye was contemplating suing McGraw for injuries he sustained during a visit to McGraw's apartment following the Lambs Club ignominy. Lackaye contended that McGraw slapped him hard enough for him to lose his balance, fall over McGraw's sofa and fracture his ankle.

The strong stretch drive Giants fans hoped their team would achieve did not materialize to the desired degree, however. Despite 20-win seasons by Nehf, Jesse Barnes and Fred Toney, and elbowing Cincinnati out of second place, the Giants were outpaced by a more balanced Brooklyn Robins team. The 86-win Giants ran second in the National League by seven games.

On October 5, the day the World Series between Brooklyn and the Cleveland Indians began, McGraw returned to Chicago to testify before a special body of the grand jury convened to continue the Giants' players probe. Accompanying McGraw to Chicago were

Larry Doyle, Benny Kauff and Fred Toney—all of whom had personal knowledge about attempts to throw games. Also in the traveling party was Charles Stoneham.

Although not accused of any wrongdoing, Stoneham and McGraw, in particular, received ringing praise from the league's highest officer during the opening session. President Heydler asserted that the New York National League club had done more for baseball than any other club in the league. "McGraw deliberately wrecked his pennant chances by getting rid of Zimmerman and Chase because of their alleged gambling and game throwing,"[11] he said.

The quote seems akin to applauding someone for throwing out the garbage lest he become covered in its stink.

McGraw's Rebuffed Realignment Plans

McGraw lent his name—and players—to another barnstorming journey to Cuba in the fall. The renowned manager did not accompany the team, leaving it under the charge of coach Johnny Evers. Fresh off a jaw-dropping, 50-home run season, Babe Ruth joined the exclusive squad in Havana about halfway through its tour. McGraw was an early Ruth critic, sticking by his own hit-and-run, base-stealing brand of baseball as being superior to Ruth's flamboyant four-base walloping. McGraw's Ruthian resentment could perhaps trace its roots to earlier in the 1920 calendar year. The previous off-season, McGraw had relocated the Giants' spring training headquarters from Texas to Florida. As part of the move, he arranged a string of exhibitions between his ball club and the Boston Red Sox, traveling up through the South in preparation for the start of the season. The Red Sox trained in Hot Springs, Arkansas.

McGraw's intent was to capitalize on Ruth's new home run-hitting appeal, previewed in 1919 with a wowing 29 long balls. But Ruth was sold by Boston to the Yankees during the last week of 1919. As it developed, winding their way toward the northeast ahead of the Giants and the Red Sox in the spring of 1920 were Ruth's new Yankees and the

McGraw and his wife, Blanche, in the sun parlor of their Pelham, New York, home in 1922.

Brooklyn Robins. The teams shared the same Jacksonville, Florida, training locale. Those two lead clubs, with prime attraction Ruth, sapped up all of the disposable income and left turnstile scraps for the trailing teams of McGraw and Boston manager Ed Barrow when they came along a day or two later.

The fall of 1920 was a hectic and anxious one for McGraw. The health of one of his beloved players had to be weighing on him, since Christy Mathewson's lung affliction had been made public. McGraw wanted his barnstorm excursion to be a financial success. He was uncertain whether that could be attained with the amount of money guaranteed to Ruth by Cuban promoter Abel Linares, which McGraw saw as certain to cut into his team's net profits. Linares was said to be subsidizing Ruth's trip with a $1,000 per-game stipend. (Some reports indicated up to twice the amount, which was probably an exaggeration.) Measured against the average major league salary, which at the time was around $5,000, the guarantees to Ruth were princely sums indeed. Ruth arrived in Havana harbor on October 30—two weeks after Evers and his contingent. The Bambino played his first game the same day.

Days prior to Ruth's arrival in Havana, McGraw was indicted in New York for violation of the country's "dry laws," emanating from the infamous Lambs Club incident. (The establishment expelled McGraw as a member, again.) While awaiting his day in court, McGraw accelerated an effort which he had begun earlier in the year to purchase an unhappy Rogers Hornsby from the St. Louis Cardinals. The attempt failed, as the Cardinals brass, headed by Branch Rickey, decided to hold on to their dissatisfied second sacker. Hitting .370, Hornsby won the first of his seven batting titles with the sixth-place Cardinals in 1920. Shortly after the World Series, the trade rumors intensified as Thanksgiving neared.

On November 16, the day before he departed for Havana on vacation, McGraw tried to put the acquisition notions to bed. "Certainly I would like to have Hornsby on my club—what manager wouldn't?" he said. "But I'm not going to give the Federal Reserve Bank for him."[12] The most reliable figure mentioned was that McGraw had offered $200,000 for the extremely talented St. Louis player. The 24-year-old Hornsby, by this time, had already been referred to as the "fiery Texan" and branded as a "temperamental star" in the St. Louis sports pages, from which many a byline advocated the trade. That was especially so after Hornsby had stated, on more than one occasion, a desire to play in the big city instead of what he called "pastiming in St. Louis."[13]

McGraw had clearly (and rather coldly) indicated that he was putting Larry Doyle out to pasture and that he wanted to shift Frankie Frisch from third base to second— after the Hornsby deal fell through. To make the move more feasible, McGraw purchased the contract of infielder Goldie Rapp from the St. Paul Saints of the American Association. But Rapp did not make the grade at third, and Frisch would spend most of another season at the hot corner.

The McGraws took up residence at the Chibas Apartments during their stay in Havana. According to Blanche McGraw, her 47-year-old husband was able to find his greatest enjoyment during the Caribbean holiday at Oriental Park. "At night, there was fun at 'our' casino," a passage from her book divulged, "with plenty of good food and excellent music."[14] Her only lament was not being able to coax John to more than one swing around the dance floor. And that came only when the band played "When Irish Eyes Are Smiling." It was McGraw's favorite song, and he never grew tired of hearing it played.

Although McGraw's attendance at the Havana race track and casino remained faithful in future years, his overall enjoyment may have waned following the mandate he and Stoneham received from Commissioner Landis to sell their interests in the gaming park. The iron-fisted rule of baseball's first commissioner came to light early with this edict cracking down on affiliations with diverse elements of gambling.

Before he finally left for Cuba in mid–November, McGraw's name had been prominently featured in all of New York's newspapers. False reports surfaced in the dailies that McGraw had made a $20,000 out-of-court settlement with John C. Slavin, the person most aggrieved in the aftermath of McGraw's headline-grabbing, over-indulgent night of drinking.

The embattled Giants manager also had to deny reports that he was planning on retiring to concentrate full-time on executive duties under the titular vice presidency he held with the Giants. Hughie Jennings, former Detroit Tigers manager, was rumored to be succeeding McGraw in the Polo Grounds' home dugout. A closing declaration from the Giants' stockholders' meeting in Jersey City, in early November, put the rumor to rest and identified an intended tailoring change in store for the Giants leader: "John J. McGraw will not appear on the field in uniform to direct his team during the next season, it was announced here today by the Giants pilot. The task of handling the team from the coaching box will be turned over to Hughie Jennings. Jennings succeeds Johnny Evers, who will lead the Cub machine next season."[15]

Also during that particularly active off-season, and again from Chicago, McGraw, Stoneham and co-minority partner Francis X. McQuade were among National League owners seen pushing for a reorganization of the two major leagues into a new, 12-club league. Under the radical plan, the eight-team National League would absorb three AL squads (Boston, New York and Chicago) and place a new team in Detroit. The insurrection was another clear attack against American League president Ban Johnson, with whom McGraw and other National League owners maintained long-standing feuds. White Sox owner Charles Comiskey had joined in the uprising, still simmering against Johnson over the league's top executive's dismissal of Comiskey's conspiracy complaint after the 1919 World Series.

The five opposing American League teams were Cleveland, Detroit, Philadelphia, St. Louis and Washington. The dissident group of franchises was led by Senators owner Clark Griffith. A baseball war was said to be on the horizon, which McGraw dispelled, stating to the press that the deal and the "new National League" was all but created. "The men who are backing the new twelve clubs are determined to go through with it," said the high-profile manager. "They [five AL owners] know they have the losing end of it, and they don't want any part of a fight. One or two of them are getting ready right now to run away from Johnson."[16]

But when threatened with legal action over ownership of major and minor league players and territorial rights, the too-presumptuous McGraw and other rebel leaders backed down. The folly of the plan became evident as NL owners realized they were threatening similar actions they had so opposed from the Federal League. The composition of the major leagues, for the everlasting good of the game, remained unchanged.

While in Chicago during this busy time, McGraw and Stoneham met Jacob Ruppert and Til Huston and agreed to renew the Yankees' lease for continued use of Stoneham's upper Manhattan ballpark for two more years through the 1922 season. This had to be particularly galling for McGraw and Stoneham because in 1920 the Yankees had outdrawn the Giants in their home ballpark by more than 350,000 fans. The businessmen swallowed their pride with more ease by nearly doubling their tenants' rent to a six-figure arrangement.

After interrupting his stay in Cuba to attend the December baseball winter meetings, held in New York, the trying fall and winter for McGraw turned much more pleasant with the succession of the changing seasons. McGraw and Blanche put aside more than three months of Havana vacationing and arrived in San Antonio, Texas, on March 5, 1921. Most of the Giants had already gathered there to commence spring training. (McGraw had changed training venues, perhaps in spiteful response to last season's disappointing exhibition arrangement with the Boston Red Sox.) Following three straight second-place finishes, McGraw whipped into shape what would turn into a world championship ball club.

Major league owners breathed a collective sigh of relief in April as the District of Columbia Court of Appeals overturned the decision in favor of the Baltimore Terrapins in the Federal League case. As if that was not enough of a reason for the moguls to smile, record-breaking inaugural day crowds in New York and Chicago advanced the belief that the public had heartily taken to the increased offense in baseball and that the tainted 1919 World Series scandal had not damaged the sport. "Opening day was the first sign that the fans had not abandoned the game and that the owners'—and Commissioner Landis's—public relations campaign was working,"[17] wrote Lyle Spatz and Steve Steinberg, co-authors of *1921: The Yankees, the Giants & the Battle for Supremacy in New York*.

In Philadelphia, the largest crowd seen since the 1915 World Series (25,000) filled the Baker Bowl to watch the John McGraw-guided Giants earn a 10–8, extra-inning victory over the Phillies on April 13. A two-run home run by High Pockets Kelly in the top of the 11th inning was the difference. Kelly, after leading the league in RBI last year, took the first stride in pacing the circuit in home runs this season with 22. McGraw used three pitchers in the game: Phil Douglas, Jesse Barnes and winner Fred Toney. The three hurlers would win 48 games among them, slightly more than half of the Giants' 94 league-leading victories on the season.

The Giants made their home debut eight days later and succumbed to the same Phillies, 6–5. A lovely spring day helped entice a crowd of 25,000, which was 12,000 fewer than the Yankees had drawn for their first home game. Giants catcher Earl Smith caught the first ball from New York Governor Al Smith, moments before receiving more pronounced tosses from starter Fred Toney. Smith's batterymate was cuffed for ten hits and four earned runs in taking the loss. Shortstop and team captain Dave Bancroft booted a grounder in the eighth inning with the bases loaded, allowing the winning run to score. First baseman Kelly banged his third home run in six games. Kelly would hit safely in his first 13 games of the season.

The disappointing April 21 home opener marked three decades of existence for the Giants' home stadium (or, rather, for the Giants' home-field location; the team moved into Polo Grounds III in 1891, rebuilt when that park burned in April 1911). Along with other interesting data perhaps not readily known to the era's casual fan, a long-standing New York journalist enlightened readers to this fact in this practiced fashion:

> The historic park was laid out in 1890 by the Brotherhood Club of the New York Players League, which assumed the name of "Giants," although the original National League club, which was owned by John B. Day and occupied the vacant lot next to the Brush Stadium, first received that popular title. Why? Because members of the champion Giants of 1888 and 1889 were all big, pow-

erfully built men. When the season of 1891 began … Brotherhood Park was formally christened the Polo Grounds.[18]

The McGraw collective was in the midst of a six-game winning streak on Monday, May 2, the day the manager had a weight lifted off of his shoulders. Some of New York was debriefed in their afternoon newspapers; others, such as the subscribers to the *New York Times*, read about it the next day, as follows: "It took a jury in Federal Court less than five minutes yesterday to find John J. McGraw, manager and part owner of the New York National League Baseball Club, not guilty of violating the Volstead Act. The defendant came into court on crutches due to a sprained ankle he received while practicing on the Polo Grounds on Sunday."[19] (The ankle sprain indicated that McGraw continued to run pre-game drills.)

Fortunately for McGraw, John C. Slavin had fully recovered (he stated that he could not remember what had happened to cause his severe injuries). Without any witnesses, a criminal case against McGraw was never brought. Slavin filed no civil complaint, either. The embarrassing Lambs Club episode was reduced to McGraw (illegally) having had "one too many," for which a sympathetic, all-male jury was obviously not prepared to condemn him.

New York won 21 of their first 30 games, but trailed the red-hot Pittsburgh Pirates (23–6) by 2½ games after games on May 20. Ten days hence, the New York club swept a morning-afternoon doubleheader at the Polo Grounds (5–1, 13–7). In between games, the dedication of the Captain Edward L. Grant memorial was conducted. The five-foot stone monument, placed within play in deepest center field, was unveiled by Grant's sisters, Florence and Louise. The regimental band from Fort Slocum led a parade of former and current soldiers across the field. Among the baseball and civic personages who spoke a few words were McGraw and Commissioner Landis.

On June 2, the contending Giants opened a Western road excursion in Pittsburgh. "John McGraw sat on the bench in 'civvies' to direct and encourage his men," penned a Pittsburgh reporter. "John J. has a sore knee which put a hamper on his field activities."[20] McGraw did not have to exert much effort during the game, as Art Nehf garnered his seventh win, in nine decisions, with a four-hit, 4–0 shutout. Winning three out of four games at Forbes Field, McGraw's group moved into a tie for first place with the Pirates. But the Giants then lost six in a row (their longest losing spell of the season) five to Cincinnati and St. Louis, and lost their grip on the top spot.

Not long afterward, McGraw let go of one of the three remaining pitchers from his 1917 pennant-winning club, when he sold Pol Perritt to the Detroit Tigers via the South Atlantic League's Columbia Comers, where Perritt had been previously shipped. Another, more complicated, trade that McGraw tried to pull off during this time did not go his way. His attempt to acquire holdout third baseman Heinie Groh from the Cincinnati Reds was disallowed by Kenesaw Mountain Landis. Groh was considered one of the top players in the league, offensively and defensively. So unhappy was he in Cincinnati and with the salary he was offered that he had decided to sit out the season. The commissioner's stance was that no player should be able to force his own trade by not fulfilling his contractual obligations and, therefore, he nullified the proposed transaction. Publicly, at least, McGraw did not disagree with the verdict against him. "Judge Landis' ruling that Groh would have to play with Cincinnati or not at all was drastic but just," he said, with an added indication of the broad powers the former federal judge had been given by major league owners. "The New York club has no kick coming. Judge Landis was elected high commissioner of baseball to administer the law in a way that he thinks is for the best interests of the game."[21]

Staying on the league-leading Pirates' heels, the Giants bashed the Philadelphia Phillies in a Baker Bowl doubleheader on June 25. Amassing 26 runs on the day, the visitors' 17 runs in the nightcap were the most tallied by the club in a game that season. Scoring four runs in each contest, the Phillies were no match for McGraw's maulers, who clubbed five home runs in the second game and six on the day. Catcher Frank Snyder, splitting duties behind the plate with Earl Smith, hit two circuit smashes, backing the one-sided win credited to Rube Benton, although the pitcher hurled only four innings. The Phils avoided a four-game sweep in the series finale by pounding Giants starter Phil Douglas. The final score was 12–8, and McGraw allowed Douglas to be raked over the coals for the full game, permitting 19 hits (five home runs).

Douglas had been obtained by McGraw in the trade for the devalued Dave Robertson two years earlier. Douglas, himself a "problem child"—before and after his arrival in New York—never acclimated to the rigorous ways of McGraw. He had walked away from his pitching obligations a month after his trade and had been suspended indefinitely by McGraw. He returned to the Giants in 1920 and posted a 14–10 record, pitching quite effectively as both a starter and reliever. The public humiliation Douglas thought McGraw had purposely subjected him to in Philadelphia was too much to take. Again he walked out on McGraw, and again was suspended. The walkout was brief, as the pitcher met the team in Boston on July 1 and was reinstated the same day.

By the first of July, McGraw had seen enough of Goldie Rapp at third base to feel he needed an upgrade. The Giants tactician engineered a trade with the Braves in which he sent Rapp, outfielders Lee King and Lance Richbourg to Boston in exchange for infielder Johnny Rawlings and outfielder Casey Stengel. King had been one of two outfielders (Curt Walker, the other) McGraw had used to replace the excommunicated Benny Kauff in center field. The key piece in the trade was Rawlings, who was having his best season in the majors—on both sides of the ball. Hitting .291 at the time of his relocation, Rawlings would lead the circuit in assists (495), putouts (342) and double plays (93), while playing the most games at second base (146).

Frankie Frisch was moved back to third base following the Rawlings acquisition. Nearly halfway through an extended homestand that mostly entertained the Western clubs, McGraw and Stoneham's outside empire experienced an expected, but no less painful, reduction. The sale of the partners' Cuban-American Jockey and Auto Club to New York businessman Thomas F. Monahan had gone through. In reporting the completed sale, W.C. Vreeland described a location that made it easy to understand the property's attraction and investment appeal to the two North Americans. "There is no finer racing plant out of doors than Oriental Park," wrote the *Brooklyn Daily Eagle* scribe. "The course is in a bowl, and the clubhouse and grandstand overlook it, thus affording a splendid view of the horses from start to finish in every race. There are tropical gardens, and the entrance is through an avenue of palms."[22]

On the last day of the homestand, July 24, the Phillies came to town for a single game. New York edged the Quaker City team, 4–3. High Pockets Kelly drove in all of his club's runs with a homer (#16) and double. Outfielder Emil "Irish" Meusel, who was hitting over .350 and was second in the circuit to Kelly in home runs with 12, was not in the Philadelphia lineup. Meusel had been benched for what was perceived as lack of hustle, or interest, in a game two days earlier. McGraw exploited the disenchantment William

McGraw (in sweater), Hughie Jennings and Cozy Dolan (hand in back pocket) in spring training, 1923. Jennings and Dolan served as McGraw's coaches that season. Dolan would be impli-
cated in a gambling scandal at the end of the 1924 season with the Giants, ending his major
league career.

Baker had with Meusel and pried the rising star away from the Phillies' owner. The exchange stipulated that McGraw give up outfielder Curt Walker, catching prospect Butch Henline and $30,000 for Meusel. The trade, which passed the purview of the commissioner, re-established the Giants' outfield—with budding superstar Youngs and the redoubtable Burns—as without peer in the league.

On the same day the homestand ended, the Giants released Rube Benton, the second of the three holdover hurlers from McGraw's 1917 NL championship staff. "Failure to keep in condition" was the reason given in more than one printed notice. Benton was 5–2 with a 2.88 ERA in 18 appearances, half of them starts. The veteran left-hander had been plagued by "off-the-field distractions" for his entire career and had been dragged into the recent federal inquiry on gambling. Every other big league team passed on Benton, and he wound up pitching for St. Paul in the American Association. He would return to the National League, but not until 1923, and pitch the remaining three years of his 15-year career with the Cincinnati Reds.

The transaction left only Slim Sallee from the Giants' 1917 World Series pitching staff. The 36-year-old Sallee was used strictly in relief by McGraw, chipping in to the team's success with a modest 6–4 record. He would complete his final big league campaign in 1921.

Irish Meusel joined his new club for their next series in Pittsburgh. He played his first game on July 27, collecting one hit in three at-bats, in a 4–1 Giants victory. Meusel's new manager was watching the action from the Forbes Field stands. The previous day, McGraw had been ejected from the game by Bill Klem. McGraw drew a rapid suspension from John Heydler for joining with Johnny Rawlings in a foul-mouthed, verbal attack on Klem afterward. Rawlings had been expelled by the no-nonsense umpire in the waning moments of the contest—won by the Giants, 9–8, in ten innings. Rawlings' actions cost him $50 but no time away from the diamond.

Later in the day of his beef with Klem, McGraw was arrested. Pittsburgh resident George M. Duffy alleged that McGraw had attacked him at the Giants' hotel during the team's first trip to the Steel City back in early June. Duffy had filed a $20,000 civil suit for damages from the attack. McGraw posted bail of $3,000 and never came close to seeing the inside of the local jail cell.

McGraw was a spectator of a different kind on July 28. The manager left Pittsburgh for Chicago to see Heydler about his suspension. While in the City of Big Shoulders, McGraw was part of the public gallery on the day the defense rested its case in the "Black Sox" trial. McGraw was seen shaking hands with one of the principals in the case, Buck Weaver. "Mac just told me he'd like to have me on his ball club if I'm cleared here and Judge Landis will let me to play,"[23] said the soon-to-be-acquitted White Sox player in a sidebar with a newspaperman.

Heydler acceded to a perfunctory three-day suspension for McGraw, and the manager rejoined his team in Cincinnati on July 29. From there, McGraw denied all tampering suspicions that were swirling about from his Midwest trip. "I met Weaver with some other of the accused players in the courtroom at Chicago, where I went in search of President Heydler," he explained. "I made no offer to him [Weaver]. If he plays ball again it is entirely up to Landis. I have nothing to say about it."[24]

The Giants split a six-game series at Cincinnati, winning the final game, 5–4, on August 1. A local writer offered an insight on McGraw's managerial tendencies, derived from that winning engagement. "McGraw is not much of a believer in the sacrifice hit," said Jack Ryder, "and usually prefers to hit and run. But he is quite partial to the squeeze. It won the game for him in the seventh inning when Burns's bunt toward first went safe."[25]

McGraw made his second trip to Chicago in two weeks, as the Giants completed their Western road tour in that city on August 9. His team rather disappointingly split a four-game series with the seventh-place Cubs. The Giants' two biggest winners, Art Nehf (14–6) and Jesse Barnes (10–6), were the victorious pitchers during the four-day encampment. The second-place club returned home three games in back of the top-tiered Pirates, exactly in the same position they had left New York 16 days ago.

McGraw used an open date on the schedule, August 10, to close on a house located on 915 Edgewood Avenue in Pelham, New York. The house was about a 12-mile drive from the Polo Grounds. The move to the suburbs cost McGraw $40,000, the sale price of the ten-room home.

In mid–August, McGraw's recent roster moves were not providing the expected jolt. Syndicated writer Henry L. Farrell of UPI was one of the first to offer a blistering analysis.

> McGraw made such drastic moves this year for the championship that he has wrecked his team. New York fans are bemoaning the trades that brought Irish Meusel, Red Causey and Stengel to the Giant fold with all the vehemence that the Pittsburgh and Boston fans protested at the trades several weeks ago. It was then charged openly that the wealthy Giants were buying the pennant by outbidding other clubs that wanted Meusel.[26]

Meusel was hitting in the low .200s since changing uniforms. The former Giant, Causey, had been re-obtained by McGraw in a trade with frequent trading partner Philadelphia on July 10. He could not crack the Giants' rotation. And Stengel was not getting much playing time.

Still in the runner-up position, the Giants faced a 7½-game deficit to the Pittsburgh on August 24, the day the Pirates began a five-game series at the Polo Grounds. McGraw's men rose up and captured all five games against the league-leaders. Art Nehf hurled two complete-game victories in the four-day battle. Phil Douglas topped his mound cohort by tossing two nine-inning gems in three days, including a shutout. Fred Toney, right behind Nehf in wins now, notched his 15th, pitching the distance in a 5–2 triumph. The second Nehf win (3–1), on Saturday, August 27, attracted the biggest crowd, 36,000. It was a dream series for the winning manager. McGraw did not make one substitution in the first four games. Not until the fifth game did he make a managerial move at all; it involved a pinch-runner.

McGraw's squad continued to chip away at the reduced lead. The Giants reeled off ten straight wins in September, taking over undisputed control of first place on September 9. When the streak ended on September 19, McGraw's charging club had moved 3½ games in front. Undeterred by having to play their final 15 games on the road, including facing the four Western clubs on hostile ground, the Giants beat back all comers. Art Nehf defeated the Cardinals, 4–1, for his 20th win, on September 26. Afterward the Giants boarded a 5:30 p.m. train scheduled to arrive in New York early the next evening. The Manhattan warriors left St. Louis with the pennant virtually assured, holding a four-game lead over Pittsburgh, with four games to play on the schedule.

The day after clinching its World Series berth, the Giants put together a benefit game to raise funds for the ailing Christy Mathewson. Replaced as Giants coach this season by Jesse Burkett and Alvin "Cozy" Dolan, Mathewson had spent the year convalescing in Lake Saranac. The team's front office brought back players from the past, and the aged athletes participated in a friendly contest against current players that lasted only five innings due to rain. The "Old-Timers" game was held prior to the regular season home finale versus the Boston Braves on September 30. The scheduled game was rained out and not made up.

The 41-year-old baseball hero conveyed his salutations from upstate New York in a prepared statement that was carried by all newswire outlets. It read:

> On this day of days at the Polo Grounds I am glad to send heartiest greetings to all my friends. It is absolutely impossible for me to put into words my feeling of pleasure and gratitude at the manner in which the New York baseball club and friends of baseball are honoring me, but it certainly is good to have friends who do not forget and who remember me so substantially. With such support I cannot fail to win my game. Here is hoping that the Giants win theirs.[27]

Mathewson also sent dozens of autographed baseballs for sale for any souvenir-minded spectator. A baseball signed by Mathewson, President Warren Harding, Vice President Calvin Coolidge, Babe Ruth, and High Pockets Kelly was auctioned off. Pittsburgh businessman Truly Nolan placed the high bid of $750 and won the special ball. The event was a success, with Mathewson receiving initial and subsequent checks totaling over $50,000.

The next day in Philadelphia, McGraw again sadistically let Phil Douglas pitch an entire game in which his stuff was not up to par. Douglas gave up ten runs (seven earned) and *20* hits in 8⅓ innings. Remarkably, Douglas had a chance to win the game entering the bottom of the ninth, when the Phillies scored twice to beat him, 10–9.

The second World Series involving teams from the same city but first with a shared ballpark began on Wednesday, October 5. The Miller Huggins-led New York Yankees had cinched their first pennant over the weekend. During the playing of the "Star Spangled Banner," a group of Yankees laid a large wreath around the Captain Eddie Grant monument in center field. In the stands, Kenesaw Mountain Landis attended his first World Series game as commissioner of baseball. The Giants acted as home team and alternated with the Yankees with each subsequent encounter. McGraw managed in uniform from the bench. Hughie Jennings and Cozy Dolan manned the coaching lines. For the Yankees, Charlie O'Leary held down the first base box for the entire game, while Babe Ruth served at third for most of the contest.

Instead of sticking with his winningest pitcher, Art Nehf (20–10), McGraw chose to rekindle his roller coaster relationship with Phil Douglas, whose last game had been a disaster. The 15-game winner was defeated, 3–0, by the Yankees' Carl Mays, the tough submariner who last season had inadvertently provided baseball with its saddest headlines. Frankie Frisch laced four of the five hits Mays permitted.

Nehf, who had stayed behind in New York to scout the Yankees while the Giants were in Philadelphia, started Game Two. For the second day in a row, the Giants were shut out. Waite Hoyt, the precocious Brooklyn boy McGraw had sold to Ed Barrow's Boston Red Sox, tossed a two-hitter, with five walks. Nehf surrendered only three hits, but with seven walks and one legitimate run. Babe Ruth, who received three of Nehf's free passes, stole second and third base in the fifth inning, with two outs. He was left stranded. "What a joke it was when the critics said, 'the Giants will show us up on the bases,'" Ruth said afterward. "It seems to me the Yankees are 'showing the Giants up.'"[28] Ruth's stolen bases were part of three on the day for the Yankees and five in two games, including two swipes of home plate. Frisch had the only steal, so far, for the National League champs. Nearly 5,000 more fans than yesterday's 30,203 total were present.

The Giants found their hitting eye in the next clash. Lashing out 20 hits against four Yankees pitchers, the McGraw tribe gave their opponents a 13–5 pasting. The Giants broke open the game with an eight-run seventh inning. Ross Youngs had two extra-base hits and drove in four runs. Frisch scored three runs and stole two of the four bases swiped by the victors. Tossing seven innings of one-run relief of starter Fred Toney, Jesse Barnes was the winning pitcher. The largest crowd of the entire series, 36,509, were enlivened by the Giants' hitting resurgence.

Rain postponed the fourth game, scheduled for Saturday. The Series-resuming Sunday affair was a tight encounter for seven innings, with the Yankees clinging to 1–0 lead behind Game One starter Mays. In the top of the eighth, the Giants broke through with three runs on four hits and held on to win, 4–2. Phil Douglas efficiently held the Yankees to seven hits, without walking a batter and striking out eight. Ruth socked his first World Series home run, with the bases empty, in the last inning. "There were no flukes about our two triumphs," said an energized McGraw after the contest. "I said at the beginning of the series that we should win because we have the better team, and I am still of the same opinion."[29]

The kid from Brooklyn stopped the Giants' momentum on Monday. Waite Hoyt outpitched Art Nehf again, winning 3–1. The run against the Yankees' right-hander was unearned, as he spaced ten hits in giving his team a leg up in the intracity confrontation. Yankees outfielder Bob Meusel, younger brother of Emil, collected a pair of hits, scored a run and plated another. A side note shed some light on McGraw's totalitarian managerial tactics.

> Exactly thirty-nine times in the fifth game the Giants' players interrupted play on the field to ask McGraw what to do. No ball is served to a Yankee batter that McGraw does not order. No Giant batter strikes at a ball, in a crucial moment, without his instructions. McGraw is the reason that Babe Ruth has fanned eight times. He orders every ball—high, low, curve, fast or slow—that is served to the Bambino. He is the mastermind. He is the works.[30]

In the last best-of-nine World Series, the Giants may not have feared elimination in the sixth game, but the team was well aware that another loss could spell doom. Rising to the challenge, McGraw's club overcame another poor start by Fred Toney and benefited from another excellent relief effort by Jesse Barnes, to beat the American Leaguers, 8–5. McGraw pulled an ineffective Toney in the first inning in favor of Barnes, who allowed only two runs in 8⅓ sterling innings. (McGraw almost surely predetermined to have Barnes ready on short notice, as the same strategy had worked so well in Game Three.) Tying the Series at three games apiece, the Giants wreaked the most damage by zeroing in on the slants of Harry Harper and Bob Shawkey. Hitting one of two home runs for the winners, Irish Meusel matched his sibling's four-base hit from yesterday. Giants catcher Frank Snyder clubbed the other circuit clout. The Yankees were without their premier long ball swatter, Babe Ruth. The masher was nursing various physical ailments, the most serious to his elbow.

In Game Seven, the man who was in and out of McGraw's doghouse all year took the mound and again outdueled counterpart Carl Mays. Phil Douglas crafted a splendid eight-hit, 2–1 victory that placed the world championship within his team's grasp. The Giants used a stolen base sandwiched between two singles to score one run and capitalized on a costly error by Yankees second baseman Aaron Ward to plate the other. Ruth missed his second game.

Following the first game's attendance total of 30,203, the Fall Classic was attracting an average of 35,000 fans to the Polo Grounds. A cold snap on October 13 reduced the spectatorship to 25,410 in the eighth encounter. Both managers brought their Game Five starters back on two days' rest. Art Nehf tossed one of the best World Series–clinching efforts in history. The Giants ace spun a five-hit, 1–0 gem to beat Waite Hoyt and crown the Giants monarchs of baseball. An unearned run in the first inning, produced on an error by shortstop Roger Peckinpaugh, accounted for all the scoring. Ruth, as the tying run, pinch-hit in the ninth and grounded to first base.

"Give all the credit to Jennings and the players," McGraw selflessly told reporters. "I can't say too much for Nehf, Snyder, Douglas, Barnes and all the other boys. Never was my heart so set on winning this time. I wanted this world's series more than I wanted anything in my whole life."[31]

A disappointed Jacob Ruppert offered unwavering support for his team in the wake of the widely-publicized defeat. "We're going to start building our own ball park next spring," said the Yankees co-owner. "That's how much I think of the Yanks."[32]

McGraw was in much demand over the off-season and did not winter as long in the Tropics as usual. He and his wife did not leave for Havana until January 28, 1922, and they returned February 27.

One of the places that welcomed McGraw while he was at home was the William Fox movie studio in nearby New Jersey. McGraw had become a fan of the "moving pictures" medium and was interested in seeing how they were made. Also part of the pressing agenda that limited his vacation time was the signing of a five-year contract to continue managing the Giants at a per annum of $65,000. McGraw's substantial salary was $10,000 below that of the President of the United States, but as a part-owner who was entitled to a share of profit distributions, McGraw's actual compensation level soared well above Warren G. Harding's. Owner Charles Stoneham actually offered McGraw a ten-year deal. But McGraw turned him down, saying that, at his age, he was not sure whether he wanted to commit to manage for another decade. The 48-year-old McGraw did state, however, that he wanted to become the first manager to win three world titles in a row. After breaking a tie last fall with Connie Mack for most pennants won (now with seven), the Giants' supreme leader could be excused for sounding as if he were getting ahead of himself.

McGraw had also been closely involved in firming up the previously nixed trade for star third baseman Heinie Groh. He sent star outfielder George Burns and third-string catcher Mike González, along with the sizable sum of $150,000, to the Cincinnati Reds for the salary-discontented Groh. The deal met with the commissioner's approval this time around and was consummated the first week of December. Groh was known for having a most unorthodox batting stance. He stood way up in the batter's box, with both toes facing the pitcher. He used a bottle-shaped bat and choked up extremely. "His freakish batting style makes him valuable for he is a perfect hit-and-run man."[33] McGraw said of his new acquisition.

Keeping the checkbook wide open, McGraw spent $75,000 for Jimmy O'Connell, a graceful outfielder owned by the San Francisco Seals, on December 7. The Groh deal allowed 24-year-old Frankie Frisch to transition from third base to second (as McGraw wanted), and sent 29-year-old Johnny Rawlings to the bench. The trade may have shored up the Giants' infield defense for the next few years, but it also left a hole in the outfield. The 32-year-old Burns (the same age as Groh) had been a fixture in left field at the Polo Grounds since 1913. On top of being an on-base and runs-scoring specialist, the reliable Burns was one of the most popular players in Giants history. Ridding himself of a perceived malcontent in Groh and fattening his wallet to such an obscene degree, while also obtaining a player the quality of Burns, must have had Garry Herrmann smiling from ear to ear for weeks.

The Giants stepped forward in search of John McGraw's eighth pennant on April 12, 1922, at the Polo Grounds. A tinge of winter was left in the air as Conway's Band entertained for more than 90 minutes before game time. Not dissuaded by the cold clime were more than 30,000 fans who came out to cheer their World Series champions. Mayor John F. Hylan performed the ritual ball toss, closely watched by the mayor of Jersey City and the governor of New Jersey. The Brooklyn Robins made clear to McGraw's men that it was a new season by downing Art Nehf, 4–3. Irish Meusel hit the Giants' first home run of the season, a fifth-inning solo shot off winning pitcher Dutch Ruether. Irish's brother Bob, serving a suspension, was among the majority who applauded the deed from the stands. Dave Bancroft batted leadoff, the lineup spot George Burns had occupied for so many seasons. He collected three of his team's nine hits. Frankie Frisch missed the game (and 13 more) due to a spiking injury suffered during spring training. The Giants unveiled thin red- and blue-piped stockings that some in the press referred to as barber pole socks.

The champions won the next three games against the Flatbush contingent, including a 17–10 slugfest in the final contest. The home club scored 11 runs in their first turn at the plate, against three Brooklyn pitchers. Ross Youngs smacked three singles and a triple, driving in five runs. New Giant Heinie Groh batted out four hits for the second game in a row. Flags at the Polo Grounds flew at half-mast to honor the passing of one of the most well-known 19th-century baseball players, Cap Anson. The controversial Anson had died the previous day, just days shy of 70.

Less than a week later, aware of his deficiency in the left field pasture, McGraw re-signed Dave Robertson. The formerly disgruntled Giants outfielder had been released by the Pittsburgh Pirates. Over the course of the season, Robertson played the last 42 games of his nine-year career, earning but a handful of starts and appearing mostly as a pinch-hitter.

Giants hitters closed the month of April with a bang, scoring 15 runs on 20 hits and hitting four home runs at Braves Field. The four-base hits, two by High Pockets Kelly and one each by Bancroft and Youngs, stayed within the broad confines of Boston's home park. Youngs scored five runs and hit for the cycle. (The major leagues would cross the 1,000 home run threshold for the first time this season.) Phil Douglas won his third game without a defeat. The 15–4 win was the fourth in a row for New York, which was on its way to an 18–4 start before slowing down a bit.

During the first week of May, John McGraw made one of those rare franchise-shaping decisions that would reap benefits for the New York Giants beyond his long tenure. Earlier in the spring, while the Giants were in Memphis, Tennessee, to play an exhibition game against the Memphis Chicks, a young Standard Oil salesman came to see McGraw at the Peabody Hotel.

The salesman, who was also a prospect, had been sent there by Norman "Kid" Elberfeld, a minor league manager and contemporary of McGraw. In McGraw's suite, an unawed Bill Terry placed a price on his services that McGraw was not prepared to meet. The 23-year-old Terry, a former minor leaguer who currently played ball on his full-time employer's semipro team, was married with a young son. He was determined not to accept the lower wages McGraw offered at the expense of his fledging family. Terry politely excused himself and left McGraw surely surprised at being turned down in his hotel suite. The meeting occurred on April 1.

Now, a little more than four weeks later, McGraw advised a front office representative to contact Terry and agree to his financial terms. The dauntless youth joined the Giants in New York, worked out and made a good impression on McGraw, who, until then, had not seen Terry play. The 6'1", 200-pound recruit was sent to the Toledo Mud Hens. What made McGraw, who was on top of the baseball world, reconsider and accede? Perhaps Elberfeld—who had seen Terry play in the Southern Association—kept up the nudging pressure. Perhaps McGraw came to admire Terry's sincere position. Perhaps a little of both. In the end, the powerful McGraw gave in, and New York Giants fans would be forever grateful. After the signing, McGraw paid Elberfeld a $750 commission for finding Terry. (The future Hall of Famer maintained his position with the oil company, for years and years, during the winter months.)

Another young prospect McGraw auditioned who turned into a signing bonanza was Loyola Academy's Frederick Charles Lindstrom. During the Giants' road trip to Chicago in mid–May, the preparatory school's baseball coach, Jake Weimer, a former big league pitcher, persuaded McGraw to look over his star player. McGraw liked what he saw in the green youngster—only 17 at the time—and signed him to a contract. Lindstrom was farmed out to Toledo as soon as school let out.

On May 24, Phil Douglas outdueled Cincinnati Reds pitcher Adolfo Luque, 2–1, in ten innings, breaking a Giants' five-game losing skid and avoiding a four-game series sweep. Before he left town with his squad, McGraw let it be known that he was extremely interested in two of the Reds' players—one of whom had not played a game all season, over a salary dispute, and the other, a tall right-hander who was delivering fine exhibitions from the mound in this, his sophomore year.

> If $150,000, cash down, and maybe some players to sweeten the deal, will buy Eddie Roush and Pete Donohue, the New York club is willing to pay the price. There is only one Roush and he ought not to be wasting the best years of his life as a holdout. And this Donohue—give him to me and I'll hold the pennant safe in New York for five years, maybe ten. He is a pitcher such as we see only once in a dozen years. There is my offer—$150,000 and six players to make it good.[34]

Garry Herrmann responded by practically labeling Donohue as untouchable, but left open all avenues when it came to his illustrious but displeased outfielder. When McGraw arrived in New York the following day, he denied making such an offer, saying that his words had been twisted around by the Cincinnati press.

Following road forays into Philadelphia and Boston, the Giants came close to losing control of first place, established during the second week of the season. A 3–2 loss to the Braves on June 3, the Giants' sixth setback in seven games, shrank the team's lead in the standings to a single game over the Pittsburgh Pirates. The road-weary club then began a 24-game Polo Grounds encampment that ended July 4 with the club 5½ games in the lead.

On the first day of the homestand, June 7, McGraw led a procession of players, behind Conway's Band, to raise the pennant-winning banner up the center field flagpole. The Giants paddled the visiting Chicago Cubs, 9–4, following the ceremony. Three days later, the Giants raised their championship flag in the same manner, purposely coinciding with the arrival of the Cincinnati Reds and a specially dedicated "George Burns Day." The former Giants outfielder, in his visitor's uniform, headed the file of Giants players to center field and then was individually honored at home plate. Surrounded by top executives of the league and other clubs, Burns was honored with gifts and verbal praise. A cane-carrying Kenesaw Mountain Landis served as master of ceremony.[35] Cheered all day long by more than 30,000 fans, Burns went 1-for-4 with a run scored. The Giants scored three runs in the ninth inning, helped by an error by infielder Sam Bohne, to pull out a 3–2 win. George Kelly doubled in the tying runs, and a two-base hit by Frank Snyder drove in the game-winner.

During the long homestand, Casey Stengel started receiving more and more playing time. McGraw had attempted to plug the hole left by Burns, using rookie Ralph Shinners (an American Association purchase) in center field and second-year man Bill Cunningham. (Burns had graciously moved to center field to accommodate Irish Meusel's arrival last season.) Stengel and Cunningham would develop into platoon specialists in the middle pasture for the remainder of the campaign. Stengel, whose playing time had been previously limited by a bad back, outperformed Cunningham, hitting .368, albeit in 250 at-bats. Stengel smacked a thrilling solo home run into the upper right field deck on June 17 to give the Giants a 2–1, ten-inning victory over the Pittsburgh Pirates.

On the penultimate day of the month, McGraw was involved in a fight with an opposing pitcher. For an unknown reason, he was sitting on the bench in the right field bullpen. He levied a few badgering words on Philadelphia Phillies pitcher George Smith, who was heading to the visitors' clubhouse after being removed from the game for a pinch-hitter. Smith was the pitcher who severely beaned Ralph Shinners back in April. Shinners, as it happened, was sitting with McGraw. Smith barked back at McGraw, and soon the three men were tangling. By happenstance, also at the game was Kenesaw Mountain Landis.

The commissioner may have left early, or was out of the sightline, for he stated he had not seen the incident, which was broken up by a few players. No disciplinary action came about for any of the warring parties, and McGraw quickly shifted the news focus by announcing a signing the next day. Kid Elberfeld, manager of the Little Rock Travelers, outfitted McGraw with another significant prize named Travis Jackson. A shortstop, the 18-year-old Jackson had been under Elberfeld's tutelage since his minor league entry into the Southern Association the prior year.

McGraw was felled by sinusitis, a recurring health problem that would plague him for the remainder of his days, on July 23, while in Cincinnati. He missed a week of games, returning on July 30, the day he executed a trade with the Boston Braves for pitcher Hugh McQuillan. The diamond strategist relinquished $100,000 and three pitchers—spot starter Fred Toney and two minor leaguers, Larry Benton (no relation to Rube) and Harry Hulihan.

McQuillan, a right-hander, would have a winning record for the Giants but not quite equal to the sum laid out for him. Even though McQuillan sported a 5–10 record with Boston, the trade was denounced by out-of-town writers as another example of the Giants organization's ability to procure a post-season installation by simply opening their bulging war chest.

A countering statement from George Washington Grant may make late 20th century nostalgics, who equated the corporatization of baseball with the advent of the players' union, think differently. "Baseball is a business proposition," said the Boston Braves owner. "If the money doesn't come through the gates, it has to come in some other way, and the money hasn't been coming through the gates. I want another pennant winner and I am going to attempt to have one. I got a tremendous amount of money for McQuillan and it's going to be spent on the team."[36] Grant had sent infield wizard Rabbit Maranville to the Pittsburgh Pirates the prior season in a player bundle that deposited $150,000 into the Braves' coffers. In less than six months, Grant would sell his team.

McGraw concurrently took a feeler on Jack Scott, a 30-year-old pitcher who had been released by Cincinnati, in May, due to a damaged arm displayed in an X-ray. Scott thought differently and came to New York to try to sell himself to McGraw. He succeeded by working out every morning at the Polo Grounds during a homestand in late July. His signing was made public on August 1. A right-hander, Scott would garner eight victories in ten decisions, as a starter and bullpen man for McGraw, over the next two months.

The 58–37 Giants owned a 1½-game lead over the second-place St. Louis Cardinals at the time of the McQuillan trade. McQuillan pitched well in his Giants debut on August 4, but lost, 3–2. After shutting out the Cubs for eight innings, he tired in the ninth. He left the game with the bases loaded, holding a 2–1 lead. Two inherited runners eventually scored against reliever Claude Jonnard. The Cardinals, managed by Branch Rickey, shortly passed the Giants in the standings.

During the stumble, McGraw lost two of his best pitchers—one for a week and the other permanently. Art Nehf (15–7) asked leave from the club to visit his seriously ill father-in-law; he was gone for six days (August 9–14). Phil Douglas succumbed to his drinking demons and was suspended by McGraw. The pitcher's absence was veiledly explained by the *Evening World's* Bozeman Bulger: "Off again on one of his periodicals, Phil is personally responsible for more grey hairs on managerial heads than old age."[37] During his detox period, Douglas (11–4) fell victim to his own antipathetic sentiments toward McGraw, which led to a career-damning error in judgment. The 32-year-old wrote to a former teammate that he was willing to be "paid off" in order never to pitch another ball for the Giants. Douglas was convinced that if he was not a part of the Giants, McGraw's gang would have a hard time winning the pennant. The teammate, Leslie Mann, now with the Cardinals, showed the letter to Rickey, who forwarded it to the commissioner. Meanwhile, the Giants left New York for Pittsburgh after their game on Sunday, August 13. McGraw stayed behind with all intents and purposes of reinstating a "dried-out" Douglas and rejoining the club presently with the misguided pitcher. The two men arrived in the Steel City after their team but were met by Commissioner Landis. In a meeting with McGraw and Landis, Douglas did not deny writing the letter, in which he said he was prepared "to go fishing" and leave the Giants to their own devices—if the price was right. He did deny that he ever threw a game. Placed on the permanently ineligible list of the New York National League Baseball Club for implications of crookedness, Douglas had no chance of finding employment with another major league club. His nine-year big league career, sprinkled with brilliance but just as often stained by a lack of self-discipline, ironically concluded with him finishing atop the National League in ERA (2.63), as well as in a couple of statistical categories—WHIP (1.199) and ERA+ (153)—created since then.

Thirteen wins in 15 games, from August 11 to 27, shot the Manhattanites into first place by seven games. The team warded off a brief challenge by the Pirates during the third week of September and claimed the flag with a final seven-game cushion over runner-up Cincinnati.

In the American League, the New York Yankees had a more difficult time successfully defending their title. Miller Huggins' club edged out the St. Louis Browns on the final weekend of the campaign to earn the right to challenge the Giants for overall supremacy of the diamond.

The best-of-seven World Series opened on Wednesday, October 4, under summer-like conditions. In a repeat of last year, the Giants suited up as the home defenders first, perhaps in deference to their ballpark or a won coin-flip, before alternating home and road uniforms with the other New York team for the remainder of the Series. Bullet Joe Bush, who had faced the Giants in the 1913 World Series with the Philadelphia A's, started for the visitors. McGraw chose Art Nehf, who was the Giants' top winner at 19–13. Bush, who led the Yankees' pitching staff with 26 wins, appeared on his way to a tightly contested victory when the Giants staged a late rally to turn the tide of imminent defeat. In the bottom the eighth inning, with the score 2–0 in the Yankees' favor, the top of the Giants' batting order—Bancroft, Groh, and Frisch—all singled to load the bases. Cleanup hitter Irish Meusel followed with a fourth consecutive safety to bring in Bancroft and Groh. Huggins replaced Bush with Waite Hoyt, pitching with runners on first and third and no one out. Ross Youngs, Hoyt's first batter, sent a long fly to center field, easily scoring Frisch from third. Hoyt fanned the next two, but the Giants had taken a 3–2 lead. In the ninth, Rosy Ryan, the collegiate pitcher McGraw had signed on the recommendation of Jesse Burkett in 1918, completed his second inning of scoreless relief to pick up the win. Ryan had fanned Babe Ruth to end the prior inning. The Bambino knocked in one of his team's runs earlier with a single.

The next day, Ruth doubled and scored the run that knotted the game at three-all in the eighth inning. The Giants had scored their three tallies on a three-run home run into the left field bleachers by Irish Meusel in the top of the first stanza. Leading off the bottom of the tenth, Ruth came up for a fifth time against Giants starter Jesse Barnes and popped up. Two outs later, the game, which began at 2 o'clock under clear skies and lasted two hours and 40 minutes, was called on account of darkness by home plate umpire George Hildebrand. The decision upset many fans, who felt the action could have continued. The majority of the players, however, agreed with the arbiter's judgment. Gate receipts amounting to over $120,000 were awarded to New York charities, including disabled soldiers, by decree from the commissioner, who was in attendance but had no say in the stoppage of play. Barnes and the Yankees' Bob Shawkey tossed the extra-inning distance, with each receiving a disappointing no-decision in the stalemate.

Every club in the league had had a chance to pick up Jack Scott for the $2,500 waiver price back in May. No club did, including the Giants, which led to Scott's outright release by Cincinnati. In Game Three, fate smiled on McGraw's regenerated right-hander like never before, as Scott hurled one of the best games of his life. A former 20-game loser with the Boston Braves, Scott baffled the American League champions, 3–0, on four hits. In the one hour and 48-minute gem, Scott made sure the encounter had no chance of falling victim to the same advances of twilight as yesterday. The Giants peppered starter Waite Hoyt and his rescuer, Sad Sam Jones, for 12 hits. The winning pitcher was not McGraw's first choice to start the game. "I was going to start McQuillan," said the manager post-game, "but as he was just not feeling right [during warm-up] … I decided to start Scott."[38]

The following day, October 7, McGraw's other August pitching supplement paid grand post-season dividends as well. The former Boston Brave and yesterday's proposed starter, Hugh McQuillan, bested Carl Mays, 4–3. Mays posted one bad inning, and it became his downfall. Slashing out five hits in the top of the fifth inning, the Giants pushed across all of their runs. McQuillan doubled and scored a run in the eventful frame. A persistent rain, which dogged the entire proceedings, interrupted the fine weather enjoyed up to that point by all baseball enthusiasts. McQuillan escaped a potentially big inning himself in the bottom of the first. The first two batters singled. At this early point, the elements gave rise to a haze, coming from the Harlem River, which enveloped the entire Polo Grounds diamond. The temporary mist made it difficult for some to see the defensive play of the game by Bill Cunningham, way out in center field. From his seat in the press box, Grantland Rice saw the gold star play distinctly. "Ruth came up and for a moment it looked as if he had peeled the epidermis off the ball," wrote the renowned sportswriter. "His long, high smash went soaring on to center, with Cunningham in swift pursuit. Backing almost against the center field fence, Cunningham made a brilliant catch, stumbled and fell at the foot of the heavy barrier."[39] Based on the description, the catch was similar to Willie Mays' famed 1954 World Series grab, in almost the same cavernous spot—but without the video to immortalize it. As in Mays' spectacular over-the-shoulder capture, the baserunner advanced only one base (from second to third). The Yankees went on to score twice in the inning, but it could have easily been more.

Every game of the Series, so far, had outdrawn the highest attended game from the last year's Fall Classic (36,509, Game Three). The fifth game on October 8 provided the biggest New York World Series crowd yet seen, 38,551. Again, as in two prior games, the undefeated Giants used a single inning to break through and carry the day. Bunching four hits and a walk in the bottom of the eighth inning, the defending champions scored three runs to defeat the Yankees, 5–3. A rainy drizzle from yesterday held over through the first two innings, and then the skies cleared for the remainder of the afternoon. Giants starter Art Nehf trotted off the field for the second year in a row with the clinching win. Bullet Joe Bush lost a late-inning lead for the second time in five days. Ross Youngs caught the final out of the game and jubilantly threw the ball over the right field bleachers into the vacant lot beyond.

"Gentlemen," Jacob Ruppert said to a large group of reporters the next morning, "all I've got to say is the better club won, and—I mean this—I'm glad that it won in four straight games. It left no room for argument. We were outclassed."[40]

McGraw was with the Yankees' owner at the time. His dutifully gracious comments contemplated not only the unexpected upset pulled off by his Giants but the openness toward gambling still surrounding the sport. "I only hope, gentlemen, that the two New York teams will play a third series," McGraw said. "We didn't expect to win four straight…. It only shows that such odds as 8 to 5 against any club in any series is foolish."[41]

That the 94-win Yankees (one more victory than the Giants) did not put up more of fight was a testament to McGraw's five pitchers. The manager made only one pitching change in the Series, and it came in Game One.

Babe Ruth was more thoroughly contained than in the prior Series. The big swatter, who clubbed 35 home runs in just 110 games on the season, hit a weak .118 (2-for-17), with only one extra-base hit. "I signaled for every ball that was pitched to Ruth during the last World Series," McGraw would pleasingly inscribe in his 1923 autobiography. "In fact, I gave the signal for practically every ball that was pitched during the series by our pitchers."[42]

The Fall Classic victory over their more turnstile-popular tenants was the third and final world championship title John McGraw would claim as a manager.

The same month of the Giants crowning victory, the U.S. Supreme Court refused a rehearing of the Baltimore Terrapins' Federal League case versus organized baseball, reinforcing its earlier decision of May 29, 1922. The refusal cemented baseball's anti-trust laws exemption.

Also in October, basking in the glow of his second consecutive World Series triumph, John McGraw gladly presented himself at a Baltimore Orioles reunion of his mid–1890s glory teams. Ned Hanlon, Hughie Jennings, Joe Kelley, Sadie McMahon, and Wilbert Robinson were among the most well-known former teammates who came together to wistfully recall a now-bygone era. Before the dynamic month ended, McGraw and his wife detoured to Scranton, Pennsylvania, to attend the wedding of Jennings' daughter, Grace.

Back in New York, McGraw completed a trade with the current Baltimore Orioles of the International League. The pitching-minded manager paid $65,000 for Jack Bentley, a 27-year-old left-hander who had come up at a young age with the Washington Senators but had been out of the major league spotlight for six years. Along with the cash, McGraw promised the Orioles owner and manager, Jack Dunn, three players to be delivered before April, or he would add $2,500 for each man. Dunn collected an additional $7,500 on the deal when McGraw decided it was easier to part with money than prospects.

In early December, McGraw attended the National Association of Professional Baseball Leagues meeting in Louisville, Kentucky. He hoped to pull off a trade, or two, but none materialized. To those more receptive ears, McGraw could have gone into detail about the diamond-encrusted rings, commemorating the Giants World Series victory, his team had recently ordered and were looking forward to receiving. (The prior year, the players had opted for diamond-studded watch fobs as their championship spoil.)

McGraw received an early Christmas present when a $30,000 lawsuit against him was dismissed during the holiday season. The plaintiff, a Mary A. Butterfield, had suffered injuries, she said, after being struck by John McGraw's automobile back in 1917. McGraw, who did not drive, was not at the wheel. The case, defended by celebrated 1880s pitcher-turned-attorney John Montgomery Ward, was swept aside by the presiding judge on the grounds that McGraw's "chauffeur was violating instructions at the time the accident occurred."[43]

Presumably, McGraw was not only breathing easier, figuratively speaking, from the summary judgment, but literally as well, from a recent cartilage-removing operation to clear up his nasal passage and relieve his sinus condition. The lingering nose damage was rooted in the errant practice ball thrown by Dummy Taylor all those springs ago.

One former Orioles teammate who did not make the reunion in Baltimore was Wee Willie Keeler. The former batting king was ill. Suffering from heart disease, Keeler died on January 1, 1923, in his Brooklyn home. Both major circuits were well represented at his funeral three days later. McGraw, Jennings, and Wid Conroy, Keeler's New York Highlanders roommate, formed part of the pallbearers' unit on a frosty day swirling with snowflakes. It was reported that the eyes of McGraw welled with tears as he viewed Keeler's body at his home prior to the requiem mass. He and Keeler, as young turks with Baltimore in 1897, had engaged in a knock-down, locker room fight in the truest Greco-Roman style. Both men were completely naked on their way to the showers when they went at each other.

Keeler was 50 years old, the same age as McGraw on Opening Day, 1923. With the exception of center field and pitcher, McGraw used the same lineup that won him the clinching game of the World Series: Bancroft (ss) Groh (3b), Frisch (2b), Meusel, (lf), Youngs (rf) Kelly (1b), and Snyder (c). To commence the new season, McGraw had handed center field to Jimmy O'Connell, his 22-year-old, $75,000 PCL purchase. Hugh McQuillan tossed a four-hit, 4–1 victory over the Boston Braves, at Braves Field, to start the Giants off on their successful National League title defense on April 17. Heinie Groh hit a two-run homer for the winners. The Giants won four out of five games against the Braves, who were now under new management that included Christy Mathewson. Jack Bentley, McGraw's $72,500 minor league acquisition, was the starter and loser in the only setback (9–2).

Mathewson was on hand, with his new team, when the Giants opened their home schedule on April 26. In the pre-game ceremony, Commissioner Landis distributed the custom-made World Series rings to the deserving Giants players. Mathewson was drawn out to the field by cheering fans and he shook hands with McGraw, dressed in a suit and overcoat. The Polo Grounds was sans flagpole in center field, as the stadium was undergoing construction upgrades.

Therefore, the flag-raising was limited to the Stars and Stripes rising atop a provisional staff on the roof of the grandstand, as Conway's Band played the national anthem. From his bunting-draped box, Mayor John F. Hylan executed his third home schedule-launching throw. Behind Art Nehf and Rosy Ryan, New York beat Boston for the fifth time in six tries, 7–3. Pitching eight innings, Nehf allowed Boston's only hit—a double by Tony Boeckel. Four Giants' errors were responsible for the Braves' runs.

Defeating Boston, Brooklyn, and Philadelphia (the eventual three worst teams in the league) a combined 15 times in their first 20 games, the Giants assumed first place by four games on May 7. The other four NL clubs then visited the Polo Grounds in succession, beginning the following day. McGraw's combine proved it was equally up to the new challenges, winning nine out of 12 against the tougher competition.

Despite the great start, all was not smooth sailing on ship McGraw. The manager had placed Johnny Rawlings on waivers. When claimed by the Phillies, the infielder refused to report. Rawlings was subsequently traded to Pittsburgh by the Phillies without playing a game for Philadelphia. McGraw indefinitely suspended Rosy Ryan for "poor conditioning," a journalistic euphemism that usually applied to repeated over-indulgences with alcohol or breaking curfew. In Ryan's case, as a young newlywed, it was more of a clash with McGraw's overbearing manner. McGraw had denied Ryan a chance to make some extra money, prior to his December wedding, by pitching in post–World Series exhibitions in the Pacific Coast League. The 25-year-old pitcher was also late reporting to spring camp because of salary squabbling. And he had failed to accompany the team on its trip to Philadelphia on May 3.

McGraw felt a need to address the Ryan issue and others circulating around his team. He naturally took to the biggest news medium available. "Rumors have come to me from various sources that several of my pitchers are not satisfied with their salaries," McGraw wrote in a widely-distributed column. "Well, right here, I will say that no club has been more liberal in the pay of their players than the one of which I am an official. I desire all of my men to be satisfied—to be unified. Teamwork is impossible without such a condition. I have no use for malcontents on my team."[44] The strict disciplinarian emphasized his regimental practices, which consisted of daily two-hour workouts, while making clear the irrefutable application of the established "My Way or the Highway" McGraw doctrine: "I expect all my players will try to perfect themselves physically and mentally so as to be fit at the time I set. If they are not, I shall take the same method as I have with pitcher Ryan. I shall insist that my method shall prevail and mine alone. My players must accept those conditions."[45]

Ryan was reinstated May 14. The next day, the Giants had to trim two players from the roster to reach the 20-man limit. McGraw cut two pitchers. He sent Fred Johnson to San Antonio and returned Rube Walberg to the Portland Beavers. McGraw had bought Walberg from the Pacific Coast League team the prior year for $15,000. The deal stipulated that if Walberg was returned by May 15, the Giants would be reimbursed the full purchase price. The decision of McGraw not only contrasted with the free-spending ways of the Giants, but it cost the team much more than the pittance that it saved. A few months later, Walberg was sold by the Beavers to the Philadelphia A's, where the left-hander would develop into an intrinsic part of Connie Mack's pitching staff for years to come. The sale price was $10,000.

While his club was riding high (33–13), McGraw rid himself of two perceived "malcontents" on June 7. He traded spring training holdout Jesse Barnes and recalcitrant catcher Earl Smith to the Boston Braves. Smith had done fine work for the Giants, mostly splitting the catching chores with Frank Snyder for the past three seasons. But he was one of the many players who butted heads with McGraw's rigid manner, and he had been suspended multiple times by the manager. Barnes was one of the suspected pitchers who had been complaining to the press about his salary. Worst of all, he had gotten off to a bad start and drew only four starting assignments as a consequence. The 30-year-old right-hander had been a consistent winner for McGraw since his acquisition in 1918, including two 20-victory seasons. Boston provided, in return, backup catcher Hank Gowdy and a back-of-the-rotation pitcher named John "Mule" Watson, who would win 15 games in two seasons with New York.

McGraw had brought 20 pitchers (a large number) into camp back in March. He may have thought he had sufficient depth, with the addition of the four-years-younger Watson, to counter the loss of his once-star pitcher. Barnes would continue to struggle with the lowly Braves, though his ERA suggested he deserved better.

June closed with the Giants splitting a doubleheader against the Boston Braves and with McGraw's soldiers holding a 4½-game advantage over the second-place Pittsburgh Pirates. The recently exchanged Jesse Barnes outdueled Art Nehf in the June 30 second game, 1–0.

Championship flag-raising ceremonies took place on Saturday, July 21, in much the same manner as last season. Conway's Brass Band led the contingent of players out to center field, where the pennant and championship banners were hoisted up separate flagpoles. The commissioner and league president Heydler were the highest-ranking sports dignitaries present.

The Giants took care of business thereafter, pummeling the St. Louis Cardinals, 14–7. Heinie Groh cranked out five hits, and Irish Meusel and Travis Jackson slammed home runs. The 19-year-old Jackson had made the team coming out of spring training and was playing in place of the injured Dave Bancroft.

When August rolled around, the Cincinnati Reds made a bid to challenge McGraw's squad. On his pitching staff, Pat Moran's club touted three eventual 20-game winners (the last NL team to sport a trio of charmed circle members). The best of the lot was Adolfo Luque, the circuit's premier pitcher. Luque boasted a 17–3 mark on the August 3 morning the Giants arrived in Cincinnati for a five-game series, scheduled to begin that day. Cincinnati trailed the Giants by three games in the standings. The Reds starter had beaten the Giants three times so far, including two Polo Grounds shutouts. Moran succumbed to the heady numbers and needlessly rearranged his rotation in order to start Luque twice in the series.

All baseball games on August 3 were postponed out of respect for the unexpected passing of President Warren Harding. The third of four American presidents to die of natural causes while in office, the 57-year-old Harding was stricken with a heart attack in San Francisco. An Ohio native, he was noted in regional papers as having been an ardent Reds rooter.

When the schedule resumed a day later, Luque hurled his worst game of the season. Knocked from the box in the fifth inning, having surrendered seven runs, he and the Reds absorbed a 14–4 defeat. Rosy Ryan pitched a complete game to improve to 10–1, in his flexible role as relief man and spot starter. The Giants won the next three games in tighter fashion, including a 2–0, high-end performance from Hugh McQuillan over Eppa Rixey (another Reds 20-game victor).

Out of desperation as much as strategy, Luque came back on August 7 and was unable to salvage the Reds' dignity—or his own. In the eighth inning, the Reds' top pitcher was the target of heavy razzing from the Giants' bench. After giving up four consecutive singles, which built up a Giants lead to 5–2, the pitcher calmly left the mound, in mid-count to Ross Youngs, and walked toward the visitors' bench.

> As he stepped over the foul line he tossed the ball to umpire Klem and continued on his way. Advancing straight upon Casey Stengel, who kept his seat, the infuriated Cuban let swing a vicious right at the center fielder's head. Casey ducked to one side just in time, and the blow glanced off his shoulder. Immediately there was a confusion of left and right swings, but it did not last long as Pep Young [sic] grabbed Adolfo by the neck, securing a firm strangle hold, and dragged him 20 feet away.[46]

Besides the agitated players, irate fans clashed with policeman as hordes swarmed the field. The ability to restore order became increasingly more difficult when Luque, after getting a drink of water, appeared with a bat in his hand, seeking more retribution against Stengel. It took the Cincinnati gendarmes to disarm the belligerent hurler, and finally calm prevailed. Both Luque and Stengel were ejected by Bill Klem. Mule Watson, aided by Rosy Ryan, was the winning pitcher in the 6–2 final.

The Giants left Cincinnati with a 7½-game lead over Pittsburgh and eight over the previously second-place Reds. Luque was suspended one week for his actions, and the whole misguided pitching design of Pat Moran cost the Reds a reasonable chance at the pennant and deprived Luque of a chance to win 30 games. Although this was an era in which pitchers were expected to be ready on short notice, there was no reason, with 50-odd games remaining, for the rotation disruption. Juggling Luque required rearranging the other staffers as well. In one of the great pitching seasons of the Liveball Era, the Reds' right-hander went 27–8 with a 1.93 ERA. He tossed a league-topping six shutouts and was denied *seven* more simply due to unearned runs. Luque was one of only two starting pitchers in the entire decade to register an ERA under 2.00 (Pete Alexander, 1.91 in 1920, was the other).

All throughout the summer, rumor clouds followed the Giants portending the team's sale, due to business misconduct by stock broker-financier Charles Stoneham. The principal owner, who was "under indictment for complicity in local bucket shop scandals,"[47] was under pressure to sell his controlling interest in his club. Any number of potential new buyers surfaced, from George Washington Grant, late of the Boston Braves, to former owner Harry Hempstead.

Speculation that, under new ownership, McGraw would become president and coach Hughie Jennings would be installed as manager abounded. But in the months that followed,

Stoneham would weather not only this indictment (for mail fraud) but a second one as well, and manage to escape prosecution from wrongdoing to continue in majority control.

The Cincinnati Reds, to their credit, did not quit following the embarrassing sweep on their home turf. The team battled to within three games of New York in early September—though, by the time the Giants left New York on their final road trip on September 9, the Reds had slipped 4½ games back. That same day, Mule Watson showed up at Grand Central Station to board the team train to Boston, intoxicated. McGraw suspended the pitcher for the rest of the year and imposed a $500 fine. The suspension was short-lived, as Giants players lobbied McGraw to give Watson another chance. After receiving an apology and a promise to behave in the future from Watson over the phone, McGraw reinstated the hurler. The manager would not relent on payment of the fine, which was deducted from the player's salary. Watson joined the club in Chicago.

At Cubs Park on September 17, High Pockets Kelly recorded the game of his career. The first baseman slugged home runs in consecutive innings (3,4,5), and banged out two other hits. He scored four times and drove in an equal total in the Giants 13–6 victory.

On September 19, the Giants were rained out in their last scheduled game in St. Louis. McGraw declined to make up the game the next day, an off-day for both the Giants and Cardinals. The Giants' next stop was Pittsburgh, and McGraw had intended on visiting Christy Mathewson in Factoryville, Pennsylvania, his hometown and place of residence. The McGraws and the Jenningses spent the off-day with Mathewson and his wife.

On September 22, after sweeping three contests from the Pirates, the Giants headed to Cincinnati for a two-game set, with their 4-game lead intact and eight games to play. The next day, a non-playing one for the team, the purchase of Lewis "Hack" Wilson was officially made known. The stout outfielder from the Virginia League debuted with the Giants later in the month.

On September 24, the Reds' Pete Donohue (the Reds' third 20-game winner) beat the Empire State front-runners, 6–3, to trim the difference. But the following day, Mule Watson outpointed Adolfo Luque, who was pitching on one day's rest, 3–2. Luque volunteered to pitch after Eppa Rixey came up with a lame arm during warm-ups. Watson, the mediocre pitcher McGraw picked up in the Barnes-Smith trade in June, beat the best pitcher in baseball for the second time in a crucial situation this season.

A few days later, McGraw became the first manager to win three pennants in a row twice. The Giants' final record was 95–58, and their final margin of victory over Cincinnati was 4½ games. The Reds were left with the minor consolation of being the only club in the league to take the season series from the first-placers.

Unlike the past two seasons, the New York Yankees' third successive pennant came in a cakewalk. The 98–54 team crushed all challengers, leading the American League field by a final tally of 16 games.

During the final week of the campaign, the Giants took advantage of scheduled off-days to practice and play an exhibition game. The first two days of practices were conducted at their former tenant's gigantic new ballpark in the Bronx. McGraw put his players through intensive batting and fielding drills and had his top seven pitchers throw batting practice to the hitters.

McGraw thought the Yankee Stadium infield was in fine shape but said he found the outfield bumpy in spots. The exhibition game, the brainchild of McGraw, was for the exclusive benefit of two old-time Giants luminaries: John B. Day and Jim Mutrie. Day was one of the founders of the 19th-century Giants franchise and Mutrie its first manager. Both men were in their 70s and in declining health. Playing Jack Dunn's Baltimore Orioles, the Giants' lineup had one startling addition—Babe Ruth. A photo of Ruth, wearing a Giants uniform and posing next to the civilian-clad McGraw on the top step of the Giants' dugout, has fortunately survived the passing of time, existing today in mass reproduction.

Six-month-old Yankee Stadium hosted the first game of the third all–New York World Series on October 10. Twenty-four players on both squads were granted eligibility. Yankees first baseman Wally Pipp had an injured ankle, and the team requested the flexibility of adding rookie Lou Gehrig to the roster in the event Pipp aggravated his injury. McGraw said no. The Giants had recently lost back-up outfielder Ralph Shinners to a bad case of influenza and did not seek a replacement.

The New York Nationals entered the Series without a pitching ace. The majority of the team's wins had been distributed among five hurlers, with Jack Scott and Rosy Ryan tying for most triumphs with 16. Hugh McQuillan earned 15 victories, while Art Nehf and Jack Bentley each notched 13. Claude Jonnard, the team's main bullpen man, finished and saved the most games in the league (25/7). Sometimes flippantly referred to as "the embalmer of lost games," Jonnard's value as a non-starter was not overlooked by the Giants.

Nehf hurled a shutout in his final start of the season on September 28. McQuillan tossed five shutouts innings in a tune-up outing eight days later. But McGraw selected eight-game winner Mule Watson—who had started the Giants' last game of the season, three days earlier—to throw the first pitch in Game One for the defending world champions. Watson threw only 38 pitches before being relieved by Ryan to start the third inning. He had surrendered three runs.

Yankees starter Waite Hoyt also experienced an abbreviated afternoon, after surrendering four runs, on four hits and a walk, in the third inning. The game was tied 4–4, entering the top of the ninth. Casey Stengel, who missed last year's Fall Classic due to a leg injury, hit a long drive to left-center field for an inside-the-park home run. Surrendering the fateful blow was Bullet Joe Bush, who had taken over for Hoyt and had held the Giants scoreless until this juncture. Ryan, who slightly outdid Bush's effort, secured the final three outs for a 5–4 victory. McGraw came out of the Giants' first base dugout once; it was before the game to pose for a picture with Babe Ruth and another with Miller Huggins. Dressed in a gray suit, the Giants manager was not seen again for the rest of what was, weather-wise, a pleasant afternoon. Ruth went 1-for-4, hitting the ball hard three times.

The next day, across the Harlem River, Ruth broke out. The Babe hit two solo home runs, the first one clearing the Polo Grounds' right field roof. Aaron Ward clocked a third four-bagger for the visitors, all of which came against Giants starter Hugh McQuillan. Scattering nine hits, Herb Pennock evened the Series for the Yankees with a 4–2 win. Irish Meusel homered in the losing cause for the home team. Miller Huggins finally had something to be encouraged over. "We have the best club in the country and we'll prove it in this series. I only hope McGraw's pitchers continue to pitch to Ruth."[48]

One of McGraw's pitchers, Art Nehf, semi-pitched to Ruth in Game Three. Nehf walked Ruth twice, was reached for a single and struck out the Bambino once. Nehf was otherwise sterling. The curve-baller, who had warmed up with Watson prior to Game One, spun a six-hit shutout over the heavy-hitting Yanks, 1–0. Casey Stengel shared the hero's spotlight with his teammate, hitting the first fence-clearing World Series home run at Yankee Stadium. The seventh-inning blow sailed over Ruth's head in right field. Nehf became the first pitcher to throw two 1–0 shutouts in the World Series. The feat has not been equaled.

Jack Scott, who had shut out the Yankees in last year's Fall Classic, could not find the same magic in the next game. Scott suffered a second-inning kayo, helped along by his own error. Two other Giants hurlers, Ryan and McQuillan, followed Scott in the inning, in which the Yankees scored six times. Bob Shawkey and Herb Pennock combined for an 8–4, Series-evening win. The largest Polo Grounds crowd of the Series, 46,302, were entertained with 13 hits by each team.

Prior to the pivotal fifth game, Huggins and Giants captain Dave Bancroft had a longer than usual meeting at home plate, exchanging the lineup cards with the umpire. Bancroft was the first batter of the game and went hitless, as did his teammates save for Irish Meusel. The Giants left fielder collected the only three Giants hits on the afternoon, as Bullet Joe Bush—making his third appearance—turned back the McGrawites, 8–1. Jack Bentley became the third Giants starter to be sent to the showers before the third inning. Topping Game Three's total, 62,817 spectators set a new World Series attendance mark.

McGraw turned to Nehf to keep the championship dreams alive on the Giants' home turf. But the game southpaw, pitching on two days' rest, wilted late in the sixth contest. In the eighth inning, holding a 4–1 lead, Nehf was allowed to face five batters. He retired the first, then surrendered, in succession, two hits and a walk, loading the bases. McGraw made no indication that he might remove Nehf. With all the bases occupied, Dave Bancroft came over to the Giants' bench to confer with the master strategist. The duration of the conference drew a protest from Huggins. Home plate umpire Hank O'Day ordered the action to resume. After walking the next batter and forcing in the first run of the inning, Nehf was finally removed. Ryan, who had been excellent out of the bullpen all season long, gave up the lead (after he excitingly struck out Ruth with the bases loaded). The five runs Huggins' team eventually plated were enough to ring up a 6–4 win and the Yankees' first championship hurrah. Pennock won his second game, assisted by a two-inning outing by Sad Sam Jones.

The weather throughout could not have been better, except for the final game. Morning showers that did not end until noon held the crowd to a little over 34,000, the smallest of the six engagements—which drew the first million-dollar gate in World Series history. A home run was hit in every game, with each team driving out five. Ruth led all hitters with three circuit smashes.

"I could not help it," said a disconsolate Nehf in the locker room. "It had been a strain all through those innings when they failed to hit me. In the eighth, after Ward was out and Schang hit, my arm would not go on."[49]

McGraw acknowledged his deserving opponents. "The better team won," he admitted, while completely oblivious to his own tactical inaction in the final contest. "The only thing I regret is that the Yanks did not bat in their winning runs in the last game instead of having them presented to them. I would like to point out that not once during the series was Babe Ruth passed intentionally."[50]

Ruth was "unintentionally" walked eight times and posted a 1.000 slugging mark.

"If the Giants again win the pennant, and we feel sure that we will repeat, much of the credit should go to Travis Jackson," said John McGraw in September 1923. "He was the man of the hour on any number of occasions. Inside of three years he should be one of the bright stars of the National League."[51] McGraw was referring to the 19-year-old Jackson's admirable job filling in for Heinie Groh and Dave Bancroft, both of whom missed parts of the season due to ailments.

In the off-season of 1923–1924, McGraw decided to push Jackson's progression along, using a partially altruistic trade that sent Bancroft to familiar trading partners. Bancroft, along with flyhawks Casey Stengel and Bill Cunningham, were sent to the Boston Braves for pitcher Joe Oeschger and outfielder Billy Southworth. "We have several reasons for making the sacrifice," McGraw said of the mid–November trade, which specified a promotion for Bancroft. "First, for the good of baseball and my desire to do something big for my old friend Matty, and finally to give Bancroft the opportunity to become a big league manager. While we feel we are giving up a great infielder in Bancroft, we feel we are securing a great outfielder in Southworth."[52]

McGraw was half-right. Bancroft was a great infielder, a fact perhaps clearer today than it was then; the 32-year-old shortstop had, we know now, led the team in WAR in 1921 and 1922, and had finished second to Frankie Frisch a year later, despite missing almost 50 games after contracting severe pneumonia. In 1924, Southworth, whose forte came later as a manager, was forced to relinquish most of the playing time in center field to rookie Hack Wilson.

Days after the Bancroft transaction, McGraw and the Mrs. left on an overseas trip with the Jenningses. The day before his European departure, McGraw held a two-hour meeting with Branch Rickey at the Waldorf-Astoria Hotel. The primary topic of conversation was said to be Rogers Hornsby. A deal between the astute baseball rivals could not be worked out. (Rickey wanted Frisch to be part of any deal.)

Perhaps because of his trip to the continent, McGraw spent only two weeks in Cuba, just before reporting to the Giants new training venue in Sarasota, Florida. Last winter, McGraw had been formally recognized for his ties with the sport on the island.

> Cuban baseball enthusiast held a big demonstration in honor of John J. McGraw, manager of the New York Giants, here. McGraw, in uniform, was escorted by a guard of honor from his hotel to Almendares Park, where he witnessed 17 innings of variegated baseball and later was presented, in the name of Cuban fans, with a handsomely engraved medal and an embossed parchment.[53]

While in Havana, McGraw hired Armando Marsans as a spring training coach, to instruct the players on base running and sliding techniques. McGraw had four coaches in Sarasota: Frank Dwyer worked with the pitchers, while Hughie Jennings and Cozy Dolan tutored the infielders and outfielders, respectively. Only Jennings and Dolan were retained throughout the season. Prior to the campaign commencing, Marsans was reassigned as player-manager of the Elmira Colonels of the New York–Penn League.

Another "reassignment" was simply perplexing. McGraw sent Jack Scott, his top winner from 1923 (tied with Rosy Ryan), to the Toledo Mud Hens in exchange for a prospect. Scott had been the unemployed pitcher with the purported bad arm McGraw had taken a chance on in 1922. He had compiled a 24–9 record in his season and a half in New York, plus a World Series shutout. Though with the team for only two months, he had been given a full share of the 1922 Fall Classic's winners' pool by his teammates. But in the spring of 1923, Scott had the temerity to hold out for more money. Scott also had reportedly shown up "sick," and unable to pitch, prior to Game One of the last World Series, possibly altering McGraw's pitching choice to the less than formidable Mule Watson. The rejuvenated pitcher had to clear waivers from every other major league club, making the transaction smell of complicity.

The Giants raised the curtain on the 1924 season on April 15, with 20-year-old Travis Jackson at shortstop and two other sparkling rookies, Bill Terry and Freddie Lindstrom, waiting in the wings. The Polo Grounds refurbishing taking place during last season's opener was complete, the centerpiece being a new clubhouse now within the stadium in center field. The franchise used the occasion to hoist a tri-pennant banner, reading, CHAMPIONS NATIONAL LEAGUE '21, '22, '23, in left-center field. On the re-established center field flagpole, the Old Glory was raised to accompanying Conway Band strains of the national anthem. Mayor John F. Hylan had already made his appearance, coming in through the center field gate. Halfway through his walk, he was met by nine Broadway showgirls, dressed in baseball uniforms, who had been performing for the crowd. The ladies escorted the mayor to his box seat. Having been raised in Brooklyn and with the Robins today's opponents, the mayor's loyalties may have been tested. Prior to Hylan's ceremonial first toss, McGraw, in a tailored suit and overcoat, was photographed shaking hands with a bespectacled Wilbert Robinson, in uniform.

Robinson's starter, Dutch Ruether, led the visiting Robins to a 3–2 win over the Giants and Rosy Ryan. Zack Wheat drove in all the runs for the road team. Forty thousand fans came out on a crisp spring day for the event. It was the largest Opening Day crowd recorded at the Polo Grounds, assisted by last season's completion of the second-deck extension along third base into left field.

Over the next fortnight, McGraw's troupe lost only one other game. On the first of May, the 9–2 club began a road trip that would keep them away from the Polo Grounds for a full month except for a doubleheader sweep over the Philadelphia Phillies on May 4, and another on May 28, when they swept Brooklyn. In the middle of this period, on May 16, High Pockets Kelly came down with a toothache. Bill Terry stepped in at first base and hit two home runs and drove in five runs in a slugfest 16–12 win at Cubs Park. That same day, McGraw twisted his knee while out for a walk and aggravated a ligament injury from more than 20 years ago. Confined to crutches, McGraw traveled with his team to Pittsburgh, the next stop, but was forced to return home when the discomfort grew too much to bear. His leg was placed in a steel cast. McGraw was unable to return to the team until July 8. He had been forced to hand over a 16–10 club to Hughie Jennings; when McGraw reassumed control, the Giants were a heady 48–25.

As McGraw reintegrated himself, one of the pitchers he had been cultivating bloomed. Several years earlier, Jesse Barnes had a direct influence in the Giants' minor league signing of his younger brother, Virgil. A right-hander like his older sibling, Virgil Barnes had spent parts of the past two years in the Giants' bullpen, before joining the starting rotation this season. The 27-year-old Virgil won seven out of ten starts from July 4 to August 21, helping to keep the Giants at the top of the league. Barnes had served in the First World War and had received the Wound Chevron, the equivalent of the Purple Heart.

Serving with Barnes as a Giants front-line staffer was Jack Bentley. The former International League pitcher was doing his best to live up to his pricey purchase. Bentley tied Barnes for most team wins with 16. Art Nehf and Hugh McQuillan were both 14-game-winners, with McQuillan's 2.69 ERA almost a run lower than Nehf's. Rosy Ryan was not quite as effective as last year in his dual starting and relieving roles; his record was 7–6, and he saved five games. Claude Jonnard, 4–5, finished 17 games (one more than Ryan) and posted the best ERA on the squad (2.41), though in 89⅔ innings.

On August 18, Ryan was the losing pitcher in the major leagues' longest game of 1924. At Redland Field, Ryan allowed the winning Cincinnati runs to cross the plate in the bottom of the 17th frame. A double by George Burns sent home Eddie Roush, whose single had tied the contest, 7–7. Pitcher Tom Sheehan, who led off the inning with an infield hit, hurled 15⅔ innings, in relief, to pick up the exhausting win. Sheehan permitted three runs, two earned, and 11 hits, with seven walks and eight strikeouts, while facing 63 batters—and accumulating a no doubt off-the-charts pitch count. Prior to the 3:45 marathon, a bronze memorial plaque, in memory of Pat Moran, was installed against the wall of the grandstand near the press box gate. The former Reds manager passed away from kidney failure in early spring. Moran's family and close friends were present for the ceremony, as well as Commissioner Landis. Several top baseball executives spoke a few words, including McGraw.

McGraw spoke with much different-toned words two days later when he released two lower-grade players on his team and asked waivers on a third. Pitcher Leon Cadore and catcher Eddie Ainsmith were sent packing, and Mule Watson was dangled from the waiver wire. The men had overstepped the boundaries of McGravian law.

> I must win pennants. That's my job in baseball.
>
> In order to win these pennants I must have discipline, and if I have to sacrifice winning the flags, I'll have it. Each ball player must be in his room at 11 p.m. He must refrain from temptations that all good or well-trained athletes keep away from. Regardless of what kind of star he is, if he does not observe the rules he cannot play for me.[54]

Cadore had been picked up a month earlier by McGraw, with the same reclamation hope as with Jack Scott. Ainsmith had played in only ten games. The players had contributed next to nothing and were easy discards, but McGraw's point could not be lost on the rest of the team. Watson was pulled back from waivers and remained with the New Yorkers the rest of the way, though he did not work much.

Entering September, the Giants had to work to give McGraw his fourth pennant in a row, facing serious challenges from the Pittsburgh Pirates and Brooklyn Robins. Pittsburgh was two games from tying the Giants, and Brooklyn was two games further back. McGraw's pace-setters split a road doubleheader with the Boston Braves on September 1. The Barnes brothers both won their starts on the day. Former Giant Jesse won the opener in 11 innings, 5–4, and Virgil, quite less stressfully, copped the nightcap, 10–2, for his 14th win. McGraw was stationed at his hotel throughout the day, the victim of heat exhaustion arising from an unforgiving heat wave.

Two days afterward, McGraw made a lineup change. He sat Irish Meusel and moved High Pockets Kelly into left field, inserting Bill Terry at first base. Used mostly as a pinch-hitter, Terry was not tearing the cover off the ball, but McGraw was obviously itching to see more of him. The left-handed swinger, whom McGraw called "the sweetest-looking batter I ever saw step to the plate"[55] back in the spring, played most of September during a heated pennant race, a testament to McGraw's early confidence in him.

It was a three-team scramble heading into the last week of the season. Losers of two home games in a row, the first-place Giants were scheduled to open a three-game series at the Polo Grounds with third-place Pittsburgh (1½ games back) on September 22. To complicate matters, McGraw had just lost Heinie Groh (knee) and Frankie Frisch (finger) to injuries in back-to-back games. After a night of showers, the Giants called off the game due to wet grounds, even though the team suited up and conducted their usual morning practice and the sun was shining before they left the field. Pirates owner Barney

Dreyfuss protested the decision—which he squarely placed on McGraw—to John Heydler. The postponement forced the Pirates to stay over an extra day in New York after McGraw refused to make up the rainout with a doubleheader. In the end, the Pirates lost a scheduled off-day prior to playing a doubleheader back in Pittsburgh on September 26. After beating the Cubs (in Brooklyn), the 90–60 Robins tied the idle 89–59 Giants on the September 22 "wet grounds" postponement day.

The Giants took advantage of the one-day respite. Like champions, the regrouped McGrawmen rose to the challenge and swept the three games from Pittsburgh. McQuillan (14–8), Barnes (16–10) and Nehf (14–4) all hurled complete games. Brooklyn, with a loss and off-day within the span, slipped 1½ games behind, with two games to play for both contenders. The inspired Giants clinched the pennant with a home win over the Philadelphia Phillies on September 27. In the 4–1 victory, Bentley (16–5) won for the fifth time in six starts, hurling his fourth straight complete game.

The 93–60 Giants had a fine hitting club. With the exception of Groh and Wilson, all the regulars hit .300 or better. High Pockets Kelly, sending a message that he was far from ready to be put out to pasture, led the team in slugging (.531) and the league in RBI (136). Frankie Frisch tied with Rogers Hornsby for most runs scored in the Senior Circuit (121) and trailed only Hornsby in WAR among NL position players. Ross Youngs batted .356 with a colossal .441 OBP. Catchers Frank Snyder and Hank Gowdy maintained productive seasons, combining for 90 RBI from a normally offense-deficient position. For the second year in a row, the Giants' 5.6 runs per game, bettered every other team, with next-closest St. Louis nearly a full run behind at 4.8.

The Washington Senators nosed out the New York Yankees for the American League pennant, spoiling a fourth consecutive all–New York match-up in the World Series. Frisch's injured finger did not prevent him from playing in the autumn showcase, but Groh's badly wrenched knee limited him to one pinch-hitting appearance. Groh's place at third base was taken by Freddie Lindstrom for the entire seven-game conflict. It was a lot to ask of Lindstrom, who was still a month away from his 19th birthday. Frisch at third, Kelly at second and Terry at first, along with shortstop Jackson, may have seemed the more viable alternative. (Kelly had played second base down the stretch when Frisch was out.) But instead, McGraw chose Lindstrom, who made only 16 starts all season, almost half of them in the waning days of the campaign, following the injuries to Frisch and Groh. McGraw went as far as to bat Lindstrom leadoff in all the World Series games.

The first World Series game in Washington franchise history was a memorable one and indicative of the bitterly contested struggle to follow. On October 4 at Griffith Stadium, Frisch, named team captain in place of the departed Bancroft, exchanged lineup cards with Senators manager Bucky Harris at home plate. President Calvin Coolidge tossed out the first ball to home plate umpire Tommy Connolly, and the "king of pitchers," Walter Johnson, hummed across the first offering of the game for the home team. A host of other government bigwigs were on hand, as well as Commissioner Landis, "who throughout the contest rested his chin on his hands, which clasped the top of a walking stick."[56] Also in the crowd of more than 35,000 were Johnson's wife and mother, to see the first World Series appearance of Johnson's 18-year career. Though not as fast as he once was, Johnson was still dominant enough to lead his league in wins, strikeouts and ERA—the so-called pitching triple crown—as well as shutouts. The great moundsman pitched his heart out for 12 innings, but came out on the losing end of the contest, 4–3, to Art Nehf, who also courageously hurled the extra-inning distance. Nehf had given up a 2–1 lead in the bottom of the ninth, but gutted through the rest of the way—especially in the 12th. In that inning, Washington scored once and had the tying run at third base with arguably their best hitter, Goose Goslin, up. Nehf retired Goslin on a ground out. In the top of the frame, Ross Youngs had delivered a tie-breaking single and Kelly followed with a sacrifice fly to provide the margin of victory. Afterwards, McGraw, who was playing with fire in the late innings with Nehf, called the nail-biter the greatest World Series game ever played.

At the same venue the next day, with left-hander Tom Zachary taking the mound for Washington, McGraw sat Terry and put Kelly back at first base. Both Terry and Kelly had homered against Johnson in Game One, with Kelly playing the outfield and Irish Meusel watching from the bench. McGraw opted to use Hack Wilson over Meusel (both right-handed swingers), but Meusel was back to fill the vacancy left by Kelly in Game Two. Late-inning heroics were again in store for the 35,922 fans, but with a much happier ending than the previous day. Trailing 3–1 in the ninth, the Giants tied the game on a walk and two hits. Frankie Frisch scored from first base on a single, the Giants' second run. After a groundout, Wilson's hit brought in the tying run from second. In the Senators' turn at bat, Roger Peckinpaugh, whose bottom-of-the-ninth-inning, two-base hit tied yesterday's game 2–2, lashed a game-winning RBI double off Giants starter Jack Bentley, who allowed a walk and a sacrifice to second. One of two left-handers on the Senators' staff, Zachary was credited with the win, though he had to be rescued, with two outs in the ninth, by Fred "Firpo" Marberry. McGraw was described by one writer as "crouched in the dugout, looking like Rodin's thinker and sounding like heavy static."[57] The manager again exhibited no move to replace his starting pitcher with the game on the line in the last inning. Lindstrom singled to lead off the game, becoming the youngest player in World Series history to record a hit.

The Series shifted to New York for the next three games. With the right-handed Marberry as Bucky Harris's choice to start the third game, Terry manned first base and Kelly went back into the outfield, with Meusel sitting again. The Giants scored three runs in the first three innings against yesterday's one-out reliever. As the Senators mounted a comeback in the fourth, McGraw yanked starter Hugh McQuillan in favor of Rosy Ryan.

The reliever escaped the inning with a 3–2 lead. Ryan homered into the upper deck in right field, earning the laurel as the first National League pitcher to hit a World Series home run. The fourth-inning blast came against Senators reliever Allen Russell. Spanking out 12 hits and cashing in on a pair of Washington errors, the Giants won, 6–4. The official scorer, at his discretion, awarded McQuillan the win, despite his pitching less than four innings. Mule Watson, the last of four Giants hurlers, saved the game by getting the final two outs with the bases loaded. Lindstrom made all three putouts in the final inning, unassisted, at third base. McGraw, calling his pitching "rotten," praised Frankie Frisch for his brilliant play in the field.

Virgil Barnes took the mound in Game Four. Known as "Zeke" to his friends, Barnes was victimized by a third-inning, three-run home run by Goose Goslin and two more runs in the fifth, forcing his removal. George Mogridge, the other southpaw on Washington's staff, pitched effectively into the eighth. Recording the final five outs was Marberry, who as a starter and reliever, in the mold of Rosy Ryan, would flourish as a Senators bullpen man in the years to come. The Senators put the game away in the eighth with two more tallies. The final was 7–4.

Art Nehf had stuck out his pitching hand to stop a batted ball in Game One, and his thumb became too bruised to permit his scheduled turn in the fifth game. Opposing Walter Johnson, instead, was Jack Bentley, the Game Two, complete-game loser.

The Giants derailed the "Big Train" with 13 hits and six runs (four earned), as Bentley—who smacked a two-run homer off Johnson—defeated the Senators, 6–2. McGraw prudently pulled Bentley, pitching on two days' rest, in the eighth, when the game was still close. McQuillan secured the final five outs, and the Giants put the game away with three runs in the eighth inning. Lindstrom collected four singles and drove in two runs against the pitcher whose major league career began when Lindstrom was a year old. (Lindstrom hit .333 in the seven games, with four RBI, validating McGraw's determined use of him.) Post-game comments by Johnson may have sounded like utter doom and gloom for Washington fans, presently and going forward. "I couldn't hold them," said the legendary pitcher. "I had two chances, but I couldn't come through; and I may not pitch next year."[58]

Bucky Harris sounded more inspiring prior to Game Six, back in Washington on October 9. (There were no off-days in the Series.) "We're far from discouraged," said the youthful player-manager of the Senators. "The breaks were against us in New York, but I think they're due for a turn in our favor."[59] In a day's time, Harris, who was a month away from his 28th birthday, would sound downright prophetic. The Washington skipper named Tom Zachary, the Game Two victor, to keep the hopes of Washington rooters alive. Zachary proved to be the pitching star and Harris the hitting hero in a low-scoring contest won by the Senators, 2–1. Art Nehf's thumb had healed sufficiently for him to take the mound. He hurled seven innings, allowing both runs, before being removed for a pinch-hitter. A clutch, two-out single by Harris delivered both Senators runs in the fifth inning. Zachary, who in a few years was destined to give up Babe Ruth's transcendent 60th home run, scattered seven hits and the lone run in the blue-chip, Series-saving effort.

On October 8 in New York, a coin flip had determined where the seventh contest, if needed, would be played. Clark Griffith correctly guessed the haphazard result and won the hosting rights for his city. The 21st World Series, thereby, became the first to incorporate the 2–3–2, eventual standard format.

The seventh game was a tense, extra-inning encounter, imbued with early intrigue and lasting drama. McGraw selected Virgil Barnes, the Game Four starter, with the aspiration of achieving an unprecedented fourth World Series title for himself. Harris chose Warren "Curly" Ogden, a right-hander and spot starter. But the selection was a ploy by the Senators' skipper, for he removed Ogden after he had faced two batters and brought in southpaw George Mogridge. The move was intended to counteract the Giants' left-handed swingers, Youngs and Terry. Both pitchers showed good stuff early on. Barnes allowed one hit through five innings—a solo home run by Harris—while Mogridge held the Giants scoreless. In the top of the sixth, the Giants broke through. Youngs walked and Kelly singled. McGraw pinch-hit Meusel for Terry, and Harris countered by bringing in righty Firpo Marberry. Meusel drove in Youngs with a sacrifice fly, and the Giants scored twice more in the inning. It was the last scoring for New York until next year.

Pitching on two days' rest, Barnes seemed on top of his game. Entering the eighth inning, he had permitted but three hits and no more scoring. In that inning, he faltered. He gave up a one-out double and infield single to put runners on the corners. McGraw did nothing. When Barnes walked the next hitter, loading the bases, McGraw still did nothing. In an eerie repeat of last year's final Fall Classic game, when McGraw let Art

Nehf practically give away a 4–1, eighth-inning lead, the Giants manager allowed Barnes to pitch to two more batters. The first flied to short left field, not deep enough to advance the runner from third. But Bucky Harris, doing it all for his club, grounded a single to left to score the tying runs. The ball took an errant hop over third baseman Freddie Lindstrom's head. McGraw then signaled for Barnes to be relieved. Yesterday's starter, Art Nehf, retired Sam Rice to end the inning.

Harris then made a call to the bullpen that lifted the spirits of the Washington fans even higher. Walter Johnson came into the game, bringing everyone in the stadium to their feet, including President Coolidge, who was attending his third game. Johnson's cross-fire delivery kept the Giants off the scoreboard for four innings, while two of McGraw's hurlers matched him through the 11th inning. In the bottom of the 12th, catcher Muddy Ruel doubled (after his counterpart, Hank Gowdy, dropped a foul popup for an error) with one out. A Jackson error let the next batter, Johnson, reach first, with Ruel not advancing. Then Senators center fielder Earl McNeely sent a hot shot down to third and—as happened in the eighth inning on Harris's single—the ball took a delinquent hop and skipped over Lindstrom's head (ruled a double), scoring Ruel with the championship run.

A group of delirious fans on the field lifted Johnson on their shoulders. They halted the celebration when the First Fan and his wife, escorted by a Secret Service detail, walked up to shake hands with the veteran pitcher.

"I'm just the happiest man in the world, that's all."[60] Johnson repeated over and over again, afterward.

SEVEN

Sidestepping More Scandal

"If I wanted a colorful player who could draw them in at the gate, I would take Babe Ruth. But if I had to choose a real ballplayer to make a team I would select Rogers Hornsby as the greatest player in baseball."—John McGraw

The 1924 Series, viewed from the "bad hop" circumstances of the extra-inning, Game Seven victory of the Senators, seemed fatefully scripted against the men from Gotham, in favor of providing iconic pitcher Walter Johnson with his only championship glory. McGraw absorbed the crushing setback in an unusually subdued manner. "I didn't feel badly about it," he told the press after the 4–3, 12-inning loss in the deciding game. "Defeat is something that must be taken in stride. It's part of life. I have had plenty of winners in my time. The breaks helped to stop us, but breaks are part of every ballgame. I was glad it was Johnson who beat us as long as someone had to."[1] Other reports had him lashing out at his dejected team in the locker room after the thrilling ending.

The day after the World Series concluded, October 11, McGraw was in New York, meeting with Kenesaw Landis, or testifying, more accurately. The commissioner was continuing his investigation into another scandal that had emerged under McGraw's nose. Prior to the first game of the last series of the season, against Philadelphia, coach Cozy Dolan and reserve outfielder Jimmy O'Connell had allegedly conspired to offer $500 to Phillies shortstop Heinie Sand to refrain from trying his best. Sand informed his superiors. Frankie Frisch, Ross Youngs and High Pockets Kelly were implicated as having knowledge beforehand of the bribe attempt. The three star players denied such knowledge.

Also denying any awareness of the occurrence, from the start, was McGraw, who was implicitly absolved by Landis when he personally handed the Giants leader the World Series proceeds check for $99,327.35, to be divided among the losing participants. Excluded from the monetary distribution were Dolan and O'Connell, who were declared ineligible to participate in the Series by Landis.

When the ugly incident came to light, days prior to the sport's premier pageant, many in the press and baseball public understandably cried foul. Old McGraw foes Ban Johnson and Barney Dreyfuss were among the loudest clamorers, and neither was willing to absolve McGraw in the slightest. "Hell is going to be popping in a few days," huffed Johnson. "I will stand for no more nonsense and I know the public is back of me in my demand that this whole nasty mess be aired and guilty ones punished. Stoneham and McGraw—these are the names we hear every time there are reports of a scandalous nature in our sport."[2] The American League president accused Landis of being too friendly with the National League and the New York Giants, and called for the baseball czar's resignation. Johnson had urged that the World Series not be played until the inquiry was fully concluded. He boycotted the 1924 Fall Classic in protest of what he considered feet-dragging by Landis.

Dreyfuss echoed Johnson's fulminations on postponing the World Series.

> I think it is an insult to the intelligence of the public to ask people to believe that two rather obscure members of a champion club could go and offer to pay someone $500 solely of their own money to have something crooked done that would benefit many other persons besides themselves. Others were to profit and I feel sure that if the investigation is carried far enough others will be found guilty.[3]

Dreyfuss also brought up an unheeded claim from last year that McGraw had sent over Cozy Dolan to "tamper" with Pie Traynor, in the hopes of souring upcoming contract negotiations.

McGraw had been delayed in New York until the day before the World Series began, by an initial conference with Commissioner Landis that included Charles Stoneham at the Waldorf-Astoria. "This is a fine way to enter the world's series," McGraw said. "They were dumb. I cannot understand why these two men did what they did when the chances were 100 to 1 that New York would win the pennant."[4]

"They're making a goat out of me," insisted 23-year-old Jimmy O'Connell. "They picked me because I knew Sand well. We played in the [Pacific] Coast League. Dolan put the proposition to me Saturday. He said the whole team would chip in to make up the $500."[5]

Landis displayed little vigor in carrying the case past his sanctioning of the primary players—which would amount to a lifetime ban for the now-pariah duo. Neither one held another job in organized baseball.

Despite McGraw's own stated pessimism prior to the games, anticipating a snub by the fans over the breaking scandal, the World Series was wonderfully attended. The three games in New York were packed with people, including two with over 49,000 patrons, one of the pair marking a new Polo Grounds World Series record. The first three contests in Washington filled the park, though surprisingly, Game Seven saw the attendance dip by about 4,000 from the previous turnouts. The weather was pleasant, often ideal, throughout.

McGraw left town soon after his sixth World Series defeat to lead an overseas barnstorm tour he had arranged with Charles Comiskey, including a contingent of White Sox players. He also met with Cozy Dolan before departing. It was printed in the October 14 edition of the *Chicago Tribune* that Dolan beseeched McGraw's help in trying to obtain another audience with Landis.

Nothing was leaked as to the outcome of the get-together. McGraw personally had to be glad of the trip's fortuitous arrangement, providing a legitimate means of taking him out of the country without making it seem he was evading anything. McGraw joined the advance group of players, headed by Hughie Jennings, in Montreal on October 15. The White Sox "team" was led by its manager, Johnny Evers, and supplemented by two Washington Senators, Sam Rice and Muddy Ruel. McGraw and coaches Jennings and Hans Lobert were accompanied by their wives, as were most of the Giants' players—including Casey Stengel, who had received a personal invitation from his former boss. The same evening, the traveling teams set sail for Europe. Charles Stoneham, incidentally, stayed in New York, awaiting his day in federal court, scheduled for November 10. He also had a second indictment (for perjury) hanging over his head. It was related to the same $1.6 million debt-failure of brokerage firm E.M. Fuller & Co. Stoneham, under oath, had denied formal association with the shady firm and had said large sums of monies transferred from Charles A. Stoneham & Co., prior to it going out of business in 1921, to E.M. Fuller & Co. were meant as loans and not equity stake purchases. The Grand Jury did not buy it.

When McGraw and company returned on December 2, he proclaimed the trip a success, though admittedly a money loser. But he made clear that the excursion was "not a money-making expedition. We went across the Atlantic for other reasons than financial ones,"[6] McGraw said. The ambitious baseball ambassador lamented the rainy weather encountered in England and Ireland, though a clement day in London brought out 7,000 fans, including King George V, to watch the foreigners engage in their indigenous sport.

According to McGraw, his touring teams were responsible for playing the first baseball game in Ireland. But selling the game of bats and balls was going to be an uphill climb, he concluded. "I am satisfied that baseball will never gain a foothold there [Europe] unless it is taught in the public schools," he assessed. "It is out of the question to make ballplayers out of adult Europeans. They have their own games and favorite sports."[7]

During the early winter, the most discussed trade having to do with McGraw was shot down before it got far off the ground. Jake Daubert, a star first baseman for the Brooklyn Robins and Cincinnati Reds, had tragically died during the World Series from appendicitis complications. The Reds, searching for someone to fill the void, came calling on McGraw, with a gleaming eye on William Harold Terry. McGraw was open to dealing the future superstar, but he wanted, in return, pitcher Pete Donohue or Eppa Rixey. Reds manager Jack Hendricks countered with Adolfo Luque. But McGraw, who admired the Cuban pitcher, could not consider it due to the eight-year differences in age between Luque and Donohue. (It was a difficult year for Cincinnati followers. The team lost Pat Moran and Daubert within seven months of each other.)

The SS *Leviathan*, upon which the McGraw expedition returned from Europe, experienced rough seas on its westward crossing of the Atlantic. Struck by hurricane-force winds on part of its journey, the ocean liner had several starboard portholes smashed in by crashing waves, and 15 people suffered injuries, some serious. None of the ballplayers or their wives were hurt. McGraw understandably had enough sailing for one off-season and skipped his usual Havana vacation.

McGraw and Blanche headed to Sarasota in February 1925, in early anticipation of the Giants' pitchers and catchers arriving. The McGraws spent some quality time cruising the Gulf of Mexico on the yacht of John Ringling, of three-ring circus fame. While doing so, the Stoneham federal case was steering to a conclusion. Rumors spread that if convicted, the Giants' owner would be forced to sell his majority stock in the team. Ringling and Colonel Til Huston, who had been bought out by Jacob Ruppert for his partnership share of the Yankees, were named as likely buyers of the stake. But Stoneham and two others were eventually acquitted of the charges, for lack of sufficient evidence. (The perjury charge remained pending—but would also not stick.) McGraw made no significant changes to his club over the winter. His starting eight were as good, if not better, than any in the league. But the lack of an ace, a consistent winner to arrest losing spells and augment winnings streaks, caught up with the club.

A former ace of McGraw's faced the Giants on Opening Day, April 14, as the National

League began its 50th season. As it did, five of the other seven managers in the league had all played under McGraw: Robinson (Brooklyn), McKechnie (Pittsburgh), Fletcher (Philadelphia), Bancroft (Boston) and Hendricks (Cincinnati).

In Boston, Jesse Barnes outdistanced Art Nehf, 5–4. Both pitchers permitted eight hits and overcame errors that increased their runs-allowed totals. McGraw was at home in New York, unable to attend due to a cold. After an off-day, the manager rejoined his team on April 16. Jack Scott, the banished hurler from last season whom every club in the majors passed on, gave the Giants their first win, 8–1. Having been recalled from his minor league exile, Scott surrendered four hits and four walks and struck out four Braves in the dandy outing. The defending circuit champions made it two out of three the next day. Wayland Dean, a high-priced pitching prospect of McGraw's from 1924, tossed his first career shutout. A few months away from his 23rd birthday, Dean silenced the Braves on four singles, 2–0.

In the next game, on April 18, the Giants and Brooklyn Robins renewed their interborough rivalry for another year. Earlier in the day, the man most responsible for molding the Brooklyn franchise into an integral component of the National League, Charles Hercules Ebbets, died from heart failure. His family wished the scheduled game to carry on, and it did. Players of both squads were equipped with black armbands, and a moment of silence was paid in tribute by all inside the deceased man's namesake ballpark. The Giants won, 7–1. National League president John Heydler ordered all games postponed on Tuesday, April 21, the day of Ebbets' funeral. McGraw was part of the Giants' delegation, including Charles Stoneham, who paid their respects.

The following day, the Giants unfurled two banners in their home opener versus the Boston Braves. The 1924 National League championship pennant and the National League's golden jubilee flag were hoisted up separate flag poles prior to the game. The Giants came out on top, 6–5, gladdening the 35,000 present, scoring the deciding run in the ninth inning on three consecutive errors by Braves infielders. New York State Supreme Court Justice Robert Wagner assumed the first ball-tossing honors. Among the usual fare of local VIPS on hand were Latin American dignitary Gerardo Machado, the president-elect of Cuba, and silent screen child star Jackie Coogan.

In a cruel twist of irony, Ebbets' successor, Edward J. McKeever, caught pneumonia at the Brooklyn president's funeral and burial on an unseasonably cold day in New York. McKeever died eight days later. His funeral was May 2. The entire Brooklyn team came out to pay their respects, led by manager Wilbert Robinson. Stoneham represented the Giants at the services. McGraw was not reported in attendance and most likely was not at the Giants-Brooklyn game later in the afternoon. He had been felled by sinusitis. It would be his worse strain to date. Although he managed to take in a couple of games in the stands during his recuperation period, McGraw did not return to the Giants' bench until June 23.

At that point, the 36–22 Giants were at their accustomed spot at the top of the standings, but by only 1½ games over the Pittsburgh Pirates. Hughie Jennings had done a particularly fine job guiding the Giants in McGraw's absence. The acting manager had to deal with a banged-up infield, with injuries to Frisch (broken thumb), Groh (knee) and Lindstrom (broken thumb). Crack outfielder Ross Youngs was slumping badly, as the kidney disease that would end his young life in a little over two years began silently manifesting itself.

When McGraw returned, some newspapers including the June 9 *Boston Globe* recklessly reported that the manager had recovered from a nervous breakdown. The Giants, and McGraw, were never forthcoming about his nasal condition. During those less sophisticated medical times, it was perhaps wiser, if not easier, to identify his illness as a severe cold or flu, rather than the possibly alarming sinusitis. Undoubtedly founded by the false nervous breakdown reports, another rumor spread shortly after McGraw came back, indicating that the long-tenured pilot would be resigning. The riled-up skipper gathered his troops in the locker room to dispel any such notion. "So I'm quitting, eh?" he told the team. "The day I quit the Giants will be the same day I'm unable to drag myself out of bed."[8]

Physically speaking, McGraw had recovered the weight he had lost during his sick leave. Another heartening sign that McGraw was back to his old self was a public beef with one of his natural-born enemies. On June 29, the Giants played the Boston Braves at the Polo Grounds. With the home team out in front, 3–1, in the bottom of the second inning, a downpour struck, halting the proceedings. After the rain completely ceased, Bill Klem inspected the field and determined it was not fit for play. Klem called the game—despite a difference of opinion from Giants head groundskeeper Henry Fabian. The decision spiked McGraw's blood pressure, needless to say. He tried to paint Klem as selfish for robbing the fans of their entertainment. The Giants slipped out of first place by percentage points following the no-decision.

In mid–July, shortstop Travis Jackson went down with an injury that would keep him out of the lineup for four weeks. Throughout the month, the Giants and Pirates see-sawed with each other for first place. Then, in early August, New York dropped six in a row to fall five games behind Pittsburgh. The Giants were on the road when McGraw decided to make a few changes. He announced the signing of American Association pitcher Freddie Fitzsimmons on August 8. The right-hander was obtained in a trade with the Indianapolis Indians, in exchange for outfielder Frank Walker and an undisclosed sum of money. The same day, he traded Hack Wilson, under option to the Toledo Mud Hens, for outfielder Earl Webb. The Virginia League pick-up of McGraw, Wilson took advantage of a broken finger suffered by Billy Southworth in June of 1924 and saw action in 107 games; he hit .295 with an admirable .486 slugging mark. Wilson started every game of the 1924 World Series.

Two days later, Hank Gowdy was let go, but the intent there was to permit Gowdy, still doing well as the backup catcher, a chance at managing the Columbus Senators. According to Freddie Fitzsimmons' biographer, Peter J. DeKever, McGraw personally traveled to Indianapolis to complete the deal for his new pitcher. This may have occurred on August 5, a rainout between the Giants and Reds. Fitzsimmons joined the Giants in Cincinnati on August 8. Interestingly, the first major league game the 24-year-old Indiana native saw was the first time he put on a big league uniform. The Giants lost that day, for the sixth time in as many games, and did not look good in the process.

> It wasn't an auspicious day. I went to my locker in the far corner of the clubhouse. The other players were sitting with their heads in their hands, like so many condemned men in the death house. I've heard men chewed out by experts, but McGraw taught me a new vocabulary as he went down the line casting doubts on each man's ancestry, intelligence and guts. And he never repeated himself during a two-hour tirade.[9]

The Giants scratched back to within two games in the standings following a win on August 19, but by the final day of the month, the deficit to Pittsburgh enlarged to 7½ games. The pitching staff was never able to find a rhythm all year. McGraw and Jennings used a five-man rotation throughout, with Virgil Barnes pacing the squad with 15 wins. Jack Scott (14–15) compiled the best ERA among regulars at 3.15 and also the team's top WAR rating at 6.0.

Rookie Kent Greenfield, another Virginia League find of McGraw's in 1923, displayed promise with a 12–8 mark. Old mainstay Art Nehf slipped to 11–9 in 29 appearances. The fifth hurler was Jack Bentley, who was hit hard but managed the same record as Nehf.

Fitzsimmons chipped in with a nice 6–3 showing and 2.65 ERA in ten games. A top contributor for the past two seasons, Hugh McQuillan, was of no help. Embroiled in a personal love triangle involving the current Miss Bronx, a Miss Helen Goebbels, the married McQuillan earned but two wins in 14 appearances. The obviously distracted pitcher did not appear in a game after July 9. He was suspended shortly after the scandalous story broke, on the pretext of failing to keep in playing condition.

McGraw bypassed the final 14 games of the season, all on the road. His team had 6½ games to make up. Perhaps his illness had taken a toll, and he was being cautious with the cooling temperatures of the early fall—or had had a minor relapse. It filtered out later that McGraw stayed behind because his wife Blanche was sick, the validity of which was difficult to corroborate.

When all was said and done, the second-place Giants trailed the champion Pirates by 8½ games. The team record was 86–66, but 51–40 under the man himself.

McGraw attended the first game of the 1925 World Series, in Pittsburgh, as a press box invitee. He had also written syndicated columns in the days leading up to the opening extravaganza, October 7. His love of the game was still evident as shown by some of his printed musings on the day of the first contest:

> Baseball is in the air—nothing else—and I am breathing it with delight. I have seen baseball grow from the time 10,000 was considered an enormous crowd until now when 40,000 will be in the stands. That feeling of fellowship and sportsmanlike spirit among people collected from people among all corners of the country makes one proud of the game he grew up with and helped to develop.[10]

McGraw saw the Series between Pittsburgh and the repeat American League champion Washington Senators as a toss-up and would only go as far as to predict that the team receiving the most "breaks" would emerge victorious.

Hours after Washington took the first game from Pittsburgh, behind Walter Johnson, the baseball world was shocked with the announcement of the death of Christy Mathewson at Saranac Lake, New York. The supreme pitcher succumbed to tuberculosis. Naturally, McGraw was hit hard by the news. His immediate comments reflected a state of detached numbness. "I regarded him as one of the finest men baseball has ever known as well as one of the greatest pitchers the game has ever known," he said. "It is indeed a great loss."[11]

Commissioner Landis's statement captured the thoughts of many, saying, "Mathewson's death is a great blow. It is especially stunning coming at a time like this."[12]

McGraw carried on with his reporting duties for Game Two, and then left with Blanche for Lewisburg, Pennsylvania, Mathewson's old, cherished college campus and burial place. McGraw was named one of the honorary pallbearers. He rejoined the Fall Classic in Washington with what one expects was a most heavy heart.

No sooner had the World Series ended, than trade talk involving McGraw began commandeering column space on the national sports pages. Bill Terry was, again, front and center in negotiations with Garry Herrmann of the Reds. Because of injuries to three of the Giants' infielders, at one time or another during the year, Terry had played virtually an entire season at first base for New York. He hit .309 with 11 home runs and 70 RBI. McGraw was supposedly willing to let Terry and Frank Snyder, whose offensive numbers had dipped considerably in 1925, go to the Reds in exchange for Adolfo Luque and catcher Eugene "Bubbles" Hargrave, a lifetime .300 hitter. When nothing happened and the proposed trade died, talks were revived later with different player chips.

But first, Brooklyn came calling for Mr. Terry. Wilbert Robinson was willing to package his famed spitballer, Burleigh Grimes, as the centerpiece in a deal for the first baseman. Grimes was five years older than Terry and commanded a much higher salary, predictably leading to McGraw's refusal of the offer. McGraw also declined Herrmann's second trade offer, this one for High Pockets Kelly and Freddie Fitzsimmons, in return for Adolfo Luque and Eddie Roush. In 1925, Kelly played second base and was once again a terrific offensive contributor (.309/20/99). It must have been clear to McGraw, by now, that Terry could do the job at first base. Luque, and especially Roush, had been on McGraw's radar in the past. But McGraw's seeming reluctance to give up a promising young pitcher outweighed all other considerations, and the effort fell by the wayside. McGraw elected to bide his time and accepted the outcome. He subsequently started the 1926 season with an overcrowded infield, relegating Terry to another year on the bench, and with deficiencies in his outfield.

Those deficiencies would not have been as great if McGraw had better assessed his outfield crop. In September, McGraw had acquired Ty Tyson from the Louisville Colonels for Earl Webb, the outfielder obtained from Toledo in the Hack Wilson trade. Coming off an impressive season with the Colonels, Tyson was a 33-year-old who had never played in the major leagues. The player shuffle and some faulty scouting notices caused damaging repercussions. McGraw chose to keep Tyson over Wilson, leaving the latter player exposed to the minor league draft. "Brilliant reports on Tyson," expanded one report, "caused the Giants to cut their strings on Hack Wilson, who recently was drafted by the Cubs. Tyson was out of baseball for five years, and came back last season with Louisville and hit .331."[13]

One assessment McGraw did not miss on—to the hosannas of all current and future Giants fans—was the practically cradle signing of one Melvin Ott. A Louisiana native, Ott, only 16 years old, had traveled to the big city to try out in front of the illustrious manager the past September. McGraw liked enough of what he saw from Ott to promise to send him a contract over the winter, with an invitation to spring training. Ott had come recommended by a casual friend of McGraw's named Harry Williams, a Mississippi businessman. To the resentment of few, if any, Giants players, 17-year-old Ott was given a spot on the 25-man roster and broke camp with the team from Sarasota, on its way north to begin the season. He stayed with the Giants the entire year, performing mostly as a pinch-hitter.

Other players were not so lucky. Heinie Groh's knees were shot, and McGraw would cut him in early May. So too, apparently, was Art Nehf's arm. Around the same time, McGraw gave the big-hearted pitcher the axe. A month later, Billy Southworth, a regular last season back from injury, was traded to the St. Louis Cardinals for Heinie Mueller, a six-years-younger outfielder. Another familiar member of the Giants was not part of the club in 1926, but for very different reasons. Hughie Jennings, who had consistently provided praiseworthy work as acting manager during McGraw's past absences, was diagnosed with tuberculosis and remanded to sanitarium care in North Carolina. Roger Bresnahan replaced Jennings as McGraw's main lieutenant.

A flatter Opening Day the Giants could not have had against Brooklyn Robins pitcher Jesse Petty. At the Polo Grounds, the 31-year-old left-hander and World War I veteran one-hit McGraw's brigade, 3–0. On a cold day in Harlem, made colder by Petty's pitching, Frankie Frisch's bloop double in the sixth inning was the only Giants safety. Due to the poor showing, the biggest cheers from the immense, partisan crowd of 45,000 were limited to Mayor James "Jimmy" Walker earlier in the afternoon. Walker entered the Polo Grounds from center field, leading the parade of players who had lined up for the national anthem (including McGraw and Wilbert Robinson) back to the infield. Walker was a former Tin Pan Alley songwriter who successfully turned his attention to politics. During the pre-game festivities, the contracted band played Walker's biggest hit, "Will You Love Me in December as You Did in May?" The crowd roared with delight at the tune, coinciding with the mayor's presence.

The next day, April 14, McGraw's new pitching addition, Jimmy Ring, hurled the Giants to a 9–5 win over the same opponents. Ring was obtained from the Philadelphia Phillies over the winter. McGraw gave up two arms, the young Wayland Dean and Jack Bentley. Before the game, a jovial-looking John McGraw was photographed taking a picture, with a box camera, of a broadly smiling Wilbert Robinson. Both men were nattily attired, wearing overcoats with wide-brimmed fedoras. The friendly incident suggests that a purported rift between the two men may not have been as accurate or deep as previously thought.

For the second season in a row, McGraw was struck with an early onset of sinusitis. One of the series he was partially able to attend was at Brooklyn. The second game, played April 23, was one that helped perpetuate the intense rivalry that historically spawned between the clubs. Burleigh Grimes was beaten by the despised visitors, 6–3. Although he did not hit a batter, *four* times Grimes threw at the head of Frankie Frisch—a player he was at odds with—the last coming in the ninth inning. In defense of his captain, Frank Snyder, from the bench, challenged Grimes to meet him under the Ebbets Field grandstand after the final out. As best as can be deciphered by varying reports, the intended one-on-one confrontation was broken up before it began in earnest by the almost simultaneous arrival of both team's managers. McGraw was accused of menacing Robins outfielder Dick Cox with a penknife as he and Cox engaged in brief scuffle. But afterwards, Robinson attested that McGraw was acting as peacemaker, not using the penknife as a weapon, rather using it to clean his fingernails prior to being summoned. "It was recalled that McGraw is usually cleaning his finger nails at one stage or another of any battle he is involved in,"[14] one local writer cynically added. (Robinson's sticking up for McGraw also casts doubt on the severity of their purported rift.)

McGraw missed ten days' worth of games with sinusitis, beginning the next day, April 24. It is uncertain whether the agitation triggered the condition.

As the Giants visited Boston without their exalted leader, that city's main newspaper passed along the following informative that could have left one impishly wondering about its effect on John McGraw's daily constitution:

> Without making much of a fuss about it, both major leagues seem due for a steady practice of using three umpires in every game. There are approximately a dozen indicator men under contract in each league now, and few indeed are the games in which there is not a third man over at the hot corner. In the World Series, there is a fourth umpire—at second base—but this is a frill appointment.[15]

The New York club was 10–8 when it embarked on its first long road trip of the season in early May. From Chicago on May 6, McGraw made his future employment intentions clear by signing a three-year contract to continue on as manager of the Giants. The new, $50,000-per-year agreement would take him through the 1929 season, kicking in after his current contract expired at the end of this season. Concurrently, from the same city, it was also revealed that baseball's best-paid manager was being sued for $14,000. A Chicago realtor, Ernest E. Olp, filed the lawsuit over a land speculation deal McGraw was promoting in Florida. It was the second lawsuit in six months McGraw faced. In October, he and Giants treasurer Francis X. McQuade were named in a breach of contract suit by William F. Peabody over lost commission arising out of the sale of the Giants back in 1918. The monetary damage amount was $66,000.

While in Chicago, McGraw was asked about his decision to part with Hack Wilson. "I let Hack go," said the Giants boss, "because he was not hitting for me. He went like wild, for a time, but then he went to pieces. I could not afford to hold him at the time, because I had to rebuild my club. I hope he does [well], for Wilson is the sort of ball player I like."[16]

After experiencing some rough treading on the western trip, the Giants stumbled back to New York with a 15–19 record. Following a 2–1 loss at Ebbets Field on May 23, the Giants canceled a scheduled return engagement with their rivals at the Polo Grounds the next day. Cold weather was the official reason. The intemperate climate did not prevent McGraw from putting his squad through an afternoon-long workout. The Giants then swept a rescheduled twin-bill the following day.

The team's play in June could be best described as inconsistent, as they won only one more game than they lost. Every spot in the order was hitting relatively well—except the catching position. Ross Youngs was hitting again, although perhaps not with the gusto of the past. In front of 35,000 Polo Grounds fans, he scored three times and stole three bases in a 10–3 win over Cincinnati on June 13. Outfielders Ty Tyson and Irish Meusel, both batting over .300, collected five hits and four RBI between them. The Giants' infield of Kelly, Frisch, Jackson and Lindstrom was as fearsome as ever. The root of the problem, therefore, lay with the men on the rubber. No starter, except for Kent Greenfield, had a winning record as June expired.

As July opened, the 34–35 Giants were in the second division, 8½ games behind the top-tiered Cincinnati Reds. On July 7, an exhibition game was held at the Polo Grounds between the Giants and Washington Senators. The beneficiary of the day's receipts was the Christy Mathewson Memorial Fund, established to build a memorial for the great slabman on the grounds of Bucknell University. Prior to the benefit game, in which Walter Johnson hurled the first two innings, some 20 early-20th-century major leaguers squared off in a three-inning exhibition of their own. Many of McGraw's past underlings participated, including Iron Man McGinnity, Fred Merkle and Art Devlin, and more recent fan favorite George Burns. Anticipated to play an inning or two, McGraw backed off and simply filed about in flannel trousers.

Back on the traveling circuit, the Giants lost the last three encounters of a four-game series at Cubs Park. The third loss was a 16–2 shellacking and dropped the club to .500 (44–44). McGraw let his team have it afterwards. He threatened to bench both High Pockets Kelly and Irish Meusel for lacking intensity. At the plate, Kelly was hitting over .300 and Meusel had gone 4-for-4 in the blowout loss; his average was .312. In the wake of his general disgust, McGraw was quoted as saying: "The trouble with the team is due to the indifference of certain players and the downright insubordination of others. The indifferent ones seem to take no interest in baseball, while the insubordinate ones will not take orders."[17]

A recent ex-player of McGraw had revealed some of the challenges of playing under the demanding manager. "I never did play up to my top form in New York," said Billy Southworth, from St. Louis, where he had been traded for another outfielder, Heinie Mueller. "During the years I was there, I was always straining and trying too hard. We had a few run-ins on the bench, but I like Mr. McGraw, and he is a fine gentleman. I simply couldn't play for him—that's all."[18]

The Giants took two of their next three games, but promptly dropped four in row. One of the losses was to the Pirates, 4–3, on July 27. McGraw took Irish Meusel out of the game at the end of the third inning for defensive inadequacies. Meusel sounded resignedly unbothered over the occurrence, as if his spirit had already been broken. "It's all part of the game," the outfielder said. "McGraw took me out of the game yesterday because I did not stop the triples of Cuyler and Traynor. I got to the balls as quickly as I could but they bumped the stands before I could get my hands on them. I guess he thought I should have stopped them. I did not argue the point with him, for he is the boss."[19]

McGraw's men won 11 out of 13 to lift their fading pennant hopes. On the morning of August 11, the club had climbed into the first division and trailed the new National League leaders, the Pittsburgh Pirates, by 5½ games. But just as strikingly, the Giants' season collapsed. The team lost 13 of the next 15 games—all but one on the road.

At the beginning of the losing skein, the Giants best player quit the club in St. Louis. Frankie Frisch took umbrage at a McGraw tongue-lashing directed at him in front of team members, for what McGraw considered a poor game in the field. In a 6–2 Cardinals win on August 20, the "Fordham Flash's" defensive lapses involved being pulled out of position by a Cardinals' hit-and-run play and failing to cover first base on 1–6–4 double play opportunity. The third out of the inning was lost, and the Cardinals scored three runs in the frame. McGraw announced after the game that he was shifting the sparkplug second baseman and hometown favorite over to third base for the next day's game. The next morning, August 21, fed up with McGraw's browbeating ways, Frisch went AWOL. He was seen leaving the Giants' hotel with his suitcase. Frisch was fined for the disappearing act and suspended. Travis Jackson was named as acting captain of the Giants.

Labeling him as a first-time offender, McGraw left the door open for the truant player's return. "Frisch always has been a well-behaved player," he said. "I am going to take his good record into account in dealing with him. The indefinite suspension may last a week or a day or a month. It all depends on the developments."[20]

The developments were that the Giants kept losing, and McGraw heavy-handedly fined his unhappy second sacker $500, plus a dock in pay for the time he missed. (One New York reporter specified that Frisch did not communicate with McGraw or Stoneham, but used High Pockets Kelly to relay and receive messages, and that the fine amounted to the bonus Frisch received as team captain.) Frisch did not put on his Giants uniform again until September 4. He was photographed shaking hands with McGraw that day at the Polo Grounds. To his credit, the disaffected player never criticized McGraw. To the press, he indicated he had simply returned to the Bronx, suffering from general fatigue from a cold and needing time to recover. Frisch blamed playing an exhibition game, on the road trip, in a sweat-drenched jersey as the root cause of the sickness.

Frisch returned to the lineup on September 8 and played most of the remaining games of the season at second base. He hit a tenth-inning, walk-off home run off the Reds' Eppa Rixey on September 17. The blow knocked the Reds out of a first-place tie with the St. Louis Cardinals, the eventual National League champions. A day earlier, the Giants accepted the self-purchased release of Irish Meusel. The 33-year-old outfielder was hitting .292 with a .754 OPS.

The Giants, with 74 wins, won their fewest number of games since 1918. The total was only good enough for fifth place.

It was not a good year for McGraw off the field, either. The previous winter, he had become involved in a land speculation project in southwest Florida that would fail, the result of a real estate crash and the image-crushing destruction left behind from the so-called "Great Miami Hurricane" of September 1926. McGraw suffered an out-of-pocket six-figure loss, the majority of which went to pay off suit-minded investors.

A loss of a different kind and closer to McGraw's heart occurred on November 8, when John McGraw, Sr., died. Living in Cortland, New York, the elder McGraw, described as being in frail health, was 82. McGraw's relationship with his father seems to have remained a distant one.

Although there were no write-ups about his attending his father's funeral, it is unlikely, at this stage of McGraw's life, that he did not. McGraw had three living siblings remaining from his original family brood of eight: sisters Helen and Anna, and brother Michael James McGraw. Another sister, Margaret, had died in 1924. The four siblings were the known McGraw children to have survived into adulthood.

In December, the annual hot stove league trade talk about Bill Terry was ignited. Instead of the Cincinnati Reds, the Boston Braves ostensibly made the strongest bid. The Braves offered Joe Genewich for the budding superstar. Genewich was a nearly 30-year-old right-hander with a sub-.500 record in the big leagues, the type of pitcher McGraw had great success in turning around when backed by his superior teams. But McGraw wasted little time in firmly declining.

Turning toward another trade avenue in St. Louis, Rogers Hornsby was demanding a three-year, $50,000 annual contract from Cardinals owner Sam Breadon. Hornsby was currently signed through 1927, making $30,000 as a player. He had assumed the field manager duties of the club from Branch Rickey in the early part of the 1925 campaign and had led the Cardinals to the 1926 World Series championship. Breadon was compensating Hornsby for managing through stock options he allowed Hornsby to acquire after Rickey's departure. The valuable options were previously owned by Rickey. (Quite often it was reported that Hornsby was receiving no salary for managing, which was technically true but infuriating to Breadon.) The Cardinals owner pledged that he was willing to meet Hornsby's price—but on a one-year basis only.

The impasse between the two strong-willed men resulted in a blockbuster trade occurring on December 20. Frankie Frisch was the obvious trading component, but Breadon asked for Bill Terry, along with Frisch, in order for the Giants to obtain the game's greatest right-handed hitter. McGraw countered with pitchers Jack Scott or Jimmy Ring, instead of Terry. Breadon chose Ring, and the straight two-for-one player transaction went through. From a public relations view, the Giants now had the closest thing in baseball to counter Babe Ruth, both at the box office and on the field of play. Hornsby inked a two-year contract worth $40,000 annually and was appointed the Giants team captain.

McGraw pulled off another advantageous trade on January 9, in which he landed pitcher Burleigh Grimes. The 33-year-old spitball artist was coming off his second straight losing season with Brooklyn and was no longer in a position to demand an elevated salary. In a three-way trade involving the Philadelphia Phillies, McGraw gave up Jack Scott and infield prospect Fresco Thompson. The Phillies sent catcher Butch Henline to the Robins.

McGraw must have been a satisfied man when he left for Cuba at the end of January. It was his first trip to the island in three winters, having bypassed it two years ago for his European goodwill excursion and last year to concentrate on his Sarasota, Florida, land deals. McGraw was in Havana when yet another high-profile trade was announced. Almost certainly negotiated before McGraw left, the exchange

McGraw and the person he called the "greatest player in baseball," Rogers Hornsby. McGraw pulled off a trading coup in obtaining Hornsby from the Cardinals prior to the 1927 campaign. But Charles Stoneham stupidly rid his team of the incredible talent a year later.

signaled the end of High Pockets Kelly's career in New York. The productive and versatile player was traded, along with cash, to the Cincinnati Reds for Edd Roush. Sought for comment at the Oriental Race Track, where he was spending the day with New York Mayor Jimmy Walker and former Boston Red Sox owner Harry Frazee, McGraw said, "I have a high regard for Kelly, but it is my belief both Kelly and Roush will be benefitted by the exchange."[21] The trade paved the way for 28-year-old Bill Terry to take over first base.

McGraw was delayed in Havana by bad weather and was not present when an advance group of players, Rogers Hornsby among them, arrived in Sarasota for the start of training on February 21. Roger Bresnahan was there to greet the men. McGraw would arrive in three days.

As the season approached, the Giants clearly had improved, as McGraw may have completed his best wheeling and dealing in one off-season as Giants manager. Excluding his slabmen, the only visible shortcomings lay at catcher and right field. Combative backstop Frank Snyder had been "waived" from the team back in August, and it was becoming more and more apparent that Ross Youngs would not be returning to baseball. After showcasing his special talent for nearly a full decade, the ill Youngs had played his final game the same month Snyder was released. After signing Hornsby in January, McGraw set out to make Edd Roush happy. But it took a while to do so. The newly obtained player would not report to camp without a contract. Finally, Roush, 34, signed an uncommon three-year deal on March 31, understood to yield $23,000 annually. McGraw expressed little worry that the outfielder would be ready for the season's inauguration, less than two weeks away.

McGraw was even more sure about the playing status of his newest and biggest star, even if the rest of baseball was not. The matter of Hornsby's partial ownership of the St. Louis Cardinals, through his stock in the team, mushroomed into a contentious issue between the league and player. John Heydler had ordered Hornsby to dispose of the stock holdings back in January. "Hornsby cannot play in New York while holding one-eighth of the stock of the St. Louis club," decreed Heydler. "I believe I will have the support of the [National League] board of directors in this stand, even to the extent of defending my position in a court of law."[22]

Hornsby was willing to sell his 1,167 shares, for which he had agreed to pay $52,515, back to Breadon. The Cardinals owner offered $75 a share. The profit of $35,010 was not enough for Hornsby, who wanted $100 per share. "There is no rule in the National League to prevent us from playing Hornsby," McGraw said. "If there was any objection it should have been raised before the trade was completed. I intend to see that he starts at second base whether he sees fit to dispose of his holdings at somebody else's price or not."[23]

After heated back-and-forth exchanges in the press, Heydler called an emergency meeting of National League owners four days before the season's opening pitch, in a last-ditch attempt to resolve things. It failed, though Heydler had the backing of all the owners save the expected one. With all three sides (including Hornsby) threatening legal action, the conflict of interest wrangle was suddenly settled 24 hours later. Convinced by the league that legal fees would exceed the disputed difference between the two parties, Breadon agreed on a per-share price that nearly doubled Hornsby's original investment. Also attached to the agreement was an additional $12,000 for Hornsby's attorney, "the exasperating William J. Fahey, of St. Louis, who made himself so obnoxious to National League owners in Pittsburgh on Friday by refusing to consider the best interests of the game."[24]

Hornsby was one of two Giants off-season acquisitions who hit home runs on Opening Day, April 12, in Philadelphia. Outfielder George Harper, who came over in the Burleigh Grimes trade, knocked another ball over the fence. Bill Terry also homered, with the bases loaded, as the Giants battered the Phillies, 15–7. Two days later, in his Giants debut, Grimes was knocked from the box without recording an out in the third inning. He was the losing pitcher in a 9–6 defeat to the Phillies. Former Giant Jack Scott, part of the three-team trade that landed Grimes in New York, hurled the victory. At the plate, Scott went 4-for-4, with a home run and four RBI.

The Giants took two out of three from Philadelphia and then split four games at Boston prior to christening their home schedule on April 20. While in Boston, appearing like a taskmaster, McGraw stood by as Hugh McQuillan, in his first start of the season, allowed six runs on 16 hits and four walks. Remarkably, McQuillan emerged victorious, 7–6, over the Braves, who left 12 men stranded. The winning runs were on base when the weary pitcher secured the final out. A year and a half removed from a public and messy divorce, McQuillan had compiled an 11–10 record in the last campaign.

The Giants struck a high note in the initial Polo Grounds game, winning, 5–1, behind Freddie Fitzsimmons. The pitcher received the first ball toss directly from Mayor Jimmy Walker. Both Hornsby and Roush were cheered enthusiastically by a gigantic crowd of close to 50,000. McGraw's silver jubilee as Giants field director was noted in the following observations by United Press correspondent Frank Getty:

> A tremendous ovation was accorded to the man who had brought ten pennants and three world championships to New York. McGraw, who came up from Baltimore to manage the Giants at the age of 29, was not in uniform for the occasion. It has been several years since John J. donned the blouse and breeches of his club. To tell the truth, his figure will no longer stand it. John J. McGraw ran his ball club Wednesday just as he has run it for 25 years—like a czar.
>
> With his eyes constantly on the Giants bench, where sat the dumpy figure of baseball's greatest manager, chunky Fred Fitzsimmons took his orders by the secret code system before he hurled each ball. Infield and outfield in new white uniforms shifted mechanically but with the utmost strategy as each Philadelphia batter, his peculiarities no mystery to the squint-eyed, grey haired man on the bench, came to the plate.[25]

McGraw sounded energized by the day's happenings, cheerfully singing his team's praises afterward. "We've got hitting strength, brainy fielding and team spirit as never before," he said. "After 25 years in the big leagues, even with all the stars I've had, I couldn't ask for a better club."[26]

Burleigh Grimes did not win his first game until May 5. The right-hander downed his former team, 4–1, pitching a six-hitter and not allowing an earned run. From then on, accruing 18 more victories, Grimes was the Giants' winningest pitcher.

As was the custom, May brought the first encounters with the non–Eastern clubs. Assuming the initial travel burdens were the teams west of the Allegheny Mountains. The first meeting between St. Louis and New York occurred at the Polo Grounds on May 11. Second-place St. Louis trailed the Giants by one game. Hornsby homered and drove in five runs as Hugh McQuillan coasted to a 10–1 win. Frisch went 0-for-4. The Cardinals, managed now by Bob O'Farrell, won one of three games played. During the series, Travis Jackson made his first appearances of the year. The shortstop had been recuperating from a six-week-old appendectomy operation.

The day after the Giants completed a three-game sweep over the Cincinnati Reds, the Pittsburgh Pirates came to New York for the first time. It was May 18, and McGraw missed all or part of the game (a 13–6 loss) due to a court appearance as defendant in a lawsuit brought by the estate of publisher Edward R. Thomas. The estate sought to recover a nearly $15,000 investment in a Sarasota, Florida, land deal gone bad. The next day, the Giants and Bucs were rained out, as was the Jack Sharkey–Jim Maloney heavyweight boxing card at Yankee Stadium.

The skies cleared enough on May 20 for aviator Charles Lindbergh to take off in his *Spirit of St. Louis* from Roosevelt Field in Mineola, Long Island, at 7:52 a.m. with the goal of making the first solo crossing of the Atlantic. Later that evening, more than 30,000 fight fans stood in silence for one minute at the rescheduled boxing match to pray for Lindbergh's safe journey. Sharkey won the bout with a decisive fifth-round knockout. By the time Lindbergh completed his 33½-hour, famously successful flight, the Corsairs had beaten the Giants twice more, on their way to a four-game road sweep. The Pirates left Manhattan in a virtual three-way tie for first place with the Giants and Chicago Cubs.

The Giants moved on to Boston and failed to play for four days because of rain and wet grounds. McGraw initially stayed behind in New York to await the judge's decision on the lawsuit. New York Supreme Court Justice John L. Walsh dismissed the case against McGraw, based primarily on lack of oral argument available from the deceased plaintiff, Mr. Thomas.

The Giants had slipped to a 4½-game disadvantage to first-place Pittsburgh, when the hour arrived to leave the East Coast for the western fringes on May 31. But not before McGraw rerouted his team to Olean, New York, on June 1—where the manager received his real baseball start 37 years ago. At nearby St. Bonaventure University, the institution of higher learning dedicated its new athletic field as McGraw-Jennings Field, in honor of McGraw and Hughie Jennings, two of their former and most famous athletic alumni. (McGraw and Jennings had attended the Franciscan university, at one time or another, in their off-season early years while with the Baltimore Orioles.)

The original plan was for the field to carry only McGraw's name. But McGraw suggested that his longtime friend should also be recognized. The Giants played an exhibition game and had their way with the college team, winning 12–2.

In Cincinnati, the first road stop, the Giants split four games. The second loss occurred on June 5 in the series' finale. New York opened a 6–0 advantage, and McGraw left the game to return to his hotel, for an unstated reason. The Reds battled back, and reliever McQuillan blew a two-run, ninth-inning lead, permitting three runs for a 10–9 Reds win. McGraw was incensed. He accompanied the team to Pittsburgh, where the Giants divided another four-game set. The manager then left his club as it traveled to Chicago and returned to Cincinnati, where he met with Garry Herrmann and Boston Braves owner Emil Fuchs. (McGraw was spared seeing four losses in a row to the Cubs.) It took two days, but McGraw engineered a trade to rid himself of the scapegoat McQuillan. He exchanged the presently disfavored and mediocre hurler, along with pitcher Kent Greenfield (2–2) and shortstop Edward "Doc" Farrell, for Braves pitcher Larry Benton, catcher Zack Taylor and utility infielder Herb Thomas. Then McGraw made a side-trip to Indianapolis, with intentions to try and sign Indians pitcher Bill Burwell.

During this same period, news arrived that Jim Johnstone had died. The retired umpire succumbed to a neck infection that developed while aboard ship during a European cruise. Johnstone was the umpire McGraw barred from the Polo Grounds in 1906, and he, along with Bill Klem, steadfastly refused a bribe attempt prior to the final game of 1908 versus the Cubs at the Polo Grounds. Though he umpired only ten years in the National League, Johnstone expelled McGraw from 13 ballgames. Johnstone was credited with designing lighter-weight catching and umpiring masks with broader sight lines. He was 54.

McGraw caught up with his club in St. Louis, where it again did no better than break even in four contests. The Giants came limping home from a 6–10 road trip on June 19.

After the last pitched ball of June 30, the team McGraw was earlier so high on sported a 33–33 record. They trailed Pittsburgh by 7½ games. Also at the end of June, Frankie Frisch was outhitting Rogers Hornsby by a dozen points—and Hornsby was batting .372. Sam Breadon, whose Cardinals were battling the Pirates for first place, pulled no punches on his thoughts of the big off-season trade. "I'd rather finish last with Frankie Frisch than win another pennant with Rogers Hornsby,"[27] he rancorously stated.

On July 19, 25 years to the day since McGraw became Giants manager, an array of luminaries came out to the Polo Grounds to commemorate McGraw's anniversary, including 30,000 fans who braved showery conditions. Among the top baseball names were

Jacob Ruppert, John Heydler, Kenesaw Mountain Landis, and former American League enemy Ban Johnson. Transatlantic air heroes of the day, Commander Richard E. Byrd and Clarence Chamberlain, headed a parade in honor of the celebrant. "Mayor Jimmy Walker presented McGraw with a waist-high silver loving cup," detailed one wire report, "on behalf of his friends in New York. On the cup was a figure of McGraw as a player in the uniform of the Baltimore Orioles."[28] The New York players gave their skipper a silver service, with Roger Bresnahan making a short dedication. The Lambs Club—which had reinstated McGraw's membership in September 1924—also gifted a silver platter, and the stadium ushers chipped in to buy McGraw a silver-headed cane. The visiting Chicago Cubs dampened, but could not spoil, the 25th anniversary sentiments with an 8–5 victory in the game that followed.

McGraw's spirits were enlivened the following day after Mel Ott delivered a pinch-hit, two-run single in the bottom of the ninth to push New York past the Cubs, 5–4. Travis Jackson homered twice for the winners.

The Giants staged another, bigger ninth-inning rally, on July 21, against the St. Louis Cardinals. The team batted around and scored five runs to tie the game 6–6. In the tenth, however, the Cards tallied the deciding run on two Giants errors. In that half-inning, McGraw was dismissed from the short remainder of the game by umpire Frank Wilson for arguing a ball called on Cardinals batter Jim Bottomley. It was McGraw's first ejection in five years. A progressive slowing down with age and the inability to come on the field without a uniform had combined to put an almost complete stop to the once ball-of-fire manager. In other, more staggering news, McGraw was informed of the sudden death of an old Baltimore Orioles teammate. Billy Gilbert died from a stroke suffered on August 8. Gilbert had been the second baseman on McGraw's first pennant and world championship teams in 1904 and 1905, respectively. A former minor league manager, Gilbert had been employed as a scout for the Newark Bears. He was 51.

In the month of August, the Giants were impeded by more lousy weather, causing numerous postponements. An entire series with the Cardinals in New York was washed out. (Bad weather plagued most teams during the year, as the Midwest and Eastern United States experienced storm fronts that dropped deluvial amounts of rain in some places.[29]) Yet the team played its best baseball of the season, winning 16 out of 21. The surge helped the New Yorkers to establish themselves firmly as legitimate pennant contenders, along with three other clubs.

But on September 3, McGraw relinquished his team to Rogers Hornsby for the remainder of the season. The manager was struck by his debilitating nasal condition, rendering him unable to perform his managerial duties. The Giants were 2½ games out of first place. Over the final 33 games under the extraordinary player, the Giants' record was 22–10 (one tie). But the 92–62 team made up only half a game in the standings to the pennant-worthier, 94–60 Pittsburgh Pirates.

Of certain speculative interest is how McGraw would have handled the egocentric Hornsby leading the Giants to the pennant in his absence—and whether McGraw would have returned to the dugout for the World Series. It is safe to say that he would have had to have been on his deathbed to be kept away. In fact, McGraw did attend the Series and was one of several baseball personalities to contribute syndicated newspaper commentary on the happenings.

McGraw began work on building a club to take to another World Series himself on

October 4. In the major league draft, he picked a pitcher turned outfielder named Francis Joseph "Lefty" O'Doul. The left-handed hitter had brief stints with both the New York Yankees and Boston Red Sox years earlier before returning to play ball in his native northern California. O'Doul, 31 at start of the 1928 season, was playing with the San Francisco Seals of the Pacific Coast League at the time of his selection.

Two weeks after the "Murderers' Row" Yankees swept the Pirates in the Fall Classic, many Giants followers were soberingly reminded that winning a World Series paled in comparison to some of life's other vagaries. On October 22, 1927, Ross Youngs, age 30, died of Bright's Disease in San Antonio, Texas. He left behind a wife and two-year-old daughter. "It was one of the saddest incidents I can remember," John McGraw said. "He was one of the finest players I ever had."[30]

After a two-month lull with only two minor transactions completed, a second bombshell involving the National League's highest-paid player was detonated 13 months after the original. "After due deliberation between President Stoneham and manager McGraw," explained the shocking press release, "and having in mind what they believe to be the best interests of the New York Giants, a trade was consummated today which involves Rogers Hornsby whereby the Giants are to receive Francis ["Shanty"] Hogan, catcher, and Jimmy Welsh, outfielder from the Boston Braves."[31] The January 10 notice, handed out to reporters, was signed by both Charles Stoneham and McGraw.

The release, ironically, was passed out by club secretary James Tierney. A bitter dispute between Hornsby and Stoneham, originating from an argument between the superstar second baseman and Tierney, instigated the unceremonious jettisoning. Traveling with the team during McGraw's absence, Tierney had criticized Hornsby's play-calling on the field, and Hornsby responded with a brutal counterattack on the executive. Tierney complained to Stoneham, and when he contacted Hornsby about the matter, the team president was not spared Hornsby's wrath either. The "Rajah" was of the opinion that neither man knew sufficiently enough about the game, or managing, to tell him what to do—and he untactfully told them so.

"We feel that we have done what is for the best, looking toward the future welfare of the organization," read part of Stoneham's statement, "and I trust that the loyal fans and supporters will bear with the club until such time as the results of this transaction are definitely decided on the playing field."[32]

The trade came as a complete surprise to Hornsby, and neither Stoneham nor McGraw was present during the two press releases. McGraw, from Savannah, Georgia (on his way to Havana), only said, "There is nothing to add to the original announcement."[33] It was the most telling of all the issued statements from the Giants' hierarchy. Stoneham had always favored and supported McGraw in the past. McGraw could now do no less.

"As a result of the trade," conjectured one report of the stunning announcement, "it is probable the Giants will use Andy Cohen, the Jewish infielder from Texas, who did so well in the International League [sic] last season at Texas. It has long been McGraw's ambition to develop a Jewish star to attract New Yorkers to the Polo Grounds, and with the departure of Hornsby the Giants manager has his opportunity."[34]

A month after the shattering Hornsby deal, the Giants also dealt away 19-game winner Burleigh Grimes, in a financially motivated deal that was not presented as such. McGraw, upon his arrival at the Giants' new training base in Augusta, Georgia, had to defend the Grimes trade. He did so in an ambiguous manner, according to this newswire explanation: "As to the swap which brought [pitcher] Vic Aldridge from Pittsburgh in exchange for Grimes, McGraw pointed out that he wanted a hurler to win games in April and May. Grimes did not get started until late last season, McGraw explained."[35] It was a most regrettable decision by the Giants manager. Grimes would win 25 games for Pittsburgh, while Aldridge won four for New York.

Because of the two big transactions, McGraw's Cuban vacation may not have been as thoroughly relaxing as in other winters. Adding to the tumult came the news of close friend Hughie Jennings' passing on February 1. Jennings, 58, died of meningitis. He was survived by his wife, Nora, and a daughter from his first marriage, identified as Mrs. Thomas P. McWilliams. Jennings was posthumously elected to the National Hall of Fame in 1945.

McGraw put his eight-year-long tiff with the Red Sox behind him, scheduling four games with the American League team during spring training. The Giants won 80 percent of their exhibition games, scoring an abundance of runs in many of the victories. Although they were without Rogers Hornsby, the squad was propped up by a grand hitting season from third baseman Freddie Lindstrom, who hit .358 in 1928, leading the league in hits (231) and driving in a team-high 107 runs. If he had not already, Bill Terry made everyone forget about High Pockets Kelly. He knocked in over 100 runs and hit .326 for the second year in a row. Shortstop Travis Jackson contributed a solid season, accruing the third-best WAR (5.4) on the team, though hitting only .270. Hornsby's replacement, Andy Cohen, produced a respectable 2.4 WAR.

Playing 94 games for the Giants, Pacific Coast League recruit Lefty O'Doul hit .319 with eight homers. He missed several weeks of the campaign due to a fractured ankle. Jimmy Welsh saw the bulk of the action in center field, and 19-year-old Mel Ott became a starter for the first of 18 consecutive seasons. Playing mostly right field, the future Hall of Famer smacked 18 home runs and pushed across 77 runs; he hit .322. Only the Pittsburgh Pirates outhit the Giants as a team, .309 to .293.

The Giants maiden game was played on April 12 at the Polo Grounds. In town were the Boston Braves, with their new, gargantuan acquisition. Rogers Hornsby and Andy Cohen posed with each other for photographers before the game, showing the renewed freshness of a new season on their beaming faces. Cohen was the game's hitting star, collecting three hits and driving in the decisive runs in the Giants' 5–2 win. The 23-year-old also scored two runs and was carried partially off the field by exuberant fans after the final out. Larry Benton, the red-headed right-hander McGraw had obtained from the Braves last June, pitched the distance. Hinting at the great season he had in store for New York fans, Benton walked none and fanned three. Despite a raw day, the turnout was a healthy 30,000. The biting temperatures did not prevent McGraw from appearing in uniform for the first time in four years. He participated in batting practice drills, along with coaches Roger Bresnahan and Hans Lobert. Raised initially with the blue field upside down, the American flag was quickly lowered and hoisted correctly as the final chords of the "Star Spangled Banner" filled the air. Following the slight pre-game hitch, with Charles Stoneham at his side, Mayor Jimmy Walker removed his black derby hat, but not his gloves, to toss out the first pitch.

During the first month of the campaign, rain or cold temperatures postponed nine of the Giants' 17 scheduled games. Inclement weather canceled four straight games in Boston the last week of April. During the inactive period, McGraw announced that he

The always dapper Giants manager strikes an assured pose in front of his Polo Grounds dugout, circa 1929. A young and jacketless Bill Terry is seated second from right.

was suspending pitcher Vic Aldridge for 30 days. The Burleigh Grimes–trade acquisition had failed to sign a contract, preferring to take the extended holdout route.

McGraw publicly challenged his team to be in first place at the time of their first Western road trip. On May 2, after Larry Benton picked up his third win in four starts, a 2–1 triumph over Brooklyn, McGraw's 9–4 Giants hit the rails with a half-game lead over second-place Cincinnati. The Queen City was the team's first stop on the five-city journey.

As McGraw and his men were settling in to begin a four-game series, news broke from New York concerning a front office shakeup. Judge Francis X. McQuade, minority owner and treasurer of the Giants since the sale of the team by Harry Hempstead, was stripped of his duties as treasurer by Charles Stoneham. A United Press staffer disclosed the back-story behind the unexpected move. "McQuade is known to have opposed both the Hornsby deal and the trade which sent Burleigh Grimes to Pittsburgh for Vic Aldridge, who has refused to report to the Giants,"[36] wrote George Kirksey.

McQuade, according to initial comments, did not sound like a man who was going to go quietly. "McGraw beat it to Cuba when Hornsby was traded and Stoneham made himself unreachable," McQuade grumbled. "Now they put me out and go west. I am right here and I'll be here all summer. When the time comes there will be a showdown. I have plenty of ammunition and am not afraid to use it."[37]

Stoneham, indeed, had left New York. He met up with McGraw in Cincinnati and silenced anyone who thought the Giants' manager and vice president might be next in line in a potential executive purge. Stoneham discarded the more than a year and a half remaining on McGraw's current contract and signed him for three more years, through 1930. McGraw declined an offered five-year extension.

New contract notwithstanding, McGraw seemed to have a hop in step this spring. In Cincinnati and Pittsburgh, he continued dressing in uniform (a departure from his previously phased-into norm) and hitting pre-game rollers to his infielders. Having won 13 out of their first 20 games, his team left Pittsburgh with a tenuous first-place stationing. But in Chicago, fortunes for the team and its manager temporarily turned. McGraw suffered a broken leg after being struck by a taxicab outside of Wrigley Field, May 14. He was stepping off the curb when hit and was unable to manage for six weeks.

After missing 40 games (overlooked in the Official Records), McGraw returned on June 30, in civilian clothes and sporting a cane. He guided his Giants to a doubleheader win (7–4, 12–5) over the Boston Braves at the Polo Grounds. The Giants, in second place, moved to within 3½ games of the St. Louis Cardinals.

While McGraw was recuperating, Edd Roush left the team in the lurch. The unhappy outfielder harbored lingering resentment over what he considered overbearing treatment from McGraw, and the feelings had not improved under acting manager Roger Bresnahan. Roush abandoned his club in Philadelphia on June 24. He was immediately suspended by the team for "breaking training rules."

"They think you are intoxicated if you take one glass of beer,"[38] stated Roush, in a clear conduct-related grievance. Roush accused the Giants of hiring private detectives to follow him away from the ballpark. The 35-year-old former batting champion had hit over .300 for ten straight years but was batting only .248 when he bolted.

Also during his healing period, McGraw acquired pitcher Joe Genewich from the team most transparently willing to partner with McGraw in player transactions. The Boston Braves received three Giants pitchers, including Virgil Barnes, and an outfielder. Earlier, to provide Shanty Hogan with some veteran backup help at catcher, McGraw traded flychaser George Harper to the St. Louis Cardinals, in return for catcher and former manager Bob O'Farrell.

McGraw's most significant deal—and his last great signing, via trade or other acquisition—occurred on July 12. On the recommendation of scout Dick Kinsella, McGraw purchased left-handed pitcher Carl Hubbell, paying $25,000 to Hubbell's Beaumont Explorers Texas League team for the privilege. Hubbell's first start, on July 26, was anything but encouraging. He lasted an inning and two-thirds against the Pirates, giving up seven runs (two earned), on seven hits. Capturing the 7–5 decision, Burleigh Grimes picked up his 16th win for the Pirates.

Edd Roush returned to the Giants at the start of August. He played a few more games before he was lost to the club for the remainder of the season with torn stomach muscles. It was in August that the Giants turned on the propulsion jets to contest the top spot in the National League with the St. Louis Cardinals. The New Yorkers won 13 out of 16 to open the month, including three consecutive 3–2 victories in St Louis from August 17 to 19. But then McGraw's horde turned into lost sheep and dropped eight games in a row to close the month. Freddie Fitzsimmons halted the bad trend with a 1–0 gem on September 1 versus Brooklyn. It was Fitzsimmons' 16th win against eight setbacks.

The victory was one of a rousing 25 wins in the month for New York. The Polo

Grounders played their last 15 games of the season at home, but adversely for the team, all were against the first-division Western clubs. Winning two out of three against circuit-heading St. Louis from September 20 to 22, McGraw's bannermen clawed to within a game of first place. The next day, pitching retread Joe Genewich tossed the game of his career, defeating the Reds' Adolfo Luque, 2–1, in 14 innings. In observance of Yom Kippur, which began at sundown, the game began earlier than usual, at 2:15, and lasted an even two hours and 30 minutes. A big Sunday gathering of 40,000 was on hand. The Giants took two more games from Cincinnati but could not draw closer to the Cardinals.

With five games remaining, in the first game of a doubleheader against the Chicago Cubs on September 25, an apparent interference play that went against the Giants helped the Cubs capture the victory and impede the pennant chances of McGraw's team. The "non-call" was made by home plate umpire Bill Klem, who ruled that Cubs catcher Gabby Hartnett did not obstruct the Giants' Andy Reese as he tried to score from third base on a fielder's choice. Reese, the tying run, was caught in a rundown, collided with Hartnett, and was then tagged out by another Cub. Adding to McGraw's indignity on the bench, Cubs starter Art Nehf shut the door on any more Giants scoring and pitched his team to a 3–2 victory. The Giants salvaged a split when 14-game winner Genewich tossed a shutout in the nightcap.

McGraw formally protested the interference play to John Heydler, who would not overrule his most senior umpire. (McGraw never forgot the incident; often over the winter, he petulantly pointed to it as having cost the Giants the pennant.) The Giants dropped the next two games to Chicago and were eliminated on the next-to-last day of the campaign. New York won ten hard-fought games on their final homestand, but, with a final record of 93–61, finished two games behind flag-waving St. Louis.

Instead of concentrating on an umpire's potentially missed call in one game, McGraw and the entire Giants organization may have been truer to their fans by retrospectively examining their personnel moves prior to the season. Larry Benton's unanticipated emergence as a 25-game-winning ace for McGraw tempered the loss of Burleigh Grimes, but Rogers Hornsby's 1928 Wins Above Replacement metric of 8.8 strongly argues that his presence would have easily put the Giants over the top. Charles Stoneham's hubris unequivocally cost his team the pennant.

EIGHT

Final Campaigns
of the "Mastermind"

"John J. McGraw, as gray as a badger and round as an old-fashioned beer keg, is in one of those finishes that delight the heart."—Damon Runyon

Weeks after the Yankees' Miller Huggins equaled John McGraw and Connie Mack for most World Series won with three, John McGraw traded Lefty O'Doul to the Philadelphia Phillies for outfielder Freddy Leach on October 29, 1928.

Eight months older than Leach, O'Doul was nicknamed the "man in the green suit" because of his affinity for wearing such garments. Over his next four big league seasons, O'Doul's stupendous hitting turned many players in baseball an envious shade of the same leafy color. O'Doul exploded with the lumber in his first season in Philadelphia, as a change in the baseball's composition generated an across-the-board rise in offense in both leagues. Playing in every game, O'Doul hit .398, leading the league in hits (254) and OBP (.465). He slugged .662, socking 32 home runs and driving home 122 runs. Amazingly, the sensational batter stuck out only *19* times in 638 at-bats.

Later in the off-season, Ray Schalk, veteran catcher and recently deposed as Cubs manager, took Roger Bresnahan's place as McGraw's top lieutenant. Bert Niehoff was also contracted as coach.

In late December 1928, a New York building contractor and political broker named William F. Kenny bought 20 percent of the National Exhibition Company stock. The purchase price of 2,500 shares of stock previously owned by a Boston syndicate of businessmen revealed the abundant prosperity of the New York Giants baseball club. Numbers crunchers, outside the team's inner circle, were able to place the value of Stoneham's corporation at around $4,000,000—the most valuable franchise in the major leagues.

Evidently pleased with his new salary and the ancillary perks of being the winningest pitcher in New York, Larry Benton was the first team member to sign his 1929 contract. He did so the first week of January, just prior to the McGraws' departure for Cuba. It was a much calmer—and longer—Cuban retreat this year compared to last, and presumably more enjoyable and relaxing for the Giants' leader. McGraw's tropical vacation lasted six weeks; he returned to New York on February 18.

McGraw reached San Antonio a week afterward and took active command of his assembled club the next day. There were two conspicuous absentees in camp—Edd Roush, a habitual late-spring training arrival, and Bill Terry, a habitual spring training holdout.

Both men reported two weeks later. Both were in the Opening Day lineup, in Philadelphia on April 18 (delayed a day by rain).

In an indication of the offensive upswing, the Giants scored 25 runs in two Baker Bowl games to open the new campaign, winning both. Carl Hubbell, who had won ten games in two-plus months last season, was the 11–9 winning pitcher in the opener, with relief help from Larry Benton. Lefty O'Doul clubbed two homers and knocked in four of the losers' runs. New York then had a series in Boston called off due to inclement weather.

The Phillies returned the inauguration favor to the Giants on April 23. In contrast to the heavy-hitting games in Philadelphia, the Giants lost, 3–1, in 11 innings. Larry Benton hurled the entire game, while having to endure his teammates leaving the bases loaded four times without scoring. A pleasant spring day was spoiled for the approximately 30,000 spectators who watched from the seats. O'Doul hit his third home run against his former team. The rakish mayor of New York, Jimmy Walker, now becoming a regular at Giants and Yankees season christenings, tossed out the ceremonial first ball.

During the early spate of weather-related postponements, a blurb in the *New York Times* appeared which may have led some to question McGraw's overall focus. "Rain stops ball games and causes John McGraw to visit the race track," vigilantly noted one writer. "The day the Giants were prevented from playing in Philadelphia by the hail and rain storm, McGraw made the long trek to Havre de Grace, and yesterday he was down at Jamaica."[1] McGraw was by no means alone with his horse-racing addiction among various sectors of the baseball establishment.

However, McGraw appeared alone in his sinus condition. The punishing affliction rendered him unable to discharge his managerial duties for 15 games in early May. The manager missed a no-hitter thrown by Carl Hubbell on May 8. Humbling the Pittsburgh Pirates at the Polo Grounds, Hubbell faced 30 batters, thanks to one walk and two errors. He struck out four in the 11–0 victory. Mel Ott slammed two of his career-high 42 home runs on the season to back his Giants roommate. McGraw had come down with a particularly bad flare-up of his sinuses, which necessitated the need for sunglasses. One day in May, the portly, ruddy-faced manager had trouble gaining access to his long-time place of work when he showed up wearing blue-tinted shades. A security guard, who did not recognize McGraw, impeded his entrance—or gave McGraw the bum's rush, as NEA service sports editor Henry L. Farrell put it.[2] The chagrined guard was then given the bum's rush himself, it was noted, when his mistake was revealed.

The 1929 Giants began the new campaign sluggishly. After his 16-day absence, McGraw rejoined a team that was playing as if its chief members were also sick. At least one national reporter was mistakenly willing to blame the Giants' 10–16 record on the lack of first-rate leadership. "The worst of it is that McGraw has been missing for rather lengthy periods in each of the last four seasons," wrote Davis J. Walsh. "The puppets were ready to dance but the master wasn't there to pull the strings; at least Hughie Jennings, Roger Bresnahan and Ray Schalk, acting mangers in three of the four emergencies, found this to be so."[3] In reality, Jennings and Bresnahan (and Hornsby) more than adequately guided the Giants during McGraw's periods of extended incapacitation.

When McGraw was his healthy self, he deliberately waited as long as he could to announce his game-day starter. "Such a [pre] announcement may help those whose business it is to bet on ballgames," he was quoted as saying shortly after his return to active duty. "Besides, I don't like to be put in a position of telling the baseball writers one fellow will pitch and then perhaps change my mind and feel as if I am not keeping faith with the writers."[4]

McGraw's masked pitching selections began responding, and the Giants bettered themselves considerably in the standings. Not hurting their cause was a ten-game stretch in June in which the Giants put up double-digit run totals eight times. The team won all eight games. On June 15 at Forbes Field, McGraw's marauders pounded out 28 hits against six Pirates pitchers. It took 14 innings, but the Giants won, 20–15. Travis Jackson hit for the circuit twice and batted home seven runs. Four days later at the Baker Bowl, Ott clocked a pair of home runs, with six RBI, as the Giants outslugged the Phillies, 15–14, in 11 innings.

After 70 games, the Giants had reversed their initial lethargy. The team was ten games over .500, in third place, within a four-game reach of the front-running Chicago Cubs.

The increased run production did not completely immunize hitters against an occasional well-pitched game. On July 6, the Giants and their bench boss were particularly frustrated by Brooklyn's Watty Clark. On a gorgeous summer afternoon, the Robins' pitcher three-hit the Giants at the Polo Grounds, 4–0. All the runs scored against Giants starter Carl Hubbell were unearned. Late in the game, McGraw suffered only his second ejection in seven years. Though McGraw's fighting personality had softened with age, a third-strike call by umpire George Magerkurth, on Travis Jackson, summoned forth some of the verbal tanning of yesteryear that he exclusively brandished upon the balls and strikes callers. Sportswriter Tommy Holmes recognized these points. "Simultaneously with the loss of his temper he lost control of his tongue," relayed the Brooklyn beat writer. "And for a brief moment the mellow McGraw was gone. In his place sat an aging gentleman with the bright, snapping eyes and biting tongue of the old McGraw, a throw-back to the rough-and-ready leader of the Giants who was the stormy petrel of baseball."[5]

Starting to slip in the standings, McGraw felt the need for a closed-door meeting with his players prior to the game at the Polo Grounds on July 18. The Giants beat Pittsburgh that day behind Carl Hubbell, but a week later things had deteriorated further. Reports about dissension within the ranks surfaced. Shanty Hogan, in spite of, or because of, his youth, was a player who had no problem speaking his mind. He raised issue with being fined $100 over a short period of time—twice for not following McGraw's orders during games and once for allegedly staying out all night in Boston. Larry Benton (who did not come close to duplicating his 25-win campaign of 1928) complained that McGraw was too often micro-managing his pitch selection. Responding to another aired grievance, McGraw admitted to fining Carl Hubbell $25 for a base running error that supposedly cost the Giants a ballgame.

McGraw and his 58–47 Giants came back to the Polo Grounds to start a homestand, on August 9, against the Western clubs. In third place, 12 games out of contention, the Giants made no headway, playing .500 ball in 16 games. Apparently looking ahead toward next year, McGraw twice left his team in September for player recruitment purposes, without bothering to return after the second time. He obtained future assets in pitcher LeRoy Parmelee from the Toledo Mud Hens and Sam Leslie, a first baseman with the Memphis Chicks. Another minor league purchase, from Newark, Hubert "Hub" Pruett, was not as fruitful. During his periods away from the club, McGraw also found time to write columns for the Christy Walsh Syndicate, one of them openly disagreeing with one of Babe Ruth's major league all-star selections. Ruth deemed the A's Jimmie Foxx as the elite first baseman in the big leagues. McGraw believed Bill Terry deserved the all-around honor. In 1929, Terry hit .372 and led the league in putouts and double plays for the second consecutive season.

A strong Chicago Cubs team, led by Rogers Hornsby and slugger Hack Wilson, finished 10½ games over the Pittsburgh Pirates and 13½ over the Giants at season's end. The Cubs were defeated in the World Series by the Philadelphia Athletics, who ended the Yankees' string of three successive AL pennants. Yankees manager Miller Huggins had grown ill as the campaign was on its last legs and died of a bacterial infection on September 25. "I am very, very sorry," McGraw said about the news. "Miller was a gallant little fellow and was one of the best managers in baseball history. It is terrible to see him go."[6] Huggins was 51.

Judged by his absence, McGraw may not have seemed interested, but for dyed-in-the-wool Giants fans, one of their own was battling for circuit home run honors, and the last days of the campaign absorbed their attention. Mel Ott was tied with the Phillies' Chuck Klein with 42 home runs entering the final two days of the campaign. On October 5, in the first game of a doubleheader, which concluded the Phillies and Klein's schedule, the Phillies' outfielder socked his 43rd round-tripper. Ott went 1-for-3, with a walk and run scored. The Phillies edged the Giants, 5–4. Lefty O'Doul smacked four hits, including his 32nd home run. In the second game, Ott was walked intentionally five times, in order to deny him a chance at equaling Klein, playing in his final game. Giants starter Bill Walker, meanwhile, challenged Klein throughout and hung an 0-for-5 collar around the slugger. The next day, Ray Schalk batted Ott leadoff in the Giants' season finale in Boston. Ott batted five times. He stroked two singles and walked once, but failed to homer.

Soon after the disastrous stock market crash of October 1929, McGraw's expected retooling of his team began with excising his coaching staff. He cut loose Ray Schalk and Bert Niehoff during the early days of November. He brought aboard two former Giants, Irish Meusel and Dave Bancroft, to take over as his assistants. Bancroft was signed as an active player and played his last ten major league games with the Giants.

In mid–November, another of McGraw's contemporaries sadly met his demise. McGraw's former inexhaustible ace, Joe McGinnity, died of complications from bladder surgery a few months earlier. "It is always hard to witness the passing of one of the old guard," McGraw said. "Joe was a real credit to the game."[7] McGraw pleasantly recalled some of the unique pitching qualities that made McGinnity stand out on the mound:

> McGinnity was not only the greatest underhand pitcher I ever saw, he was one of the greatest pitchers I ever saw.
> McGinnity studied that underhand form of delivery … and when he released the ball his right knee was practically on the ground. The ball came up at you. It rose and it had a peculiar hop on it. But McGinnity could also pitch overhand. When he pitched those doubleheaders for us he used to pitch the first game overhand and the second game underhand. It was as different as if two pitchers had been working.[8]

Perhaps thinking that the minor leaguers he had acquired over the past few months would make an immediate impact, McGraw let the winter come and go without making any frontline changes to his squad. As far as the offense was concerned, there was not much need, or room, for an upgrade. In the upcoming peak Liveball year, in which six out of the eight National League teams registered a batting average over .300, the Giants would lead all of baseball with a .319 collective mark.

Leading the hitting vanguard was Bill Terry, who hit .401 in 1930 while amassing a league record–tying 254 hits. The last National League player to hit .400, Terry was one of six Giants first-stringers whose batting average exceeded .300. Missing out on the hitting celebration was Edd Roush. The headstrong outfielder could not come to an agreement with McGraw over a new contract, and he sat out the entire season. Reaching the end of his three-year deal, Roush had hit .324 last season, but McGraw proposed to cut his pay to $15,000. The fact that Roush had started only 107 games in the outfield, and only 39 the prior year, contributed to the offered decrease.

McGraw filled his center field slot mostly with Wally Roettger. The third-year outfielder was obtained from the St. Louis Cardinals days before the regular season. The Giants gave up minor league pitcher George "Show-

McGraw and Philadelphia Phillies manager Burt Shotton. In a display of poor sportsmanship, Shotton ordered Mel Ott intentionally passed five times in the penultimate game of the 1929 season in an attempt to preserve the home run title for the Phillies' Chuck Klein.

boat" Fisher and Doc Farrell. The dentist-turned-ballplayer Farrell had been reacquired last June from the Boston Braves for outfielder Jimmy Welsh. Roaming left field, Freddy Leach would present McGraw with a good year with a .327 batting average, 13 triples, 13 homers, and 71 RBI. Mel Ott's home run total's slid to 25, but he hit .349 and racked up 119 RBI—second on the team to Terry's 129. "Master Melvin," still only 21 years of age, led the league in OBP (.458), assisted by 103 walks.

McGraw had a fine trio of starters in Bill Walker, Freddie Fitzsimmons and Carl Hubbell. A 14-game winner in his first full season in 1929, Walker was a $25,000 signee from Denver, Colorado, who had made good quickly. A left-hander, his 3.09 ERA led the senior circuit. All three hurlers proved reliable innings-eaters for McGraw. After "the Big Three," as it were, the staff was spread rather thinly.

While McGraw was in Cuba in early February, Francis X. McQuade's legal attempt to be reinstated as treasurer of the Giants, with back pay, was dismissed in New York magistrate court. McQuade argued that he, Stoneham and McGraw had a verbal agreement, dating back to 1919, in which each agreed to use their office's influence to perpetuate the others' positions. (The ruling would be overturned by an Appellate Court in late spring.)

Also in February, McGraw's younger brother died. James Michael McGraw was club secretary of the Toledo Mud Hens, the quasi–minor league affiliate of the Giants. Complications following an appendicitis operation was the disclosed cause of death. Eight years John McGraw's junior, James was 48.

McGraw arrived in San Antonio (via Miami) and took command of his team on February 26, directing two intra-squad games that day. The morning affair lasted five innings; in the afternoon, six innings were played. The majority of the exhibition schedule was to be played against the Chicago White Sox, who were also training in the Texas city. Apart from Roush, two other team stars were conspicuously absent at this early training stage, Freddie Lindstrom and Bill Terry. Although halted by a tonsillitis operation in August, Lindstrom was coming off a season in which he hit .319 and drove in 91 runs in 130 games. Within two weeks, both men had acceded to terms.

In late March, side-by-side photographs of McGraw and Connie Mack, at work, appeared across the national sports pages. The photos were taken from the men's respective training camps, and the caption, in effect, touted the pair—the longest-tenured managers in the big leagues—as not being afraid of getting their hands dirty. McGraw was shown hitting fungoes. He was wearing a five-gallon hat with black band pulled down over his eyes, a black button-down sweater and cuffed, pinstriped dress pants with two-toned spats. From Ft. Myers, Florida, a hatless Mack was pictured in a three-piece suit, winding back to throw a baseball—which, unlike McGraw's, appears to be a posed shot. The Giants experienced a cold and rainy spring in San Antonio, explaining some of McGraw's attire.

Two weeks before the start of the 1930 season, McGraw announced his Opening Day lineup. Andy Reese, a Southern Association purchase and utility infielder for the Giants the last few seasons, would be the new second baseman, taking over for the discarded Andy Cohen. Minor leaguer Johnny Mostil would take Roush's place (this was before the Roettger trade). Bill Walker, McGraw announced, would be the campaign's first starter.

As 35,000 fans applauded, two "Walkers"—Mayor Jimmy and pitcher Bill—threw initial pitches on April 15 in what one writer referred to as "long underwear weather at the Polo Grounds."[9] Most of the same big crowd cheered as Freddy Leach brought in second baseman Eddie Marshall with a double in the bottom of the ninth inning to boost the Giants to a 3–2 win over the Boston Braves. Marshall, a former Beaumont Explorer, had beaten out Andy Reese at the starting keystone position. Bill Walker was credited with the complete-game victory.

Following three straight rainouts, the Giants won three more games. One of them was claimed thanks to a two-out, two-run, bottom of the ninth inning single by Wally Roettger on April 19. The base hit gave the Giants a 3–2 win over the Philadelphia Phillies. Then, for the second year in a row, an entire April series was postponed in Boston, due to rain and cold temperatures. The Giants won another three games before suffering their first defeat of the season. At 7–3, the club packed up their travel trunks for the first of three occidental road trips.

In Pittsburgh, the *Pittsburgh Press*' Ralph Davis questioned whether McGraw was still motivated sufficiently by the game. He alluded to McGraw's lack of field mobility—by the manager's own design—as a chief dampener.

John J. McGraw doesn't get the thrill out of baseball he once did. Once a notable figure on the coaching lines, he now sits on the bench, clad in civilian clothes. He still dominates his team. Only yesterday he lingered in the stands on his way to the bench to talk to a friend. It was time for the pitchers to warm up, but nobody in the Giants party was willing to take the initiative. He may dictate every ball pitched, every bat swing, but if he does, it is from the cover of the bench, and the spectators do not get a chance to cheer, or deride him, as their feelings may be. The Little Napoleon may still rule, but the fan army misses him from the role he once filled. And it's a safe bet that they miss him no more than he misses those old thrills himself.[10]

In their series in the Steel City, the Giants scored 41 runs in four games, and won three of them. Later, in St. Louis, McGraw tried to address his lack of pitching depth. He swung an exchange of pitchers with the Cardinals' front office. McGraw received 39-year-old veteran hurler Clarence Mitchell for ten years-younger Ralph Judd. A left-hander with a spitball that was not as effective as most (shown by a career below-.500 record), Mitchell pleasantly provided short-term dividends for McGraw. (Mitchell is perhaps best remembered for lining into the only unassisted triple play in World Series history in 1920.) Judd, one of a group declared free agents by Kenesaw Mountain Landis in 1929, was signed by the Giants from the Birmingham Barons roster. The right-hander never panned out and was no loss to the Gothamites.

The Giants returned to New York in mid–May with two players on the sick list. Travis Jackson contracted the mumps. Wally Roettger had been the first to catch the contagious disease. He suspected he may have been infected by then-teammate, Cardinals outfielder Homer Peel, in the spring. McGraw feared a mumps outbreak on his squad but, luckily, it never happened.

Several games into the homestand, McGraw pulled off another trade. He took care of the annoying deficiency in his infield by obtaining Cincinnati Reds veteran Hughie Critz. Considered the best defensive second baseman in the league, Critz had become available due to a more than year-long hitting slump. McGraw sent the no longer effective Larry Benton to the Reds in the one-for-one exchange. "I hate to see Larry go," said McGraw, "but he couldn't seem to win for us anymore. The addition of Critz will make a big difference for us in our team and plug a spot that has given us trouble."[11]

McGraw and the Reds executed another trade a few days before the expiration of May. With an abundance of infielders now on his team, the Giants' chief dealt unproven second baseman Pat Crawford to Cincinnati for outfielder Ethan Allen and once-stud pitcher Pete Donohue. The gamble on Crawford did not pay off for Herrmann, while Allen and Donohue were short-term contributors for New York.

A recovered Travis Jackson returned to the lineup on June 6, providing McGraw for the first time the infield he envisioned when he traded for Hughie Critz. That infield produced nine hits in a 10–7 home win against St. Louis. The next day the Giants were 9–7 winners over the Cardinals as Mel Ott belted two home runs, his 11th and 12th, and drove in six. Every Giants position player recorded at least one hit. New York, a disappointing 24–22, trailed the upstart Brooklyn Robins, at the top of the National League, by five games—but with a long way to go.

McGraw, as he was apt to do, attended the Max Schmeling-Jack Sharkey heavyweight championship fight, held at Yankee Stadium on June 12. Along with a local and national VIP contingent, several Giants and Robins players were on hand. Also taking in the bout, which ended on a fourth round, low-blow disqualification of Sharkey, were members of the Cincinnati Reds, in town playing at Ebbets Field.

As the calendar page flipped into July, one Giant's all-around performance gained more and more notice. "Bill Terry is probably the world's greatest first baseman, hitting, fielding and throwing, and everything else taken into consideration. Terry is a finished ball player without weakness."[12] The graceful first sacker entered July hitting .387; he closed the month with a .396 average. But he trailed three other National League hitters in the batting race, including Lefty O'Doul.

On July 25, Terry garnered three hits, including a solo home run, in the Giants' 3–1 win over the Pittsburgh Pirates. Prior to the contest, McGraw left New York for Montreal on a scouting expedition. The Giants upped their record to 50–42, 4½ games out of the running. But, unaccountably, McGraw sounded like someone who was throwing in the towel, and even worse, employing excuses. "The Giants need pitchers," he said from the French-Canadian city. "My team would have had a good chance of winning the flag had our pitchers come through. The rabbit ball and poor umpiring are making baseball unpopular. Bunting is gone and base running has disappeared. The public liked that."[13]

Giants fans, at least, were developing a new taste for what Bill Terry was doing. On August 5, versus Brooklyn, the first baseman collected five hits, including a home run, to raise his batting average to .407—best in the league.

McGraw bowed out on the team and the rest of the season on September 1, as the Giants departed on a sojourn to Philadelphia and Boston. The 71–55 Giants were five games behind the Chicago Cubs, the new league leaders. Rumors began circulating about McGraw's time with the Giants reaching its end. Fueling the talk were the widely known overtures surrounding "millionaire bricklayer" J. Henry McNally's supposed on-the-table offer to buy the team from Charles Stoneham. McGraw was said to be contemplating resigning, if the sale went through, making him available for Jacob Ruppert to hire. All such hearsay came to a screeching halt on September 3, when Stoneham announced that he and McGraw had agreed on a five-year contract, beginning in 1931, for McGraw to stay on as manager. McGraw would be paid $70,000 a year, maintaining his current $50,000 managerial compensation, with an additional $20,000 salary as vice-president. The Giants also revealed that McGraw indeed had been ill but was expected to recover fully.

The extended illness was officially attributed to heat exhaustion, and not sinusitis.

> Not until yesterday when Stoneham announced that McGraw had signed a new long-term contract, did it become known that the veteran manager was under doctor's orders to remain off the bench. It is known, however, that during his absence from the team McGraw appeared at the race track in Saratoga Springs. This was taken to mean in some quarters that he had definitely lost interest in the Giants and planned to transfer his services elsewhere.[14]

At least one of his players expressed his pleasure over the progression of events.

"McGraw still is, as he always has been, the greatest manager in baseball," said captain Travis Jackson. "and we are glad to know that he will continue as our leader. We mean to fight to the last for this year's pennant and do not consider the race over by any means."[15]

While Jackson and the team were in Boston, John and Blanche McGraw decided to follow through on a plan to downsize their habitation and purchased a new home in the village of Pelham Manor, just south of their current residence. The new place, at 620 Ely Avenue, had nine rooms and three baths.

On the diamond, the torrid St. Louis Cardinals took control of the race for the National League's ultimate prize. The Cardinals won 21 of 25 games in September, passing three clubs ahead of them, including the Giants, to haul away their third pennant in five years.

Of some personal consolation for Giants fans, no one could pass Bill Terry with the stick. "Memphis Bill" beat out Brooklyn's Babe Herman by eight points for the batting title, which curiously played up more in the press than his hitting .400. Or not so curiously, since hitting .400 had been accomplished by a few other players in the past decade.

McGraw's theory about the public liking bunting and stealing may have been true, but based on ballpark crowds since the beginning of the prior decade, fans liked the increased hitting more. Attendance in the National League, in 1930, hit its pre–World War II peak at 5,445,532, a more than 10 percent increase from the previous year. In the American League, attendance held steady at 4.6 million.[16] The figures attested that the great stock market crash had yet to affect the disposal income of the average American. But that would soon drastically change.

Over the winter, the Giants released Irish Meusel as coach and contracted former hurler Chief Bender to work exclusively with the pitchers. Delighting many New Yorkers, George Burns was also hired as coach. Dave Bancroft was retained as McGraw's top assistant. The coaches were already in camp when McGraw arrived in San Antonio, with new designs for his ball club, on February 24.

McGraw had the acknowledged best infield in baseball, with Bill Terry (1B), Hughie Critz (2B), Travis Jackson (SS) and Freddie Lindstrom (3B). But he decided to convert Lindstrom into an outfielder. The "Chicago Swede," as Lindstrom was sometimes pegged in the press, had become an accomplished player and star in the league. An independent talent-evaluating report, at the time, praised the player in this manner: "For seven seasons, Lindstrom was a great third baseman, ranked as Pie Traynor's closest rival in fielding and fully Traynor's equal at bat."[17]

The change produced unsettled results, as Lindstrom missed more than half the 1931 season due to injury. The new scheme also required "piano-legged" Mel Ott to play center field, in order for Lindstrom to roam in right field. Ott held his own defensively in center, but Lindstrom, when he played, was a defensive downgrade in his new position.

Apart from this highly questionable decision, comments made by McGraw in spring training suggested a manager out of touch with his personnel. "Last year we missed winning the pennant due to spotty pitching," he said. "If we can get [Pete] Donohue or [Joe] Genewich to win the share of ball games they are capable of, you'll see us around first place all summer."[18]

McGraw was expecting what were washed-up pitchers to supplement a projected rotation of Freddie Fitzsimmons, Carl Hubbell, Bill Walker and Clarence Mitchell. Donohue, a former three-time 20-game winner, had been a shell of his former self for the past several seasons and had fewer than 50 major league innings left in his arm. Genewich had already played his last big league game.

McGraw's plan for third base was a snappy, young fielder named Johnny Vergez. A Pacific Coast League product, Vergez had been purchased by McGraw from the Oakland Oaks last October. Vergez, 24, hit .278 in 152 games in the forthcoming season; his 81 RBI were third-best on the Giants. McGraw evidently had no plans for Edd Roush and placed the obdurate holdout on waivers in March. The veteran outfielder was claimed by the Cincinnati Reds, and he played his final big league campaign with the team of his greatest glory.

At the end of March, Byron Bancroft Johnson died at age 67. The father and founder of the American League succumbed to diabetes. He had resigned as president of the league he had built into the equal of its older counterpart in 1927. His successor, Ernest S. Barnard, coincidentally died March 27, a day prior to Johnson. Many of the same American League owners attended Barnard's funeral on March 31, and then Johnson's the next day. McGraw provided these comments about the pair: "The fact that there is an American League today is due more to Johnson than anybody else and the league stands as a monument to his genius. The death of Barnard is a distinct loss not only to the American League, but all of baseball."[19]

Less than a month later, the man whose former club had become an active trading partner of McGraw over the past few years died. Garry Herrmann had relinquished ownership of his team following the 1927 season due to health reasons. The chairman of the old National Commission was 71. At the time of Herrmann's death, the Giants were ten games into the 1931 season. Their record was 6–3 (one tie).

Changes were occurring at the Polo Grounds to keep up with the evolving times. In 1930, a public address system was installed. At the start of this season, the press box was moved from its field level location to just below the upper deck boxes. Writers had often complained about actors, women and other personalities invading their sanctuary. The scribes soon gagged among themselves that they had seen the last of the actors, who could not be plainly seen by the general public from the new writers' perch.

Changes also occurred on the diamond with respect to a revised scoring rule and altered equipment. McGraw weighed in on both developments.

Undoubtedly the really skillful pitchers have been helped by the new ball with higher seams. While the new ball appears to have curbed the fluke hitting, it hasn't hurt the really good hitters. The general averages may be slightly lower as well due to the abolishing of the sacrifice fly. Another striking effect to the less lively ball has been to the infielders. The throwing to bases this spring has been exceptionally good."[20]

The Giants opened the 1931 season with eight games on the road, winning five. At the Polo Grounds on April 22, the home schedule commenced in a pleasing manner with a 5–4 win over the Philadelphia Phillies. Johnny Vergez, playing in his first Giants home game, had two hits and two RBI. Hughie Critz hit his second home run and the first by a Giants player at home. Prior to the close game, Mayor Walker assumed added ceremonial duties by involving himself in flag-raising chores. The Polo Grounds, its stands draped in gold and white bunting commemorating the 50th year of a New York franchise in the National League, could now accommodate 55,000 patrons. The Giants closed April with a 9–4 mark.

Because of rain and cold weather, the team was limited to 23 games in the season's second month. The Giants won 14 of them. McGraw's unit was boosted by Freddie Fitzsimmons' 5–0 start. The Giants also benefited from an early shot in the arm by Clarence Mitchell. The 40-year-old spitballer won five of his first six decisions.

As June began, at 23–13, the Giants were right on the tail of the league's premier team of the past half-decade, the St. Louis Cardinals. Playing the third-place Chicago Cubs on June 22, the Giants trailed, 5–2, entering the ninth inning. It was a sedate Monday afternoon at the Polo Grounds with only 5,000 fans on hand. Sedate—until the final inning. McGraw called on 20-year-old Hal Schumacher to relieve. Schumacher had been signed on New Year's Day, right off the campus of St. Lawrence University in upstate New York. A right-hander, Schumacher had come to McGraw's attention thanks to Al

Kinney, McGraw's first manager at Olean, "back in the day when the players wore mustaches,"[21] as one newspaper described the era. McGraw had taken an immediate liking to Schumacher, in much the same paternal way he had with Mel Ott, during the youngster's first spring camps. While facing the inning's third batter, Kiki Cuyler, Schumacher's batterymate Shanty Hogan thought umpire Dolly Stark missed a called strike three. Hogan let Stark know about it, dropping a few non-endearing terms. Hogan was tossed. Sticking up for Hogan and Schumacher, McGraw lashed out at the umpire from the bench with some of his vintage vitriol. One of the band of writers covering the Giants described what happened next: "'*You* get out of the park, too!' yelled Stark, whipping off his mask and dancing grotesquely."[22] McGraw's ejection was but his third in nine years.

The Giants stayed around first place for only a portion of the summer, during which John McGraw received his last career ejection on July 18, 1931. From the dugout, the manager too jarringly chastised an out call at first base by Bob Clarke. It was the top of the eighth inning at Sportsman's Park in St. Louis when the arbiter prematurely ended McGraw's afternoon.

The Giants held a 3–0 lead over the Cardinals. The final score was 4–0. Bill Walker, 8–4, spun a two-hitter. The next day, McGraw was slapped with a three-day suspension for berating Clarke, who filed a complaint with John Heydler. McGraw received a telegram notifying him of his forced mini-vacation at the Chase Hotel, where he and the team were staying. The veteran manager became livid. Heydler, who happened to be in St. Louis at the time, was confronted by McGraw near the press gate at Sportsman's Park on July 19.

McGraw popped off at the league's top executive, within earshot of several witnesses. "This is a fine thing you did to me," shouted McGraw. "Here I am trying to stir my ball club … and I'm suspended for criticizing a rotten ump." Proving he was not the type to forget past grievances, McGraw continued. "You're still backing up the rotten umpires, just as you backed up Klem in 1929 when he refused to allow that interference on Reese in that game with the Cubs. Clarke is a rotten umpire, has been for years, and you know it."[23]

After the heated harangue, McGraw later tried to squirm his way back into the dugout in an executive capacity, invoking a technicality of sorts. But Heydler would have none of it. "Just because McGraw is vice-president of the New York club as well as its manager," stated the NL chief, "is no reason why he can have privileges on the bench. He was suspended because of the abusive language he used on umpire Clarke."[24] The team played three more games in St. Louis during the suspension and lost all three. Dave Bancroft was the acting manager.

In prior years, McGraw's warriors would have been inspired by their leader's fiery outburst against Heydler. But no longer. New York Giants historian Peter Williams wrote that "there was hardly a player left who still had any respect for the 'old man'"[25] during this time. His stature as a field general had also suffered. This newspaper snippet alluded to McGraw's sagging reputation, while announcing a possible player transaction by New York early the following season: "Frank Packard heading to the New York Giants? John McGraw, formerly referred to as the 'mastermind' of the New York Giants, but lately termed 'just another manager,' is said to be sold on the former Colt."[26] On top of this, the 58-year-old McGraw—who had been previously described by sports scribe Jimmy Powers as a "grey-haired, squinty-eyed man, with fat red cheeks and ample nose"[27]—was showing the physical ravages of years of over-indulgences.

At the close of play August 31, the Cardinals threatened to run away with the pennant, opening up a ten-game advantage on New York and 14 on third-place Chicago. Using an eight-game winning streak begun the same day, the Harlemites clawed back to with 5½ games of the Cardinals on September 5. But it was as close to first place the Giants would get under their long-time administrator until next April.

Four days later, McGraw managed a game at Yankee Stadium in not quite the manner he envisioned at the start of the campaign. In a grand gesture, the owners of the three New York teams agreed to play charity games, against one another, for the benefit of the growing rolls of unemployed workers in the city. The speculation bust on Wall Street had driven banks to virtually stop lending money. Continued economic growth, without the normal lending risk behind it, was impossible. Corporate expansion was grinding to a halt. Businesses slashed their payrolls and scaled back on production. Without the powerful engine of consumer spending to drive product demand, the nation was facing the greatest socio-economic downturn of the century. In a matter of weeks, sequential collapses in world currencies triggered what became known in the United States, and the industrialized world, as the Great Depression. Across every major city in the country, relief stations, more popularly known as "soup kitchens," would soon begin popping up to provide a means of sustenance to an expanding, disenfranchised labor market.

A crowd of over 60,000 came out, each paying one dollar for their ticket (including reporters), to see the two glamour teams of New York battle. Both second-place clubs started their aces—18-game winner Lefty Gómez for the New York Americans and 17-game victor Freddie Fitzsimmons for the Giants. The Yankees broke a 3–3 tie, scoring four runs in the eighth inning, one of them on a long Babe Ruth home run, to win, 7–3. For the first four and a half innings, the Reach-trademarked American League ball was used, one which had not undergone a dampening change in composition from last year. One run was scored. In the second half of the game, the "less lively"—as McGraw had put it—Spalding-brand National League ball was employed, during which nine runners scurried across the plate. Both pitchers hurled nine innings.

Two weeks later, the Brooklyn Robins did their part for the less fortunate of New York, joining their city counterparts at the Polo Grounds on September 24. (The Giants had been eliminated from pennant contention the prior week.) Brooklyn was on both bills of the benefit doubleheader, playing the Giants in the first game and facing off against the Bronx borough team in the second. Mayor Jimmy Walker had been traveling in Europe and had missed the Giants-Yankees affair on September 9. But the debonair city official made up for it with a showy entrance on the field with Charles Stoneham, Jacob Ruppert and Frank York (president of Brooklyn) at his side, along with John Heydler, McGraw and Joe McCarthy, manager of the Yankees. The band from the NYC Department of Sanitation, created during Walker's first term in office, accompanied the dignitaries with spirited music. Fans from the five New York boroughs, numbering 44,000, watched the Giants defeat the Robins, 3–1, behind Bill Walker, their second-best pitcher (14–9). Brooklyn also dropped the second game, 5–1, to the Yankees' Ed Wells. Lou Gehrig blasted a towering home run which rattled the rafters of the roof in deep right field.

A few days later, the Giants, 87–65, achieved their 11th second-place finish under McGraw. The club, however, was no match against another powerful, pennant-winning St. Louis Cardinals squad that won 101 games.

NINE

"Last of the
Swashbuckling Managers"

"McGraw remarked that baseball had become 'something of a pink tea.' It
was nothing like that when he played nor in the years afterward when he
was less mellow than he is today."—Ralph Davis, *Pittsburgh Press*

At his New York Giants office on West 42nd Street, overlooking Bryant Park, John
McGraw brought down the sliding cover of his roll-top desk with a loud thump. He
announced to the gathered press that he had concluded business for the year in New
York and was departing for Cuba later that New Year's Eve, 1931. "I can think of no better
way to start a new year than with a vacation,"[1] he announced. Before he left on his winter
pilgrimage, McGraw indicated to the assembled journalists in his office that he would
return to New York in six weeks to make final preparations to meet his team for spring
training.

The entrenched New York Giants manager and Blanche left New York, and its freez-
ing temperatures, via train to Miami, where they took a connecting ship to Havana.
Umpire Bill Klem, who resided in Miami, was on hand to wish the McGraws a bon
voyage. Klem's and McGraw's history dated back more than a quarter-century now. The
future Hall of Fame arbiter had sent McGraw, as a manager, to an early shower no fewer
than 15 times, dating back to 1905—more than any single umpire. (Klem threw out more
players and managers than any baseball arbiter, with 305 lifetime ejections, per Official
Records.) Klem, with his gesture, distinctly left those past contentious issues on the field.

McGraw and Blanche arrived in Havana on New Year's Day, 1932. Fifteen days after
the McGraws' continental departure, the *Chicago Daily Tribune* published a story that
indicated Charles Stoneham was ready to trade Giants star first baseman Bill Terry to
the Chicago Cubs for pitcher Pat Malone and another player to be named presently. The
veteran Terry, according to Stoneham, was being obstinate in contract demands. "He has
made trouble about signing every year since he was a rookie,"[2] Stoneham said. The Giants
owner also called Terry "a detriment to the ball club." Stoneham was keeping the vacationing McGraw apprised of the situation with regular dispatches.

Early into his tropical stay, news came to McGraw that his former Orioles teammate
Kid Gleason had died. Gleason was the first of several close teammates, or old playing
associates, of McGraw's to pass away in 1932, including Dan Brouthers and Candy
LaChance. Less than a month later, McGraw received the news that old opponent Barney
Dreyfuss had expired. The Pittsburgh Pirates owner was a few weeks shy of 67.

Toward the end of his Havana furlough, McGraw acquired a pitcher he had coveted for years. When McGraw arrived in Havana harbor on the first of the year, Adolfo Luque was property of the Brooklyn Robins. Three weeks later, the Robins released the 41-year-old hurler. McGraw likely visited Luque at his place of residence in central Havana, *calle* Jesús Peregrino #87, or perhaps spent time with the pitcher at Oriental Park or elsewhere. By the tenth of February, McGraw had convinced Luque to join the Giants to bolster the team's bullpen.

McGraw unquestionably knew he was also receiving the added bonus of Luque's accumulated pitching wisdom, which would benefit the entire Giants pitching staff. Ironically, the acquisition would pay its biggest dividend not for McGraw personally, but for his presently unhappy employee Terry, the following season.

Terry obviously was not traded to the Cubs by the Giants. (The great player had been edged out of a second straight batting crown on the last day of the season by the Cardinals' Chick Hafey, .3488 to .3486.) The report of the first baseman's threatened exchange was doubtlessly voiced to the press by a posturing Stoneham during a difficult point in the negotiation standoff. McGraw himself secured Terry's signature on his 1932 contract during a stopover in New Orleans, from New York, on his way to the Giants' West Coast training camp site. It occurred on February 19, a few days after the 58-year-old manager returned stateside from Havana.

In 1932, after 24 years of utilizing pre-season conditioning facilities in Texas, Florida and Georgia, McGraw booked his team for a cross-country training excursion in Los Angeles. It was written that McGraw had been lured to the West Coast by Universal Pictures to make "a series of baseball pictures." It can be recalled that, in the winter of 1912–1913, capitalizing on his recent World Series appearances, McGraw had engaged in a high-paid, 13-week vaudeville stage show run with Hughie Jennings. One sportswriter quipped that he could not wait to see the rough and tumble "Mugsy" McGraw after going through his first session of "painting and powdering" for the big screen.

The Giants' top field man arrived in Los Angeles on February 23, accompanied by Blanche. He immediately announced that there would be two practices a day for his team, commencing the following day. All practices would be closed to the public. Keeping away the fans, McGraw rationalized, would build curiosity and excitement for the start of exhibition games. On that latter front, the Giants had the major league company of the Chicago Cubs, Detroit Tigers and Pittsburgh Pirates, all training in California and available to provide competitive exhibition matches leading up to the start of the season.

The Giants trained at Wrigley Field, the seven-year-old park in South Los Angeles. It was named after chewing gum mogul William Wrigley, Jr., who owned the ballpark's primary tenants, the Los Angeles Angels of the Pacific Coast League. It had to be considered somewhat of a coup for Wrigley to lure the Giants to California, as he had done. His own Chicago Cubs had previously established training roots on Catalina Island. (After one weekend exhibition game with the Cubs, the Giants were treated to a barbeque at Wrigley's island complex.)

The Giants had trained once before in Los Angeles, in 1907. McGraw was then in his sixth year as Giants manager. Now, he was starting his 31st season at the helm of his beloved New York team. His last pennant had come in 1924, making him the first manager to capture four consecutive league flags. He had won three World Series, though not consecutively as he had wished to do. Connie Mack, though also denied winning three consecutive world titles by the St. Louis Cardinals last fall, had captured five Fall Classic rings.

The annual holiday in Cuba provided its usual reinvigorating therapy, and, come the spring, McGraw showed little sign that he was not up to the challenge of another marathon season. "I've been in baseball too long to go around making predictions," said McGraw at the outset of spring training. "But I think the Giants will be much improved over last year. Naturally, St. Louis is the team to beat."[3]

Though the Giants had finished a distant second to St. Louis, there were several reasons for McGraw's optimistic outlook. He was expecting a bounce-back year from second baseman Hughie Crtiz, who was out for much of 1931 with an injured arm, and the full-time return of Freddie Lindstrom from an instep fracture. The manager had shored up his bullpen with the acquisition of Luque and Herman "Hi" Bell, former St. Louis Cardinals reliever, picked up from that team's Rochester minor league affiliate. There were also high expectations for rookie outfielder Len Koenecke. Incumbent left fielder Freddy Leach was sold to the Boston Braves in March with the intentions of giving Koenecke the job.

On Wednesday, March 29, 1932, the Seattle Indians defeated a split squad of New York Giants, 18–4, in front of the largest exhibition crowd of spring training so far to see the East Coast Giants against a non–major league club. The game was held at Community Park in Santa Cruz and attracted 3,000 fans. The rest of the Giants' squad, including most of the first-stringers were in San Francisco, losing to the San Francisco Seals, 9–4. Carl Hubbell pitched the distance and allowed six runs in the eight frames. Only 350 fans showed up for the game.

The contest against the Seals was more indicative of the crowds in front of which the Giants played. Attendance in the National League had dropped more than 18 percent in 1931 from 1930 (4,583,815 from 5,446,532). To offset the decrease and cut down on expenses in the face of the mounting fiscal pressure, owners not only began towing the line with salaries but now, for 1932, teams trimmed the roster limit from the previously expanded 25 to 23 players. Remarking over the low attendance in the spring, McGraw stated, "We've got to do something to attract more fans. Lack of fight is responsible."[4] Referred to as the "apostle of aggression" in one storyline, McGraw faulted the players for what he termed, "too much pacifism."[5] The manager believed that crowds would turn out more to see the "ballplayers exhibit the scrappy spirit characteristic of his own playing days."[6]

"There is only one function for an umpire," replied second-year American League president William Harridge in the same vein as his predecessor, Ban Johnson, "and that is to render decisions to the best of his ability. His belligerency or lack of it should have nothing to do with gate receipts."[7]

Earlier, on the roster squeeze, McGraw had commented, "I am going to keep three catchers, nine pitchers, six infielders and five outfielders. Some good men will probably get away no matter what happens."[8]

Somewhat past the mid-point of training camp, news was delivered to McGraw that one of his former players had died. All printed reports of the death tied the veteran skipper to the deceased utility player. "McGraw noted the regularity with which Sammy Strang hit in the pinches," read one of the obituary notices. "So he called him a 'pinch-hitter' and the term stuck."[9] Strang was a player McGraw famously fined in 1905 for missing a bunt sign, even though Strang hit a home run. McGraw reasoned that he could have just as easily hit into a double play. Under replicated circumstances in the years to come, a slew of future managers followed McGraw in this questionable disciplinary response.

The same week of the 55-year-old Strang's passing, McGraw took advantage of a Giants off-day to visit the Agua Caliente Race Track in Tijuana, Mexico. A large contingent of Giants players accompanied him. Before the opening bugle, everyone enjoyed a luncheon in the clubhouse "at which pretty Mexican girls danced to the music of a string orchestra."[10] The most circulated newspaper tattle about the jaunt surrounded a quip by the horse-racing-aficionado leader of the Giants. "Fixing a beady eye on the racing program," one of several wire services transmitted, "McGraw noticed one of the heats was called 'the Giants handicap.'"[11] The manager was overheard snidely remarking that the race was named in honor of Bill Klem.

Toward the end of the month, in the midst of the greatest financial catastrophe the country had ever faced, the U.S. Federal Government attempted to balance the national budget by imprudently raising taxes on its citizenry. The House of Representatives approved a sweeping taxation bill on March 30 (to take effect June 21), adopting levies on everything from telephone calls to match boxes. The price of a first-class stamp was bumped up a penny to three cents. An amusement tax of 10 percent on admissions above 45 cents was included in the measure (shortly revised to 40 cents). The latter tax was expected to yield $1,000,000 from each major league and an estimated $2,500,000 from college football gates. An amendment by a California representative to exclude the admissions tax on tickets for the upcoming summer Olympics in Los Angeles was soundly defeated. Carry-over capital gain losses were also abolished until 1934.

Four days later, the Giants closed their California exhibition schedule with weekend games against the San Francisco Seals in San Francisco and the Mission Reds in Woodland. The team concluded its West Coast exhibition schedule with a 20–8 record. McGraw was so pleased with training conditions and the pleasant weather, which had not disrupted his players' routines for one day, that he made arrangements to bring the Giants back to Los Angeles next spring. The only complaint McGraw had voiced, in fact, concerned several scheduled night games against Pacific Coast League teams. McGraw was loathe to play games under the lights. Finally, McGraw did not follow through on any of the acting inclinations he was said to have had during his stay in the burgeoning Tinseltown. The earlier report proved to be false or, as happens in the film industry, did not develop.

As the Giants headed east on Monday, April 4, the Lindbergh baby kidnapping case, which had gripped the nation since its occurrence on March 1, was now in its 34th unsolved day.

For Giants fans, there was no mystery behind McGraw's decision to start Bill Walker in the season's opener against the Philadelphia Phillies on April 12. Walker, in 1931, had led the National League in ERA (2.26) and shutouts (six) and had been the club's second-winningest pitcher with 16. On a wintry day at the Polo Grounds, Walker was rocked for seven earned runs on seven hits, unable to record an out in the second inning prior to his removal. The Phillies defeated the Giants, 13–5. Eighteen thousand fans braved the nippy temperatures and the embarrassing effort by their club.

Prior to the game, McGraw received the following telegram from an influential politician—one who obviously had not followed McGraw's career very closely or was feeling in much need of re-election support from whatever quarter he could find: "I send you my heartiest congratulations upon beginning the 30th year of your great career as manager of the New York Giants, in which you have done so much to uphold the traditions of clean sportsmanship in the most beloved national game. Signed, President Herbert Hoover."[12] Going forward, neither McGraw nor Hoover, nor the constituencies they led, had a very good year, also like Mayor Jimmy Walker, who threw out his final ceremonial pitch for the Giants. The raw climate may have reminded the flamboyant public official of Lake Placid, New York, where he had eminently consorted at the Winter Olympics, two months earlier. The high-ranking civil servant was soon to be brought down by the too-well-known stigma of political corruption.

The Opening Day loss by the Giants became a recurring theme for the club. McGraw's band was in the cellar, at 5–10, on May 4, when it set off to St. Louis on its first lengthy road swing. The manager blamed the poor start on his pitchers receiving irregular work due to the rash of rainouts the squad encountered in the season's first weeks. The club won three out of four from the Cardinals from May 5 to May 8. On the final day of the series, Carl Hubbell vanquished Gabby Street's Redbirds, 4–1, in the first game of a doubleheader. It was the last win John McGraw would manage.

After two games in Chicago and a three-game set at Forbes Field were washed away, the team moved on to Cincinnati. Starting May 15, McGraw missed the four-game set with the third-place Reds. He was laid up by separate reports of "indigestion" and "ptomaine poisoning," references to the stomach problems McGraw had been suffering from, off and on, for the past two years. The indisposed pilot made it to Redland Field prior to the game of May 17, but only long enough to find Bill Klem and give him an earful over the previous day's actions. "The Old Arbitrator" had made the Giants play through a sudden rainstorm that cropped up in the bottom of the sixth inning. Ahead, 2–0, Freddie Fitzsimmons was tossing a three-hit shutout. The Reds scored six runs, while the Giants and their pitcher, McGraw contended, were forced to play with a "slippery ball." Having had his say, the infirm manager retreated to his Cincinnati hotel room and eventually returned to New York ahead of the team.

On May 30, the Giants swept a pair of games from the Boston Braves at Braves Field, with McGraw still unfit for duty. A writer close to the team enlightened the New York public that McGraw was sicker than previously believed. The details were reprinted in *The Sporting News* as follows: "Manager John McGraw, who was stricken with illness while the Giants were idle in Pittsburgh, recently, has not been allowed to take his place on the bench. He is suffering from sinus trouble, which has affected his vision and given him much pain. His physician has advised him to stay at home until real hot weather sets in."[13]

The following day, after losing to Boston, 7–2, the team returned home. On June 1, the club was beaten by the Philadelphia Phillies, 4–2. McGraw made only a brief appearance in the clubhouse prior to the game, hoping to inspire his men. It did not work.

The next day, the *New York World-Telegram* broke one of the biggest baseball stories in history. Obtaining the presses-stopping scoop was sportswriter Tom Meany. Most New York scribes veered away from the Polo Grounds on June 2, after seeing the "No Game" sign posted outside, canceling the scheduled double engagement between the Giants and Phillies, supposedly due to a chance of showers. But the enterprising Meany thought he might be able to scrounge up a "filler" story if he poked around a bit inside. Pressing forward, Meany encountered a hot dog vendor near the clubhouse entrance steps.

"Did you hear McGraw is out?" asked the vendor. "He quit and Terry is the new manager."[14]

On December 15, 1932, the Giants club physician, William J. Walsh, was shot and killed by an unstable person who ended up taking his own life. Walsh, McGraw's primary doctor, had prescribed rest for his esteemed patient in 1932, a recommendation that finally delivered McGraw's sudden and widely unexpected retirement.

"For over two years, due to ill health," McGraw's prepared statement read at the time of the announcement, "I have been contemplating the necessity of turning over the management of the Giants to someone else. My doctor advises me, because of my sinus condition, that it would be inadvisable for me to attempt another road trip with the club this season. So I suggested to Mr. Stoneham that another manager be appointed." McGraw also made clear that he had something to do with Bill Terry's installation. "It was my desire that a man be appointed who was thoroughly familiar with my methods. And who had learned baseball under me."[15]

The McGraws, who were childless throughout their marriage, left for Havana two weeks after they attended the unfortunate doctor's funeral. It was McGraw's last trip to his foreign, winter home away from home. In mid–January 1933, McGraw received a surprise call from the president of the New York Chapter of the Baseball Writers' Association of America, Dan Daniel. The reporter notified McGraw that he had been selected as recipient of the Bill Slocum Award, in recognition of his long and meritorious service to baseball. (Slocum was a former president of the BBWAA and respected sportswriter and editor.) McGraw interrupted his tropical vacation and returned to New York to accept the award on February 5.

At the award dinner, in the grand ballroom of the Commodore Hotel, also attended by new Giants manager Bill Terry, McGraw received an ovation and heard a telegram from Connie Mack read out loud that referred to McGraw as baseball's greatest manager. The man, who many local writers in the audience softheartedly referred to as "ol' Jawn," regaled the over 500 attendees who came out to see him. The manager with the most National League pennants in history reminisced about his early days with the Baltimore Orioles and told humorous stories of his 1913–1914 barnstorm tour to the Far East. The dumpy, white-haired former manager also used the platform to set the record straight on the rea-

Enjoying his last winter in Cuba, McGraw attentively eyes the field from the clubhouse lawn of Oriental Race Track in Havana in January 1933.

son for his abrupt retirement from the game eight months earlier. "I resigned as manager of the Giants because my doctor ordered it," McGraw said from the dais. "There was no quarrel with me and Mr. Stoneham. He treated me squarely, like both predecessors under whom I worked."[16]

In attendance were Branch Rickey and a slew of the greatest baseball writers of the day. One of those writers, John Kieran, donned a white wig and lampooned the white-maned Kenesaw Mountain Landis, in one of the evening's highlights. The commissioner was not present.

McGraw packed up his award and returned to the warmer Caribbean climate, to the Hotel Nacional, where he and his wife were staying. McGraw gave one interview while in Havana, an informal one at that, to Burris Jenkins, Jr., the sports cartoonist of the *New York Evening Journal*. Jenkins Jr. caught up with McGraw at the Oriental Race-track. He quoted McGraw as saying, "You'd be surprised how little I keep up with baseball news. I read scarcely anything about it. Even last year, when I went to a game, I couldn't sit through more than a few innings. You see, now that I'm out of it…. If you don't mind, I'd like to watch these two-year-olds come in."[17]

McGraw may have been trying to put on a brave face with the comments. Or he may have been trying to steer attention away from himself, for the benefit of his former team.

The couple returned to New York in the spring of 1933, with John McGraw "looking better than he had in quite some time."[18] Bill Terry and the Giants were training in Los Angeles—the first spring training in 43 years unattended by McGraw. On the day McGraw celebrated his 60th and last birthday, April 7, 1933, the Giants pounded the Detroit Tigers, 17–7, in an exhibition game in Norfolk, Virginia.

Thirteen days later, the Giants opened their home schedule, with McGraw, maintaining the executive title of vice president of the club, in attendance. On a frigid day, only 15,000 fans assembled to see Carl Hubbell shut out the Boston Braves, 1–0. McGraw joined in the pregame festivities, marching behind New York City Mayor John P. O'Brien for flag-raising ceremonies. Cheered every step of the way, McGraw strode back to the dugout, wished his former team luck and slipped into the stands, eventually retreating to the center field clubhouse to watch the brilliantly pitched game.

The next significant appearance by McGraw on a ball field came in early July. At the inaugural All-Star Game, McGraw's last game in control of the lineup card resulted in a 4–2 defeat, with old nemesis Babe Ruth delivering the decisive blow. In the home Comiskey Park dugout, sat 70-year-old Connie Mack, who would famously render tribute to his opposing field tactician by stating, "There has been only one manager—and his name [is] McGraw."

McGraw continued his duties as a high-ranking team executive through the remainder of the season, making regular trips to the club offices in Manhattan. He followed, with a great deal of satisfaction and perhaps a bit of envy, his former team's run to the National League pennant and the World Series championship. "They had wonderful pitching," he stated, "and Terry handled his team in wonderful shape. Every man on the team did his part."[19] All of McGraw's post–Series assessments were crafted with the unpretentious mention of Terry's fine leadership. No one could accuse his compliments toward Terry of being insincere.

Right after the World Series, print rumors circulated that McGraw had been offered the presidency of the Chicago Cubs, to fill the void left by the recently deceased William

Veeck. McGraw strongly denied any basis to the story and more vehemently squashed the notion that he would ever consider leaving the Giants. McGraw also made it clear that he was not part of an ownership group, led by millionaire sportsman John Hay Whitney, supposedly intent on buying the New York Giants franchise.

Through the fall and early winter, McGraw's health began deteriorating. His kidneys were not flushing out body toxins properly and his intestines and prostate were being overrun by cancerous bacteria. McGraw and his wife decided not to travel to Cuba at the end of the year.

McGraw's last public appearance came in early February 1934, at the National League owners' meeting, hosted by Charles Stoneham, at the Waldorf-Astoria. McGraw stayed but one hour before exiting to an awaiting car. He was driven back home by his trusted driver, Edward Stanley. A few days earlier, McGraw had tried to attend the annual Baseball Writers' soiree at the Commodore Hotel, but halfway through dressing for the event at his home he was stricken by his infirmities and ordered to bed by the summoned physician.

McGraw weathered that attack and gave several signs of recovery over the next weeks. But on February 17, he suffered a relapse and was admitted to the hospital, where he was administered the last rites of the Roman Catholic Church. A week later, February 24, he lapsed into a coma from which he never awoke. He died from uremic poisoning the next day at 11:50 a.m. Present at his bedside were Blanche, Stoneham and several friends and relatives. "Everyone regrets his death, but none more than I,"[20] said the Giants owner.

"John had the mind of a man and the heart of a boy," Mrs. McGraw passed along amid her sorrow. "At the end he wasn't a day older in spirit than when he took charge of the Giants 32 years ago. Being Irish, he naturally loved a good fight. But when it was over he was willing to forget and forgive. He always tried to leave the ballgame in the ball park, but I always thought every defeat took something out of him just as every victory seemed to add new zest to his life."[21]

As in the wake of most deaths, commentary was delivered that was both elevating and softening of character. "Those who know McGraw best, know him to be a thorough little gentlemen generous and kind to a fault and a prince of good fellows."[22] The quote, attributed to baseball editor and author A.H. Spink, cast a light on McGraw's off-the-field attributes.

"Some will remember his baseball greatness but all will remember his unselfish acts of charity to those in need,"[23] echoed Emil Fuchs, owner of the Boston Braves.

"He was an outstanding figure in baseball, and while actively engaged, added much color and enthusiasm to the national game,"[24] AL president William Harridge diplomatically stated.

No one could doubt the genuineness behind Wilbert Robinson's released statement. "This is one of the saddest messages that has ever come to me,"[25] said McGraw's earliest lifelong baseball contemporary. Robinson would also pass away later the same year at age 70.

Jacob Ruppert declared of the man who helped engineer his purchase of the New York Yankees, "He was the first man of prominence in baseball I ever knew, and one of the finest."[26]

And Casey Stengel, newly appointed manager of Brooklyn, commented: "There was a great man. He hired and fired me. But when I was down he came to the front for me."[27]

One of the many McGraw disciples who became managers, Stengel would also provide, with the emotion-reducing distance of the passing years, an often-referred-to McGraw quote. Soon after batting helmets came into use in the league, Stengel stated that if these protection guards had existed when he played for McGraw, the manager "would have made us get hit in the head with the pitched ball [to get on base]."

Bill Terry's remarks at the time of McGraw's death reflected honest praise and balanced sincerity: "McGraw was far and away the greatest manager of all time. I doubt if his records, achievements and personality will ever be equaled. There were times, in my playing days under him, when we had our differences, but deep down in my heart I always loved and respected the old man and never lost sight of the fact that I owe to him all the essential knowledge I have about baseball."[28]

During the move to Ely Avenue, McGraw came across a box filled with slips of papers. He sat down with the box in front of the fireplace and began tossing the papers, a handful at a time, into the flames. The papers were a multitude of unpaid promissory notes collected by McGraw for loans he had handed out to friends and acquaintances.

"How much?" asked his wife, slipping in beside him.

"I don't know," answered McGraw, watching the papers dissolve into ashes. "Ten or fifteen thousand. They'd have paid. They just didn't have it."[29]

McGraw's benevolent nature was confirmed a few years before his death by Frank J. Bruen, general manager of Madison Square Garden. "John McGraw, friend of many, many years, is the most generous human being I have ever known, and a man who never said 'no' to any acquaintance in financial distress,"[30] stated Bruen, one of McGraw's numerous associates in the sports entertainment field.

The day of John McGraw's funeral services, the coldest February on record in New York City since record-keeping was established in 1871, came to a close with high temperatures reaching only the upper teens. The February 28 requiem mass was held at St. Patrick's Cathedral on Fifth Avenue. Celebrated people from all walks of life, from business tycoons to billiards players, from politicians to promoters, from supreme court justices to speakeasy singers, turned out. Crowd estimates ranged up to 5,000. "A detail of veteran ushers from the Polo Grounds," one report apprised, "wearing their brilliant scarlet coats and caps, formed an honor guard across the sidewalk before the cathedral as the service began at 10:00 a.m."[31] Afterwards, McGraw's body was transported by rail to the Bonnie Brae Cemetery (now New Cathedral) in Baltimore, for placement into a temporary vault, to await a spring interment.

The previous two days, February 26 and 27, Blanche McGraw had opened her suburban home to the general public, while her husband lay in state in the parlor where the two often played cards. "They were a devoted and loveable pair," relayed Eddie Brannick, the long-time front office man of the Giants and one close enough to McGraw to know. "Mrs. McGraw was his best companion. When the team struck a losing streak, John would become blue. She was the only one able to console him."[32]

Blanche's intention behind opening up her house was to permit the ordinary man an opportunity to say a final goodbye to John. A heavy snowfall, however, kept many of the common people from paying their respects to the man Kenesaw Mountain Landis eulogized as someone far removed from the commonplace. Among those present, with almost certainty, were McGraw's two surviving siblings, sisters referred to in the press as Mrs. Frank Gray of Canaan, Connecticut, and Mrs. James F. Connelly of Camillus, New York. Anna Gray and Helen Connelly received their brother's 80 shares of stock in the National Exhibition Company; it was the only stock McGraw was known to have held, and therefore he was spared any financial hardship in the great equities and commodities plunge of 1929. Blanche was bequeathed her husband's entire estate. Also in attendance were Christy Mathewson's wife, Jane, and his namesake son, and Frankie Frisch. "John was one of the best friends I ever had and the man who taught me most of the baseball I know,"[33] said Frisch from McGraw's home. Bill Terry also reached the residence from Florida to pay his respects.

The following newspaper abstract of the man, printed in the wake of his resignation in 1932, conveyed the wide scope of influence McGraw had left behind: "A fighter, a master showman, and a leader who was willing to take chances, attracted the greatest players of his time to the Giants and gave the paying customers their money's worth. It is generally believed that no man associated with sport in the United States has matched the lasting imprint which McGraw, as manager of the Giants, has left on our game."[34]

Brooklyn sportswriter Harold C. Burr may have summed up McGraw's life closest to the manager's heart with his post-mortem tribute: "The last of the swashbuckling managers has climbed the Last Dugout's steps with the sudden passing of John Joseph McGraw, the man who made the Giants fanatically hated, respected and beloved throughout the National League for 30 years."[35]

TEN

Absenteeism as a Manager

Baltimore Orioles

Year	Games	Dates	Reason	Team Record
1899	13	August 28–September 9	Bereavement	6–7
1901	1	May 17	Suspension	0–1
	9	July 15–22	Injury (kneecap).	5–4
	27	August 21–September 16	Injury (torn knee cartilage)	6–21
1902	4	May 4–8	Suspension	0–4
	26	May 26–June 22	Injury (spiking)	12–14
	6	July 1–7	Suspension	3–3

In 1899, McGraw's first year as a pilot with the Baltimore Orioles, he was unable to attend two weeks' worth of games when his first wife Minnie unexpectedly died. The Orioles' record during his bereavement leave was 6–7. In July 1901, after an earlier suspension caused a one-game absence, the 28-year-old McGraw was forced away from his duties for nine games due to a dislocated kneecap. Aggravating the same injury later in the season caused the young skipper to forego his baseball responsibilities again for 27 games, August 21 to September 16.

The following season, 1902, McGraw managed in fewer than half the games Official Records show. He was suspended for five days (four games) in May. Later in the month, the player-manager missed four weeks of the schedule following a severe spiking he suffered. Shortly after his return, he was suspended indefinitely by American League president Ban Johnson. After securing his release, he jumped leagues, signing on as manager of Andrew Freedman's New York Giants on July 19. McGraw, however, spent much of the remainder of the season away from the club on player recruiting jaunts. He managed a total of 62 games in 1902, 27 (14–13) with Baltimore and 35 (15–20) with the Giants.

Year	Games	Dates	Reason	Team Record
1902	5	August 14–17, August 19	Recruitment of players	3–2
	8	August 23–September 1	Recruitment of players	3–5
	15	September 15–October 4	Recruitment of players	4–11
1903	2	April 27–28	Broken nose	2–0
	2	May 1–2	Severe nose bleed	1–1
1904	3	August 23–24	Suspension	2–1
	10	September 6–13	Ankle injury	8–2
	1	September 28	Unexplained absence	0–1
	4	October 3–8	Indifference	2–2
1905	10	May 27–June 6	Suspension	8–2

Year	Games	Dates	Reason	Team Record
1906	3	May 2–4	Suspension	2–1
	1	May 7	Soreness/auto accident	0–1
	16	August 8–24	Suspension	10–6
1907	1	April 11	Sick with the grippe	0–1
	3	August 8–9	Suspension	2–1
1908	3	June 17–18	Suspension	2–1
	1	July 6	Scouting	1–0

A fateful smash to his nose by a thrown baseball prompted McGraw to take a recovery leave of four games in 1903. A two-day suspension in 1904, his first in the National League, and a field accident involving overzealous fans cut into his dugout time by more than a dozen games. He remained off the bench on crutches from September 6 through at least September 13. "After they clinched the pennant on September 22, McGraw started taking in the early races at any of various tracks around the city, then rushing to the Polo Grounds by four o'clock for that afternoon's game,"[1] writes Charles Alexander. McGraw, Bresnahan and Billy Gilbert were declared absent for their game on September 28 by the *New York Times*. Bresnahan was said to have returned home to Ohio, but no reason was given for the non-appearance of the other two. It may not be wild speculation to deduce that the pair played hooky together following a day at the races. In between games of a Polo Grounds doubleheader on October 1, McGraw "was presented with a gold watch by some of his most enthusiastic friends."[2] With his first pennant secured, the uninterested manager permitted 46-year-old Dan Brouthers to suit up and manage the Giants in their next games, October 3 and 4, against the St. Louis Cardinals. The latter day was a doubleheader in which the Giants forfeited the nightcap, after three home team players were ejected and the club petulantly declined to continue with the action. A former Orioles teammate of McGraw, Brouthers appeared in two of the three games.

In 1905, McGraw was disqualified for ten games—the result of another suspension— after instigating a stinging verbal encounter with Pittsburgh Pirates owner Barney Dreyfuss. A year later, two more suspensions, following altercations with umpires, cost McGraw nearly three weeks of time away from the Giants' dugout.

In 1907 and 1908, the overly assertive manager accepted his eighth and ninth suspensions, separating him from his team for six games. In the former year, a bad cold necessitated his skipping the Giants' first game of the season. In the latter season, a summer side-trip to Columbus, Ohio, with John T. Brush to meet new purchase Rube Marquard deprived McGraw of another contest.

Year	Games	Dates	Reason	Team Record
1909	2	April 15–16	Infected split finger	1–1
	1	April 22	Infected split finge	1–0
	8	April 30–May 10	Infected split finger	3–5
1910	6	August 19–August 24	Suspension	3–3
1911	3	May 17–19	Suspension	1–2
	6	May 30–June 5	Wife ill	4–2
	3	July 27–29	Suspension	1–2
1912	2	April 20–24	Suspension.	2–0
	1	September 30	Personal day	1–0
	1	October 1	World Series scouting	0–1
1913	2	May 15–17	Suspension	1–1
	5	July 3–7	Suspension	5–0
	1	September 30	Split squad practice	0–1

Year	Games	Dates	Reason	Team Record
	1	October 3	World Series scouting	1–0
1914	5	August 4–8	Suspension	3–2
	7	October 1–6	Indifference	4–3
1915	2	October 4	Indifference	0–2
	1	October 7	Indifference	1–0

An infected, split finger robbed McGraw of 11 games in the dugout early in the 1909 campaign. From 1910 through 1912, insulting umpires prompted the league to suspend McGraw on four occasions and for a total of 14 games. A brief illness to Blanche in 1911 and World Series scouting in 1912 resulted in eight more unseen contests.

Two more suspensions in 1913, one for engaging in fisticuffs with an opposing player, sacked the Giants pilot for seven contests. He purposely ignored two games at the end of the campaign while preparing for his World Series opponents.

National League suspension number 16 and late-season indifference trimmed 12 games from McGraw's managerial ledger in 1914. During a season-closing homestand, the manager eschewed the last seven home games, four of which were against the Boston Braves. The absence versus the Braves reflected poorly on McGraw; it was the first meeting of the teams since Boston had passed McGraw's front-runners in early September. Mike Donlin managed in place of McGraw, who was vaguely identified as being sick but who returned one day after the season closed to skipper a post-season series between the Giants and the New York Yankees.

A full season at the helm—which would have been his first as Giants manager—was within reach in 1915, when McGraw decided to kick back at a doubleheader at Braves Field, October 4, and watch the proceedings with the regular folk. He could not stay out of trouble. "McGraw watched the games from a seat in the grandstand," noted the *Boston Globe*, "and had quite a spirited run-in with Walter Jackson, otherwise known as the 'Salem Kid.'" Jackson said that during the wordy battle, the New York manager had a knife in his hand, and he left the grounds vowing that he would cause McGraw's arrest for threatening him with the knife and also abusing him by the application of epithets."[3] The Giants lost both games. Two days later, a Brighton District Court judge threw out Jackson's complaint, after hearing McGraw and other witnesses' testimony. McGraw then skipped out on the Giants' final game of the season, October 7, in Beantown.

Year	Games	Dates	Reason	Team Record
1916	1	July 20	Christy Mathewson trade	0–1
	2	October 4–5	Quit team	1–1
1917	13	June 9–23	Suspension	9–4
	2	September 30	Traveling to see Buck Herzog	0–2
1918	1	August 29	Personal day	1–0
1919	1	May 8	Meeting with Branch Rickey	0–1
	12	September 16–28	Internal gambling probe; quit team	7–5
1920	5	May 19–23	Suspension	2–3
	5	June 1–4	Undisclosed illness	3–2
	11	August 8–17	Recovery from Lambs Club brawl	7–4
	2	September 6	With Charles Stoneham	1–1
	4	September 27–October 1	National gambling probe; reorganization of National Commission	2–2

Year	Games	Dates	Reason	Team Record
1921	3	July 27–July 29	Suspension	3–0
1922	1	June 4	Cold	1–0
	10	July 23–30	Sinusitis	6–4
	1	August 15	Phil Douglas issue	1–0
	2	October 1	Indifference	1–1

In July 1916, McGraw missed a game to travel to Cincinnati to complete the Christy Mathewson trade, and, in a fit a pique, he quit the team with two games to go on the schedule.

The following year, a serious run-in with an umpire handed McGraw a 16-day suspension. The Giants played 13 games without him. With an eye on the World Series, McGraw left the flag-clinched Giants in Cincinnati on September 30, and headed east ahead of the team to call on Buck Herzog at his Baltimore farm. The dissatisfied infielder had left the club three weeks earlier to rest a haggard body. Substitute skipper Art Fletcher could not prevent a pair of losses that day. In the season-abridged competition of 1918, McGraw neglected at least one game during the final few days of the campaign.

A May 1919 meeting with Branch Rickey held important enough trade implications for McGraw to step out on his club for a day with the Giants in action. Months after that, a Notes of the Game addendum in the September 16, 1919, *Cincinnati Enquirer* advised that "John McGraw has pulled a Jess Willard by heaving a sponge into the ring. McGraw did not put on his baseball togs, then left the game early and caught the 5 o'clock train to New York. He left Mathewson in command of the club." From that point, the Giants manager shunned the last 12 games on the team's schedule ostensibly in order to confront a more pressing matter involving gambling accusations levied against two of his players.

The following season, 1920, the almost annual ritual of suspension shaved five games from McGraw's managing record, as did an undisclosed illness (probably sinus-related). In August, a physical beating he incurred following an all-night drinking binge prevented McGraw from appearing at 11 games on the bench while he healed. Later on, the Giants left New York on the midnight train to Boston on September 6 for a Labor Day doubleheader. McGraw was not with them. He arrived at Braves Field as the first game was concluding and watched the second game with Charles Stoneham in the grandstand. As the same month was expiring, the federal gambling investigation in the wake of the 1919 World Series compelled McGraw to appear in Chicago and offer insights on dishonest players Heinie Zimmerman and Hal Chase. Acting as Giants Vice President, McGraw stayed over in town to affix his signature on a reorganization proposal for the National Commission. Supported by other high-ranking baseball executives, the plan signaled doom for baseball's three-person governing body and cleared the way for the establishment of the new post of Commissioner of Baseball in November. McGraw missed at least four games. Johnny Evers acted as manager pro tempore of the Giants during the season.

More umpire-baiting in 1921 brought out a three-day pink slip from the league. In July 1922, physical ailments occasioned the bellicose figure to bypass ten games at the helm. A cold and dealing with the self-destructive Phil Douglas caused him to sacrifice two other playing dates. On the last day of the season, McGraw and Stoneham entertained a group of dignitaries under the Polo Grounds grandstand while the Giants were playing a doubleheader with the Boston Braves. Among the invited guests were Braves owner George Washington Grant and former managers Fred Clarke and Jack Dunn. Commissioner Landis also mingled about with a slew of old-time Giants the likes of Dan Brouthers and Amos Rusie.

Year	Games	Dates	Reason	Team Record
1923	2	May 30	Unexplained absence	1–1
	2	August 15	Toothache	0–2
1924	47	May 17–July 6	Knee injury	32–15
	5	September 1–3	Heat exhaustion	3–2
1925	1	April 14	Cold	0–1
	45	May 2–June 21	Sinusitis	27–18
	1	August 27	Unexplained	0–1
	14	Sept 14–October 3	Personal leave/indifference	8–6
1926	10	April 24–May 3	Sinusitis	3–7
	4	July 12–15	Scouting trip	2–2
1927	1	May 18	Court date	0–1
	4	June 11–14	Trading; scouting	0–4
	7	July 27–August 2	Scouting trip	5–2
	32	September 3–October 2	Sinusitis	22–10
1928	40	May 15–June 28	Broken leg	24–16
	3	August 28–29	Cold	0–3

In 1923, during the third year of a four-season pennant run, McGraw was truant on two dates at the Polo Grounds, each, coincidentally, doubleheaders.

"Illness and infirmity kept him away from his team at least a third of the time, beginning about 1924,"[4] Charles Alexander wrote in his 1988 book on McGraw. The manager was gone for 47 games in 1924, the aggravation of his old knee injury the root cause. (Official Records has made an incomplete note of this non-attendance period.) Heat exhaustion prevented the venerable leader from attending a five-game set at Braves Field in early September.

In 1925, as in 1907, an inopportune cold cost him another Opening Day memory. In May and June, plagued by his bedeviling sinus condition, McGraw's was absent a total of 45 games, from May 2 until his return on June 23. On the day of his return, at home against Brooklyn, the *Times'* Harry Cross wrote that "although McGraw joined the club in Chicago [June 8–11] he has not yet sat on the bench since he was taken ill late in April."[5] The latter date reference point strongly confirms that McGraw was not present for the May 2 game versus Brooklyn, the day of Edward J. McKeever's funeral (see page 155 in the text). (Official Records reflects McGraw's absence beginning with the following game, May 4, and places his return prematurely on June 9.) Then, halfway through September, McGraw appeared to lose interest in finishing the campaign. The second-place Giants were 6½ games off the pace at the time. Staunch McGraw press backer Joe Vila reported that Mrs. McGraw was ill and that her husband stayed by her side during the period. (Official Records accounts for a little more than half the time McGraw was actually gone during the season.) As he had the prior year, Hughie Jennings stepped in for his good pal as field director.

McGraw's troublesome sinuses flared up on him again in April 1926, forcing the Giants manager to forgo the team's first road trip—a limited Eastern jaunt in which his club ticked ten games off the schedule without him. Roger Bresnahan managed the club. Later in the summer, McGraw began indulging in scouting trips, mostly during Giants road trips in the West. Diverting from Cincinnati for four days, July 12–15, he went to Louisville in search of potential major league players. These in-season trips would continue with regularity until his penultimate year as manager.

The next season, a court date mandated a brief withdrawal from his club on May 18. On July 27, the Giants arrived in Chicago to begin a 12-game Western road foray without their leader. McGraw was off touring the lower-level Southern leagues for players. Coincidentally, McGraw had also shunned his club's first trip into Chicago, in June, for the same reason. McGraw then took ill at the beginning of September, and Rogers Hornsby took over the Giants. (The Hornsby games in September are accounted for in OR but not the other contests McGraw declined to attend.)

The following year, 1928, the aging pilot broke his leg when struck by a taxicab outside Wrigley Field. The accident occurred on May 14, after Cubs hurler Charlie Root had beaten Freddie Fitzsimmons, 8–2, inside the ball yard. Six weeks of convalescence followed, with an accrued 40 games away from the dugout. A summer cold knocked McGraw for a loop in late August. The Giants played three times before he licked it.

Year	Games	Dates	Reason	Team Record
1929	15	May 7–May 22	Sinusitis	5–10
	3	June 19–20	Heat exhaustion	3–0
	2	July 26–27	Scouting trip	1–1
	1	July 29	Scouting trip	1–0
	3	September 1–2	Scouting trip	1–2
	23	September 9–October 6	Scouting/indifference	16–7
1930	4	May 17–18	Unexplained Absence	1–3
	1	June 4	Scouting	1–0
	2	July 25–26	Scouting in Montreal	2–0
	20	August 2–August 24	Personal matters/sinusitis	12–8
	28	September 1–28	Sinusitis	16–12
1931	3	July 19–21	Suspension	0–3
	22	July 25–August 14	Scouting/sinusitis/scouting	14–8
	3	September 10–12	Scouting	1–2
	2	September 16	Scouting	0–2
	1	September 19	Meeting with Norman Perry	1–0
	1	September 27	Indifference	0–1
1932	20	May 15–June 1	Sinusitis	9–11

In May of 1929, the seasonal sinus scourge caused an interval of 15 games. McGraw was also felled by heat exhaustion in the second game of a doubleheader at Ebbets Field on June 18. Prior to his getting back on his feet, the Giants played and won three games in Philadelphia. Later on, McGraw excused himself from multiple contests. Nine games behind the Chicago Cubs on July 25, McGraw put Ray Schalk in charge while he went on a short recruiting trip. No sooner had he returned (July 28) than he took off again for another brief interlude. A third absence from the team was made with Charles Stoneham shortly afterward, August 3. A rainout and off-day spared any additional marks on McGraw's attendance record, as he reunited with his club in Pittsburgh two days later. The sojourns occurred during a road trip through the cities of Chicago, St. Louis and Cincinnati. The end result was the signing of Ray Lucas, an American Association pitcher who never won a game for McGraw. On August 31, the Giants headed to Boston; McGraw headed to Buffalo. The Giants manager took in a game between the Toronto Maple Leafs and Buffalo Bisons. McGraw threw in the campaign towel shortly thereafter. He shucked his duties as manager for the last 23 games of the season, starting September 9. The manager's absence was repeatedly explained as his being in search of new talent, even after the minor league season ended. McGraw defended his time away, while sounding much like a man with homemade excuses. "Inasmuch as the Giants have been beaten out of the pennant by a string of misfortunes," he said, "I think that it is better for me to hunt for new material without depending entirely on scouts."[6] Although he could not find time for his team, McGraw did attend Miller Huggins' funeral in New York on September 27. The Giants were off that day, while the American League postponed all action in their circuit.

Implied estate business involving his deceased brother and recurring bouts of his nasal affliction wrecked the last two months of his 1930 season, although he was once again healthy enough to report from the World Series in syndicated columns. At the beginning of August, five games in arrears of Brooklyn, McGraw passed the managerial baton to Dave Bancroft and did not take it back until weeks later. "When the Giants returned from their last western trip to engage the Robins in a four-game series at the Polo Grounds [August 27–30]," clarified the *Sun*'s Joe Vila, "McGraw took over the reins and informed his intimate friends that he had been attending to his late brother's affairs, but also had been under his doctor's care."[7]

Vila explained why the manager could not be with his team in the trenches during the entire month of September:

> McGraw, beset by a recurrence of sinus trouble that he suffered a couple of years ago, and along with it an infection of the upper jaw, was a very sick man as the Giants fought their way down the stretch … but against the advice of both friends and his physician, he refused to quit work before the season ended, and sat every afternoon in a window of the Polo Grounds clubhouse directing his players by remote control.[8]

While it is improbable that McGraw attended every one of the Giants' 17 September home games, he can no more be given official credit for "managing" 500 feet away than he could when he sat in a box near the Giants' dugout during his numerous suspensions.

Previously, McGraw had missed back-to-back doubleheaders on May 17 and 18. Two and a half weeks later, accompanied by Charles Stoneham, he crossed the Hudson to see prospect Carl Fischer of the New Jersey Skeeters pitch. The June 4 excursion to West Side Park veered McGraw away from the Giants' game versus the Cincinnati Reds at the Polo Grounds. In search of more minor league talent, McGraw had traveled across the border, by himself, on July 25–26, to watch the Montreal Royals. He returned to the Polo Grounds and his team on July 27.

In the summer of 1931, McGraw absorbed his 20th and final career suspension. Handed down in St. Louis, its duration was three games. Following that Cardinals series, after which the Giants found themselves 7½ games behind the league leaders, the club traveled to Cincinnati. The reinstated McGraw went scouting in nearby Louisville on July 25. His object of interest was Colonels second baseman Billy Herman. Rejoining the team in Pittsburgh two days later, he was struck by his respiratory affliction. He took more time away from the team to recover and then made another talent discovery trip to Indianapolis, where he was seen in the grandstand at Washington Park on August 8. A few days later, the acquisition of Indianapolis Indians outfielder Len Koenecke for four players under control of the Giants became big news. "The extraordinary feature of the deal, for these baseball times," illuminated one report, "was that Indianapolis president N.A. Perry refused $75,000 payment in cash for Koenecke and insisted on the delivery of players equivalent to value placed on the outfielder's services."[9] Although the official exchange was four players for one, the press would invariably refer to Koenecke as McGraw's $75,000 purchase.

McGraw's absences were now attracting attention outside of New York. "Like a man who walks out on a play that does not strike his fancy," disclosed national sportswriter Copeland C. Burg, "manager John McGraw of the New York Giants has deserted his team in the 1931 baseball race and is busy trying to do something about 1932. It was learned today Charles A. Stoneham has dug down in his sock and produced some $250,000 to buy players and McGraw and Chief Bender have been going up and down the land looking for first-class ivory."[10] McGraw sent Bender to the West Coast to scout, among others, pitcher Sam Gibson. The San Francisco Missions hurler was purchased by the Giants not long afterward.

McGraw returned to the Giants several games into a homestand, August 16, only to break away from his men on another scouting jaunt a few games later. Seemingly consumed more by trying to improve his team for next year, and beyond, than making a stretch run for the pennant, the manager did not accompany his squad to Pittsburgh for a three-game series from September 10 to 12. He waived off a doubleheader on September 16 in Cincinnati, the city within easy reach of the hotbed minor league towns of Louisville and Indianapolis. On September 19, the roving manager left the Giants in St. Louis under Dave Bancroft, while he went ahead to Chicago, the next road stop for New York. This time McGraw incorporated a personal business agenda ahead of the club's interests. McGraw had scheduled a meeting with Indianapolis owner Norman Perry about a possible ownership stake in the Giants.

In 1932, McGraw, apparently suffering from sinusitis, was absent from the bench for 20 straight games in May, leading up to his news-making resignation announcement on June 2.

In all, the Hall of Famer missed at least 679 games while manager, more than six times the number recorded in the official record, which accounts for 108 games (44 in 1924, and 32 in both 1925 and 1927). The official record also has McGraw managing only until June 28 in 1902. Although suspended for belligerency that day, he was still Orioles manager until given his release by the club on July 8. Like all other games missed because of suspensions, the unattended six games (July 1 thru 7) in the interim are included above.

Appendix A:
Transactions as a Manager

Retrosheet.org provided the source for the majority of the transactional information that follows, although some transactions were found in newspapers of the period. I used three ratings for signings, trades, and sales judged to be positive: "Outstanding," "Good" and "Effective." Outstanding transactions generally involved elite players who contributed significantly to New York's success over seasons. Good transactions had an extended, constructive effect on the organization. Moves that simply turned out to favor the Giants over the other club I considered effective. In rating McGraw's player sales, I took into account the amount received and the future value that the sold Giant player provided to his new team.

Conversely, those transactions I viewed as negative were labeled as "Bad," "Poor" and "Ineffective." In addition, there are several moves I describe as "Incomplete" or "Inconsequential." In the former cases, the players involved were all ticketed for future trades, which received separate grades. The inconsequential exchanges I evaluated as virtually pointless for the club, not worth the paperwork, as it were. Poor trades, signings, and sales were those that, simply put, weakened the Giants.

Date	Players	Rating
June 18, 1899	Sold INF John O'Brien to the Pittsburgh Pirates.	Effective
July 17, 1899	INF Dave Fultz signed as a free agent.	Inconsequential
August 5, 1899	Purchased INF Aleck Smith from the Washington Nationals.	Effective
February 1901	Signed pitcher Joe McGinnity as an implied free agent.	Outstanding
March 14, 1901	Signed catcher Roger Bresnahan from the Toledo Mud Hens (American Association).	Good
March 25, 1901	Signed INF Jimmy Williams as an implied free agent.	Effective
April 22, 1901	Signed OF Cy Seymour as an implied free agent.	Effective
April 23, 1901	Signed OF Jim Jackson as an amateur free agent.	Ineffective
May 11, 1901	Signed pitcher Jack Dunn as a free agent.	Inconsequential
June 10, 1901	Signed pitcher Frank Foreman as a free agent.	Effective
December 4, 1901	Signed OF Kip Selbach as an implied free agent.	Effective
December 1901	Signed OF Joe Kelley as an implied free agent.	Effective
February 1902	Signed 1B Dan McGann as an implied free agent.	Effective
February 1902	Signed pitcher Tom Hughes as an implied free agent.	Ineffective

Date	Players	Rating
February 1902	Signed INF Billy Gilbert as an implied free agent.	Effective
July 21, 1902	Purchased OF George Browne from the Philadelphia Phillies.	Effective
August 1902	Signed OF Sam Mertes as an implied free agent.	Effective
August 17, 1903	Purchased Red Ames from the Ilion Typewriters (New York State League) for $1,500.	Good
August 18, 1903	Purchased INF Art Devlin from the Newark Indians (Eastern League).	Good
December 12, 1903	Obtained SS Bill Dahlen from the Brooklyn Superbas in exchange for SS Charlie Babb, pitcher Jack Cronin and $6,000.	Effective
January 26, 1904	Purchased contract of P Hooks Wiltse from the Troy Trojans (New York State League).	Good
August 7, 1904	Obtained OF Mike Donlin from the Cincinnati Reds in a three-way trade. The Giants sent OF Moose McCormick to the Pittsburgh Pirates; the Pirates sent OF Jimmy Sebring to the Reds.	Effective
December 20, 1904	Sold catcher Jack Warner to the St. Louis Cardinals.	Effective
January 7, 1905	Purchased INF/OF Sammy Strang from the Brooklyn Superbas.	Effective
August 1905	Acquired pitcher Claude Elliot [as player to be named] from the Louisville Colonels (American Association) in exchange for pitcher Claude Ferguson.	Effective
April 6, 1905	Signed INF/C Boileryard Clarke as a free agent. [Player sold to the American Association in February 1906.]	Ineffective
July 12, 1906	Purchased OF Cy Seymour from the Cincinnati Reds for $12,000.	Effective
July 13, 1906	Acquired OF Spike Shannon from the St. Louis Cardinals in exchange for OF Sam Mertes and INF Doc Marshall.	Effective
December 14, 1906	Purchased INF Tommy Corcoran from the Cincinnati Reds. [Released outright the following season.]	Ineffective
January 11, 1907	Sold INF Billy Gilbert to the Newark Indians (Eastern League).	Effective
July 20, 1907	Purchased Larry Doyle from the Springfield Babes (Central League) for $4,500.	Good
August 9, 1907	Purchased OF Josh Devore from the Meridian White Ribbons (Cotton States League) for $750.	Effective
September 1, 1907	Drafted pitcher Doc Crandall from Cedar Rapids Rabbits (Three-I League) in the major league draft.	Effective
September 1, 1907	Drafted infielder Buck Herzog from the Reading Pretzels (Tri-State League).	Effective
September 21, 1907	Signed 1B Fred Merkle from the Tecumseh Indians (Southern Michigan League).	Effective
December 13, 1907	Obtained Fred Tenney, Al Bridwell and Tom Needham from the Boston Doves in exchange for Dan McGann, Frank Bowerman, Bill Dahlen, George Brown and Cecil Ferguson.	Effective
July 1, 1908	Purchased Rube Marquard from the Indianapolis Indians (American Association).	Good

Date	Players	Rating
July 1, 1908	Purchased Chief Meyers from the St. Paul Saints (American Association) for $6,000.	Good
July 1, 1908	Purchased Art Fletcher from the Dallas Giants (Texas League) for $1,500.	Good
July 8, 1908	Claimed pitcher Bob Spade from the Cincinnati Reds on waivers.	Ineffective
July 10, 1908	Acquired pitcher Jack Weimer and INF Dave Brain from the Cincinnati Reds in exchange for pitcher Bob Spade and $5,000.	Ineffective
July 22, 1908	Lost Spike Shannon on waivers to the Pittsburgh Pirates.	Effective
August 3, 1908	Purchased INF/OF Shad Barry from the St. Louis cardinals.	Ineffective
December 12, 1908	Acquired pitcher Bugs Raymond, catcher Admiral Schlei and OF Red Murray from the St. Louis Cardinals in exchange for catcher Roger Bresnahan.	Effective
January 30, 1909	Sold catcher Tom Needham to the St. Paul Saints (American Association) for $1,000.	Effective
February 9, 1909	Signed OF Bill O'Hara as a free agent.	Ineffective
February 2, 1909	Sold pitcher Dummy Taylor to the Buffalo Bisons (Eastern League).	Effective
February 27, 1909	Sold pitcher Joe McGinnity to the Newark Indians (Eastern League).	Poor
August 3, 1909	Purchased pitcher Louis Drucke from the Dallas Giants (Texas League).	Effective
April 4, 1910	Traded INF Buck Herzog and OF Bill Collins to the Boston Doves in exchange for OF Beals Becker.	Ineffective
May 7, 1910	Purchased OF Wee Willie Keeler as a free agent.	Inconsequential
July 23, 1910	Purchased INF Hank Gowdy from the Dallas Giants (Texas League).	Ineffective
August 23, 1910	Purchased pitcher Jeff Tesreau from Shreveport for $3,000.	Good
August 24, 1910	Released OF Cy Seymour.	Effective
July 8, 1911	Purchased Heinie Groh from Decatur Commodores (Three-I League) for $3,500.	Effective
July 22, 1911	Acquired INF Buck Herzog from the Boston Rustlers in exchange for INFs Al Bridwell and Hank Gowdy.	Effective
September 12, 1911	Purchased OF George Burns from the Utica Utes (New York State League) for $4,000.	Good
April 10, 1912	Sold INF Art Devlin to the Boston Braves.	Effective
June 1912	Purchased OF Dave Robertson from the Norfolk Tars (Virginia League).	Effective
July 31, 1912	Purchased pitcher Al Demaree from Mobile Sea Gulls (Southern Association) for $7,000.	Effective
August 19, 1912	Purchased pitcher Ferdie Schupp from the Decatur Commodores (Three-I League) for $4,000.	Effective
February 1, 1913	Signed Jim Thorpe as an amateur free agent for $18,000 over three years.	Ineffective
May 22, 1913	Acquired pitcher Art Fromme from Cincinnati Reds in exchange for pitcher Red Ames, INF Heinie Groh, OF Josh Devore and $20,000.	Poor

Date	Players	Rating
June 3, 1913	Purchased 3B Eddie Grant from the Cincinnati Reds for $3,500.	Ineffective
June 18, 1913	Purchased pitcher Rube Schauer from the Superior Red Sox (Northern League) for $10,000.	Ineffective
August 6, 1913	Acquired catcher Larry McLean from the St. Louis Cardinals in exchange for pitcher Doc Crandall.	Effective
September 25, 1913	Acquired 3B Milt Stock from the Boston Braves in exchange for minor league player Arthur Duchesnil.	Effective
August 29, 1914	Released pitcher Hooks Wiltse.	Effective
January 4, 1915	Traded pitcher Al Demaree, INF Milt Stock and catcher Bert Adams to the Philadelphia Phillies in exchange for INF Hans Lobert.	Poor
March 25, 1915	Acquired pitcher Pol Perritt from the St. Louis Cardinals for outfielder Bob Brescher and cash.	Effective
July 28, 1915	Purchased 1B High Pockets Kelly from the Victoria Bees (Northwestern League) for $1,200.	Good
August 18, 1915	Released OF Fred Snodgrass.	Effective
August 19, 1915	Purchased Rube Benton from the Cincinnati Reds for $3,000.	Effective
August 26, 1915	Signed amateur pitcher Waite Hoyt.	Incomplete

(See transaction January 2, 1919.)

Date	Players	Rating
August 31, 1915	Released pitcher Rube Marquard on waivers to the Brooklyn Superbas for $2,500.	Effective
December 23, 1915	Purchased OF Benny Kauff from the Newark Peppers (Federal League) for $35,000.	Effective
December 23, 1915	Purchased OF Edd Roush from the Newark Peppers (Federal League).	Incomplete

(See transaction July 20, 1916.)

Date	Players	Rating
January 17, 1916	Purchased catcher Bill Rariden from the Newark Peppers (Federal League).	Effective
January 17, 1916	Purchased pitcher Fred Anderson from the Buffalo Blues (Federal League).	Effective
February 10, 1916	Sold catcher Chief Meyers on waivers to the Brooklyn Superbas.	Effective
July 16, 1916	Purchased pitcher Slim Sallee from the St. Louis Cardinals for $10,000.	Effective
July 20, 1916	Acquired INF Buck Herzog and OF Red Killefer in exchange for pitcher Christy Mathewson, INF Bill McKechnie and OF Edd Roush.	Bad
August 14, 1916	Purchased OF Ross Youngs from the Sherman Lions (Western Association) for $2,000.	Outstanding
August 28, 1916	Acquired 3B Heinie Zimmerman from the Chicago Cubs in exchange for INFs Larry Doyle, Herb Hunter and OF Merwin Jacobson.	Effective
September 15, 1916	Selected pitcher Red Causey from the Waco Navigators (Texas League) in the major league draft.	Effective
April 23, 1917	OF Jim Thorpe sold to the Cincinnati Reds on waivers for $2,500.	Ineffective

(Thorpe returned to the Giants by Cincinnati on August 23.)

Date	Players	Rating
January 8, 1918	Acquired INF Larry Doyle and pitcher Jesse Barnes in exchange for INF Buck Herzog.	Good
June 20, 1918	Signed pitcher Rosy Ryan as a non-drafted free agent.	Effective
July 22, 1918	Purchased pitcher Fred Toney from the Cincinnati Reds.	Effective
January 2, 1919	Acquired catcher Earl Smith from the Rochester Hustlers (International League) in exchange for pitchers Waite Hoyt and Joe Ogden, OF Joe Wilhoit, INF José Rodríguez and cash.	Poor
March 11, 1919	Released pitcher Slim Sallee on waivers to the Cincinnati Reds.	Ineffective
April 22, 1919	Purchased pitcher Jean Dubuc from the Salt Lake City Bees (Pacific Coast League).	Effective
May 19, 1919	Purchased catcher Mike González from the St. Louis Cardinals.	Inconsequential
June 14, 1919	Signed INF Frankie Frisch as a non-drafted free agent.	Outstanding
July 16, 1919	Acquired catcher Frank Snyder from the St. Louis Cardinals for pitcher Ferdie Schupp.	Effective
July 25, 1919	Acquired pitcher Phil Douglas from the Chicago Cubs in exchange for OF Dave Robertson.	Effective
August 1, 1919	Acquired pitcher Art Nehf from the Boston Braves in exchange for pitchers Joe Oeschger, Red Causey and Johnny Jones, and catcher Mickey O'Neil and $55,000.	Good
November 20, 1919	Purchased pitcher Virgil Barnes from the Sioux City Indians (Western League) for $30,000.	Effective
June 7, 1920	Acquired shortstop Dave Bancroft from the Philadelphia Phillies in exchange for pitcher Bill Hubbell and $100,000.	Good
July 2, 1920	Acquired OF Vern Spencer from the Toronto Maple Leafs in exchange for OF Benny Kauff and cash.	Ineffective
June 1921	Sold pitcher Pol Perritt to the Detroit Tigers.	Effective
July 1, 1921	Acquired INF Johnny Rawlings and OF Casey Stengel from the Philadelphia Phillies in exchange for INF Goldie Rapp, and OFs Lance Richbourg and Lee King.	Effective
July 6, 1921	Purchased OF Bill Cunningham from the Seattle Rainiers (Pacific Coast League).	Ineffective
July 25, 1921	Acquired OF Irish Meusel from the Philadelphia Phillies in exchange for OF Curt Walker, catcher Butch Henline and $30,000.	Effective
September 12, 1921	Purchased outfielder Ralph Shinners from Indianapolis Indians (American Association) for $35,000.	Ineffective
December 6, 1921	Acquired INF Heinie Groh from the Cincinnati Reds in exchange for catcher Mike González, OF George Burns and $150,000.	Ineffective
December 7, 1921	Purchased outfielder Jimmy O'Connell from the San Francisco Seals (Pacific Coast League) for $75,000.	Poor
May 10, 1922	Signed INF Bill Terry as a free agent.	Outstanding
May 31, 1922	Signed INF Freddie Lindstrom as a free agent.	Good
June 30, 1922	Purchased Travis Jackson from the Little Rock Travelers (Southern Association) for $20,000.	Good

Date	Players	Rating
Date	*Players*	*Rating*
July 30, 1922	Acquired pitcher Hugh McQuillan from the Boston Braves in exchange for pitchers Larry Benton, Fred Toney, Harry Hulihan, and $100,000.	Ineffective
August 1, 1922	Purchased pitcher Jack Scott as a free agent.	Effective
September 10, 1922	Purchased pitcher Rube Walberg from the Portland Beavers (Pacific Coast League) for $15,000.	Incomplete
	(see transaction May 15, 1923)	
October 30, 1922	Purchased pitcher Jack Bentley from the Baltimore Orioles (International League) for $72,500.	Ineffective
May 15, 1923	Returned pitcher Rube Walberg to the Portland Beavers (Pacific Coast League).	Poor
June 7, 1923	Acquired catcher Hank Gowdy and pitcher Mule Watson from the Boston Braves in exchange for catcher Earl Smith and pitcher Jesse Barnes.	Ineffective
September 6, 1923	Purchased Hack Wilson from the Portsmouth Truckers (Virginia League) for $5,000.	Incomplete
	(see transaction August 8, 1925)	
November 12, 1923	Acquired INF Billy Southworth and pitcher Joe Oeschger from the Boston Braves in exchange for OFs Casey Stengel, Bill Cunningham and INF Dave Bancroft.	Ineffective
January 5, 1924	Purchased pitcher Wayland Dean from the Louisville Colonels (American Association) for $50,000.	Ineffective
April 17, 1925	Acquired pitcher Tim McNamara from the Boston Braves in exchange for pitcher Rosy Ryan.	Effective
August 8, 1925	Acquired OF Earl Webb from the Toledo Mud Hens in exchange for outfielders Hack Wilson and Pip Koehler.	Incomplete
	(see transaction September 25, 1925)	
August 8, 1925	Acquired pitcher Freddie Fitzsimmons from the Indianapolis Indians (American Association) for outfielder Frank Walker and an undisclosed amount of cash.	Good
September 3, 1925	Acquired OF Ty Tyson from the Louisville Colonels (American Association) for a player to be named later.	Incomplete
	(See next transaction.)	
September 25, 1925	Sent OF Earl Webb, as player to be named, to the Louisville Colonels, completing previous acquisition of outfielder Ty Tyson. (Previously lost Hack Wilson in obtaining Webb, then lost Webb.)	Bad
December 30, 1925	Acquired pitcher Jimmy Ring from the Philadelphia Phillies in exchange for pitchers Wayland Dean and Jack Bentley.	Effective
January 1926	Signed OF Mel Ott as an amateur free agent.	Outstanding
June 14, 1926	Acquired OF Heine Mueller from the St. Louis Cardinals in exchange for OF Billy Southworth.	Ineffective
September 16, 1926	Accepted self-purchased release of OF Irish Meusel.	Effective
December 20, 1926	Acquired INF Rogers Hornsby from the St. Louis Cardinals in exchange for INF Frankie Frisch and pitcher Jimmy Ring.	Outstanding

Date	Players	Rating
January 9, 1927	Acquired pitcher Burleigh Grimes from the Brooklyn Robins and OF George Harper from the Philadelphia Phillies in a three-team trade. The Giants sent INF Fresco Thompson and pitcher Jack Scott to the Phillies; Brooklyn received catcher Butch Henline from the Phillies.	Effective
June 12, 1927	Acquired catcher Zach Taylor, pitcher Larry Benton and INF Herb Thomas from the Boston Braves in exchange for pitchers Hugh McQuillan, Kent Greenfield and INF Doc Farrell.	Effective
July 16, 1927	Purchased pitcher Bill Walker from the Denver Bears (Western League) for $25,000.	Good
October 4, 1927	Selected pitcher Lefty O'Doul from the San Francisco Seals (Pacific Coast League) in the major league draft.	Effective
February 11, 1928	Acquired pitcher Vic Aldridge from the Pittsburgh Pirates in exchange for pitcher Burleigh Grimes.	Bad
May 10, 1928	Acquired catcher Bob O'Farrell from the St. Louis Cardinals in exchange for OF George Harper.	Effective
June 15, 1928	Acquired pitcher Joe Genewich from the Boston Braves in exchange for pitchers Ben Cantwell, Virgil Barnes, Bill Clarkson and OF Al Spohrer.	Ineffective
July 12, 1928	Purchased pitcher Carl Hubbell from the Beaumont Exporters (Texas League) for $25,000.	Outstanding
October 29, 1928	Acquired OF Freddy Leach from the Philadelphia Phillies in exchange for OF Lefty O'Doul and unspecified cash.	Bad
August 1929	Purchased pitcher Ray Lucas from the Toledo Mud Hens (American Association).	Inconsequential
September 2, 1929	Purchased INF Sam Leslie from the Memphis Chicks (Southern Association).	Effective
September 13, 1929	Purchased pitcher Roy Parmelee from the Toledo Mud Hens (American Association).	Effective
April 10, 1930	Acquired OF Wally Roettger from the St. Louis Cardinals in exchange for OF Showboat Fisher and INF Doc Farrell.	Effective
May 15, 1930	Acquired pitcher Clarence Mitchell from the St. Louis Cardinals in exchange for pitcher Ralph Judd.	Effective
May 21, 1930	Acquired INF Hughie Critz from the Cincinnati Reds in exchange for pitcher Larry Benton.	Effective
May 27, 1930	Acquired pitcher Pete Donohoe and OF Ethan Allen from the Cincinnati Reds, in exchange for INF Pat Crawford.	Effective
August 20, 1930	Purchased pitcher Jim Mooney from the Charlotte Hornets (South Atlantic League).	Ineffective
October 9, 1930	Purchased INF Johnny Vergez from the Oakland Oaks (Pacific Coast League).	Effective
October, 29, 1930	Sold OF Wally Roettger to the Cincinnati Reds.	Inconsequential
January 1, 1931	Signed pitcher Hal Schumacher as a non-drafted free agent.	Good
August 11, 1931	Acquired OF Len Koenecke from the Indianapolis Indians (American Association) for pitchers Johnny Cooney, Joe Heving, Jack Berly and OF Harry Rosenberg.	Inconsequential

Date	Players	Rating
August 21, 1931	Purchased pitcher Sam Gibson from the San Francisco Missions (Pacific Coast League).	Ineffective
September 30, 1931	Selected pitcher Hi Bell from the Rochester Red Wings (International League) in the major league draft.	Effective
February 10, 1932	Signed pitcher Adolfo Luque as a free agent.	Effective
March 10, 1932	Sold OF Freddy Leach to the Boston Braves for $10,000	Effective

Giants' Trades Not Initiated by McGraw

December 12, 1913	Acquired OF Bob Bescher from the Cincinnati Reds in exchange for INF Buck Herzog and catcher Grover Hartley.	Ineffective
January 10, 1928	Acquired catcher Shanty Hogan and outfielder Jimmy Welsh from the Boston Braves in exchange for INF Rogers Hornsby.	Bad

Appendix B:
Ejections and Suspensions

Ejections as a Player

Date	Where	Umpire	Reason
July 5, 1893	Exposition Park	Mike McLaughlin	Balls and strikes on the Pirates' Frank Killen.
July 26, 1893	Polo Grounds	Pop Snyder	HBP-non call.
June 22, 1895	Union Park	Bob Emslie	Called out at first base.
July 16, 1895	League Park (Cleveland)	Jim McDonald or Ed Andrews	Called out for "cutting" third base attempting to score.
May 20, 1897, League Park (Cincinnati)		Jack Sheridan	Called out at home plate.
May 21, 1897	League Park (Cincinnati)	Jack Sheridan	McGraw deliberately spiked first baseman Farmer Vaughn's heel.
June 10, 1898	Union Park	Ed Andrews	Abusive language.
June 30, 1898	Eclipse Park	Hank O'Day	Undetermined.
September 20, 1898	Union Park	Tom Brown	Undetermined.
September 29, 1898	Union Park	John Hunt	Balls and strikes.
June 2, 1900	West End Grounds	Bob Emslie	Out call at first base on Jesse Burkett.
July 19, 1900	Union Park	Adonis Terry	Safe call at first base on the Giants' Win Mercer.
September 8, 1900	Polo Grounds	John Gaffney	Called out at home plate.
September 19, 1900	West End Grounds	John Gaffney	Safe call at home plate on the Superbas' Duke Farrell.

Led the league in ejections in 1893 and 1900. Total: 14

Ejections and Suspensions as a Player-Manager

Date	Where	Umpire	Reason
June 5, 1899	Union Park	Ed Swartwood	Balls and strikes (as a batter).
July 4, 1899	Union Park	Jim McDonald	Called out at home plate.

Date	Where	Umpire	Reason
July 18, 1899	Union Park	Tom Lynch	Fighting with the Reds' Tommy Corcoran (as a player).
July 27, 1899 (2)	Union Park	Pop Snyder	Called out at third base.
August 26, 1899	Eclipse Park	John Hunt	Out call at third base on the Colonels' Billy Cunningham.
May 7, 1901	Columbia Park	Jack Haskell	Abusive language.
*May 15, 1901	Oriole Park	Joe Cantillon	Abusive language.
May 27, 1901	South Side Park	Al Mannassau	Abusive language.
**July 9, 1901	American League Park	Al Mannassau	Called out at third base.
August 15, 1901	Oriole Park	Tommy Connolly	Balls and strikes (as a batter).
April 19, 1902	Hunnington Avenue Grounds	Tommy Connolly	Abusive language.
*May 1, 1902	Oriole Park	Jack Sheridan	HBP non-call (as a batter).
May 23, 1902	Oriole Park	Silk O'Laughlin	Interference call on Joe Kelley.
*June 28, 1902	Oriole Park	Tommy Connolly	Out call on an appeal on Cy Seymour for failing to touch a base.
May 19, 1903	Polo Grounds	Bob Emslie	Non-HBP call on Billy Laudner.
June 6, 1903	West Side Grounds	Bob Emslie	Balls and strikes on Dan McGann.
**August 15, 1903	Polo Grounds	Bob Emslie	Abusive language.
August 26, 1903 (1)	South End Grounds	Augie Moran	Out call at home plate on Roger Bresnaham.
September 18, 1903	Palace of the Fans	Hank O'Day	Abusive language.
May 12, 1904	Palace of the Fans	Bob Emslie	Grabbing umpire's arm, following out call at third base on George Browne.

Retrosheet lists ejection date as May 14.

Date	Where	Umpire	Reason
June 2, 1904	Polo Grounds	Chief Zimmer	Out call on pick-off of Frank Bowerman at first base.
June 10, 1904	Polo Grounds	Chief Zimmer	Abusive language from coaching box.
July 6, 1904	Baker Bowl	Bill Carpenter	Undetermined.
August 12, 1904 (2)	Polo Grounds	Bob Emslie	Abusive language from coaching box.
*/**August 19, 1904	Polo Grounds	Jim Johnstone	Out call at second base on Mike Devlin.
August 26, 1904	West Side Grounds	Bob Emslie	Disputed fair call on two-base hit by the Cubs' Doc Casey.

Date	Where	Umpire	Reason
August 29, 1904	Robison Field	Chief Zimmer	Undetermined.
April 27, 1905	Washington Park	Jim Johnstone	Pick-off call at second base on Mike Donlin.
May 15, 1905	Polo Grounds	Bill Klem	Non-balk call on the Cubs' Three Finger Brown.
*May 19, 1905	Polo Grounds	Jim Johnstone	Abusive language.
May 20, 1905	Polo Grounds	Jim Johnstone	Invectives hurled at each other by McGraw and Pittsburgh manager Frank Clarke.
July 3, 1905	Baker Bowl	Bob Emslie	Shouting from bench.

Retrosheet lists McGraw, Roger Bresnahan and Babe Dahlen ejected on July 12 by unspecified umpires and causes. This appears to be a duplication from July 3, when the same three men were ejected by Bob Emslie.

Date	Where	Umpire	Reason
August 21, 1905	Polo Grounds	Jim Johnstone	Excessive arguing.
August 22, 1905	Polo Grounds	Jim Johnstone	Out call at first base on Frank Bowerman.
August 24, 1905 (2)	Polo Grounds	George Bausewine	Umpire Baiting.
August 29, 1905	Polo Grounds	Jim Johnstone	Out call at home plate on Mike Donlin.
September 1, 1905	Polo Grounds	Jim Johnstone	Strike out called on Sammy Strang.
April 26, 1906	Polo Grounds	John Conway	Berating umpire.
*May 1, 1906	South End Grounds	John Conway	Bench jockeying.
May 12, 1906	Palace of the Fans	Hank O'Day	Out call at second base on an undetermined runner.

Retrosheet lists umpire as Jim Johnstone. Changed to Hank O'Day, per the Cincinnati Enquirer *of May 13, 1906.*

Date	Where	Umpire	Reason
June 21, 1906	Polo Grounds	Bob Emslie	Balls and strikes.
June 30, 1906	Polo Grounds	John Conway	Bench jockeying.
July 10, 1906	Palace of the Fans	Bill Carpenter	Balls and strikes.
July 26, 1906	Polo Grounds	Jim Johnstone	Safe call at first base on the Reds' Frank Jude.
*August 6, 1906	Polo Grounds	Jim Johnstone	Out call at home plate on Art Devlin.

Retrosheet lists a McGraw ejection on August 16, 1906. McGraw was suspended on this date of the schedule, the culmination of his verbal assault of August 6 on Jim Johnstone and the following day's action leading to a forfeit.

Date	Where	Umpire	Reason
September 4, 1906	Polo Grounds	Bill Carpenter	Abusive behavior from coaching box.
May 11, 1907	Polo Grounds	Hank O'Day	Bench jockeying.
*August 5, 1907	West Side Grounds	Bill Klem	Safe call at home plate on the Cubs' Jimmy Slagle.

Date	Where	Umpire	Reason
September 4, 1907 (2)	Polo Grounds	Hank O'Day	Injury time out called by umpire, stopping run from scoring.
September 23, 1907	Exposition Park	Bill Klem	Disputing fair call on the Pirates' Ed Abbitacchio's hit.

Led the league in ejections in 1899, 1904, 1905, 1906, 1907.
*Included suspension.
**Retrosheet does not reflect ejection from July 9, 1901. Sources: *Multiple.*
**Retrosheet does not reflect ejection from August 15, 1903. Sources: *Multiple.*
**Retrosheet does not reflect ejection from August 19, 1904. Source: *Washington Times,* August 25.
Ejections and Suspensions as a Player-Manager: Ejections: 50 Suspensions: 8
Subtotals as a Player and Manager: Ejections: 64 Suspensions: 8

McGraw's Ejections and Suspensions as a Manager

> *Retrosheet lists McGraw and Mike Donlin ejected on May 5, 1908, for unspecified reasons by unspecified umpires.* The New York Times *and* New York Tribune *do not mention the OR stated expulsions for this date. The Giants played the game on May 5 with nine players in the lineup, including Donlin. No substitutions were recorded for any of the Giants' players.*

Date	Where	Umpire	Reason
May 25, 1908	West Side Grounds	Bob Emslie	Foul strike called on Roger Bresnahan.
*/**June 13, 1908	Polo Grounds	Jim Johnstone	Strike three called on Spike Shannon.
July 2, 1908	Polo Grounds	Cy Rigler	Undetermined.
August 11, 1908	Polo Grounds	Hank O'Day	Excessive arguing
August 25, 1908	Exposition Park	Hank O'Day	Called strike three on Roger Bresnahan.
September 3, 1908	South End Grounds	Bill Klem	Out call at first base on Larry Doyle.
September 16, 1908	Polo Grounds	Hank O'Day	Out call at first base on Mike Donlin.
September 21, 1908	Polo Grounds	Bill Klem	Safe call at first base Pirates' Chief Wilson.
June 5, 1909	Robison Field	Harry Truby	Out call at first base on Larry Doyle.
July 16, 1909	Polo Grounds	Jim Johnstone	Fair ball call on high chopper hit off home plate hit by Al Bridwell.
September 3, 1909	Polo Grounds	Bob Emslie	Out call on swipe tag on Cy Seymour at third base.
April 25, 1910	Polo Grounds	Bill Klem	Balk called on undetermined pitcher.
May 4, 1910	Washington Park	Cy Rigler	Safe call at third base on the Superbas' Zach Wheat.
May 10, 1910	West Side Grounds	Augie Moran	Safe call at first base on the Cubs' Ginger Beaumont.

Date	Where	Umpire	Reason
July 17, 1910	Palace of the Fans	Jim Johnstone	Balls and strikes
July 28, 1910	Polo Grounds	Mal Eason	Out call at second base on Beals Becker.
August 15, 1910 (1)	Polo Grounds	Cy Rigler	Foul call on liner along third base hit by Fred Merkle.

McGraw was suspended, August 18 through 24, for actions occurring on August 16 and 17, deemed as umpire baiting by league president Thomas J. Lynch. He was not ejected in either game.

Date	Where	Umpire	Reason
August 26, 1910	West Side Grounds	Cy Rigler	Non-obstruction call on Cubs' third base coach Harry Steinfeldt.
September 3, 1910	Baker Bowl	Bill Brennan	Undetermined call at first base.
September 8, 1910	Polo Grounds	Bill Klem	Called third strike on Larry Doyle.
September 16, 1910	Polo Grounds	Hank O'Day	Called third strike on Larry Doyle.
May 6, 1911	South End Grounds	Bill Klem	Called strike on Larry Doyle.
May 12, 1911	Hilltop Park	Hank O'Day	Called strike on Larry Doyle.
May 15, 1911	Hilltop Park	Cy Rigler	Ground rule dispute on ball hit by Red Murray.
*May 16, 1911	Hilltop Park	Bill Finneran	Balls and strikes.
July 13, 1911	Polo Grounds	Bill Finneran	Out call at third base on Fred Merkle.
*July 25, 1911	Palace of the Fans	Jim Johnstone	Safe call at home on the Reds' Mike Mitchell.

Retrosheet lists ejection date as July 26.

Date	Where	Umpire	Reason
August 21, 1911	Polo Grounds	Bill Klem	Called third strike on Art Devlin.
April 13, 1912	Washington Park	Garnet Bush	Out call at third base on Tillie Shafer.
*April 19, 1912	Polo Grounds	Bill Finneran	Out call at second base on Red Murray.
May 3, 1912	Polo Grounds	Bill Klem	Strike call on Larry Doyle.
April 30, 1913	Ebbets Field	Cy Rigler	Called third strike on Art Fletcher.
*May 14, 1913	Polo Grounds	Bill Klem	Out call at third base on Art Wilson.

McGraw was suspended, July 4–8, 1913, for his part in a fight with the Phillies' Addison Brennan on June 30. Fight occurred after the game.

Date	Where	Umpire	Reason
September 6, 1913	Polo Grounds	Mal Eason	Non-HBP call on Fred Snodgrass.

Date	Where	Umpire	Reason
June 18, 1914	Polo Grounds	Bob Emslie	Out call at third base on George Burns.
July 18, 1914 (1)	Forbes Field	Lord Byron	Non-foul ball call on bunt by the Pirates' Max Carey.
**July 18, 1914 (2)	Forbes Field	Lord Byron	Punitive expulsion from conduct in first game.
July 27, 1914	Polo Grounds	Mal Eason	Out call at home plate on Fred Merkle.
July 30, 1914	Polo Grounds	Steamboat Johnson	Bench Jockeying.
July 31, 1914	Polo Grounds	Steamboat Johnson	Out call at second base on Fred Snodgrass.
*August 3, 1914 (2)	Polo Grounds	Lord Byron	Bench Jockeying.
September 7, 1914 (1)	Fenway Park	Bob Emslie	Out call on Giants' baserunner.
**September 7, 1914 (2)	Fenway Park	Bob Emslie	Punitive expulsion from conduct in first game.
September 26, 1914 (2)	Polo Grounds	Cy Rigler	Non-foul tip call on pitch thrown by Mathewson.
September 28, 1914 (1)	Polo Grounds	Bill Hart	Called third strike on Fred Snodgrass.
**September 28, 1914 (2)	Polo Grounds	Bill Hart	Punitive expulsion from conduct in first game.
April 20, 1915	Polo Grounds	Lord Byron	Bench Jockeying.
May 25, 1915	Polo Grounds	Cy Rigler	Out call at home plate on George Burns.
May 28, 1915	Polo Grounds	Mal Eason	Non-balk call on the Cardinals' Hub Perdue.
June 26, 1915	Polo Grounds	Lord Byron	Called third strike on Art Fletcher.
July 2, 1915	Ebbets Field	Mal Eason	Safe call at third base on the Robins' George Cutshaw.
July 12, 1915	Polo Grounds	Lord Byron	Balls and strikes.
July 15, 1915	Polo Grounds	Mal Eason	Out call at third base on Art Fletcher.
July 17, 1915	Polo Grounds	Ernie Quigley	Non-foul bunt call on the Cardinals' Miller Huggins.
July 23, 1915 (2)	Polo Grounds	Bill Klem	Balls and strikes.
September 17, 1915 (2)	Forbes Field	Cy Rigler	Balls and strikes on Eddie Grant.

Date	Where	Umpire	Reason
April 25, 1916	Braves Field	Bill Klem	Umpire baiting.
April 27, 1916	Braves Field	Bill Klem	Umpire baiting.
June 2, 1916	Polo Grounds	Mal Eason	Out call at first base on Fred Merkle.
July 18, 1916	Robison Field	Bob Emslie	Out call at third base on Benny Kauff.
August 11, 1916	Polo Grounds	Ernie Quigley	Out call at first base on Larry Doyle.
September 2, 1916 (1)	Braves Field	Lord Byron	Called third strike on Hans Lobert.
June 5, 1917	Redland Field	Lord Byron	Non-interference call on Reds batter Edd Roush during a steal of second base.
*June 8, 1917	Redland Field	Ernie Quigley	Non-call for leaving early from third base on a tag play on the Reds' Heinie Groh.

Retrosheet lists umpire as Lord Byron. Changed to Ernie Quigley per the Cincinnati Enquirer, *June 9, 1917.*

**June 8, 1918 (2)	Polo Grounds	Lord Byron	Non-out call on catch attempt by Ross Youngs.
June 19, 1919	Robison Field	Cy Rigler	Umpire baiting.
*May 18, 1920	Cubs Park	Charlie Moran	Umpire baiting.
*July 26, 1921	Forbes Field	Bill Klem	Bench Jockeying.
August 8, 1922	Polo Grounds	Cy Rigler	Out call at first base on a Giants runner.
July 21, 1927	Polo Grounds	Frank Wilson	Balls and strikes on the Cardinals' Jim Bottomley.
July 6, 1929	Polo Grounds	George Magerkurth	Called third strike on Travis Jackson.
June 22, 1931	Polo Grounds	Dolly Stark	Balls and Strikes on the Cubs' Kiki Cuyler.
*July 18, 1931	Sportsman's Park	Bob Clarke	Out call at first base on Chick Fullis.

Led the league in ejections in 1908, 1910, 1914, 1915, 1916, 1931.

*Included suspension.
**Retrosheet does not reflect ejection from June 13, 1908. Sources: *New York Times* and *New York Tribune,* June 14, 1908.
**Retrosheet does not reflect ejection from July 18, 1914, second game of doubleheader. Sources: *The New York Times* and *Pittsburgh Daily Post,* July 19, 1914.
**Retrosheet does not reflect ejection from September 7, 1914, second game of doubleheader. Sources: *New York Tribune* and *Dunkirk Evening Observer*, September 8, 1914.

**Retrosheet does not reflect ejection from September 28, 1914, second game of doubleheader. Source: *The New York Times*, September 29, 1914.

**Retrosheet does not reflect ejection from June 8, 1918. Sources: *New York Times* and the *Brooklyn Daily Eagle*, June 9, 1918.

Ejections and Suspensions Subtotal as a Manager: 73 Suspensions: 12

Grand Total: Ejections: 137 Suspensions: 20

Appendix C:
Career Managerial Record

Year		Team	Record	Percentage	Accepted	Record Percentage
1899		Balt. Orioles	80–55	.592	86–62	.581
1901		Balt. Orioles	57–39	.593	68–65	.511
1902		Balt. Orioles	14–13	.518	26–31 [29–34*]	.456
1902		N.Y. Giants	15–20	.429	25–38	.397
1903		N.Y. Giants	81–54	.600	84–55	.604
1904	+	N.Y. Giants	94–41	.696	106–47	.693
1905	+ >	N.Y. Giants	97–46	.678	105–48	.686
1906		N.Y. Giants	84–48	.636	96–56	.632
1907		N.Y. Giants	80–68	.540	82–70	.539
1908		N.Y. Giants	95–55	.633	98–56	.636
1909		N.Y. Giants	87–55	.612	92–61	.601
1910		N.Y. Giants	88–60	.594	91–63	.591
1911	+ <	N.Y. Giants	93–48	.659	99–54	.647
1912	+ <	N.Y. Giants	100–47	.680	103–48	.682
1913	+ <	N.Y. Giants	94–49	.657	101–51	.664
1914		N.Y. Giants	77–65	.546	84–70	.545
1915		N.Y. Giants	68–81	.456	69–83	.454
1916		N.Y. Giants	85–64	.570	86–66	.566
1917	+ <	N.Y. Giants	89–50	.640	98–56	.636
1918		N.Y. Giants	70–53	.569	71–53	.573
1919		N.Y. Giants	80–47	.629	87–53	.621
1920		N.Y. Giants	71–56	.559	86–68	.558
1921	+ >	N.Y. Giants	91–59	.606	94–59	.614
1922	+ >	N.Y. Giants	84–56	.600	93–61	.604
1923	+ <	N.Y. Giants	94–55	.630	95–58	.621
1924	+ <	N.Y. Giants	58–43	.574	61–48	.560
1925		N.Y. Giants	51–40	.508	65–55	.542
1926		N.Y. Giants	69–68	.503	74–77	.490
1927		N.Y. Giants	65–45	.590	70–52	.574
1928		N.Y. Giants	69–42	.621	93–61	.604
1929		N.Y. Giants	56–47	.548	84–67	.556
1930		N.Y. Giants	55–44	.555	87–67	.565
1931		N.Y. Giants	71–49	.591	87–65	.572
1932		N.Y. Giants	8–12	.400	17–23	.425
Totals		33 Seasons	2,470–1,674	.596	2,763–1,947	.587
					[2,766–1,950*]	.587

*Discrepancy with accepted record
Does not include tie games
+Won pennant, no World Series played
+ >Won pennant, won World Series
+ < Won pennant, lost World Series

All-Time Winningest Managers

In the table below, McGraw's revised record and winning percentage are used to place him anew among the all-time leaders in wins. Only his total differs from the accepted record.

		Record	Percentage	Years Managed
1.	Connie Mack	3,731–3,948	.486	53 (1894–1950)
2.	Tony LaRussa	2,728–2,365	.536	33 (1979–2011)
3.	Bobby Cox	2,504–2,001	.556	29 (1978–1985; 1990–2010)
4.	**John McGraw**	**2,470–1,674**	**.596**	**33 (1899; 1901–32)**
5.	Joe Torre	2,326–1,997	.538	29 (1977–1984; 1990–2010)
6.	Sparky Anderson	2,194–1,834	.545	26 (1970–1995)
7.	Bucky Harris	2,158–2,219	.493	29 (1924–1943; 1947–48; 1950–56)
8.	Joe McCarthy	2,125–1,333	.615	24 (1926–1946; 1948–1950)
9.	Walter Alston	2,040–1,613	.558	23 (1954–1976)
10.	Leo Durocher	2,008–1,709	.540	24 (1939–1946; 1948–55; 1966–73)

Chapter Notes

Preface

1. Chris Jaffe, *Evaluating Baseball's Managers: A History and Analysis of Performance in the Major Leagues, 1876–2008* (Jefferson, NC: McFarland, 2010), 105.

2. Lawrence Ritter, *The Glory of Their Times: The Story of the Early Days of Baseball Told by the Men Who Played It* (New York: Macmillan, 1966), 131.

Introduction

1. Bill James, *The Bill James Guide to Baseball Managers from 1870 to Today*. New York: Scribner, 1997, 53.

2. News Notes and Highlights, *Sporting Life*, April 7, 1917, 4.

3. James, *Bill James Guide to Baseball Managers*, 64.

Chapter One

1. "McGraw, Veteran Giant Pilot Is 59 Today; Old 'Firebrand' Started Career 42 Years Ago," *Sandusky (OH) Register*, April 7, 1932.

2. *Ibid.*

3. Mrs. John J. McGraw [Mary Blanche Sindall McGraw], *The Real McGraw*, ed. by Arthur Mann (New York: David McKay, 1953), 47.

4. Jack Veiock. "Yanks Planning to Take Honors Before Ending." *Washington Times*, October 14, 1921

5. Charles C. Alexander, *John McGraw* (Lincoln: University of Nebraska Press, 1988), 34.

6. "The Baltimores Shutout," *Pittsburgh Daily Post*, July 6, 1893.

7. "Three Straight Victories. Giants Are in a Winning Mood Nowadays," *New York Times*, July 27, 1893.

8. Terry Gottschall, "May 15, 1894: It Was a Hot Game, Sure Enough!" SABR Baseball Games Project, http://sabr.org/gamesproject.

9. "Flag Flyers Lose," *Atlanta Constitution*, October 7, 1894.

10. "First for New York," *Chicago Inter Ocean*, October 5, 1894.

11. "Mr. Byrne Is Kingpin," *Brooklyn Daily Eagle*, October 5, 1894. The Temple Cup trustees were Tem-ple, NL president Nick Young, and Brooklyn club pres-ident Charles H. Byrne. Alexander wrote that capitu-lation came from the Giants' players: "Each [Orioles player] found a Giant who was willing to split an in-dividual share 50–50. McGraw, for example, paired with George Davis, the Giants shortstop, while Kelley paired with Amos Rusie and Keeler arranged his split with first baseman Jack Doyle." Alexander, *John McGraw*, 43.

12. "Baseball for the Cup," *New York Evening World*. October 5, 1894. It appears that these uniforms first debuted for the Temple Cup games.

13. "Baseball Equipment History," Epic Sports (website), n.d., https://epicsports.com/baseball-equip ment-history.html.

14. "McGraw Is 59 Years Old Today; 30 Years as Giant," *Burlington (IA) Hawkeye*, April 7, 1932.

15. "Spiders Win. First Blood for Cleveland in Tem-ple Cup Series," *Boston Post*, October 3, 1895.

16. "Baltimore Shut the Spiders Out in the First Game in the East," *New York Times*, October 8, 1895.

17. "Caylor's Ball Gossip," *Roanoke (VA) Times*, April 24, 1896.

18. "Johnny M'graw Married," *Lake County (IN) Times*, February 4, 1897.

19. "Another Plucky Victory for the Reds," *Cincin-nati Enquirer*, May 21, 1897.

20. "Mugsy McGraw Again Put Out of Game," *Cincinnati Enquirer*, May 22, 1897.

21. "Temple Cup Stays with Orioles," *Atlanta Con-stitution*, October 12, 1897.

22. "Rain Robs Senators of Chance for Victory," *Washington Times*, May 6, 1903.

23. "Opening Day in Harlem," *New York Sun*, Oc-tober 22, 1899.

24. "Griffith Sent to the Bench," *Chicago Tribune*, June 6, 1899.

25. "Cincinnati Wins Hotly Contested Game from Baltimore," *Sayre (PA) Morning Times*, July 19, 1899.

26. "Baltimore 8–9, Cleveland 5–4," *Kansas City (MO) Journal*, July 28, 1899.

27. "Louisville 5, Baltimore 1," *Chicago Inter Ocean*, August 27, 1899.

28. "McGraw's Wife Buried," *Louisville (KY) Cou-rier-Journal*, September 4, 1899.

29. "Won't Go to St. Louis," *Wilkes-Barre News*," March 23, 1900.

30. "Brooklyns Win in St. Louis," *Brooklyn Daily Eagle*, May 14, 1900.

31. "Baseball Gossip," *Cincinnati Enquirer*, August 16, 1900.

32. "St. Louis 6, New York 5," *Chicago Inter Ocean*, September 9, 1900.

Chapter Two

1. "Big Baseball Deal Completed National and American Leagues Are Acting in Concert," *Louisville (KY) Courier-Journal*, November 14, 1900.

2. *Ibid.* Alexander stated that McGraw's contract with St. Louis did not include the reserve clause, facilitating his skipping out on the team. This may also be how Wilbert Robinson and Bill Keister, who had accompanied McGraw to St. Louis, were able to join McGraw in Baltimore in 1901. McGraw's reference to the money owed him, also according to McGraw's biographer, was for docked pay due to McGraw's late joining of the team.

3. Michael Wells, "Joe McGinnity," SABR Baseball Biography Project," www.sabr.org/bioproj/person/f75cf09d.

4. "Charley Zimmer in Pittsburgh," *Pittsburgh Daily Post*, February 18, 1901.

5. Alexander, *John McGraw*, 76.

6. "Mugsy McGraw at Old Tactics," *Pittsburgh Gazette Times*, May 8, 1901.

7. "They Must Behave. Ban Johnson Enforces Discipline in American League," *Allentown (PA) Leader*, May 21, 1901.

8. "McGraw's Timely Triple Caused the Athletics Defeat at Baltimore," *New York Times*, May 16, 1901.

9. "Johnson Scents Trouble," *Washington Times*, July 27, 1901.

10. "American League," *Minneapolis Journal*, August 16, 1901.

11. "More Fines for the Orioles," *Chicago Tribune*, August 21, 1901.

12. McGraw, *The Real McGraw*, 16.

13. *Ibid.*, 17.

14. Alexander, *John McGraw*, 88.

15. "Will Not Tamper with Baltimore Players," *Louisville (KY) Courier-Journal*," July 9, 1902.

16. Langdon Smith, "Crowd Cheers Mathewson's Work Against Brooklyn," *New York Evening World*, July 28, 1902.

17. "McGraw and His Pitchers," *Louisville (KY) Courier-Journal*, May 19, 1904.

18. "Giants Line 'Em Out Hard," *New York Evening World*, May 6, 1903.

19. Frank Deford, *The Old Ball Game: How John McGraw, Christy Mathewson and the New York Giants Created Modern Baseball* (New York: Grove Press, 2005), 51.

20. John J. McGraw, *My Thirty Years in Baseball* (New York: Boni and Liveright, 1923; Lincoln: University of Nebraska Press, 1995), 144. Page references to the 1995 edition.

21. "McGraw Becomes Abusive," *Harrisburg (PA) Daily Independent*, April 19, 1904.

22. "Giants on the Bases," *Washington Post*, September 25, 1904.

23. Though the crowd ringingly indicated that Sunday baseball was welcomed by the populace, Sabbath "blue laws" in New York City would not be overcome for another decade and a half. "On April 19, 1919, Governor Smith signed into law the Walker Act, and ten days later the New York Board of Alderman followed suit.… The first legal Sunday baseball game was played at Ebbets Field on May 4, 1919." John G. Zinn and Paul G. Zinn, *Ebbets Field: Essays and Memories of Brooklyn's Historic Ballpark, 1913–1960* (Jefferson, NC: McFarland, 2013), 25.

24. "Pulliam Suspends Manager M'graw," *Washington Times*, August 25, 1904.

25. McGraw, *My Thirty Years in Baseball*, 144. McGraw, in his book, attempts to squirm away from the decision not to play the World Series, placing the onus squarely on Brush. But for anyone familiar with McGraw and his relationship with Ban Johnson at this time, it would be hard to accept that he, McGraw, was not the driving force behind the poor decision to boycott. Additionally, the manager wrote a lengthy statement, published in *Sporting Life*, that he assumed full responsibility for the unwillingness to meet the American League champions: "Blame should rest on my shoulders, not Mr. Brush's, for I and I alone am responsible for the club's action," he said. "Shoulders the Blame," *Sporting Life*, October 14, 1904, 6.

26. "Star Pitchers Will Not Play Post-Season Series," *Rochester (NY) Democrat and Chronicle*, September 20, 1904.

27. "Giants Benefit Will Be a Success," *New York Evening World*, September 29, 1904.

28. "M'graw's Salty Dose," *Pittsburgh Daily Post*, May 28, 1905.

29. Stephen V. Rice, "Sam Mertes," SABR Baseball Biography Project, www.sabr.org/bioproj/person/77318d62.

30. "McGraw Prefers White Sox," *Indianapolis News*, October 2, 1905.

31. The governing body of baseball at this time was the National Commission, consisting of one league president and Cincinnati Reds owner Garry Herrmann as chairman. The magnates of each circuit elected the presidents in charge of both circuits, and their opinions influenced most inter-league rulings made by the executives. The three-member association was dissolved with the naming of Kenesaw Mountain Landis as commissioner on November, 12, 1920.

32. McGraw, *My Thirty Years in Baseball*, 157.

33. *Ibid.*, 158. Not everyone cared for the Giants' new look. The *Chicago Tribune* described the Giants as "wearing funeral garb" and looking like a "flock of blackbirds that had waded in lime."

34. *Ibid.*, 159.

Chapter Three

1. "Rowdy Tactics by the Giants," *Chicago Daily Tribune*," May 2, 1906.

2. "Self-Defense the Plea of New York's Manager," *Rochester (NY) Democrat and Chronicle,* May 19, 1906.

3. "M'graw Discharged," *Pittsburgh Daily Post,* May 20, 1906.

4. Deford, *The Old Ball Game,* 109.

5. "Hoodlumism at Baseball Games," *Brooklyn Daily Eagle,* August 7, 1906.

6. "Umpire Barred; Giant Killers Win by Forfeit," *Chicago Inter Ocean,* August 8 1906.

7. *Ibid.*

8. "President Pulliam Approves the Suspension of Manager McGraw," *Raleigh (NC) Evening Times,* August 24, 1906.

9. *Ibid.* Pulliam is obliquely referring to the constraints placed on him by National League owners.

10. "Superbas Lose Fourth Game Through Batting Rally by Phillies," *Brooklyn Daily Eagle,* September 5, 1906.

11. Since McClellan's election victory in 1903, the Williamsburg Bridge had opened and the Manhattan Bridge was three-quarters complete. In his early 40s, McClellan oversaw the opening of the city's first subway tunnel in October 1904. The young mayor pushed forward the important waterfront projects of the Battery Maritime Terminal, for local denizens, and the Chelsea Piers, which provided over-sized docks for large European ocean liners. The future architectural landmarks of the Grand Central Terminal and New York Public Library were in various stages of expansion and new construction, respectively.

12. "Lively at Hearing on Sunday Baseball," *New York Times,* June 13, 1907. A similar, state-wide bill, known as the Burke bill, proposing Sunday amateur baseball, was defeated in Albany, the state capital, back in February 1903.

13. "McGraw's Comment on Doyle," *Decatur (IL) Herald,* August 1, 1907.

14. "National League News," *Great Bend (KS) Weekly Tribune,* September 20, 1907.

15. "McGraw Suspended," *Scranton (PA) Republic,* August 8, 1907.

16. "McGraw Again in Trouble," *Harrisburg (PA) Star-Independent,* September 24, 1907. Klem, according to the *Chicago Inter Ocean,* stayed calm, wiped his face and said, "Thank you," following McGraw's obnoxious actions.

17. Bowerman was also the catcher who caught the second-most games by Mathewson with 133.

18. "Ball Players Fight," *Washington Herald,* April 30, 1908.

19. "Dan McGann Fights Manager M'graw," *Wilkes-Barre (PA) Record,* May 1, 1908.

20. Jack Ryder, "Giants Ready to Crush the Reds," *Cincinnati Enquirer,* June 17, 1908.

21. *Ibid.*

22. "Giants and Tigers, Says John M'graw," *Washington Times,* September 19, 1908.

23. "Blunder Costs Giants Victory," *New York Times,* September 24, 1908.

24. Charles Dryden, "Battle of Cubs and Giants Ends in Row. Umpire Calling It 'No Contest.'" *Chicago Tribune,* September 24, 1908.

25. Bill Lamberty, "Harry Pulliam" SABR Baseball Biography Project, www.sabr.org/bioproj/person/6e05 b19c.

26. "The Cubs Win the Pennant," *New York Times,* October 9, 1908.

27. *Ibid.*

28. Irvin S. Cobb. "Crowds Gathered Early, but Failed to Avoid the Rush," *New York Evening World,* October 8, 1908.

29. "Fans Are in Camp," *Washington Post,* October 8, 1908.

30. Irvin S. Cobb, "Crowds Gathered Early, but Failed to Avoid the Rush," *New York Evening World,* October 8, 1908.

31. "Cubs Win Out in National League," *Springfield (MA) Republican,* October 9, 1908.

32. "Detroit Wild Over Big Series," *Atlanta Constitution,* October 10, 1908.

33. "Bill Dahlen Takes the Blame for That Ninth Inning Blunder," *Brooklyn Daily Eagle,* May 5, 1910.

34. "Manager McGraw Suspended; Charged with Umpire Baiting," *Brooklyn Daily Eagle,* August 19, 1910.

35. "Baseball Gossip," *Baltimore Evening Sun,* August 25, 1910, 8.

Chapter Four

1. "Fire Sweeps New York's Polo Grounds," *Virginia City (NV) Evening Chronicle,* April 14, 1911.

2. "Stands Burned at Polo Grounds," *St. Louis Post Dispatch,* April 14, 1911.

3. *Ibid.*

4. Jack Ryder, "Kinston Can Call Out the Band," *Cincinnati Enquirer, July 26, 1911.*

5. "Giants Will Play Series in Cuba," *Harrisburg Daily Independent,*" October 28, 1911.

6. "McGraw Says Cubans Are Poor Batters," *Chicago Inter Ocean,* December 24, 1911.

7. "Fine for M'graw in Cuba," *New York Herald Tribune,* December 5, 1911.

8. Stew Thornley, *Land of the Giants: New York's Polo Grounds* (Philadelphia: Temple University Press, 2000), 65.

9. Harry Daniel, "Come-Back Cubs Stop Marquard's Streak," *Chicago Inter Ocean,* July 9, 1912.

10. Frank Graham, *McGraw of the Giants: An Informal Biography* (New York: G.P. Putnam's Sons, 1944), 122.

11. Tip Wright, "Mugsy McGraw Opens 1911 Baseball Season," *Winnipeg (MB) Tribune,* January 28, 1911. From Alexander's *John McGraw,* page 4: "Give him the military uniform," wrote one admirer [of McGraw] in 1911, "And you would see Napoleon—the attitude, the

quiet decision, the folded arms, and even the funny little protruding stomach—all are there." The quote cited was from "What Is Inside Baseball?" *Outing*, 53 (July 1911), 497. Alexander adds: "It was nearly inevitable that the New York baseball writers should dub him (somewhat redundantly) 'the Little Napoleon.'" The *Boston Globe*, on July 6, 1910, referred to the Giants' pilot as "Napoleon McGraw."

12. John J. McGraw, "No One Is Blamed Least of All Snodgrass," *San Francisco Chronicle*, October 12, 1912.

13. "A 'golden pitch' can only be thrown in Game Seven of the World Series (since 1922) and only in the bottom of the ninth inning when the road team has the lead (or in the bottom of the extra inning, if the road team scores in the top, as was the case in Game Eight (because of the tie) of the 1912 World Series,"— Wade Kapszukiewicz, "Golden Pitches, the Ultimate Last-At-Bat, Game Seven Scenario," *Baseball Research Journal* 45, no. 1 (2016). (Mariano Rivera threw a total of six "Golden Pitches" in the 2001 World Series. This and Mathewson's seven "Golden Pitches" in 1912 were also from Kapszukiewicz's article.)

14. Noel Hynd, *Giants of the Polo Grounds: The Glorious Times of Baseball's New York Giants*. (Dallas: Taylor, 1996), 178.

15. "McGraw and Jennings to Enter Vaudeville," *St. Louis Post Dispatch*, October 20,1912.

16. "Magnates Pay Tribute to Late John T. Brush—McGraw at Funeral," *Indianapolis News*, November 27, 1912.

17. *Ibid*.

18. "Manager McGraw Suspended," *Brooklyn Daily Eagle*, July 13, 1913.

19. "McGraw Knocked Out by Pitcher Brennan After Game," *Salt Lake City Tribune*, July 1, 1913.

20. "Phila Rooters Mob Umpire Who Gave N.Y. Game," *Philadelphia Inquirer*, August 30, 1913. As indicated by the conference he had with Brennan and Emslie, McGraw had doubtlessly told McCormick to complain to Brennan—later getting much more than he bargained for in the process. The coatless bleacherites had not been let into the center field section until the fifth inning. The Giants had scored all of their runs in the first three innings. Philadelphia scored all of their runs from the sixth inning on.

21. *Ibid*.

22. "I Never Had a Better Club—Mack," *New York Sun*, October 10, 1913.

23. McGraw, *My Thirty Years in Baseball*, 244.

24. "Damon Runyon's Live News," *Sporting Life*, February 28, 1914, 6.

25. John J. McGraw, "Giants Concluded Chicago Series with No Appreciable Change in Standings," *Houston Post*, July 20, 1914.

26. "Boston Tie with Giants Again," *Dunkirk (NY) Evening Observer*, September 8, 1914.

27. Heywoud Broun, "Jealous Giants Ruin Pirates Long Slump by Breaking Even," *New York Tribune*, September 27, 1914.

28. "Bruggy Goes," *Boston Daily Globe*, May 1, 1915.

29. "Giants Twirlers in Poor Condition, Declares McGraw," *Winnipeg (MB) Tribune*, August 14, 1915.

30. "Benny Kauff Better Than Larry Doyle; He Admits It's True," *Evansville (IN) Press*, December 31, 1915.

Chapter Five

1. Ed Ballinger, "Buccaneer Bingles and Bunts," *Pittsburgh Daily Post*," May 10, 1916.

2. John J. McGraw "McGraw Says He Never Thought Seriously of Quitting Baseball," *New York Evening World*, August 14, 1916.

3. "Giants of '16 the Greatest Aggregation of All-Time," *Ogden (UT) Standard*, August 12, 1916.

4. "If Charges M'graw Made Are True His League Should Quit Baseball," *New York Evening World*, October 4, 1916.

5. *Ibid*.

6. "Herzog May Succeed M'graw as Manager," *Washington Herald*, October 6, 1916.

7. *Ibid*.

8. *Ibid*.

9. "McGraw Stands by Original Statement," *New York Sun*, October 5, 1916.

10. "Baseball One of the Arts; Can Not Be Unionized, Says McGraw," *Indianapolis News*, January 25, 1917.

11. Ralph Davis, "Working Under a Strain," *Pittsburgh Press*, August 15, 1917.

12. Landis displayed purposeful inaction in the important case, as co-authors and case law authorities Louis H. Schiff and Robert M. Jarvis explain: "[Landis] was reluctant to rule against the major leagues, fearing that any such decision would be a blow to the national psyche. As a result, he urged the parties to try mediation and allowed the case to languish on his docket until a settlement was reached." *Baseball and the Law: Cases and Materials* (Durham, NC: Carolina Academic Press, 2015), 52.

13. "Both McGraw and Rowland Claim Series," *New York Tribune*, October 8, 1917.

14. *Ibid*.

15. *Ibid*.

16. "Ban Johnson Elated Over AL Victory," *Trenton (NJ) Evening Times*, October 16, 1917, 8.

17. "Johnson Happy Over Triumph of White Sox," *New York Tribune*, October 16, 1917.

18. *Ibid*.

19. *Ibid*.

20. Gabriel Schechter, "Buck Herzog," SABR Biography Project, www.sabr.org/bioproj/person/4d0cbe1b.

21. "McGraw's Views," *Huntington (WV) Herald*, January 30, 1918.

22. "Sport Notes," *Wichita (KS) Daily Eagle*, January 20, 1918.

23. Hugh S. Fullerton, "McGraw Had Hot Race Tip, So Game Was Called Off," *New York Evening World*, June 11, 1918.

24. "Benny Kauff Bids Farewell to Fans," *New York Times*, June 23, 1918.

25. Hugh S. Fullerton, "Giants Have Best Chance

of Winning Pennant Flag," *New York Evening World,* July 28, 1918.

26. "New York Giants Sold to Syndicate Price, $1,000,000," *Brooklyn Daily Eagle,* January 14, 1919.

27. Charles A. Taylor, "McGraw and Others Purchase New York Giants for Over One Million Dollars," *New York Tribune,* January 15, 1918. Alexander noted that McGraw had to borrow most of the large transaction fee for his part of the purchase from Stoneham himself. Though a high-income earner for years, McGraw was not fiscally wise with his earnings. As an inveterate gambler and free-style money lender, he squandered much of his assets.

28. "Around the Bases," *Harrisburg (PA) Telegraph,* February 12, 1919. Raymond had died tragically in a lower-income hotel in Chicago on September 7, 1912. McGraw would not have him back after expelling him from the team in 1911. A coroner's report placed the cause of death as a skull fracture, allegedly sustained at the hands of a man with whom he had had a row a few days earlier. Raymond was 30 years old and was separated from his wife. He had recently lost his five-year-old daughter to influenza.

29. W.J. Macbeth, "Christopher Mathewson, Old Time King of Pitchers, Comes Back to Polo Grounds," *New York Tribune,* March 8, 1919.

30. Louis A. Dougher, "Robertson Quits Game, Ask Series Revision," *Washington Times,* May 23, 1919.

Chapter Six

1. Bozeman Bulger, "Young Fordham Player Helps Giants to Turn Tables on the Reds," *New York Evening World,* August 15, 1919.

2. "McGraw Says Spitball Is Disgusting and Dangerous," *Rochester (NY) Democrat and Chronicle,* Feb 27 1918.

3. "With McGraw Away, the Giants Thrive," *Sun and New York Herald,* May 20, 1920.

4. Dan Daniel, "Giants Beaten by Grimes, Dodgers and Soggy Play," *Sun and New York Herald,* June 7, 1920.

5. "Hitting Epidemic a Mystery. 1920 Baseball Seems Livelier," *El Paso (TX) Herald,* June 18, 1920.

6. Hugh S. Fullerton, "In Matty's Passing Baseball Has Lost Its Greatest Idol," *New York Evening World,* August 2, 1920.

7. "Soft Grounds Keep Bucs and Giants Apart," *Pittsburgh Gazette Times,* July 20, 1920.

8. "John McGraw's Record as Maiden Class Fighter," *Sun and New York Herald,* August 11, 1920.

9. "McGraw Is Missing at Probe of Odd Injury to Slavin," *Brooklyn Daily Eagle,* August 12, 1920.

10. McGraw Hit Bottle; Bottle Hit McGraw; Mind Void," *Brooklyn Daily Eagle,* August 15, 1920.

11. "It Is Black Mail, Says Comiskey; Robins Win Flag," *Sun and New York Herald,* September 28, 1920.

12. "Rumors About Hornsby Are Denied by McGraw," *Willoughby (OH) News-Herald,* November 17, 1920.

13. "Hornsby Tired of St. Louis; May Play with the Giants," *Appleton (WI) Post-Crescent,* November 6, 1920.

14. McGraw, *The Real McGraw,* 279.

15. "McGraw to Direct Team from Dugout," *Washington Herald,* November 10, 1920.

16. "War Clouds Begin to Move Away in Major League Conflict," *Rochester (NY) Democrat and Chronicle,* November 11, 1920.

17. Lyle Spatz and Steven Steinberg, *1921: The Yankees, the Giants and the Battle for Supremacy in New York* (Lincoln: University of Nebraska Press, 2010), 89.

18. Joe Vila, Polo Grounds in Use Thirty Years," *Philadelphia Inquirer,* April 22, 1921. According to ball parks.com, John B. Day's New York Gothams began play at the Polo Grounds I in 1883. Located north of Central Park, between 5th and 6th Avenue, the original locale drew its name from the equestrian sport that was first played there. In 1889, Day's team was unceremoniously moved out by local authorities and established a new residency on the southern end of Coogan's Hollow (Manhattan Field). When the Players' League disbanded after only one year, Day's club moved into the larger northern plot previously occupied by the PL's Brotherhood Club, transitioning into the Polo Grounds III in 1891. The accepted fourth incarnation of the Polo Grounds followed its 1911 fire.

19. "McGraw Is Freed of Liquor Charge," *New York Times,* May 3, 1921.

20. Chilly Doyle, "Chilly Sauce," *Pittsburgh Gazette Times,* June 3, 1921.

21. Myron Townsend, "Spicy Tips on Sporting Topics Served Red Hot El Paso Style," *El Paso (TX) Herald,* June 17, 1921.

22. W.C. Vreeland, "Stoneham and McGraw Sell Havana Track," *Brooklyn Daily Eagle,* July 14, 1921.

23. "White Sox Put Crimp in Part of Burns Story," *Escanaba (MI) Morning Press,"* July 29, 1921.

24. "McGraw Denies Any Offer to Buck Weaver," *Oregon Daily Journal (Portland),* July 31, 1921.

25. Jack Ryder, "Notes of the Game," *Cincinnati Enquirer,* August 2, 1921.

26. Henry L. Farrell, "Irish Meusel Disappoints with Giants," *Oakland (CA) Tribune,* August 14, 1921.

27. Myron Townsend, "Spicy Tips on Sporting Topics Served Red Hot El Paso Style," *El Paso (TX) Herald,* October 7, 1921.

28. "Rain Halts Fourth Game of World Series," *Coffeyville (KS) Daily Journal,* October 8, 1921.

29. R.J. Kelly, "McGraw Feels Mays Is as Good as Driven from Series," *New York Tribune,* October 10, 1921.

30. "McGraw Operates Great Wireless," *Nashville Tennessean,* October 12, 1921.

31. "Giants Greatest and Gamest Club in World, McGraw Says," *Joplin (MO) Globe,* October 14, 1921.

32. Jack Veiock, "Yanks Planning to Take Honors Before Ending," *Washington Times,* October 14, 1921.

33. "McGraw Selects All-Time All-Stars, Picks Old Timers and New Comers," *Ottawa (KS) Journal,* December 30, 1922.

34. "John McGraw After Donohue and Roush," *Bridgeport (CT) Telegram,* May 27, 1922.

35. So respected was Burns as a player and person

that the National League magnates scheduled their mid-season meeting in New York to be on hand for his special recognition. For Landis, it was his first trip to the Polo Grounds since the World Series. Burns was presented with gifts from the Giants and New York baseball writers—a diamond-encrusted platinum watch with platinum chain and a silver cigarette case, respectively. Later in the evening, members of both clubs gathered at the Riverside Theatre for "George Burns Night," where Burns received a pair of silver cufflinks. The *New York Times* described the Giants' championship banner as "solid blue, with a red border and white letters," The letters read, "New York Nationals, 1921 World's Series Champions."

36. "McGraw, Beating the Law a Day, Gets McQuillan," *Brooklyn Daily Eagle*, July 31, 1922.

37. Bozeman Bulger, "Manager McGraw Utilizes Reinforcements," *New York Evening World* August 5, 1922.

38. "Series Sidelights," *Houston Post*, October 7, 1922.

39. Grantland Rice, "Giants Maul Mays to Win Third Tilt, 4–3," *Washington Times*, October 8, 1922.

40. Bozeman Bulger, "Quick Thinking Won Four Games and Series," *New York Evening World*, October 9, 1922.

41. *Ibid.*

42. McGraw, *My Thirty Years in Baseball*, 5.

43. "Ward Wins for McGraw; Damage Suit Dismissed," *New Castle (PA) News*, December 20, 1922.

44. John J. McGraw, "Suspension of Ryan Should Help Giants," *Detroit Free Press*, May 13, 1923.

45. *Ibid.*

46. Jack Ryder, "Rough House Scrap Mars Final Game of New York Series," *Cincinnati Enquirer*, August 8, 1923. The reference to Pep Young is to Ross Youngs. Writers around the country, likely following the lead of New York papers, cut off the "s" in Youngs' last name and imposed the nickname of "Pep" on the Giants' star outfielder. As far as what set off Luque, more of the same report from Ryder explained: "On reaching the clubhouse, Luque, who was still white with anger, said that Stengel had hurled a highly improper epithet at him just after he had pitched the first ball to Young [*sic*]. The Cuban stated that he would never, under any circumstances, stand for what Stengel is alleged to have called him, so he took the matter into his own hands and set out to inflict the penalty where he believed it to be deserved."

47. Davis J. Walsh, "Plan to Oust Giants' Owner," *Winnipeg (MB) Tribune*, Sept 11, 1923.

48. "Huggins Hilarious; John McGraw Grim," *New Castle (PA) News*, October 12, 1923.

49. "Curtain Falls on Last Series Scene," *Fort Wayne (IN) Journal-Gazette,* October 17, 1923.

50. *Ibid.*

51. "McGraw Rates Jackson Year's Best Recruit," *Olean (NY) Evening Times*, September 24, 1923.

52. "Jackson Will Play Short, Says McGraw," *Indianapolis Star*, November 14, 1923.

53. "McGraw Is Honored by Fans in Havana," *Pittsburgh Daily Post*, February 23, 1923.

54. "Ed Ainsmith and Leon Cadore Are Through for Season," *Pittsburgh Post-Gazette*, August 21, 1924.

55. "Kelly May Lose Job to Giant Recruit," *Ottawa (KS) Journal*, April 3, 1924.

56. "Crowds Mourn Defeat of Idol, Walter Johnson," *Brooklyn Daily Eagle*, October 5, 1924.

57. Herbert Corey, "Failure of Young to Obey McGraw in the First Inning Helped Nationals Win," *Louisville (KY) Courier Journal,* October 6, 1924.

58. "Johnson May Be Through with Baseball," *Louisville (KY) Courier Journal,* October 9, 1924.

59. "Senators Hopes Are on Zachary; Giants Use Nehf," *Brooklyn Daily Eagle*, October 9, 1924.

60. Ballplayers Mobbed By Capital Fanatics," *Scranton (PA) Republic*, October 11, 1924

Chapter Seven

1. David J. Walsh, "Chesty Giants Are Still Thinking Best Ball Club Lost World Series," *Zanesville (OH) Times Recorder*, October 11, 1924.

2. "Johnson After Heads of Landis, McGraw and Giants Owner," *Anniston (AL) Star*, October 4, 1924.

3. "Only Beginning," *Traverse City (MI) Record-Eagle,* October 2, 1924.

4. *Ibid.*

5. David Sentner, "'Making Goat of Me,' Says Jimmy," *Oakland (CA) Tribune*, October 2, 1924.

6. "McGraw Is Home; Pleased with Trip," *New York Times*, December 3, 1924.

7. *Ibid.*

8. "Terry Succeeds McGraw as Manager," *Delaware County (PA) Daily Times,* June 4, 1932.

9. Peter J. DeKever, *Freddie Fitzsimmons: A Baseball Life* (Bloomington, IN: AuthorHouse, 2013), 32.

10. John J. McGraw, "McGraw Gets Kick from Big Series; Talks on Johnson," *El Paso (TX) Herald*, October 7, 1925.

11. George Barry, "Baseball Moguls Pay High Tribute on Death of Christy Mathewson," *New Castle (PA) News*, October 8, 1925.

12. *Ibid.*

13. "McGraw Encouraged Over News of Tyson; Now Wants Burwell," *Louisville (KY) Courier-Journal*, October 28, 1925.

14. Will Murphy "Baseball Stars in Fist Fight, McGraw in Brooklyn Affray," *Cincinnati Enquirer.* April 25, 1926.

15. Melville Webb, Jr., "No Matter What May Be in Store for Giants, Braves Gave Them There First Jolt," *Boston Daily Globe*, May 1, 1926.

16. "Why Giants Released Wilson," *Pittsburgh Press*, May 10, 1926.

17. Ralph Davis, "John McGraw Decries Attitude of Athletes," *Pittsburgh Press*, July 24, 1926.

18. Ralph Davis, "Could Not Play for McGraw, He Says," *Pittsburgh Press*, July 28, 1926.

19. Chilly Doyle, "Mr Meusel Unburdens Himself," *Pittsburgh Daily-Post*, July 29, 1926.

20. "McGraw Says Frisch Has Always Been Good," *Cedar Rapids (IA) Republican*, August 23, 1926.

21. "McGraw Thinks Trade Will Help Both Stars," *Reading (PA) Times*, February 10, 1927.

22. "Hornsby Tangle Heads for Court," *Asbury Park (NJ) Press,* April 1, 1927.

23. *Ibid.*

24. Westbrook Pegler, "New of Hornsby's Sale of Cardinal Stock Spreads at Polo Grounds Opening Game," *Rochester (NY) Democrat and Chronicle*, April 10, 1927.

25. Frank Getty, "40,000 Celebrate McGraw's 25th Anniversary with the Giants," *Decatur (IL) Herald*, April 27, 1927.

26. *Ibid.*

27. "All Parties Seem Satisfied After Hornsby-Frisch Deal," *Indianapolis Star*, July 3, 1927.

28. "McGraw's Silver Jubilee Is Observed in New York," *Reading (PA) Times*, July 20, 1927.

29. In the spring, before migrating east, excessive rainfall had saturated tributaries and swollen banks of the Mississippi River like never before in the country's recorded annals, causing what became known as the Great Flood of 1927. The historic inundation of middle America left more than 16,000,000 acres of normally dry land under water and more than 600,000 people homeless. The Mighty Mississippi remained at flood stage for 153 consecutive days.

30. "Ross Young [*sic*] Dead," *Mount Carmel (PA) News*, October 25, 1926. McGraw was said to have had only two photographs of ballplayers in his Polo Grounds office: one of Youngs, presumably placed there shortly after his death, and the other of Christy Mathewson.

31. "Rogers Hornsby Traded to Boston by New York Giants for Two Youngsters," *Arizona Republic*, January 11, 1928.

32. "Hornsby Traded to Avoid Strife, Says Stoneham," *Brooklyn Daily Eagle,* January 11, 1928.

33. *Ibid.*

34. "The Hornsby Trade Creates a Sensation," *Chillicothe (OH) Constitution*, January 11, 1928.

35. "McGraw Defends Trading Players Hornsby, Grimes," *Fitchburg (MA) Sentinel*, February 20, 1928.

36. George Kirksey, "The Giants Flag Chances May Be Ruined by Dissension," *Pittsburgh Press*, May 4, 1928.

37. *Ibid.* The ammunition McQuade was referring to was knowledge of a $155,000 loan made by the NEC's board of directors to Stoneham. The Giants' owner diverted the loans to non-baseball ventures. The notes were eventually repaid by Stoneham, who became upset at McQuade for compelling the repayment with interest. Stoneham then nominated his attorney, Leo J. Bondy, for the post of Giants treasurer in place of McQuade. Shortly afterward, the Board sued McQuade for "Planning and Scheming to Wreck the Property, Assets and Earning Capacity" of the Giants franchise. The suit amount was $250,000. McGraw was in Cuba and could not testify on behalf of the plaintiffs. The suit was later dropped. McQuade sued the Giants to recuperate his lost wages. An appellate court ruled on behalf of McQuade in January 1932, and the former treasurer received his back pay, with nearly four years of accrued interest. He did not return to his post.

38. "Eddie Roush Jumps Giants," *Decatur (IL) Herald,* June 24, 1928.

Chapter Eight

1. "Bugle and Barrier," *New York Times,* April 26, 1929.

2. Henry L. Farrell, Hooks and Slides (syndicated column), *Muncie (IN) Evening Press*, May 30, 1929, 7.

3. Davis J. Walsh, "With John McGraw Back Giants Are Changed Club," *Springfield (MO) Leader,* May 27, 1929. The three "rather lengthy periods" apply to 1925, 1927, and 1928.

4. "McGraw Likes Secretive Policy of Giant Hurlers," *Reading (PA) Times,* May 27, 1929.

5. Tommy Holmes, "John McGraw Banished by Umpire as Watson Clark Hurls Three-Hit Shutout," *Brooklyn Daily Eagle*, July 7, 1929.

6. "McGraw First to Pay Tribute to Rival Gotham Pilot," *Wilkes-Barre (PA) Record,*" September 26, 1929.

7. "Joe McGinnity, Ex-Butte Skipper, Is Called," *Montana Standard (Butte)*, November 15, 1929.

8. Walter Trumbull, "Giant Leader Tells About Early Career of Noted Moundsman," *Montana Standard (Butte)*, November 15, 1929.

9. Joe Williams, "Joe Williams Says," *Pittsburgh Press*, April 16, 1930.

10. Ralph Davis, "Ralph Davis Says," *Pittsburgh Press*, May 8, 1930.

11. George Kirksey, "Starling Trade with the Reds Will Give New York One of Best Infields," *San Bernardino County (CA) Sun*, May 22, 1930.

12. Tommy Holmes, "Bissonette's Scoops on Low Throws Make Him Great Target for Infielders," *Brooklyn Daily Eagle*, May 27, 1930.

13. "McGraw Abandons All Hope of Winning," *Detroit Free Press*, July 27, 1930.

14. George Kirksey, "Signing of Giant Contract Quiets Several Rumors," *Oshkosh (WI) Daily Northwestern*, September 4, 1930.

15. "Players Are Pleased," *New York Times*, September 4, 1930.

16. Figures are from David George Surdam's book *Wins, Losses, and Empty Seats: How Baseball Outlasted the Great Depression* (Lincoln: University of Nebraska Press, 2011), 317. Attendance in the American League in 1929 was 4,662,470, followed by a slight uptick to 4,685,730 in 1930. Original source cited by Surdam as Thorn, Palmer and Gershman, *Total Baseball* (Kingston, NY: Total Sports, 1999).

17. Tommy Holmes, "Lindstrom May Be Going Still in 1946," *Brooklyn Daily Eagle,* April 28, 1931.

18. Werner Laufer, *"New York Giants Are Bound to Be Title Contender,"* Piqua (KS) Daily Call*, March 31, 1931.

19. "Sport World Offers Tributes to Ban Johnson and Barnard," *The Sporting News*, April 2, 1931, 4.

20. John J. McGraw, "New Baseball Aids Fielding Says Manager of Giants," *St. Louis Post Dispatch*, May 17, 1931. Unlike the National League, the junior circuit did not adopt alterations to their ball from last year.

21. "Giants Greatest and Gamest Club in World, McGraw Says," *Joplin (MO) Globe*, October 14, 1921.

22. "Cubs Rally in Final Frame Is Fatal to Giants," *Brooklyn Daily Eagle*, June 23, 1931.

23. Ed Kelly, "Kel-E-Graphs," *Scranton (PA) Republican*, July 21, 1931.

24. "McGraw Tells Off Baseball Chief at St. Louis Park," *Ottawa (KS) Evening Journal*, July 20, 1931.

25. Peter Williams, *When the Giants Were Giants: Bill Terry and the Golden Age of New York Baseball* (Chapel Hill, NC: Algonquin, 1994), 109.

26. Jimmy Powers, "John McGraw Philosopher. His Sermon: Always Play to Win," *Freeport (IL) Journal Standard*, July 30, 1927.

27. "Frank Packard Sought by New York Giants," *Cumberland (MD) Evening Times*, June 2, 1932.

Chapter Nine

1. "McGraw Departs for Vacation in Havana," *New York Times*, January 1, 1932.

2. "Terry to Rule with Firm Hand," *Moberly (MO) Monitor-Index*, June 4, 1932.

3. Paul Zimmerman, "McGraw Views His Giants as Greatly Improved Team," *Miami (OK) Daily News-Record*, March 13, 1932.

4. "McGraw Worried at Lack of Game Gates," *Harlingen (TX) Valley Morning Star* April 1, 1932. The 25-man roster did not return until 1939.

5. Frank G. Menke, "McGraw Believes Baseball Should Be More Aggressive," *Kane (PA) Republican*, April 4, 1932.

6. Alan Gould, "Baseball Season Worries Owners Who Fear Slump," *Las Vegas Daily Optic*, April 1, 1932.

7. "Big Leagues Differ on Ballyhoo Ideas; Harridge Opposed," *Montana Standard (Butte)*, April 2, 1932.

8. "In the Training Camps," *Brownsville (TX) Herald*, March 14, 1932.

9. "First Pinch Hitter in Baseball Dies," *Miami (OK) Daily News-Record*, March 14, 1932.

10. Graham, *McGraw of the Giants*, 252.

11. William Braucher, "Hooks and Slides," *Scranton (PA) Republic*, March 24, 1932.

12. "Greeting to 'Jawn' Sent by President," *San Bernardino County (CA) Sun*, April 13, 1932.

13. Joe Villa, "Absence of McGraw Handicaps Giants," *The Sporting News*, June 2, 1932, 3.

14. Graham, *McGraw of the Giants*, 258.

15. "McGraw's Resignation Ends 30 Year Reign as Giants' Boss," *San Bernardino County (CA) Sun, June 4, 1932*.

16. McGraw, *The Real McGraw*, 327–328.

17. *Ibid.*, 330.

18. Graham, *McGraw of the Giants*, 263.

19. "Giants Go Wild," *Kansas City (MO) Star*, October 8, 1933.

20. "Baseball Heads Express Sorrow," *Uniontown (PA) Evening Standard*, February 26, 1934.

21. Pat Robinson, "Mourners Gather to Pay Respects to John McGraw," *Coshocton (OH) Tribune*, February 27, 1934.

22. "John J. McGraw, Giants Manager Thirty Years, Dies," *Sedalia (MO) Democrat*, February 26, 1934.

23. "Allow Public to File Past McGraw Bier," *White Plains (NY) Journal News*, February 27, 1934.

24. *Ibid.*

25. *Ibid.*

26. Joe Kelly, "Glancing at Sports," *Kingston (NY) Daily Freeman*, February 28, 1932. McGraw had helped broker Ruppert's co-purchase of the New York Yankees.

27. *Ibid.*

28. Alan Gould, "Baseball Men in South Pay Tribute to McGraw," *Oil City (PA) Derrick*, February 26, 1934.

29. McGraw, *The Real McGraw*, 325.

30. Frank G. Menke, "Giants' Hard-Boiled Boss Really Soft and Big-Hearted," *Lincoln (NE) Star*, May 11, 1930.

31. "Notables Attend McGraw's Funeral at St. Patrick's," *Reading (PA) Times*, March 1, 1934.

32. Robert J. Cavagnaro, "Blanche McGraw Club's Advisor," *Canandaigua (NY) Daily Messenger*, February 27, 1934.

33. "Notables Will Carry McGraw to Final Rest," *Canandaigua (NY) Evening Standard*, February 27 1934.

34. "McGraw's Resignation Ends Thirty Year Reign as Giants' Boss," *San Bernardino County (CA) Sun*, June 4, 1932.

35. Harold C. Burr, "McGraw Last of the Old School Managers," *Brooklyn Daily Eagle*, February 26, 1934.

Chapter Ten

1. Alexander, *John McGraw*, 108.

2. "Giants Still in Depressing Form," *New York Herald*, October 2, 1904.

3. "McGraw and Fan Have a Word-Fight," *Boston Daily Globe*, October 5, 1915.

4. Alexander, *John McGraw*, 323.

5. Harry Cross, "Giants and Robins Play Twice Today," *New York Times*, June 23, 1925.

6. "McGraw Does a Bit of Scouting," *Louisville (KY) Courier-Journal*, October 2, 1929.

7. Joe Vila, "Giants Take Up Stand at Home in Final Bid to Capture Flag," *The Sporting News*, September 11, 1930, 1.

8. Joe Vila, "Yankees to Sign Joe M'carthy When Series Moves Off Stage," *The Sporting News*, October 9, 1930, 1.

9. Alan Gould, "Giants Prepare for 1932 Race," *Altoona (PA) Tribune*, August 12, 1931.

10. Copeland C. Burg, "Diamond Dust," *Belvidere (IL) Daily Republican*, August 19, 1931.

Bibliography

Newspapers

Allentown (PA) Leader
Altoona (PA) Tribune
Anniston (AL) Star
Appleton (WI) Post-Crescent
Arizona Republic
Asbury Park (NJ) Press
Atlanta Constitution
Belvidere (IL) Daily Republican
Boston Globe
Boston Post
Bridgeport (CT) Telegram
Brooklyn Daily Eagle
Brownsville (TX) Herald
Burlington (IA) Hawkeye
Canandaigua (NY) Daily Messenger
Cedar Rapids (IA) Republican
Chicago Inter Ocean
Chicago Tribune
Chillico (MO) Constitution
Cincinnati Enquirer
Coffeyville (KS) Daily Journal
Coshocton (OH) Tribune
Cumberland (MD) Evening Times
Decatur (IL) Herald
Delaware County (PA) Daily Times
Detroit Free Press
Dunkirk (NY) Evening Observer
El Paso (TX) Herald
Escanaba (MI) Morning Press
Evansville (IN) Press
Fitchburg (MA) Sentinel
Fort Wayne (IN) Journal-Gazette
Freeport (IL) Journal Standard
Great Bend (KS) Weekly Tribune
Harlingen (TX) Valley Morning Star
Harrisburg (PA) Daily Independent
Harrisburg (PA) Star-Independent
Harrisburg (PA) Telegraph
Houston Post
Huntington (WV) Herald

Indianapolis News
Indianapolis Star
Joplin (MO) Globe
Kane (PA) Republican
Kansas City (MO) Journal
Kingston (NY) Daily Freeman
Lake County (IN) Times
Las Vegas Daily Optic
Lincoln (NE) Star
Louisville (KY) Courier-Journal
Miami (OK) Daily News-Record
Minneapolis Journal
Moberly (MO) Monitor Index
Montana Standard (Butte)
Mount Carmel (PA) News
Nashville Tennesseean
New Castle (PA) News
New York Evening World
New York Herald Tribune
New York Sun
New York Times
New York Tribune
Oakland (CA) Tribune
Ogden (UT) Standard
Oil City (PA) Derrick
Olean (NY) Evening Times
Oregon Daily Journal (Portland)
Oshkosh (WI) Daily Northwestern
Ottawa (KS) Evening Journal
Philadelphia Inquirer
Piqua (KS) Daily Call
Pittsburgh Daily Post
Pittsburgh Gazette Times
Raleigh (NC) Evening Times
Roanoke (VA) Times
Rochester (NY) Democrat and Chronicle
St. Louis Post Dispatch
Salt Lake City Tribune
San Bernardino (CA) County Sun
Sandusky (OH) Register
Sayre (PA) Morning Times
Scranton (PA) Republic

Sedalia (MO) Democrat
Springfield (MA) Republican
Springfield (MO) Leader
Traverse City (MI) Record-Eagle
Uniontown (PA) Evening Standard
Virginia City (NV) Evening Chronicle
Washington Herald
Washington Post
Washington Times
White Plains (NY) Journal News
Wichita (KS) Daily Eagle
Wilkes-Barre (PA) News
Willoughby (OH) News-Herald
Winnipeg (MB) Tribune
Zanesville (OH) Times Recorder

SABR Baseball Biography Project (www.sabr.org/bioproject)

Anderson, David W. "Jim Johnstone," "Bill Klem," "Hank O'Day," and "Dummy Taylor."
Betzold, Michael. "Mike Donlin."
Bishop, Bill. "Rube Benton."
Bohn, Terry. "Jimmy Hart."
Erion, Greg. "Travis Jackson."
Faber, Charles F. "Bill Rariden," "Clarence Mitchell," and "Freddy Lindstrom."
Finkel, Jan. "Art Devlin."
Frierson, Eddie. "Christy Mathewson."
Gagnon, Cappy. "Red Murray."
Gordon, Peter M. "Art Fletcher" and "Josh Devore."
Jensen, Don. "Bugs Raymond," "Dan McGann," "John McGraw," and "Jim Thorpe."
Johnson, Janice. "Virgil Barnes."
Jones, David. "Benny Kauff" and "Heinie Zimmerman."
Keenan, Jimmy. "Joe Kelley."
Kirwin, Bill. "Cy Seymour."
Lackey, Mike. "Larry McLean."
Lahman, Sean. "Heinie Groh."
Lamb, Bill. "Andrew Freedman," "Bert Niehoff," "Joe Corbett," and "The Brush Family Women."
Lamberty, Bill. "Harry Pulliam."
Lesch, R.J. "Doc Crandall," "Chief Meyers," "George Burns," "Jeff Tesreau," and "Red Ames."
Levitt, Daniel R. "Ferdie Schupp" and "Pat Moran."
Lynch, Mike. "Phil Douglas."
Mansch, Larry. "Rube Marquard."
McKenna, Brian. "Bethlehem Steel League," "Charlie Grant," and "Lefty O'Doul."
Nowlin, Bill. "Kip Selbach."
Rice, Stephen V. "Al Bridwell," "Irish Meusel," "Sam Mertes," and "Sammy Strang."
Rogers, C. Paul, III. "Hughie Jennings."
Saccoman, John. "Garry Herrmann" and "John T. Brush."
Sallee, Paul, and Eric Sallee. "Slim Sallee."
Sandoval, Jim. "Edd Roush."
Santry, Joe, and Cindy Thomson. "Ban Johnson."
Schechter, Gabriel. "Fred Snodgrass" and "Hooks Wiltse."
Schuld, Fred. "Charles Somers."
Semchuck, Alex. "Wilbert Robinson."
Simon, Tom. "Eddie Grant."
Skipper, Doug. "Willie Keeler."
Stein, Fred. "Bill Terry," "Carl Hubbell," "Frankie Frisch," and "Mel Ott."
Sternman, Mark. "Fred Tenney"
Stewart, Mark. "George Kelly."
Strecker, Trey. "Dave Bancroft" and "Fred Merkle."
Thomas, Joan M. "Frank Robison," "Roger Bresnahan," and "Stanley Robison."
Triscuit, Zack. "Ned Hanlon."
Wells, Michael. "Joe McGinnity."
Wolf, Gregory H. "Waite Hoyt."

Articles

"Baltimore Terrapins History." Baseball Chronology.com. baseballchronology.com/baseball/leagues/Federal/Baltimore/default.asp#Legacy.
Bell, Blake. "First-Hand Diary Account of Battle of Pelham on October 18, 1776." Historic Pelham (blog), October 17, 2010. historicpelham.blogspot.com/2014/10.
Clavin, Tom. "The Inside Story of Baseball's Grand World Tour of 1914." Smithsonian.com, March 21, 2014.
croixrougefarm.org/history-42nd/
"Famous Trainer of Baseball Players Dead from Pneumonia." *New York Age*, June 17, 1922.
Felber, Bill. "1920: The Babe, The Exposure, And The Judge." National Pastime Museum (website), February 24, 2016. https://www.thenationalpastimemuseum.com/article/1920-babe-exposure-and-judge.
Goldman, Steven. "John McGraw's American Boyhood." National Pastime Museum (website), June 30, 2016 https://www.thenationalpastimemuseum.com/article/john-mcgraw-s-american-boyhood.
History.com Staff. "Stock Market Crash of 1929." History.com, accessed December 5, 2016. http://www.history.com/topics/1929-stock-market-crash.
"John McGraw and the Small Town in Texas." Sports photography.mlblogs.com, December 7, 2015.
Kapszukiewicz, Wade. "Golden Pitches." *The Baseball Research Journal* 45, no. 1 (Spring 2016): 5–10.
"Know Your Mayors: John F. Hylan." The Bowery Boys: New York City History (website), April 30, 2008. boweryboyshistory.com/2008/04/know-your-mayors-john-f-hylan.

"Know Your Mayors: The Boy Mayor of New York." The Bowery Boys: New York City History, April 9, 2008. boweryboyshistory.com/2008/04/know-your-mayors-boy-mayor-of-new-york.

"Know Your Mayors: William J. Gaynor." The Bowery Boys: New York City History, March 4, 2008. boweryboyshistory.com/2008/03/know-your-mayors-william-jay-gaynor.

Lynch, Mike. "A Season of Firsts and Lasts." National Pastime Museum (website), February 17, 2016. https://www.thenationalpastimemuseum.com/article/1922-season-firsts-and-lasts.

"Mayor Jimmy Walker: A Finer Class of Corruption." The Bowery Boys: New York City History, May 27, 2009. boweryboyshistory.com/2009/05/mayor-jimmy-walker-finer-class-of.

Pomrenke, Jacob. "1912." National Pastime Museum (website), March 9, 2016. https://www.thenationalpastimemuseum.com/article/1912.

Schechter, Gabriel. "The 1911 Season: The Cream Rises to the Top." National Pastime Museum (website), February 10, 2016. https://www.thenationalpastimemuseum.com/article/1911-season-cream-rises-top.

"The Sinking of the Lusitania" Eyewitness to History (website), 2007. http://www.eyewitnesstohistory.com/lusitania.htm.

Tourtellotte, Shane. "Did John McGraw Have a Bullpen Edge?" Hardball Times (website), June 20, 2016. www.hardballtimes.com/did-john-mcgraw-have-a-bullpen-edge/.

Wilson, Walt. "Christy Mathewson's Battery Mates." Catching Hall of Fame Pitchers (website). Bb_catchers.tripod.com/catchers/battery-hof37.htm.

Books

Alexander, Charles C. *John McGraw*. Lincoln: University of Nebraska Press, 1988.

Allen, Eric H. *1931: The Year of the Great Worldwide Financial Crash*. Self-published, 2011.

Bak, Richard. *New York Giants: A Baseball Album*. Charleston, SC: Arcadia, 1999.

Bryson, Bill. *One Summer: America 1927*. New York: Anchor Books, 2013.

Deford, Frank. *The Old Ball Game: How John McGraw, Christy Mathewson and the New York Giants Created Modern Baseball*. New York: Grove Press, 2005.

DeKever, Peter J. *Freddie Fitzsimmons: A Baseball Life*. Bloomington, IN: AuthorHouse, 2013.

Epting, Chris. *The Early Polo Grounds: Images of Baseball*. Charleston, SC: Arcadia, 2009.

Figueredo, Jorge S. *Cuban Baseball: A Statistical History 1878–1961*. Jefferson, NC: McFarland, 2003.

Goldblatt, Andrew. *The Giants and the Dodgers: Four Cities, Two Teams, One Rivalry*. Jefferson, NC: McFarland, 2003.

Graham, Frank. *McGraw of the Giants: An Informal Biography,* New York: G. P. Putnam's Sons, 1944.

Hynd, Noel. *The Giants of the Polo Grounds: The Glorious Times of Baseball's New York Giants*. Dallas, TX: Taylor, 1988.

Jaffe, Chris. *Evaluating Baseball's Managers: History and Analysis of Performance in the Major Leagues, 1876–2008*. Jefferson, NC: McFarland, 2010.

James, Bill. *The Bill James Guide to Baseball Managers from 1870 to Today*. New York: Scribner, 1997.

Klein, Maury. *Stealing Games: How John McGraw Transformed Baseball with the 1911 New York Giants*. New York: Bloomsbury, 2016.

McGraw, John J. *My Thirty Years in Baseball*. Lincoln, NE: Bison Books, 1995.

Schiff, Louis H., and Robert M. Jarvis. *Baseball and the Law*. Durham, NC: Carolina Academic Press, 2016.

Skipper, John C. *A Biographical Dictionary of Major League Baseball Managers*. Jefferson, NC: McFarland, 2003.

Spatz, Lyle, and Steve Steinberg. *1921: The Yankees, the Giants, and the Battle for Baseball Supremacy in New York*. Lincoln: University of Nebraska Press, 2010.

Stein, Fred. *Mel Ott: The Little Giant of Baseball*. Jefferson, NC: McFarland, 1999.

Surdam, David George. *Wins, Losses & Empty Seats: How Baseball Outlasted the Great Depression*. Lincoln: University of Nebraska Press, 2011.

Thornley, Stew. *New York's Polo Grounds: Land of the Giants*. Philadelphia: Temple University Press, 2000.

Williams, Peter. *When Giants Were Giants*. Introduction by W.P. Kinsella. Chapel Hill, NC: Algonquin, 1994.

Zinn, John G., and Paul G. Zinn. *Ebbets Field: Essays and Memories of Brooklyn's Historic Ballpark, 1913–1960*. Jefferson, NC: McFarland, 2013.

Websites (General)

Baseball-almanac.com
Baseballchronolgy.com
Baseballhall.org
Baseball-reference.com
Boweryboyshistory.com
Epicsports.com
Retrosheet.org
Thelambsclub.com
Wikipedia.org

Index

Numbers in *bold italics* indicate pages with illustrations